XML
in *Office 2003*

The Charles F. Goldfarb Definitive XML Series™

Holman
- Definitive XSLT and XPath

Walmsley
- Definitive XML Schema

Garshol
- Definitive XML Application Development

Hocek and Cuddihy
- Definitive VoiceXML

Holman
- Definitive XSL-FO

Goldfarb and Prescod

Charles F. Goldfarb's XML Handbook™ Fifth Edition

Goldfarb and Walmsley
- XML in *Office 2003*: Information Sharing with Desktop XML

Kirsanov
- XSLT 2.0 Web Development

Walmsley
- Definitive XQuery

Titles in this series are produced using XML, SGML, and/or XSL. XSL-FO documents are rendered into PDF by the *XEP Rendering Engine* from RenderX: www.renderx.com

About the Series Editor
Charles F. Goldfarb is the father of XML technology. He invented SGML, the Standard Generalized Markup Language on which both XML and HTML are based. You can find him on the Web at: www.xmlbooks.com

About the Series Logo
The rebus is an ancient literary tradition, dating from 16th century Picardy, and is especially appropriate to a series involving fine distinctions between markup and text, metadata and data. The logo is a rebus incorporating the series name within a stylized XML comment declaration.

XML
in *Office 2003*
INFORMATION SHARING
WITH DESKTOP XML

Charles F. Goldfarb • Priscilla Walmsley

Prentice Hall PTR
Upper Saddle River, NJ 07458
www.phptr.com

Cataloging-in-Publication Data available from the Library of Congress.

Editorial/Production Supervisor: *Faye Gemmellaro*
Editor-in-Chief: *Mark L. Taub*
Editorial Assistant: *Noreen Regina*
Marketing Manager: *Curt Johnson*
Manufacturing Buyer: *Maura Zaldivar*
Cover Designer: *Anthony Gemmellaro*
Cover Design Director: *Jerry Votta*
Series Designer: *Gail Cocker-Bogusz*

© 2004 Charles F. Goldfarb
Published by Pearson Education, Inc.
Publishing as Prentice Hall PTR
Upper Saddle River, NJ 07458

Prentice Hall PTR offers discounts on this book when ordered in quantity for bulk purchases
or special sales. For more information, please contact: U.S. Corporate and Government Sales,
1-800-382-3419, corpsales@pearsontechgroup.com. For sales outside of the United States, please
contact: International Sales, 1-317-581-3793, international@pearsontechgroup.com.

Printed in the United States of America

First Printing
ISBN 0-13-142193-X

Pearson Education Ltd.
Pearson Education Australia Pty. Limited
Pearson Education Singapore, Pte.Ltd.
Pearson Education North Asia Ltd.
Pearson Education Canada, Ltd.
Pearson Educación de Mexico, S.A. de C.V.
Pearson Education—Japan
Pearson Education Malaysia, Pte. Ltd.

To Linda – With love, awe, and gratitude.

Charles F. Goldfarb

To Doug, my SH.

Priscilla Walmsley

Overview

Contents

Preface

What do you give the software that has everything?

XML, of course!

Microsoft Office is the most successful productivity product in the history of computers, with over 300 million users around the world. Few of them use all of the features in Office now, so why add something new?

It wasn't just the needs of the information worker that motivated this extraordinary enhancement to Office, it was the needs of the information itself. Thanks to the Internet, local networks, business integration and the very ubiquity of Office, key enterprise data is not available in one convenient place. Some of it is in managed central stores, but much more is in desktop systems, departmental repositories, and even in the systems of vendors and customers.

Past versions of Office have provided tools for coping with this problem, but solution implementation has been cumbersome and often required advanced development skills. That was in part because every data source typically has its own data format. In addition to accessing the information, a solution often had to decode it as well.

In the past few years, XML has emerged to solve that problem; it has become the universal information interchange representation. XML software for machine-to-machine functions is virtually standard equipment for all platforms. But until September, 2003, the only generally useful XML on the desktop was strictly in specialized products. Common productivity tools like office suites supported only specific XML document types, when they supported XML at all.

Microsoft Office Professional Edition 2003 changed that situation forever, by accepting any user-defined XML document as a first-class citizen. As a result, millions of desktop computers have been transformed from mere word processors into potential rich clients for Web services, editing front-ends for XML content management systems, and portals for XML-based application integration.

This book shows you how to use the XML features of Office to realize that potential. You'll learn to share information among Office products and between Office and the rest of the XML universe.

XML in Office 2003 will make it easier to collaborate with co-workers and utilize the information resources of your enterprise and the Web.

Who is this book for?

You don't have to be a professional developer to use the Office XML features. We've written this book so that office users who are comfortable with preference settings and macros will be able to tap into these resources. If you can deal with scripts – or are willing to copy and modify ours – you'll be able to do even more. And if you are a pro, you'll find that we don't talk down to you: you'll easily see the added possibilities for real program code.

And XML knowledge isn't a prerequisite for this book either. It includes a bonus section of tutorials on XML and its related technologies, adapted from the best-selling *XML Handbook*.

How much XML?

Chapter 2 of this book is an introduction to XML that should be sufficient for learning the XML features of Office 2003. However, if you plan to use XML products other than Office, develop your own schemas, or use Office to share data with enterprise systems and Web services, you'll want to learn more about XML.

As our readers will have differing experience with XML and different requirements for its use, there seemed no sensible way to intersperse detailed XML education with the Office XML tasks that are the focus of the book.

Instead we've put the detailed tutorials and references on the XML language and related standards where you can easily find them when you need them. They are in Part Three. The book's Table of Contents and Index can guide you to specific subjects, and we also provide appropriate cross-references to them from the Office XML task chapters in Part Two.

While we chose and edited the XML tutorials to emphasize the aspects that are supported in Office, we did so fully aware that the focus of the book is on sharing information, including between Office and other systems that could have more complete XML support. For that reason, we also cover, though in less detail, XML facilities that Office does not support fully.

About the products

The Office suite is packaged and distributed in multiple editions and the XML support varies among them:

- Native XML file formats for Word and Excel are available in all editions.
- Custom schema support is only available in the Professional and Professional Enterprise editions.
- The new InfoPath product is only available in the Professional Enterprise edition and as an individual purchase.

Almost all of the Office material in this book involves custom schemas. The general XML material, of course, is not product-specific.

When the book talks about "the Office products" without further qualification, it means those with XML support: Word, Excel, InfoPath, Access, and FrontPage.

Although Visio also has XML support, it is sufficiently different from the other products that we don't cover it in the book. Its XML capabilities can be summarized as follows:

- It has its own XML data representation, called VDX.
- It can import SVG drawings as shapes and export complete diagrams in SVG.[1]

■ It is possible to attach XML data in any schema to objects in a Visio diagram.

These things are mentioned here to avoid cluttering the book with disclaimers like "if you have the Professional edition you can also do this" and "all of the products (except Visio and non-XML-enabled products) can do that".

How to use this book

XML in Office 2003 has three parts, consisting of 24 chapters. We won't try to describe the full scope here, as you can easily look at the Table of Contents. But we do include some tips that will help you get the most from the book.

Part One introduces the applications of desktop XML, the XML language and technology, and the XML features of Office. Please read it first as it is the foundation for the rest of the book.

Part Two teaches the XML features of Office in detail, with working examples and step-by-step walk-throughs. Each chapter has a subtitle that indicates the level of implementation task it describes: power user or script developer. The Office product name is also included if it isn't in the chapter title.

You can read Part Two with only Part One as background, although technical readers may want to complete the XML tutorials first; others can dip into them as needed. All of the examples used in Part Two can be found at the book's website: www.XMLinOffice.com

There are two considerations to keep in mind regarding the examples:

■ **Web services change.** Any Web service described in this book might not be exactly the same, or even still exist, at the time you read about it. Before testing the example code, please check the Web service at the provided URL to see if anything has changed.

■ **URLs do not contain line breaks.** URLs can be very long and they cannot contain line breaks. When you see a URL in this book that is split over several lines, the line breaks are *not* part

---

1. SVG is an XML-based graphics notation.

of the actual URL; they were inserted so that the URL could
fit within the page width of the book.

The XML tutorials can be found in Part Three. We strove to keep them
friendly and understandable for readers without a background in subjects
not covered in this book. Tutorials whose subject matter thwarted that goal
are labeled as being a tad tougher so you will know what to expect, but not
to discourage you from reading them.

There is an extensive index that also serves as a "glossary-in-context". We
believe that the meaning of a term is best understood in context – in several
contexts if they add to understanding, or the term has multiple meanings.
Therefore, an index entry identifies the page(s) where its term is defined
separately from the entry's other pages.

Acknowledgments

Our first acknowledgment is to the people at Microsoft who brought
XML to the desktop. Jean Paoli conceived the idea and spent more than
three years bringing it to life.

We especially thank him and Peter Pathe, VP of Office, for the day they
spent visiting Charles and showing off their brainchild. They aroused the
enthusiasm that led directly to this book project.

Among the Office and InfoPath team members who helped us get the
job done, we are particularly indebted to Melinda Lewison and Jeune Ji. We
also thank Jacob Jaffe for supplying the InfoPath trial CDs.

Faye Gemmellaro supervised the project for the publisher; we thank her
for her dedication, attention to detail, and unfailing kindness and patience.

We owe a very special thank you to Andrew Goldfarb who tackled a variety of editing and production tasks, in addition to serving as art director
and artist-on-demand.

Mark Taub, our Editor-in-Chief at Prentice Hall PTR, showed enormous enthusiasm for this project from the very start. We thank him for his
help, encouragement, and guidance.

Charles F. Goldfarb
Priscilla Walmsley
November 26, 2003

A new era for XML, a new beginning for office documents

■ By Jean Paoli
XML Architect,
Information Worker (Office, InfoPath) Groups,
Microsoft Corporation
Co-editor of the XML 1.0 Recommendation

■ *Redmond, October 2, 2003*

Foreword

It is my strong belief that Office 2003 XML represents a milestone in the history of electronic documents. It will help realize the full potential of XML.

What you will read in this book is more than information about a new release of a product or about a particular technology. This is a book on re-inventing the way millions of people write and interact with documents.

Finding a way to describe the meaning contained in a document has been a central focus of the XML community for nearly 20 years, back to when the primary technology was SGML. Traditionally, when a document is created, there is no information included about its actual content. All that is captured is the content's presentation – its size, whether the words are bold or italicized, the font, and so on. For example, a resume does not "know" it is a resume – it is just a collection of words that only has meaning when a human being interprets it a certain way.

Those of us in the XML field have long believed that if we could provide a means to separate the actual meaning of the content from its presentation, then users would be able to "tag" parts of a document with labels that meant something to them. So in a resume, for instance, a user could tag the name, address, career goals, qualifications, and so on. More importantly, different types of documents (resume, healthcare report) would contain different sets of tags, each set appropriate to the kind of information its document type contains. In this way, documents of any kind could become a source of information as rich as a database, enabling rich search, processing and reuse.

I believed in that vision when I joined Microsoft in 1996 and helped create the XML standard in the W3C. I collaborated with my colleagues from the SGML community to create that standard; our idea was to change the world of information.

Very early on, XML took off in the industry like wildfire! Adoption started first on the server side, where information is traditionally processed and stored. The advent of XML Web services enabled the transfer of information from server to server and server to client, even in cross-platform environments.

But until Office 2003 XML, a major piece of the information-processing infrastructure was missing. The desktop, the place where documents are created and analyzed by millions of information workers, could not easily participate in this exchange of information.

And today's businesses thrive on information. Information is generated by many channels and exists in many forms: as raw data collected from operational systems, as content and documents that are published and shared, and in countless e-mail messages exchanged and stored locally by users throughout a company.

With Office 2003 XML, Microsoft is addressing a fundamental concern that we have heard over and over again from our customers: Too often, business-critical information is locked inside data storage systems or individual documents, forcing companies to adopt inefficient and duplicative business processes.

Needed data might be located in a database that employees aren't aware of or don't know how to access, in a text document that a co-worker has stored on her PC, or perhaps somewhere on the Internet. To address this issue, Microsoft is evolving the existing document paradigm for Office by broadly supporting XML in its products: Word, Excel, Access, FrontPage, Visio and a new XML-based forms product, InfoPath.

Although there are well-established methods for storing and managing some types of data (for example, numerical data in databases), a significant portion of the information created in the business environment is not captured in any meaningful way. Workers everywhere generate reports, e-mail messages, and spreadsheets that contain vital, valuable information.

But to reuse this information, these same workers may need to spend significant time searching for the appropriate files. They may also spend effort to re-key, cut and paste, or otherwise import the relevant information into another document. The way documents are created and handled limits the extent and ease of using information outside its original document.

While there is a well-established methodology for data capture and validation in traditional data management, similar technology for gathering and managing the information contained in text-based reports and other common business documents has not been available. Originally, when my colleagues and I created XML, it was to solve this problem.

XML enables businesses to capture all manner of business information in a way that maximizes its value. By facilitating reuse, indexing, search, storage, aggregation, and other practices more often associated with management of relational databases, XML brings the power of traditional data management to documents.

But as significant as this new functionality is, there is an even greater and more innovative benefit of XML: Companies can create their own document type schemas, specific to their business, defining the structure and type of data that a document's data elements can contain.

Support for custom-defined schemas is at the core of Microsoft's "XML Vision for the Desktop". It opens up a whole new realm of possibilities, not only for end users, but also for the business itself. Now organizations can capture and reuse critical information that in the past has been lost or gone unused.

Bringing XML to the masses with Office 2003 is the result of more than 20 years' work in the field of structured documents, sharing ideas and dreams with many people whom it was an honor to know:

- The Microsoft Office team that believed in the "XML Vision for the Desktop" and, with its talent and experience for building user interfaces, designed and implemented the XML features in Office 2003. The team created a multitude of innovations that enabled those ideas and dreams to finally become reality for the information worker.
- My original Microsoft XML team and Adam Bosworth, with whom I jump-started the XML activity in Microsoft, building msxml in Internet Explorer and Windows and in the many server teams in Microsoft.
- The SGML and XML community that I have been a part of for so many years and that dreamed about a world where

documents are semantically marked. This community is my extended family.

■ The French and European scientific community and the INRIA laboratories, where I had the honor to meet, study and learn with incredible people such as Gilles Kahn, Jean-Francois Abramatic and Vincent Quint.

■ The W3C and Tim Berners-Lee in particular, whom I had the honor to meet very early on and work with in W3C projects.

And of course Dr. Charles F. Goldfarb.

As the inventor of SGML and father of markup languages, Charles was uniquely qualified to create this book. It succeeds in communicating the novel underlying vision of Office 2003 XML while focusing on task-oriented, hands-on skills for using the product.

Charles' co-author is the extremely gifted Priscilla Walmsley, W3C expert and author of *Definitive XML Schema*, a great reference and tutorial for the W3C XML Schema specification.

I will always remember the happiness on Charles' face when I visited him a year ago to show him an early version of the product. It confirmed my belief that Office 2003 XML is finally bringing the original markup language vision to the desktop for millions of users.

Enjoy the book!

Jean Paoli
XML Architect,
Information Worker (Office, InfoPath) Groups, Microsoft Corporation
Co-editor of the XML 1.0 Recommendation
Redmond, October 2, 2003

Introducing
Desktop XML

- Why Desktop XML?
- XML concepts for Office users
- XML in Office

Part One

XML is a major innovation for Microsoft Office. You can now use a truly product-neutral data format with Office – and with any of the thousands of other products and systems that also support XML.

XML lets software know what your data *means* – not just what a particular product does with it. That means you can share Office documents more easily with other people, regardless of what those people do with them. You can also gather information from sources such as enterprise data stores or Web services, and integrate it easily into your own documents.

In this Part we show you why XML can do these and other useful things. We teach enough XML for you to understand how Office uses it (even if you have no prior XML experience), and we illustrate the XML features that are now available in the Office suite.

Desktop XML: The reason why

■ Information sharing and integration

■ Documents as information assets

■ Sharing information on the Web

Chapter

1

Attention information workers!

- Are you tired of cutting and pasting from one document to another?
- Are you frustrated because people outside your work group can't find your reports?
- Are you concerned that your spreadsheet analyses may not be using the latest data?
- Do you have that tired, worn-out feeling?

Well, we can't help you with the last item, unless you've been losing sleep over the first three! But Microsoft has a cure for those: They've added a powerful dose of the miracle ingredient XML to your favorite Office tools.

XML is a neutral way to represent data in a computer file. By "neutral" we mean that XML is not associated with a single vendor's computer programs, nor is it limited to a particular structure or type of information. XML is therefore ideal for sharing information among programs. In fact, it is recommended for that purpose by the World Wide Web Consortium

5

(W3C) and is supported by hundreds of products from every important software vendor.

XML allows you to share the data in your Office documents in new and more useful ways. It can help to automate routine drudgery. It can allow your documents to become first-class information citizens, managed and protected like the other data assets in your organization.

As an example, let's look at the large and successful (and utterly imaginary) Worldwide Widget Corporation (NASDAQ: W2C) before it began using XML.

1.1 | Office before XML

Doug writes a monthly Sales Update article for the company newsletter that is widely read and appreciated for its up-to-the-minute data and inspirational prose. He types the article into Microsoft Word and saves it as a `.doc` file.

He formats the article using different styles; for example, "Heading 1" for the title and "Heading 2" for the section headers. He also puts the author name and date in bold. (See Figure 1-1.)

Doug then submits the article by email to Denise, who is responsible for compiling the newsletter. Denise opens all the article documents that are submitted and cuts and pastes them into a new Word document. She reassigns styles to the various article titles and section headers to make them consistent.

Denise fixes any problems with the submissions, such as articles that are missing author names or dates. She does some general formatting, such as putting the company logo in the corner and changing the margins. She then saves her new `.doc` document in a directory named "newsletters" and distributes it by email to the entire company.

Although this approach accomplishes the goal of getting the newsletter out, it has several drawbacks:

rendered content

When Doug created his article, his focus was on creating a formatted rendition. He applied styles so that a human reading the article could see that the author is "Doug Jones" and that the article date is February 3, 2004. A computer, though, would have

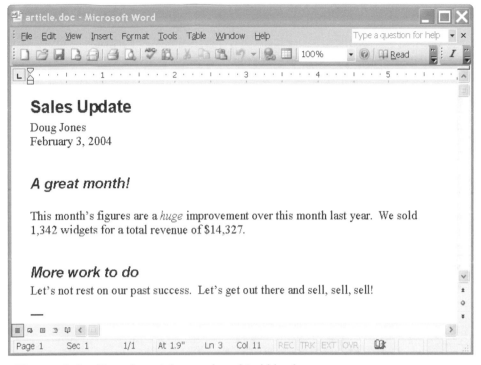

Figure 1-1   Doug's article, rendered in Word

no way of knowing this. As a result, there is no automated way to search the articles, say, for all articles whose author is Doug Jones, or all articles that were written after a particular date. In addition, there is no way to enforce rules for the article documents to make them consistent; for example, that at least one author is required, or that the title must be between 10 and 72 characters long.

inflexible rendition

Because the style information is tied directly to the content, there is a lot of repetitive manual reformatting. To change the style of all the author names, each author name needs to be changed separately. If the newsletter is to be presented in more than one way – for example, both as a printed document and as a Web page – the content of the document needs to be manually reformatted and stored redundantly. Templates could alleviate this problem somewhat, but only when the alternative renditions have similar structures.

lack of integration with enterprise data

Incorporating data from other parts of the organization requires either precise manual effort, or significant programming skills. For example, Doug needs to do careful, error-prone copying and reformatting to get the current sales statistics into his article every month.

proprietary format

The proprietary `.doc` format of Microsoft Word means that the text written by Doug, which may be a useful reference, is never integrated into a company database or content management system. It probably is abandoned on a file server somewhere.

All of these issues can be addressed by using XML in Office.

1.2 | Office documents as information assets

These days, no one seems to doubt that data is a valuable company asset. Business data that is more up-to-date and accessible can lead to more accurate planning, improved customer service, and more efficient business processes.

Technologists therefore treat data with great care. They carefully design databases and make them available to a variety of business processes. They organize these databases so that the data can be quickly and easily queried, joined, sorted and summarized. They protect them using security measures and disaster recovery plans.

All too often, though, this great care is extended only to databases containing operational data about customers, products, sales, and suppliers. There is a vast wealth of equally important data, stored in documents, that is largely ignored. It may include legal contracts, Web pages, memos, budget spreadsheets, product specifications, press releases, marketing brochures, conference presentations, product manuals and company policies and procedures.

These documents are often isolated and inaccessible. They are stored in proprietary binary formats on file servers, using inconsistent directories, names and versioning strategies. They are in rendered form, and therefore cannot be searched, summarized or indexed consistently in any meaningful way.

To coin a phrase, the data in documents isn't *integrated* with the other data of the enterprise. Using XML in Office allows that data to be integrated. Ironically, XML enables integration by separation:

- Separating the document representation from the software.

  Because XML is a non-proprietary, open file format, a wide variety of software tools can act on your documents. This means that these documents can be integrated into your business processes just like any data in a database.

- Separating the data content from style information.

  In order to use your data effectively, you need to understand what it means rather than just what it looks like. XML lets you identify and describe the content of your document, not just its outward appearance.

Without delving too far into the technical details just yet, let's take a closer look at how these two separations can help you.

1.2.1 *Separating the document representation from the software*

Previous versions of Office primarily used proprietary formats, such as `.doc` and `.xls` files, to store documents. These binary formats could effectively be used only by the software that created them. If you've ever tried to open up a `.doc` file in Notepad, as shown in Figure 1-2, you know that the format is indecipherable to the human reader, and it is largely indecipherable to other software applications as well. Only the Microsoft Word application knows how to make complete sense of it.

We are so accustomed to this state of affairs that we do not think of the documents separately from the software. A document is a "Word document" or an "Excel worksheet" that has no use outside Office.

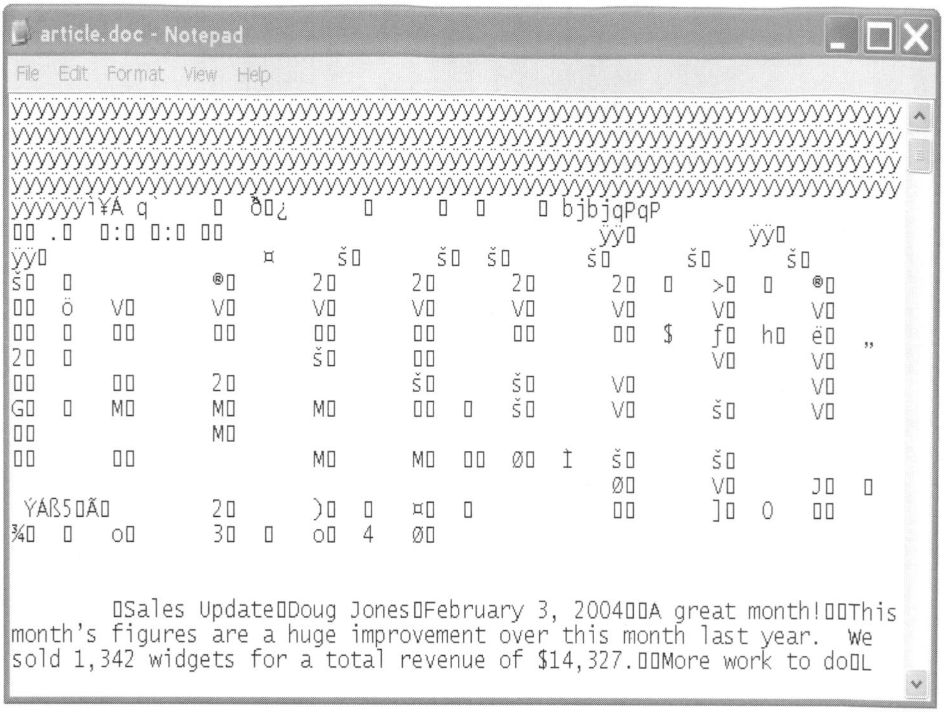

Figure 1-2   Word .doc document viewed in a text editor

XML, in contrast, is a non-proprietary character-based data representation that can be processed both by humans and, more importantly, by hundreds of computer programs. When an Office document is saved as XML, it can be used by other tools in addition to Microsoft Word.

The document is no longer a "Word document", but an XML document that can be edited in, or processed by, whatever tool makes the most sense for a given task. The document can be queried, transformed, sorted, viewed on the Web, passed around in e-commerce business processes, validated, stored in a database, shared with non-Office users and archived and indexed.

Separating the document format from the software makes the Office software more useful, too. Suddenly Office applications can be used to edit a wider variety of documents. The analytical tools of Excel can be used on any data that can be represented as XML, not just data that is stored in an Excel worksheet. Word can be used to edit any XML document.

Example 1-1 shows Doug's article represented as an XML document. Tags, such as `<title>` and `</title>`, are used to mark the start and end of data elements. Doug didn't type those tags; Word did it for him. In fact, Office users don't even have to see them on the screen if they don't want to.

There is more information in Chapter 2, "XML concepts for Office users", on page 20.

Example 1-1. Doug's article, represented in XML

```
<?xml version="1.0" encoding="UTF-8" standalone="yes"?>
<article xmlns="http://xmlinoffice.com/article"
         type="sales" id="A123">
  <title>Sales Update</title>
  <author>Doug Jones</author>
  <date>February 3, 2004</date>
  <body>
   <section>
     <header>A great month!</header>
     <para>This month's figures are a <em>huge</em> improvement over
this month last year. We sold 1,342 widgets for a total revenue of
$14,327.</para>
   </section>
   <section>
     <header>More work to do</header>
     <para>Let's not rest on our past success. Let's get out there
and sell, sell, sell!</para>
   </section>
  </body>
</article>
```

1.2.2 *Separating data content from style information*

One thing you may have noticed about our XML example is the absence of formatting information. Nothing in the document tells an application to indent a particular paragraph, display a word as bold, or use any particular font for a header. Rather, the tags convey the meaning and structure of the document.

There are tags that identify simple data elements, such as `date` and `title`. There are also elements with complex structures, such as `para` and `section`.

The vocabulary in the tags was created just for articles, which assures that there is a way to identify everything the company thinks is important about an article.

Separating the data content of the document from its formatting is one of the important principles of XML. The content itself is stored as an XML document, and different stylesheets are applied to it to achieve different renditions. This separation has two important benefits: self-describing content and flexible rendering.

1.2.2.1   Self-describing content

Describing the data rather than the style means that applications can identify what the document contains rather than what it looks like. The document becomes *self-describing*.

For example, in Doug's article, we know exactly where to find the author name, because tags identify it as an `author` element. Otherwise, we might have to assume that the author name is "that thing in bold on the second line".

Being able to identify data elements is powerful because it allows you to perform all kinds of automated functions on the document, such as:

- searching for all articles whose author is "Doug Jones" (not just articles that contain the words "Doug Jones")
- specifying rules for article documents, such as "at least one author must be specified", or "the title must be between 10 and 72 characters long"
- automatically generating a list of all the article titles, authors and dates
- generating a summary calculation of the average number of paragraphs in an article

1.2.2.2   Flexible rendering

Another advantage of separating data from style is that it provides flexibility in the formatting. If the same material is to be presented in more than one way, it does not have to be written (and maintained) multiple times.

For example, suppose Doug's article is to appear in a printed newsletter and also be available on the Web. Perhaps the Web version has links and some sidebar information that does not appear in the print version. The look is different, too: the fonts are larger on the website, and the text is continuous rather than being broken into pages.

In this situation, the unrendered (*abstract*) data content is in a single XML document. There are two different stylesheets that create different renditions of the content. If the content must be changed, it only needs to be modified in one place.

You can also create different subsets or views of the same data. For example, if:

- Different readers are interested in different aspects of the document.
- Security concerns allow only part of an article to be read by a particular audience.
- On the Web, you want to provide just the first paragraph of the article as a tease before requiring a reader to sign up for a service.
- The document contains information that is not normally presented, such as search keywords, or information about who last updated the document and when.

In each of these situations, you can write a stylesheet that shows only the relevant parts of the article.

Supporting multiple renditions of the same content is increasingly necessary. Browsing the Web has come to mean a lot more than just looking at HTML pages in a Web browser on a PC. People now use telephones, PDAs and other handheld devices to browse the Web, and they are inventing new ways of using the Web all the time. Different devices have different screen sizes and memory limits, and therefore need information presented in a different way.

When style information is kept separate, it is easier to change it without affecting the content. For example, if you decide you want the author name to appear in italics, you can simply change the stylesheet once, rather than restyling the author name in every article document.

1.3 | Enterprise data integration

We have seen that XML in Office can help integrate data by making it easier to share, search and process. This data sharing goes beyond making data in Office documents available to the enterprise. XML also makes it easier to import enterprise data into Office documents for reuse and analysis, and even to use Office as a front-end to manage enterprise data.

1.3.1 *Importing enterprise data*

You know the data – that valuable information about sales, customers, products, inventory, and employees. It is stored in database management systems, software packages (such as ERP and accounting packages) and files on a variety of computer platforms around the organization. If you are lucky, you can at least access this data in useful ways using a reporting tool or custom application provided by your IT department. If you are not so lucky, you get canned reports that aren't exactly what you need and cannot be reused. Even worse, you have to get an IT person involved every time you want to query the data in a new way.

That is all changing. Enterprise data is rapidly becoming available as XML. All major relational database vendors now offer an XML front-end, which allows data to be queried and extracted as XML. A lot of information that is stored and managed by ERP and other software packages can be exported as XML. In addition, there is a whole body of data whose native format is XML: both in XML databases and as documents in repositories and file systems.

1.3.2 *Reusing enterprise data*

Remember Doug? He includes the past month's sales figures in his article for the newsletter. Before XML he went to an intranet site and ran a report that returned the results in a Web page. He then cut and pasted the information into his article in Word.

He had to do some reformatting, because the data came back without dollar signs and the columns did not line up properly when pasted into Word. In addition, there were some figures, such as total sales and average amount of sale, which he calculated by hand.

For Doug to do this once, with relatively static data, would not be a huge amount of extra work. But Doug includes some or all of the sales figures in his article every month. He had to go through this same cutting, pasting and reformatting process repeatedly. This was tedious, and prone to error. In addition, the data is updated regularly. In order to have the most up-to-date numbers in the article, he needed to wait until the last minute or redo the formatting again before publication.

Office 2003 has greatly improved this situation using XML. All Doug needs to do now is click a button in the Word document to import the sales figures, formatted the way he wants them. When he wants to refresh the data, it is as simple as clicking that button again.

Of course, there is some setup required. A link to the database that stores the sales data needs to be created to generate an XML document. Also, a mapping needs to be defined between the resulting XML and its formatting in Word. For repetitive tasks like this one, it is well worth the time spent for setup.

1.3.3 *Analyzing enterprise data*

Another reason to import enterprise data is to allow the use of the familiar Office environment for data analysis and reporting. In particular, Excel has tools for performing complex, multi-step mathematical calculations on data, and for easily creating graphs and charts. Users are already familiar with Excel's features and want to continue to use them rather than learn new reporting tools for different kinds of enterprise data.

Before XML, program code had to be written before Excel could import anything but text files that contained tabular data (*flat files*). And those had to be reformatted, just like Doug's sales figures.

Importing XML does not require program code. Moreover, it allows Excel to import from a large number of possible data sources, without users having to understand the technical details of those sources.

The enterprise data is imported into areas of Excel worksheets that were previously set up to analyze that kind of data. For example, Doug could create a spreadsheet to generate graphs of the sales figures, as well as summary statistics. He could import the latest sales figures with a single click each month, and the graphs and statistics would automatically be updated.

1.3.4 *Office as an enterprise data front-end*

One of the exciting new capabilities of Office is not just *reading* enterprise data, but also acting as a front-end to create and update it. You can use Word, Excel and the new forms tool, InfoPath, for this purpose. With them you can create new business documents and data that you can store in a database or feed automatically to non-Office applications.

For example, Ellen works in the accounting department of Worldwide Widget Corporation. The company uses an accounting package that allows the import of transactions from XML documents. Employees used to fill out their monthly expense reports in Excel and email them to Ellen. Ellen checked the expense reports and entered the totals manually into the accounting package in order to issue reimbursement checks.

This worked out fine when there were only 15 traveling employees, but as the company grew, the task became unmanageable. There was the problem of invalid expense reports; employees often entered invalid dates or cost center codes. There was also the extra work of entering information into the accounting system, a process that was time consuming and subject to human error. In addition, there was very little querying and reporting capability.

Ellen considered purchasing a Web-based expense reporting tool that employees could use when they are on the road. Instead, when XML in Office became available she realized that the employees could use it to create expense reports. She identified the cells in the Excel expense report as elements in the XML vocabulary required by the accounting package, created a set of validation rules, and rolled it out to the employees.

Expense reports are now submitted as XML documents, although the employees continue to create them with the same tag-less Excel spreadsheet. Not only can Ellen validate and query these new expense reports far more easily, she can automatically import them into the accounting system.

In situations like this one, Microsoft Office has huge potential as a simple, inexpensive XML editing tool. It requires no additional software for the users. The minimal amount of setup needed does not require advanced programming skills.

1.4 | Next stop: the Web

So far, we have looked at information integration within a single organization. With the arrival of the Web, companies have increasingly focused on information sharing *among* organizations.

Traditionally, companies wishing to share business data either did it the old-fashioned way, by printed reports, phone calls and faxes, or by using expensive EDI systems. The Web has completely changed the face of business by making it possible to share information – and therefore conduct business transactions – far more easily using a standard set of open protocols. Organizations share business documents such as product catalogs, purchase orders and invoices via the Web. Almost invariably the transactional documents are represented in XML.

In addition to passing XML documents back and forth over the Internet, businesses have begun to share data with a new class of software called *Web services*. Web services allow applications to communicate with one another (and even discover each other!) without human involvement.

For example, a provider may offer a Web service that returns a stock quote, or the current exchange rate for a particular pair of currencies. A Web service could also be something more complex, such as a service that accepts or places an order. Other applications can execute these services over the Web without any human intervention.

Obviously, not all Web services are intended for the public at large. Some are available only to partners with whom a business relationship already exists. But public or private, the Web services software works the same way.

Web services use XML to represent requests to a service as well as the information that the service returns. As a result, you can integrate Microsoft Office with XML Web services. You can use InfoPath, Word and Excel to enter inputs to many Web services and to display the results.

1.4.1 *Retrieving data from Web services*

You can request information from a trusted source on the Web, and have it automatically included in an Office document. At Worldwide Widget Corporation, many of the sales reps and consultants travel internationally. When filling out their expense reports, they enter the currency in which their expenses were paid and the exchange rate, on that date, in US dollars.

Of course, it is possible for Ellen to direct the employees to a particular website and have them manually look up the exchange rate. However, it would be more efficient and accurate to have the exchange rate included in the expense report automatically. By using Excel to request the rate from a Web service, the consultants can retrieve it and apply it to the expense item.

1.4.2 *Office as a front-end to Web services*

In 1.3.4, "Office as an enterprise data front-end", on page 16, we talked about using Office as a front-end editor for an enterprise application. This use of Office is not limited to internal applications; you can use it across the Web as well.

Worldwide Widget Corporation buys parts from a huge number of suppliers, large and small. The smaller suppliers have no real e-commerce systems in place, although they do have PCs in their offices and access to the Web. They receive purchase orders from Worldwide and send it invoices, by phone, fax and email.

Worldwide wants to move all the suppliers over to a Web-based ordering system because it is cheaper and less prone to error than the manual process. It develops a set of Web services that allow a supplier to retrieve XML purchase order documents and submit XML invoice documents.

The medium and large suppliers have IT departments that can write code to call these Web services automatically from their enterprise accounting systems. The code processes the purchase orders and generates the invoices.

The small suppliers, unfortunately, don't have such systems, so they need a human interface to the Web services. Worldwide Widget could develop a Web-based front-end that would allow them to log on and view their purchase orders and create invoices. However, that would require software development skills and time, which are in short supply.

Instead, Worldwide designs InfoPath forms for the invoices and purchase orders. They allow the small suppliers to display the POs and prepare invoices that can be submitted as XML documents.

1.5 | What next?

Now you've learned about some of the potential uses for desktop XML. Perhaps some of the scenarios described in this chapter seem familiar, and address goals you have for your own documents: better data sharing, self-describing documents, flexible rendering, and integration with enterprise data stores and the Web.

In the next chapter, we'll go into some more detail about XML. We'll cover the basic concepts that are relevant to its use with Office.

Then we'll complete our introduction with a chapter on all the XML-enabled products in the Office suite, with examples of their XML capabilities.

XML concepts
for Office users

Introductory Discussion

- What is XML, really?
- Four principles of generalized markup
- Abstraction vs. rendition
- Elements and attributes
- XML and the Web

Chapter

2

irtually every influential company in the software industry is promoting XML as the next step in the Web's evolution. Why? Because it enables *information sharing*, and that is the key to electronic commerce, application integration, and many other desirable things.

And now Microsoft has bet the future of the world's most successful office suite on XML. How can these companies be so confident about something so new? More important: how can *you* be sure that your time invested in learning and using XML will be profitable?

We can all safely bet on XML because its technology is in fact very old and has been proven effective over several decades and thousands of projects. The easiest way to understand the central ideas of XML is to go back to their source, the *Standard Generalized Markup Language* (SGML).

XML is, in fact, a streamlined subset of SGML, so SGML's track record is XML's as well. SGML enables information interchange within and between some of the world's largest companies. Its extensible markup technology was first used for document processing, but over time it has become clear that data and documents are the same thing! To be precise, documents are the interchangeable form of data.

If you understand where XML comes from, you'll better understand what it is, how to use it, and where it and the desktop are going.

2.1 | Formatting markup

XML comes from a rich history of text processing systems. Markup actually predates the computer. Figure 2-1 shows a marked-up manuscript that might have been submitted to a human who would compose the type for printing.

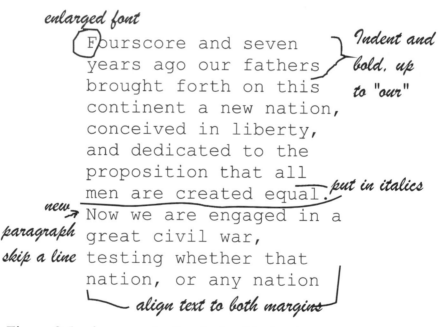

Figure 2-1   A manuscript "marked up" by hand

The first wave of automated text processing was computer typesetting. An author would type a document and include style codes to describe how the document should be formatted. The computer would read the style codes and the rest of the text and print the document with the described formatting.

The file that contains the data of the document, plus the description of the desired format, is called a *rendition*. The style codes in the rendition file are called *formatting markup*.

The system interprets the formatting markup and converts the rendition into something physically perceivable by a human being – a *presentation*. The presentation medium was originally paper, but eventually electronic display was added.

This scenario isn't totally history. You and Word work with renditions today. It's just that Word gives you a nicer interface to manipulate them.

Word's user interface to the rendition (that is, to the .doc file with the style codes in it) is designed to look like the presentation (the finished paper product). The interface is called a *What You See Is What You Get (WYSI-WYG)* interface. Since a rendition describes a presentation, it is convenient to have the user interface reflect the end-product.

More than convenient. For Word it is essential, as we saw in 1.2.1, "Separating the document representation from the software", on page 9. Word's native binary .doc rendition file format is unfathomable to humans, and to virtually all non-Microsoft software.

For interchange (and virus avoidance) Word also offers a plain-text equivalent called *Rich Text Format (RTF)*. While computers can handle it better than .doc, humans won't find it much of an improvement, as a glance at Example 2-1 will demonstrate.[1]

2.2 | Generalized markup

Formatting markup is sufficient if your only goal is to create a single rendition and then print it. In 1969, IBM asked a young researcher named Charles Goldfarb (the name may sound familiar) to build a system for editing, searching, managing, and publishing legal documents.

Goldfarb found that there were IBM products for each of these tasks but they could not communicate with each other. They could not share information! Each of them used different markup. They could not read each other's files, just as you may have had trouble loading *WordPerfect* files into *Word* or vice versa.

---

1. Whitespace added for attempted readability. Prolog with font definitions, style definitions, etc. omitted for the same reason.

Example 2-1. Doug's article, represented in RTF (article.rtf)

```
\pard\plain\s1\ql \li0\ri0\sb240\sa60\keepn\widctlpar\aspalpha
\aspnum\faauto\outlinelevel0\adjustright\rin0\lin0\itap0
\pararsid13583126 \b\f1\fs32\lang1033\langfe1033\kerning32\cgrid
\langnp1033\langfenp1033
{\insrsid13583126\par }
\pard \s1\ql \li0\ri0\sb240\sa60\keepn\widctlpar\aspalpha\aspnum
\faauto\outlinelevel0\adjustright\rin0\lin0\itap0\pararsid5243775
{\insrsid10036224 Sales Update\par }
\pard\plain \ql \li0\ri0\widctlpar\aspalpha\aspnum\faauto
\adjustright\rin0\lin0\itap0\pararsid10036224 \fs24\lang1033
\langfe1033\cgrid\langnp1033\langfenp1033
{\insrsid16529125 Doug Jones}
{\insrsid10036224\par February 3, 2004\par }
{\insrsid10036224\charrsid10036224\par }
\pard\plain \s2\ql \li0\ri0\sb240\sa60\keepn\widctlpar
\aspalpha\aspnum\faauto\outlinelevel1\adjustright\rin0\lin0\itap0
\pararsid12923755 \b\i\f1\fs28\lang1033\langfe1033\cgrid\langnp1033
\langfenp1033
{\insrsid10036224 A great month!}
{\insrsid1358312\par }
\pard\plain \ql \li0\ri0\widctlpar\aspalpha\aspnum\faauto
\adjustright\rin0\lin0\itap0 \fs24\lang1033\langfe1033\cgrid
\langnp1033\langfenp1033
{\insrsid10036224\par This month\rquote s figures are a }
{\i\insrsid10036224\charrsid10036224 huge}
{\insrsid10036224  improvement over this month last year.  We }
{\insrsid12923755 sold 1,342 widgets for a total revenue of
$14,327.}
{\insrsid10036224\par\par }
\pard\plain \s2\ql \li0\ri0\sb240\sa60\keepn\widctlpar\aspalpha
\aspnum\faauto\outlinelevel1\adjustright\rin0\lin0\itap0
\pararsid12923755 \b\i\f1\fs28\lang1033\langfe1033\cgrid\langnp1033
\langfenp1033
{\insrsid10036224 More work to do\par }
\pard\plain \ql \li0\ri0\widctlpar\aspalpha\aspnum\faauto
\adjustright\rin0\lin0\itap0 \fs24\lang1033\langfe1033\cgrid
\langnp1033\langfenp1033
{\insrsid10036224 Let\rquote s not rest on}{\insrsid12923755  our
past success.  Let\rquote s get out there and sell, sell, sell!}
{\insrsid10036224\par }{\insrsid13583126\par }
```

The problem then, as now, was that to integrate these diverse products, a neutral *document representation*[2] was needed for the information – one that wasn't designed for a single product.

---

2. Sometimes called a file format.

Goldfarb – later joined by two other IBM researchers, Ed Mosher and Ray Lorie – set out to solve this problem. The team recognized (eventually) that the solution would need to satisfy four principles:

neutral data representation (markup language)
   Various computer programs and systems would need to be able to read and write information in the same representation.

extensible markup
   There is an immeasurable variety of types of information that must be exchanged. The markup language must be extensible enough to support them all.

rule-based markup
   There must be a formal way of describing the rules followed by documents of the same type. Computers must be able to read and enforce the rules.[3]

stylesheets
   For sharing to work, it must be possible to create document types that aren't renditions. The real information must be accessible in the abstract, independent of the formatting – or any other processing – instructions. Ideally, the latter should be in separate stylesheets.

These principles are important far beyond the exchange of traditional documentation. In fact they underlie the exchange of any form of information.

The IBM team's solution was the *Generalized Markup Language (GML)*, which Goldfarb later drew on for his invention of the *Standard Generalized Markup Language (SGML)* – the parent of HTML and XML.

In the following sections, we'll look at each of these principles in a bit more detail and see how they apply to Word.

---

3. History is being compressed here somewhat. Computers that could "read and enforce the rules" didn't enter the picture until SGML.

2.2.1 *Neutral data representation (markup language)*

The need for a neutral data representation is easy to understand. Tools cannot interchange information if they do not speak the same language.

2.2.2 *Extensible markup*

The IBM team realized that the neutral representation should be *specific* to legal documents while at the same time being general enough to be used for things that are completely unrelated to the law. This seems like a paradox but it is not as impossible as it sounds!

2.2.2.1   Vocabularies

This idea is a little more subtle to grasp, but vital to understanding XML. For example, lawyers and scientists both use Latin, but they do not use the same vocabulary.

Similarly, in Example 2-2 we have Doug's newsletter article in XML, using a vocabulary that was designed for newsletter articles. In Example 2-3, however, we have the same article represented using a different vocabulary.

Before we look at the differences between the two XML representations, let's use Example 2-2 to learn the basics of XML: elements and tags, content and data, and attributes.

elements and tags
> The document has one `title` element. It begins with a start-tag (`<title>`) and ends with a corresponding end-tag (`</title>`). The forward slash differentiates an end-tag from a start-tag. The purpose of the tags is to identify the type of element (`title`, in this case) and show where it starts and ends.

content and data
> The text in between the tags is the *content* of the element. In the case of `title` the content is entirely data characters. However, the content of `body` has only markup that represents elements, and

Example 2-2. Doug's article, represented in `article` XML

```
<?xml version="1.0" encoding="UTF-8" standalone="yes"?>
<article xmlns="http://xmlinoffice.com/article"
         type="sales" id="A123">
  <title>Sales Update</title>
  <author>Doug Jones</author>
  <date>February 3, 2004</date>
  <body>
   <section>
     <header>A great month!</header>
     <para>This month's figures are a <em>huge</em> improvement over
this month last year. We sold 1,342 widgets for a total revenue of
$14,327.</para>
   </section>
   <section>
     <header>More work to do</header>
     <para>Let's not rest on our past success. Let's get out there
and sell, sell, sell!</para>
   </section>
  </body>
</article>
```

the first `para` has mixed content: data and an element (`em`). Elements that occur in the content of elements form a hierarchy. At the top is the document element (or root element): in this case, `article`.

attributes
    An element can have properties besides its element-type name and content. These are represented by name-value pairs called *attributes*. In the example, only `article` has attributes. The value of the one named `id` is the name of this particular `article` element, which is useful when a group of articles is combined in a newsletter. The `xmlns` attribute declares a namespace, which we explain in 2.6, "Namespaces", on page 39.

    The attribute names and element-type names, such as `title`, comprise a custom vocabulary specifically designed to describe newsletter articles. In contrast, Example 2-3 uses a vocabulary called the *Word Markup Language (WordML)*.[4]

---

4. Whitespace added for readability.

Example 2-3. Doug's article, represented in WordML XML (article WordML.xml)

```
<w:body>
 <wx:sect>
  <wx:sub-section>
   <w:p><w:pPr><w:pStyle w:val="Heading1"/></w:pPr></w:p>
  </wx:sub-section>
  <wx:sub-section>
   <w:p>
    <w:pPr><w:pStyle w:val="Heading1"/></w:pPr>
    <w:r><w:t>Sales Update</w:t></w:r></w:p>
   <w:p><w:r><w:t>Doug Jones</w:t></w:r></w:p>
   <w:p><w:r><w:t>February 3, 2004</w:t></w:r></w:p><w:p/>
   <wx:sub-section>
    <w:p>
     <w:pPr><w:pStyle w:val="Heading2"/></w:pPr>
     <w:r><w:t>A great month!</w:t></w:r></w:p>
    <w:p/>
    <w:p>
     <w:r><w:t>This month's figures are a </w:t></w:r>
     <w:r><w:rPr><w:i/></w:rPr><w:t>huge</w:t></w:r>
     <w:r><w:t> improvement over this month last year. We sold 1,342
widgets for </w:t></w:r><w:proofErr w:type="gramStart"/>
     <w:r><w:t>a total</w:t></w:r><w:proofErr w:type="gramEnd"/>
     <w:r><w:t> revenue of $14,327.</w:t></w:r></w:p><w:p/>
   </wx:sub-section>
   <wx:sub-section>
    <w:p>
     <w:pPr><w:pStyle w:val="Heading2"/></w:pPr>
     <w:r><w:t>More work to do</w:t></w:r></w:p>
    <w:p><w:r><w:t>Let's not rest on our past success. Let's get out
there and sell, sell, sell!</w:t></w:r></w:p><w:p/>
     <w:sectPr>
      <w:pgSz w:w="12240" w:h="15840"/>
      <w:pgMar w:top="1440" w:right="1800" w:bottom="1440"
       w:left="1800" w:header="720" w:footer="720" w:gutter="0"/>
      <w:cols w:space="720"/><w:docGrid w:line-pitch="360"/>
     </w:sectPr>
   </wx:sub-section>
  </wx:sub-section>
 </wx:sect>
</w:body>
```

WordML uses XML, as do thousands of other data representations. However, the WordML vocabulary is unique. It was designed by Microsoft to be the XML equivalent of .doc and RTF. As such, it describes components and properties of the Word formatting model. Even if one of its element-type names were the same as one in some other vocabulary, it would probably not identify the same type of thing. (We explain WordML in detail in Chapter 5, "Rendering and presenting XML documents", on page 86.)

The reason that generalized markup became successful is that users can create their own vocabularies to meet their needs. But all vocabularies use the standard markup language syntax (and other language constructs), so tools can be developed to do the large amount of common processing that is necessary for all vocabularies.

2.2.2.2 Abstractions and renditions

Computers are not as smart as we are. If we want the computer to consider a piece of text to be written in a foreign language (for instance for spell-checking purposes) then we must label it explicitly `foreign-phrase` and not just put it in italics! The "foreign phrase" is the *abstraction* that we are trying to represent; italics is just a particular rendition of that abstraction for visual presentations. For audible presentations, the rendition might be a voice with an accent.

Formatting markup is specific to a particular use of the information. Search engines cannot do very useful searching on italics because they do not know why something is italicized. It could be a foreign phrase but it could also be a citation of another document.

In contrast, the search engine could do something very helpful with suitably-marked `citation` elements: it could return a list of those documents that are cited by other documents.

Italics are a form of markup specific to a particular application: formatting. In contrast, the citation element is markup that can be used by a variety of applications. That is why Goldfarb named this form of markup *generalized markup.* Generalized markup is the alternative to formatting markup and other specialized single-use coding schemes.

Caution   *Generalized markup is often called* **structured markup** *and the act of using it* **structuring a document.** *Unfortunately, "structured" is the most misused term in markup languages, with at least four different meanings (see 20.1, "Structured vs. unstructured", on page 430). This use of it implies that only abstractions have structure, which Figure 2-2 clearly refutes. It shows the Word template* `ProfessionalReport.dot` *with the* **Document Map** *and* **Style Area** *in view. The structural hierarchy is in the left pane and style codes are in the center. A Word template is not just a stylesheet, but also a guide to the structure of the rendition.*

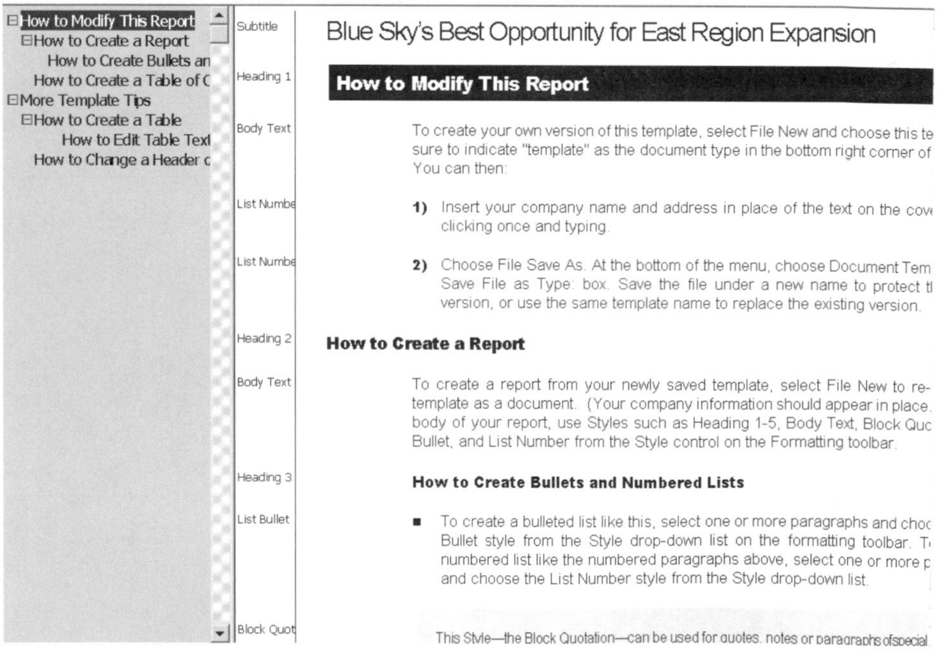

Figure 2-2   Structure of a rendition

2.2.3 *Rule-based markup*

If computer systems are to work with documents reliably, the documents have to follow certain rules. In retrospect we can see that this is important for interchanging information of all sorts, whether it is traditionally considered a document or not.

For instance a courtroom transcript might be required to have the name of the judge, defendant, both attorneys and (optionally) the names of members of the jury (if there is one). Since humans are prone to make mistakes, the computer would have to enforce the rules for us.

In other words the legal markup language should be specified in some formal way that would restrict elements appropriately. If the court stenographer tried to submit a transcript to the system without these elements being properly filled in, the system would check its *validity* and complain that it was *invalid*.

Once again, this concept is today very common in the database world. Database people typically have several layers of checking to guarantee that improper data cannot appear in their databases. For instance *syntactic checks* guarantee that phone numbers are composed of digits and that people's names are not. *Semantic checks* ensure that business rules are followed (such as "purchase order numbers must be unique"). The database world calls the set of constraints on the database structure a *schema*. This word has also caught on in the XML world.

Of course, court transcripts have a different structure from wills, which in turn have a different structure from memos. So you would need to rigorously define what it means for each type of document to be valid. In markup language terminology, each of these is a *document type* and the formal definition that describes each type is called a *document type definition* (DTD) or *schema definition*. These terms refer both to the vocabulary and the constraints on the vocabulary's use.

Example 2-4 shows a simple DTD expressed with three XML element-type declarations. Example 2-5 shows the equivalent schema definition expressed using the *XML Schema Definition Language (XSDL)*.[5]

Example 2-4. Markup declarations

```
<!ELEMENT Q-AND-A (QUESTION,ANSWER)+>
<!-- This allows: question, answer, question, answer ... -->
<!ELEMENT QUESTION (#PCDATA)>
<!-- Questions are just made up of textual data -->
<!ELEMENT ANSWER (#PCDATA)>
<!-- Answers are just made up of textual data -->
```

Example 2-5. Schema definition

```
<schema xmlns='http://www.w3.org/2001/XMLSchema'
        xmlns:qa='http://www.q.and.a.com/'
        targetNamespace='http://www.q.and.a.com/'>
 <element name="Q-AND-A">
 <complexType>
  <sequence minOccurs="1" maxOccurs="unbounded">
   <element ref="qa:QUESTION"/>
   <element ref="qa:ANSWER"/>
  </sequence>
 </complexType>
 </element>
<!-- This allows: question, answer, question, answer ... -->
 <element name="QUESTION" type="string"/>
<!-- Questions are just made up of textual data -->
 <element name="ANSWER" type="string"/>
<!-- Answers are just made up of textual data -->
</schema>
```

2.2.4 *Stylesheets*

Of course, if you are using XML for publishing, you must still be able to generate high quality print and online renditions of the document. Your readers do not want to read XML text directly. Instead of directly inserting the formatting commands in the XML document, we usually tell the computer how to generate formatted renditions *from* the XML abstraction.

---

5. XSDL is the only schema language that Office 2003 can support. We explain it in detail in Chapter 22, "XML Schema (XSDL)", on page 466.

For example in a print presentation, we can make the content of TITLE elements bold and large, insert page breaks before the beginning of chapters, and turn emphasis, citations and foreign words into italics. These rules are specified in a file called a *stylesheet*. The stylesheet is where human designers can express their creativity and understanding of formatting conventions. The stylesheet allows the computer to automatically convert the document from the abstraction to a formatted rendition.

Stylesheets for XML invariably conform to the Extensible Style Language Transformations (XSLT) W3C recommendation. XSLT can do much more processing than formatting markup ever could. Often it is used for tasks that don't involve formatting at all.

Moreover, XSLT stylesheets are normally written to apply to all documents of a given type, rather than a single document. Just as the DTD or schema sets the rules for markup, an XSLT stylesheet is a set of rules for processing, as depicted in Figure 2-3.[6]

2.3 | Elements and the logical structure

Most documents (for example books and magazines) can easily be broken down into components (chapters and articles). These can also be broken down into components (titles, paragraphs, figures and so forth). And those components can be broken down into components until we get to the textual data itself – words and sentences. At this point we would typically stop breaking the document into components unless we were interested in linguistic research.

It turns out that every document can be viewed this way, though some fit the model more naturally than others. In fact all information can be viewed this way...with the same caveat!

In XML, these components are called *elements*. Each element represents a logical component of a document. Elements can contain other elements and can also contain the words and sentences that you would usually think of as the text of the document. XML calls this text the document's *character data*. This hierarchical view of XML documents is demonstrated in Figure 2-4.

---

6. We teach you how to create an XSLT stylesheet in Chapter 18, "XSL Transformations (XSLT)", on page 392.

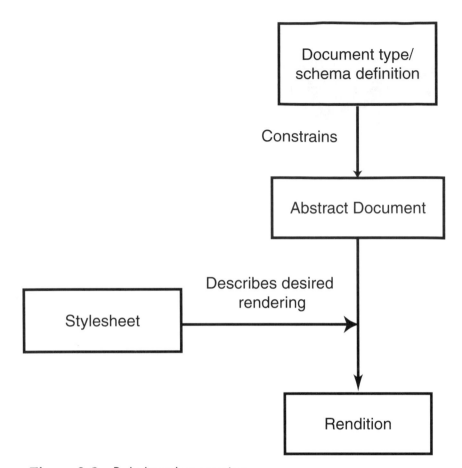

Figure 2-3   Rule-based processing

Markup professionals call this the *tree structure* of the document. The element that contains all of the others (e.g. Book, Article or Memo) is known as the *root element*. This name captures the fact that it is the only element that does not "hang" off of some other element. The root element is also referred to as the *document element* because it holds the entire logical document within it. The terms *root element* and *document element* are interchangeable.

The elements that are contained in the root are called its *subelements*. They may contain subelements themselves. If they do, we will call them *branches*. If they do not, we will call them *leaves*.

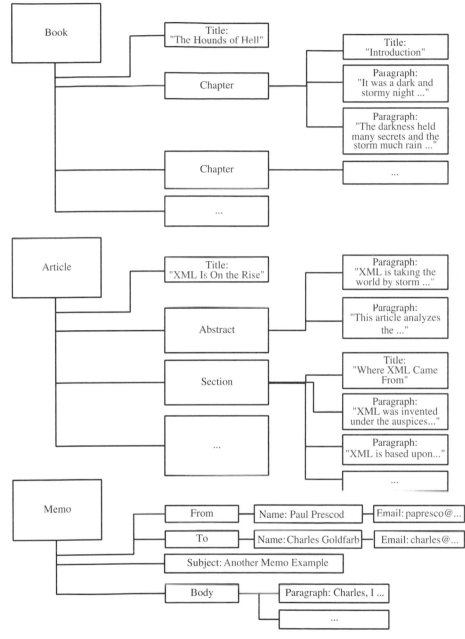

Figure 2-4 Hierarchical views of documents

Thus, the `Chapter` and `Section` elements are branches (because they have subelements), but the `Paragraph` and `Title` elements are leaves (because they only contain character data).

Elements can also have extra information attached to them called *attributes*. Attributes describe properties of elements. For instance a `CIA-record` element might have a security attribute that gives the security rating for that element. A CIA database might only release certain records to certain people depending on their security rating. It is somewhat of a judgement call which aspects of a document should be represented with elements and which should be represented with attributes.

Real-world documents do not always fit this tree model perfectly. They often have non-hierarchical features such as cross-references or hypertext links from one section of the tree to another. XML can represent these structures too.

A WordML document also has an element structure. But as the WordML document type is a complex rendition with over 400 element types, the structure isn't usually as clear as the abstraction in Figure 2-4.

2.4 | Well-formedness and validity

Every language has rules about what is or is not correct in the language. In human languages that takes many forms: words have a particular correct pronunciation (or range of pronunciations) and they can be combined in certain ways to make valid sentences (grammar). Similarly XML has two different notions of "correct". The first is merely that the markup is intelligible: the XML equivalent of "getting the pronunciation right". A document with intelligible markup is called a *well-formed* document. One important goal of XML was that these basic rules should be simple so that they could be strictly adhered to.

The XML equivalent of "using the right words in the right place" is called *validity* and is related to the notion of document types. A document is *valid* if it declares conformance to a DTD in a document type declaration and actually conforms to that DTD.

A document could also (or exclusively) be identified as conforming to a schema. If it actually does conform, it is said to be *schema valid* (commonly shortened to "valid").

2.5 | XML and the World Wide Web

When the Web began it was pretty simple. You entered a Web address into your browser and it displayed the page from that address. The address was a *Uniform Resource Locator (URL)* and the page was marked up in HTML.

The W3C maintains a DTD for HTML, but many HTML documents don't conform to it. So browsers attempted to cope with errors rather than report them to the users (who couldn't correct them in any case).

The Web has since diverged from that simple model, both in terms of the addresses and the delivered pages. The addressing model has gotten richer, and the pages mostly don't exist until they hit your browser.

2.5.1 *Web addresses: URL and URN and URI and IRI*

"U R kidding!", U might think, but we R not!

There really are four different things that look like URLs, and act like them as well. You can safely treat them as equivalent when reading this book, unless we make a point of the difference in a specific context. They are:

URI

A *Uniform Resource Identifier (URI)* is the basic form of address on the Web.

URL

The *Uniform Resource Locator (URL)* is the most common form of URI.

URN

A newer form of URI, *Uniform Resource Name (URN)*, isn't location-dependent and perhaps will reduce the number of broken links. However, it has yet to catch on because it requires more sophisticated software support (although that doesn't stop it being used to declare namespaces, as we shall see shortly).

IRI

> An *Internationalized Resource Identifier (IRI)* is a form of URI that allows non-ASCII characters.

Now when you see *URI* in the text, you'll know that it isn't a typo!

2.5.2 *Web services*

Web addresses can be extended to become *URI references*, meaning they have parameters after the actual URI, as in:

```
http://www.amazon.com/exec/obidos/ASIN/0130651982/ref
%3Dase_charlesfgoldfars/103-3982805-1512612
```

The reason for the parameters is because large websites no longer keep repositories of static HTML pages. Instead, they analyze the parameters to determine the information you've requested and they generate a page that contains the results. The Web *address* has become a *request* and the Web *page* has become a *Web service*.

In practice, though, Web-based services that are actually offered under the name "Web services" return XML documents, not HTML. The services may offer a REST interface and/or a SOAP interface.[7]

REST

> A REST Web services interface is the same as the interface to any Web resource: your service request is a URI reference that addresses the result document.

SOAP

> The SOAP interface treats the service request and response as messages in a business transaction. The result document is encapsulated in the response message; it is not a Web resource and the service request is not its address.

Office products access a REST Web service as they would any network-addressable XML document; REST requires no special treatment

---

7. REST and SOAP are explained in Chapter 19, "Web services introduction", on page 414.

(although you may want to write a macro to help users build a particularly complex parameter string).

Therefore, any explicitly-identified Web service support in Office is only for SOAP; in fact, for a specific variety of SOAP called "document-style". That interface is more complex than REST, for two reasons:

- The service request could be an arbitrarily complex XML document.
- Both the request and the response are wrapped in a SOAP message, itself a complex XML document that is dynamically customized for each Web service operation.

In this book, we'll mention SOAP or REST explicitly unless the interface to the Web service isn't important in context. And whenever we mention external XML documents, that would also include those returned by REST Web services.

2.5.3 *XHTML*

Another way in which Web pages are changing is that a new version of HTML is starting to be used. It retains the HTML vocabulary, but uses XML syntax.

XHTML – unlike HTML – tends to be valid, as it is usually generated by software. It is used in several components of Office.

2.6 | Namespaces

There is a problem that arises when you allow anybody to pick names as XML does. The problem is that different people in different places will invariably use the same names for different things. This makes it very difficult to build systems that work with documents from multiple independent sources because a publisher could use the element-type name PAR to mean paragraph while a military vocabulary could use an element type with the same name to mean paratrooper. A mathematician might use an element type with that name to label paradoxes!

2.6.1 *Prefixes*

There is a standard that addresses this problem. It is known as *Namespaces in XML.*

A *namespace* is a conceptual universe within which a defined term – a *name* – is unique. An XML namespace is slightly different: it is divided into *namespace partitions* for different kinds of names so that, for example, an element-type name can be the same as an attribute name.

Within a namespace partition (also called a *symbol space*), each name is unique. It is declared only once and the declared definition applies wherever in the scope of the namespace partition the name is used.

A vocabulary is a namespace. Without the namespaces standard, a document type could only have a single vocabulary, consisting of its element-type and attribute names. The standard lets you mix vocabularies in a document by creating vocabulary nicknames (i.e. abbreviations) that you can prefix to the names to show the vocabulary to which they belong.

For example, you might choose to prefix names from a meteorological information vocabulary with `met:`. So a document might have elements such as `met:temperature`, `met:humidity` and so forth. It could also have `health:temperature`, from a different vocabulary. To the computer, `met:temperature` and `health:temperature` are clearly different names.

2.6.2 *Identifiers*

Of course, this solution appears to create its own problem: How can you be sure that different XML designers will use `met` to refer to the same vocabulary? The short and happy answer is: They don't have to!

That's because within your document `met` – which, remember, is just a nickname – is associated with an unambiguous identifier of the vocabulary. That identifier is a URI reference and could look something like `http://www.weatherworld.com`. Other documents might use a different abbreviation for that vocabulary or use `met:` to prefix a different vocabulary.

In practice, though, vocabulary developers recommend prefixes and people tend to use the recommended ones.

Note The URI of a namespace does not have to address a real Web page. The Web addressing system is just being used as a namespace within which all URIs – and therefore namespace names – are unique.

2.7 | Other XML constructs

There are a few more XML constructs that you may need to know about, but which you will use less often – if at all – than those previously discussed. The details, including information about the nature and extent of Word's support for them, can be found in Chapter 15, "The XML language", on page 350.

There are two, however, that show up in the examples that illustrate Part Two: *processing instructions (PIs)* and *comments*. They are both markup that is not part of the document structure or data. They are essentially messages: to software in the case of PIs, and to people in the case of comments.

2.7.1 Processing instructions

Example 2-6 shows two processing instructions. The first word in each is the *PI target*, a nickname for the program for which the PI is intended.

The first PI is intended for the XML processor itself. It is called an *XML declaration* and it tells the processor the character encoding that is being used. Other software, such as Office, looks for this PI to recognize that a document is an XML document.

The second PI is intended for Microsoft Office applications. It identifies the application that created the document.

Example 2-6. Processing instructions

```
<?xml version="1.0" encoding="UTF-8"?>
<?mso-application progid="Word.Document"?>
```

2.7.2 *Comments*

Comments can be used as reminders to yourself or as messages to other people working on the document. They are discarded when a document is parsed.

Example 2-7. Comment

```
<!-- Help, I'm a prisoner in a publishing house! -->
```

2.8 | More on XML

If you plan to use XML products other than Office, develop your own schemas, or use Office to share data with enterprise systems and Web services, you'll want to learn more about XML. As our readers will have differing experience with XML and different requirements for its use, there seemed no sensible way to intersperse detailed XML education with the Office XML tasks that are the focus of the book.

Instead we've put the detailed tutorials and references on the XML language and related standards where you can easily find them when you need them. They are in Part 3, "XML Tutorials", on page 348. The book's Table of Contents and Index can guide you to specific subjects, and we also provide appropriate cross-references to the tutorials from the Office XML task chapters in Part Two.

XML in Office

- Meet the family! Word, Excel, InfoPath, Access, and FrontPage

- Information capture and reuse

- End-user data connection

- Data-driven application enhancement

his chapter is an overview of the XML features of Office. We discuss the XML-enabled Office products – Word, Excel, Access, FrontPage and the newly introduced InfoPath – in the context of several information sharing scenarios.

But the products are really just the supporting cast. The true stars are the advances that XML in Office brings to:

- information capture and reuse;
- end-user data connection; and
- data-driven application enhancement.

3.1 | Information capture and reuse

For all the valuable abstract data that is managed in database systems, there is even more that is hidden in rendered word processing documents. That fact represents an enormous intellectual property loss for enterprises, of course, but it also represents a nuisance and a time-waster for the information workers who work with those documents.

Consider the articles written for a company's websites and newsletters. Every one is likely to contain a title, author, and date within it, but more often than not that information has to be retyped, or individually copied and pasted, to get it into a catalog entry. That's because there is no reliable way for a computer to recognize those data items in order to extract them.

3.1.1   *Word processing*

In contrast, look at Figure 3-1, which shows an article being edited in Microsoft Word.

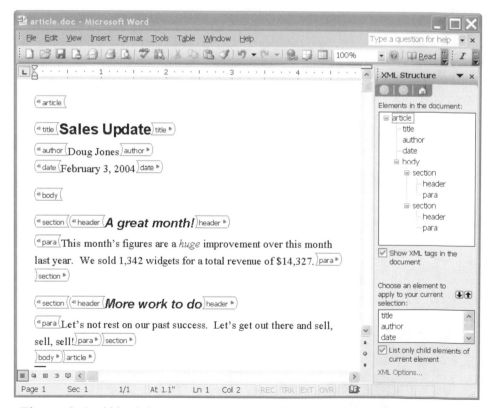

Figure 3-1   Word document showing optional tag icons and task pane with XML structure

The article is actually an XML document that conforms to a schema of the user's choosing, in this case `article`. The user has opted to display icons that represent the start- and end-tags. Note that there are distinct elements for the `title`, `author`, and `date`.

Solution developers can use the XML elements to check and normalize information as it is entered, whether or not the tag icons are displayed. An application, for example, could notify the user if the text entered for a `date` element isn't really a valid date. Or it could automatically supply the current year if none was entered.

The right-hand pane is called the *task pane*; it can be used for various purposes. In the figure, the top of the task pane shows the XML structure of the document. At the bottom is a list of the types of element that are valid at the current point in the document, according to the `article` schema.

The document is also a normal Word document, so Word's formatting features can be used in the usual way.

There are three ways to save this document as XML:

WordML

> *WordML* is Word's native XML file format. It preserves the Word document just as the DOC format would, including formatting and hyperlinks. However, it doesn't include any of the `article` markup, so we won't discuss this option further here. (We cover it in Chapter 5, "Rendering and presenting XML documents", on page 86.)

custom XML

> The document can be saved as an XML document conforming to a custom schema; in this case, `article`. A custom schema would normally be defined by an enterprise, or by a committee set up by an industry to which the enterprise belongs. For that reason, it would be designed to preserve the abstract data needed for the user's applications. For example, the `title`, `author`, and `date` can easily be identified by software and extracted for use in a catalog of articles.

mixed XML

> The saved document could contain both WordML and the `article` markup, since the two are in different namespaces. This option preserves the formatting applied by the user, while still

preserving the abstract data and distinguishing it from the rendition information.

In our example, the article is the entire Word document, but that isn't a requirement. It is possible to intersperse short XML documents within a larger Word document. For example, a travel guide might include multiple XML structures that describe hotels, with subelements for the name, address, number of rooms, rates, etc.

Using XML with Word documents enables companies to capture more of the intellectual property that is created informally by individuals and work groups, and that typically remains inaccessible to enterprise information systems. As XML, that property becomes a portable asset that can be reused as needed.[1]

3.1.2 *Forms*

For many purposes, a data entry form is more suitable for information capture than a typically larger and less constrained word processing document. InfoPath lets you design and use forms that are really XML documents that conform to your own custom schemas.[2]

Figure 3-2 shows the layout of an order form in InfoPath's design mode. The structure of the order schema is shown in the task pane on the right, from which element types can be dragged onto the form.

Note that there is only one item line in the form design. Because the order schema allows item elements to be repeated, a user entering data will be able to add item lines as needed. Had customer elements been repeatable, the form would expand to allow insertion of the group of customer information fields.

Unlike Word, InfoPath generates an XSLT stylesheet to control the rendering of the form. The formatting can even be based on the data entered in the form. For example, the dialog box in Figure 3-3 specifies that negative prices should be shown in a different color.

---

1. We cover the details in Chapter 4, "Creating and editing XML documents", on page 60.
2. InfoPath is available in the Office Professional Enterprise Edition and individually.

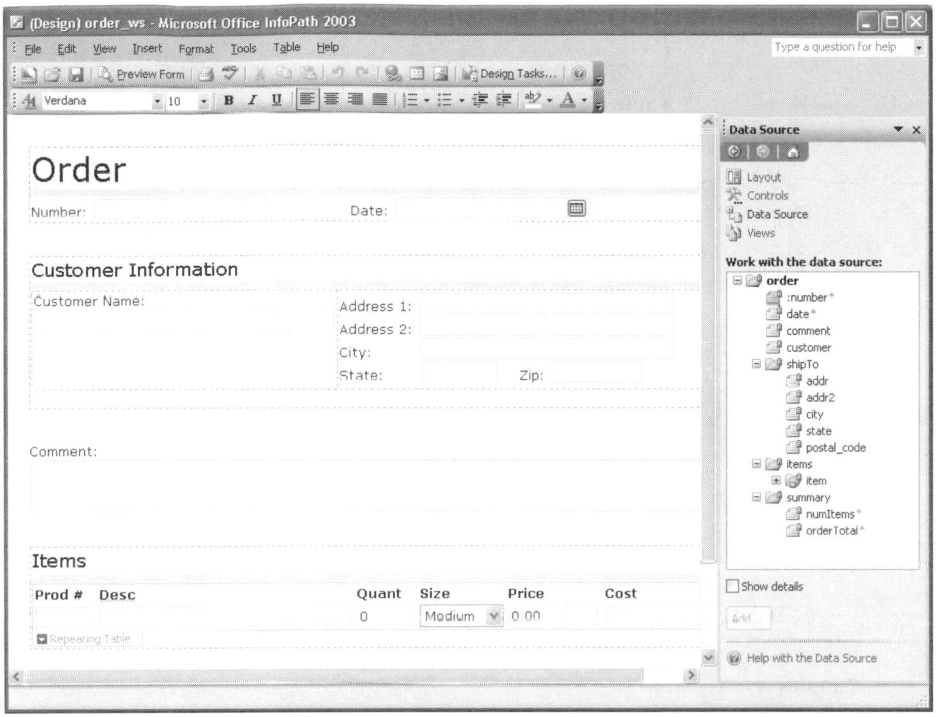

Figure 3-2 InfoPath design interface with data source in task pane

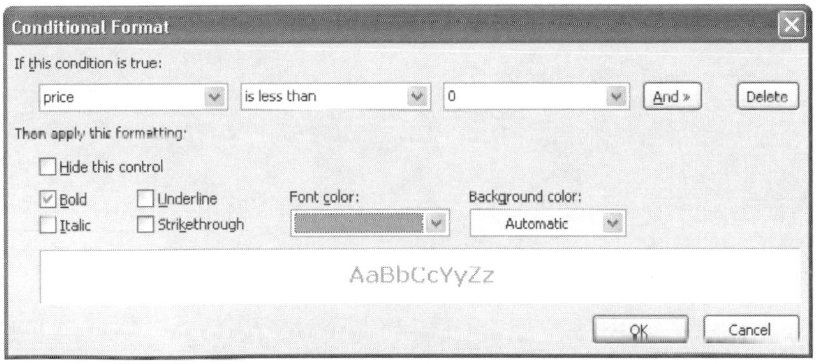

Figure 3-3 InfoPath conditional formatting dialog

InfoPath is described in detail in Chapter 9, "Designing and using forms", on page 180.

3.1.3 *Relational data*

XML elements, whether captured in Word or Excel or InfoPath (or any other way, for that matter), are as well-defined and predictable as the columns and tables of a database. XML documents of all kinds are therefore a source of information as rich as any other operational data store. Companies can aggregate, parse, search, manage, and reuse the data in documents in the same way they do the transactional data that is typically captured for relational databases.

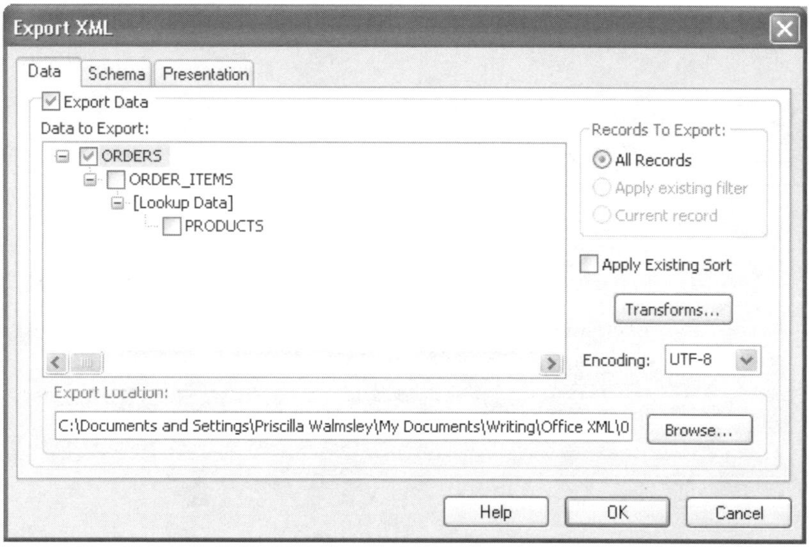

Figure 3-4   Access dialog for exporting data as XML

They can also import the document data into a database and use it in conjunction with data from other sources. In addition, they can export DBMS data as XML documents.

Figure 3-4, for example, shows the options Access offers when exporting data as XML. You can specify which tables and records to export and how to sort and/or transform them.

Figure 3-5 shows the options for exporting a schema as XML. You can choose whether or not to export the schema, and whether it should be exported within the data document or as an independent schema document.[3]

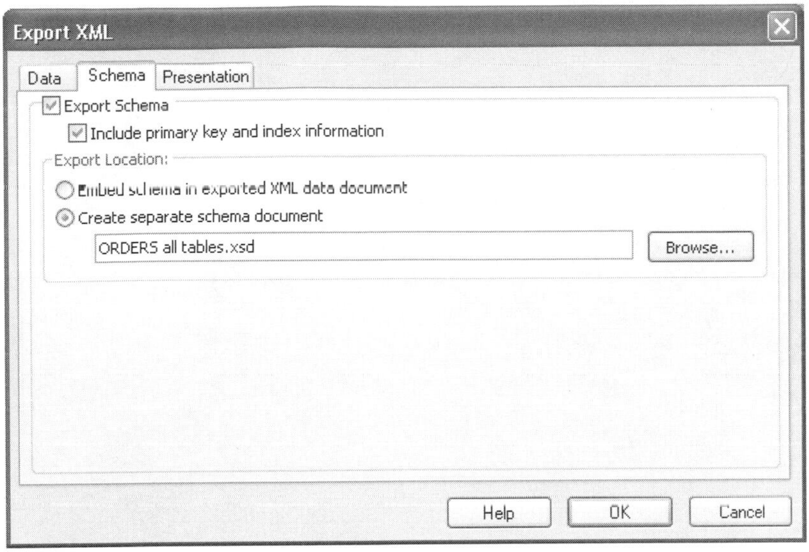

Figure 3-5   Access dialog for exporting schema as XML

3.2 | End-user data connection

Including custom XML elements in Office documents presents companies with new opportunities for business process integration.

For example, an end-user can connect directly to enterprise systems and data sources using a Web services interface. The products do the heavy lifting: natively, in the case of InfoPath, and via VBA or an external extension, in the case of Word and Excel.

The data from the Web service can be cached by the product, which can then disconnect from the server. The user still maintains the ability to work with that data, even while disconnected. For this reason, Microsoft refers to

---

3. See Chapter 12, "Access databases and XML", on page 266 for details on Access.

Word, InfoPath, and Excel as *smart clients*.[4] Once reconnected to the corporate server, the smart client can update the data sources.

The individual end-user also benefits from this ability to search for specific information and to aggregate information from multiple sources. It eliminates such time-consuming, error-prone tasks as:

- opening and closing files to find information;
- cutting and pasting information between documents; and
- searching for labels to combine data in like fields.

3.2.1 *Spreadsheets*

Consider how a smart client can assist in the creation and processing of expense reports.

Prior to leaving on a trip, during which she won't have access to the corporate network, Ellen opens the Excel worksheet shown in Figure 3-6. Its cells are mapped to the element types of the expenseReport schema, as shown in the task pane.

Each mapped element type corresponds to an area of the worksheet, either a single cell or a column of cells. The mapping allows XML data to be imported into, and exported from, the appropriate areas of the worksheet.

Ellen enters her employee number and the business purpose of her trip. The other cells that are visible in the example are populated automatically from the enterprise data store.

- Her name comes from the human resources records, based on the employee number that she entered.
- The lodging and airfare amounts come from the bookings made by the travel department.
- The per diem is based on the location in the hotel booking.
- The mileage is the calculated distance between the airport and Ellen's home address, also taken from the human resources records.

---

4. What Microsoft calls a "smart client" is essentially what the industry calls a "rich client". Perhaps Microsoft believes that if you're smart, you ought to be rich. Our readers – smart by definition – should agree!

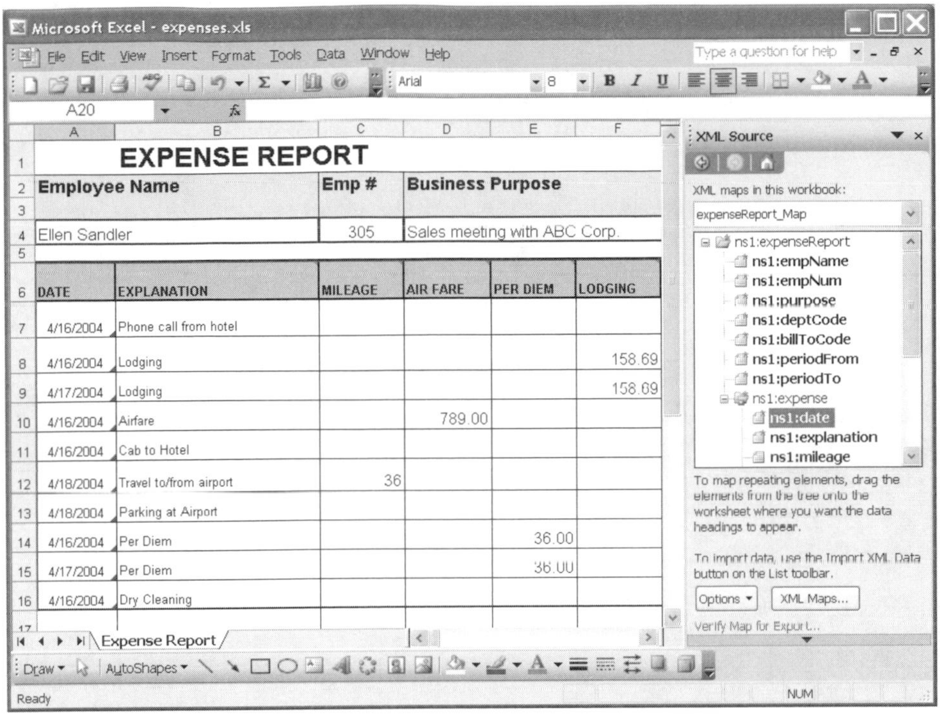

Figure 3-6   Excel worksheet and task pane with XML source map

Ellen adds more items to the worksheet during the trip, even without the network connection. When she returns, she completes the report and exports the mapped cells as an XML document conforming to the expenseReport schema.[5]

3.2.2 *Web pages*

Ellen next wants to submit her report for management approval. It needs five levels of sign-off, so she decides to post it to an internal website where all the managers can read it.[6]

---

5. We cover Excel's XML features in Chapter 7, "Using XML data in spread-sheets", on page 132.
6. Yes, in most organizations five levels of management would be, er, over the top!

Figure 3-7 shows how FrontPage is used to design a Web page based on an XML document. Elements can be dragged from the expenseReport structure in the task pane onto the main page, and styles and other formatting options can be used to present the data.

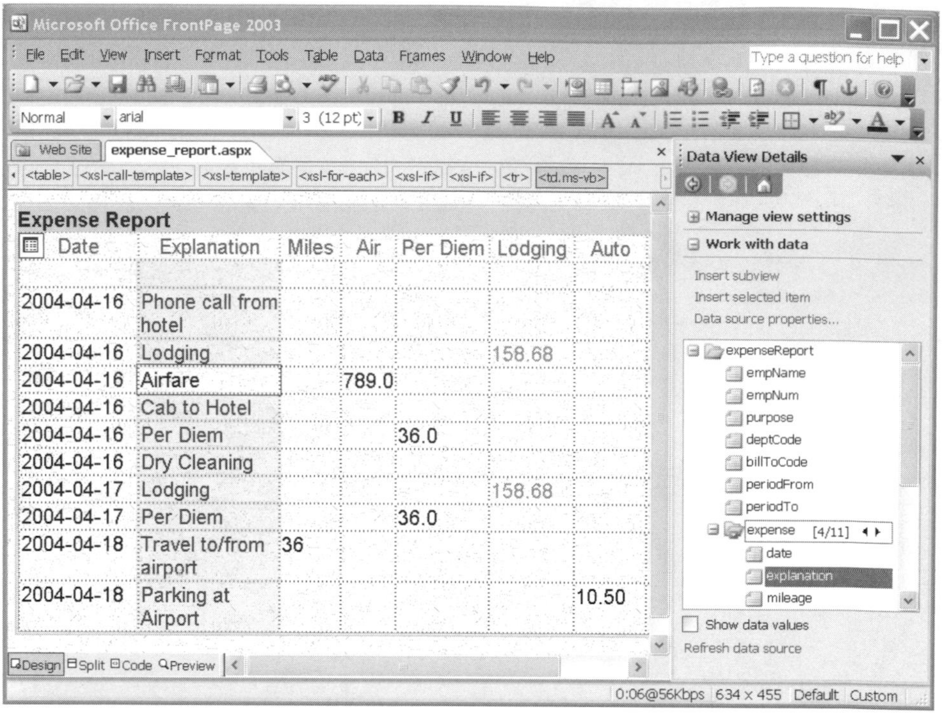

Figure 3-7   FrontPage website view with data view details in task pane

Any XML document could be used as the data source, as could databases and Web services. Sorting, grouping, filtering, and conditional formatting of the data are supported.

FrontPage generates an XSLT stylesheet from the WYSIWYG display.[7]

After Ellen's expense report is approved, the XML document is sent to the accounting department's system, which deposits the reimbursement in her bank account.

---

7. The FrontPage XML features are covered in Chapter 13, "Publishing XML to the Web with FrontPage", on page 294.

3.3 | Data-driven application enhancement

There are ways to enhance Ellen's experience with her expense report. Raising the per diem would undoubtedly provide the most satisfaction, but we have to stick to improvements enabled by mapping XML to the spreadsheet.

Solution developers have several ways to take advantage of the document knowledge that XML gives them: custom renditions, smart tags, and smart documents.

3.3.1 *Custom renditions*

The classic technique for data-driven application enhancement dates back to the dawn of markup languages, when GML first separated abstract data from presentation. It is to render the same data in different ways for different tasks or users.

In our scenario, for example, a report to the accounting department might contain only the summary totals from Ellen's spreadsheet, while her management gets to see every detail.

3.3.2 *Smart tags*

Office has a facility called *smart tags* that allows actions to be associated with words and phrases in a document. The "tags" don't have to be delimited, as XML tags are. Instead, they are defined by a program or by a lookup table that contains character strings and their associated actions. The product recognizes the matching strings in the document.[8]

Usually, an icon is displayed when the cursor is over a smart tag. When the user clicks on it, the associated list of actions pops up.

---

8. Instead of a specific character string, recognition could be based on a kind of pattern for strings that computer scientists call a *regular expression*. In this case, any character string in the document that matched the pattern would be recognized and considered a smart tag.

It is also possible to define smart tags so that an action will take place automatically when the tag is recognized. For example, recognition of the employee number in Ellen's worksheet invoked an action to send the Web service request for her employee name, which was entered into the appropriate worksheet cell.

3.3.3 *Smart documents*

The ultimate data-driven application enhancement is to respond intelligently to user input, offering context-sensitive actions and guidance, suggesting content, and providing supporting data or links to related information.

The XML facilities we've looked at so far can be used in combination to approach that goal. Add a customized task pane and even more can be done. You have what in Office-speak is called a *smart document solution.*

For example, as a user moves the cursor to different elements in a document, the task pane could display help details, related data, tools to work with the document, or related graphics. Ellen could click in a lodging cell and see the hotel contact information displayed in the task pane. She could then click on the hotel's email address and send a quick note advising the hotel of her arrival time.[9]

3.3.4 *Using the Office tools*

While all these features sound useful, there is some setup required. Fortunately, you have this book to guide you through the process. We have identified typical implementation tasks, each of which is explained in a chapter. In the context of these tasks, we present the XML features of each of the Office products. Finally, in the last part, we cover in detail some of the technologies, such as schemas and stylesheets, you may use to get there.

---

9. See Chapter 14, "Developing Office XML applications", on page 318 for more on smart tags and smart documents.

Working with XML in Office

- Word
- Excel
- InfoPath
- Access
- FrontPage

Part Two

In this Part we show you, in great detail, how to use the XML features of Office to accomplish real-world tasks. You'll learn how to create XML documents with Word and format them with the Word Markup Language. You'll also learn how to analyze XML data with Excel, store and retrieve it from Access databases, and publish it to the Web with FrontPage.

We also teach you how to design and complete forms with Info-Path, and how to use Web services with these products.

The chapters are labeled by product name and required Office skills. A *Power User* knows the Office products and is able to set up new things (styles, etc.) using the normal user interface. A *Script Developer* has, in addition, a basic knowledge of VBA, VBScript, or JScript.

However, the Script Developer chapters are written so that Power Users should be able to pick up what they need of those skills while reading and customizing the examples for their own use.

Creating and editing XML documents

- Creating and using schemas
- Opening a document
- Validation
- Working with attributes
- Saving a document
- Combining documents

Chapter

4

his chapter describes how to use Word to create and edit XML documents. We don't include WordML documents in this category because Word treats them just like .doc or RTF documents – as native Word documents.[1]

> *Skills required*   Experience using Microsoft Word to perform basic tasks such as creating and editing documents.

4.1 | Creating and using schemas

The real power of XML lies in using a vocabulary that describes the meaning of the document, not its outward appearance. For example, Example

---

1. Which is not to say that WordML isn't important. There are a lot of useful things that can be done with WordML, as we'll show you in Chapter 5, "Rendering and presenting XML documents", on page 86.

4-1 shows Doug's article marked up using a custom schema called article.[2]

Example 4-1. An article using the `article` schema (article.xml)

```
<?xml version="1.0" encoding="UTF-8" standalone="yes"?>
<article xmlns="http://xmlinoffice.com/article"
         type="sales" id="A123">
  <title>Sales Update</title>
  <author>Doug Jones</author>
  <date>February 3, 2004</date>
  <body>
   <section>
     <header>A great month!</header>
     <para>This month's figures are a <em>huge</em>
improvement over this month last year. We sold 1,342 widgets for a
total revenue of $14,327.</para>
   </section>
   <section>
     <header>More work to do</header>
     <para>Let's not rest on our past success. Let's get out there
and sell, sell, sell!</para>
   </section>
  </body>
</article>
```

This XML document identifies the meaning of the data elements, not just their location in the document. The author is identified by an `<author>` tag, and the title is identified by a `<title>` tag. The document uses a namespace, `http://xmlinoffice.com/article`, to identify the vocabulary used.

4.1.1 *Vocabularies and schemas*

A schema defines an XML vocabulary for documents of a particular type (such as `article` documents). The vocabulary includes the element-type names, such as `author` and `title`. The schema also constrains the order in which elements and attributes can appear.

---

2. You can download all example files used in the book from the companion Web site, `http://www.XMLinOffice.com`.

Industry organizations and standards committees have defined XML vocabularies for subjects as varied as computer graphics and accounting statements, many with one or more schemas that employ the vocabularies.[3] Any of those schemas – or any other – can be used with Word; there is no specific set of "supported schemas." However, a definition of the schema must be available in the W3C XML Schema definition language (XSDL), as no other schema language is supported.

Alternatively, you can define your own vocabulary by writing your own schema. Microsoft Office does not provide a GUI editor for defining a schema; you will have to create yours with a text editor or an available schema editing tool. Chapter 22, "XML Schema (XSDL)", on page 466 explains schemas in more detail and gives some guidelines for writing your own schemas.

Schemas are used in Word both to validate documents, and to provide hints on the structure of a document while it is being edited.

4.1.2 The `article` *schema*

The `article` schema definition is shown in Example 4-2.

The schema definition uses `xs:element` elements to declare the element types allowed in an `article` document. For example:

```
<xs:element name="title" type="xs:string"/>
```

declares that `title` elements contain data characters ("strings").

Some of the element types, such as `article` and `section`, are complex, which means that their elements can have child elements and/or attributes.

4.1.3 *Adding a schema to the library*

When Word opens an XML document it checks to see if the document is associated with the known schemas in its Schema Library. It does so by comparing the namespace of the document (i.e., of its root element) with the target namespace of each schema in the Schema Library until it finds a match.

---

3. *The XML Handbook* has a directory of more than 300 such public vocabulary projects.

Example 4-2. Schema for `article` documents (article.xsd)

```
<?xml version="1.0"?>
<xs:schema targetNamespace="http://xmlinoffice.com/article"
           xmlns="http://xmlinoffice.com/article"
           xmlns:xs="http://www.w3.org/2001/XMLSchema"
           elementFormDefault="qualified">
  <xs:element name="article" type="ArticleType"/>
  <xs:complexType name="ArticleType">
    <xs:sequence>
      <xs:element name="title" type="xs:string"/>
      <xs:element name="author" type="xs:string"/>
      <xs:element name="date" type="xs:string"/>
      <xs:element name="body" type="BodyType"/>
    </xs:sequence>
    <xs:attribute name="id" type="xs:ID"/>
    <xs:attribute name="type" type="xs:string"/>
  </xs:complexType>
  <xs:complexType name="BodyType">
    <xs:sequence>
      <xs:element name="section" type="SectionType" maxOccurs=
      "unbounded"/>
    </xs:sequence>
  </xs:complexType>
  <xs:complexType name="SectionType">
    <xs:sequence>
      <xs:element name="header" type="xs:string"/>
      <xs:element name="para" type="ParaType" maxOccurs="unbounded"/
      >
    </xs:sequence>
  </xs:complexType>
  <xs:complexType name="ParaType" mixed="true">
    <xs:choice minOccurs="0" maxOccurs="unbounded">
      <xs:element name="em" type="xs:string"/>
      <xs:element name="cite" type="xs:string"/>
      <xs:element name="url" type="xs:string"/>
    </xs:choice>
  </xs:complexType>
</xs:schema>
```

For example, the schema in Example 4-2 has a target namespace, specified by the `targetNamespace` attribute, of:

`http://xmlinoffice.com/article`

This is the same namespace that is declared for Doug's `article` document in Example 4-1. By adding the schema to Word's Schema Library, we can assure that it will be associated with Doug's article or any other `article` document that is opened in Word.

To add a schema:

1. On the **Tools** menu, click **Templates and Add-Ins**.
2. Click the **XML Schema** tab, shown in Figure 4-1.
3. Click **Add Schema**.
4. Select the schema file, in this case `article.xsd`, and click **Open**. This will bring up the **Schema Settings** dialog shown in Figure 4-2.
5. Type the word `article` in the **Alias** box. This will serve as a nickname for the `article` namespace. It is good practice to use the document type (i.e. the root element-type name) as the alias.

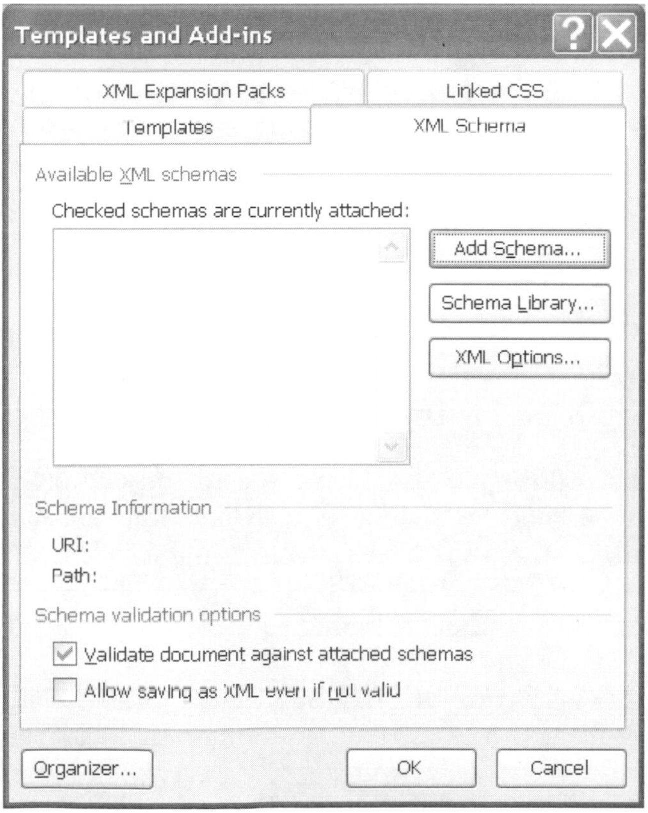

Figure 4-1   The XML Schema tab

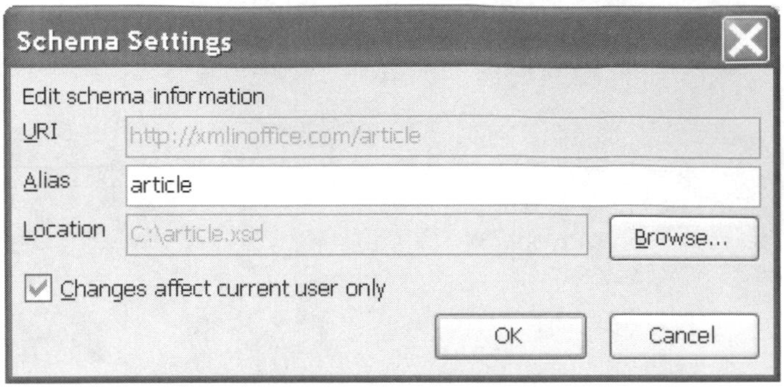

Figure 4-2   The Schema Settings dialog

If you attempt to add an invalid schema, you will be advised that the schema is invalid and prevented from adding it. Once you have added the schema, it will appear in the **Available XML schemas** list, as shown in Figure 4-3. When it is selected, the pane will show the namespace URI and the path to the schema definition file.

These settings will be saved in your Word configuration. From now on, every time you open an XML document whose root element is in the `http://xmlinoffice.com/article` namespace, the `article.xsd` schema is automatically used for that document. It is *not* possible to add more than one schema for a given namespace.

4.1.4 *Using the Schema Library*

The Schema Library, shown in Figure 4-4, allows you to add and delete schemas, as well as give them mnemonic aliases (usually the document-type name). Word uses the alias as the name of the schema; without one it will use the entire namespace URI.

To access the Schema Library, click **Schema Library** on the **XML Schema** tab of the **Templates and Add-Ins** dialog.

The Schema Library also allows you to associate *solutions* with schemas. These are XSLT stylesheets that can be used to transform XML documents when Word opens or saves them, as we will see in 5.3.2.1, "Associating stylesheets with schemas", on page 108.

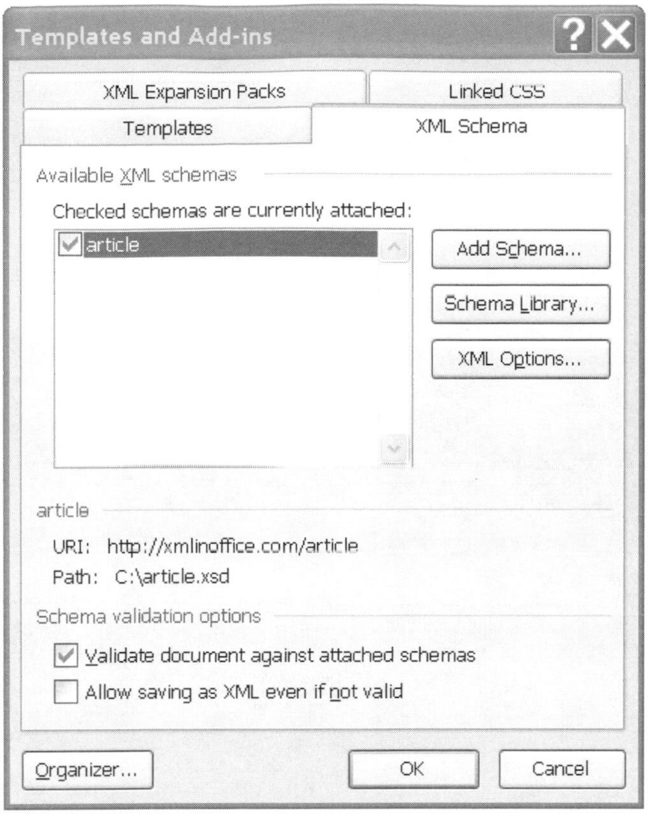

Figure 4-3 Available XML schemas

4.2 | Opening a document

Once you have added the necessary schemas to the Schema Library, there are several ways to open an XML document for editing:

- Open an existing or new Word document and mark it up according to a schema.
- Open an existing XML document.
- Open an XML template that you've created for a particular schema.

First, let's look at converting Doug's article.doc to article.xml.

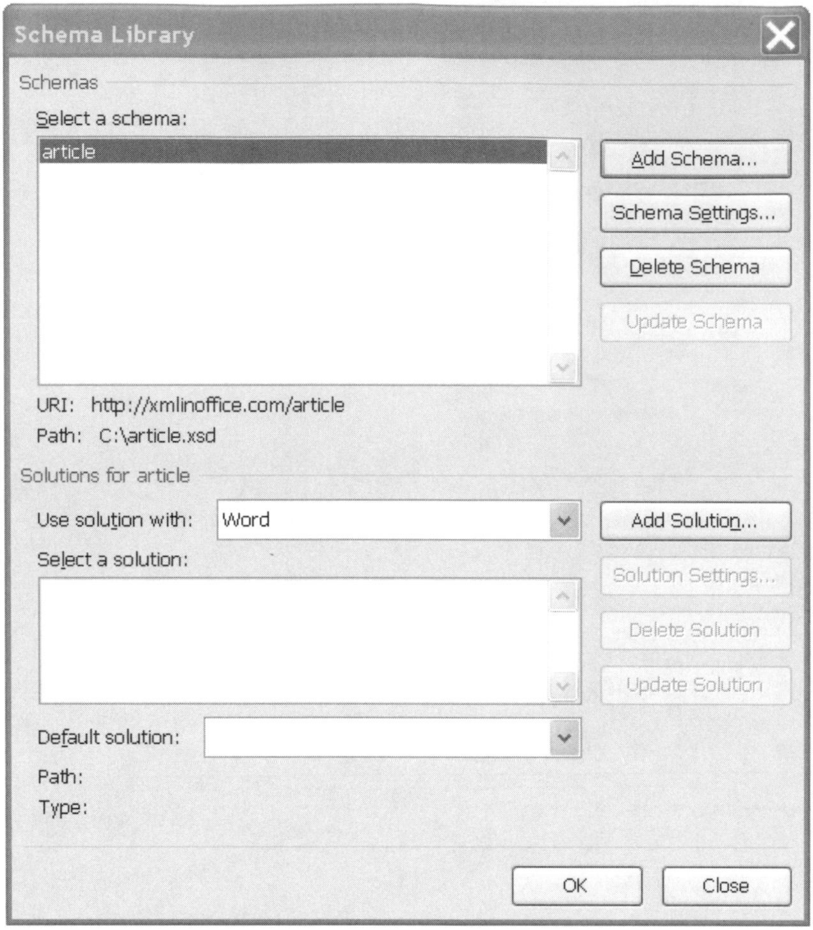

Figure 4-4   The Schema Library

4.2.1 *Opening a Word document*

To convert a Word document to XML – either an existing one or a new empty one – there are two steps. First you associate a schema with the document, and then you apply markup to its elements.

4.2.1.1   Associating a schema

A new document, or a Word document that has never been converted to XML, has no schema associated with it. Before you can begin to mark it up, you need to associate a schema. To do this (using `article.doc` as an example):

1. Open `article.doc` in Word.
2. On the **Tools** menu, click **Templates and Add-Ins**.
3. Click the **XML Schema** tab.
4. Check the box next to `article` and click **OK**.

You will now see the XML Structure pane on the right side of the Word window, as shown in Figure 4-5.

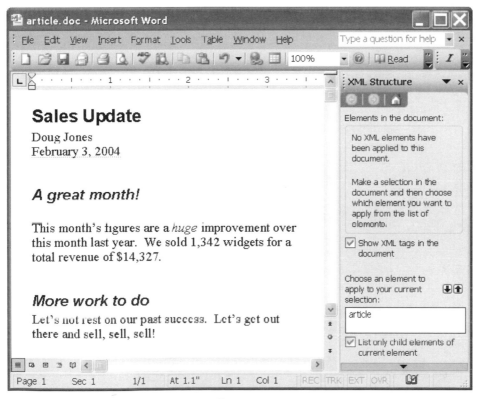

Figure 4-5   The XML Structure Pane

The XML Structure pane has two parts:

- The top part shows the hierarchical structure of the current document, based on the elements that have already been identified. When we first apply the schema to `article.doc`, no structure is shown because the document has not yet been tagged.
- The bottom part of the XML Structure task pane shows the available element types from the vocabulary. By default, it only shows the types of elements that can be validly inserted at the point in the document where the cursor is positioned.

Tip   *If you ever lose the XML Structure task pane, or close it accidentally, click* **Task Pane** *on the* **View** *menu. Then, click the top bar of the task pane and click* **XML Structure***.*

4.2.1.2   Applying markup to elements

The first order of business is to identify the root element, in this case `article`. To do this:

1. Select the word `article` in the bottom part of the XML Structure task pane.
2. This will bring up a dialog that asks whether the element to be tagged is the entire document, or the current selection only. Click **Apply to Entire Document**.

You will notice that a start-tag icon appears at the beginning of the article, and an end-tag icon at the end of the article. In addition, `article` now appears in the top part of the XML Structure pane, indicating that an `article` element has been identified in the document.

To tag the rest of the document, you can simply select a section of the text and choose its element-type in the bottom part of the XML Structure task pane. Alternatively, you can select the text and right-click, click **Apply XML Element**, then choose the element-type name.

> *Note*   You aren't really "applying an element" to anything; the element is there in the document. Think of the term as shorthand for "apply **markup to** XML element".

You can also insert a new element. To do this, position the cursor at the desired location and choose the desired element-type name in the bottom part of the XML Structure task pane. You can then type text between the start-tag and end-tag icons. This procedure is also followed when creating an XML document from a new empty Word document and when adding elements to an existing XML document.

Once marked up, our document looks something like Figure 4-6.

> *Tip*   Start applying markup at the root element and work down the tree structure. For example, tag the `body` element before either of the `section` elements. This technique allows the appropriate valid element-types to appear in the bottom part of the XML Structure task pane.

4.2.2 *Opening an XML document*

You can open and edit any XML document in Word, even documents that have no schema in Word's Schema Library (or even no schema at all).

To do so, you use the standard procedure for opening a document: that is, clicking **Open** on the **File** menu and selecting the document of interest.

The XML document must have an XML declaration as its first line. This is the only way Word will identify it as an XML document; the file extension is ignored. For example:

```
<?xml version="1.0" encoding="UTF-8"?>
```

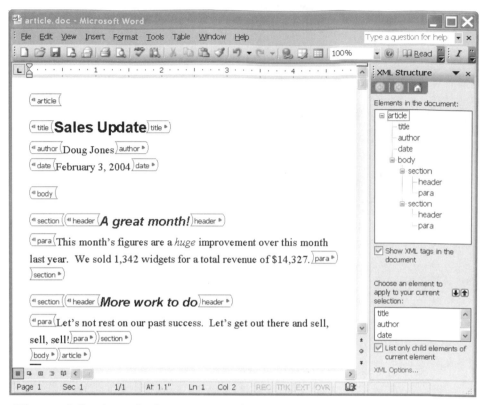

Figure 4-6   A marked up `article` document

In addition, the document must be well-formed, meaning that it follows all the rules of the XML language.[4] Upon opening the document, Word displays the XML Structure task pane.

Word then attempts to associate a schema with the document, as described in 4.1.3, "Adding a schema to the library", on page 63. If it fails, it allows all element types found in the document to occur anywhere in the document; no other element types are permitted. You can associate a schema with the document after it is opened, using the procedure described in 4.2.1.1, "Associating a schema", on page 69.

If there is an associated schema, the document need not be valid with respect to it. Word will flag the errors in the XML Structure pane (see 4.3, "Validation", on page 74).

---

4. These are described in Chapter 15, "The XML language", on page 350.

4.2.3 *Opening a skeleton document*

Rather than starting a new XML document from scratch, you can take advantage of a document type's predictable structure by creating a *skeleton document*. A skeleton serves the same purpose as a Word template. It is a sample document that an end user can modify to create the actual document he wants.

Figure 4-7 shows a skeleton document for the `article` schema. It uses *placeholder text* for all the elements, allowing the article writer simply to fill in the fields. When the user wants to enter content for an element, he just clicks the placeholder text and starts typing, much as if it were a field in a form.

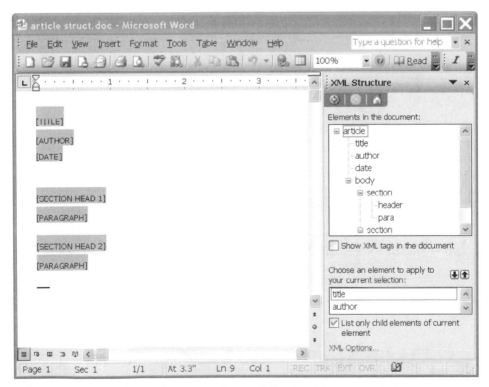

Figure 4-7   Skeleton document for articles (article struct.doc)

Placeholder text is only displayed when the tag icons are not shown, and only for elements that have empty content. Note that **Show XML tags in the document** is unchecked. Checking it will show the icons and hide the placeholder text (although the text will not be deleted permanently).

You can create a skeleton by starting with an existing XML document and deleting the data content. Alternatively, you can start with a new empty document, associate a schema, and insert the desired elements (again without any data content).

You can then specify placeholder text for each of the elements. When an element is empty, the placeholder text appears where the data content would normally appear.

To specify placeholder text for an element:

1. Right-click that element in the top part of the XML Structure pane, or in the document pane, and click **Attributes** on the context menu.
2. Type the placeholder text at the bottom of the dialog, and click **OK**.

Note that placeholder text is associated with an individual element in the document, not with an element type. In Figure 4-7, for example, the first header element has the placeholder text "[SECTION HEAD 1]" while the second header element has the placeholder text "[SECTION HEAD 2]".

Tip   Choose placeholder text that is clearly not the actual content, and that explains what data to enter if it isn't obvious. Enclose the text in square brackets to make it look more like a field for data entry.

4.3 | Validation

You may have noticed that Word validates your document as you mark it up. Word is constantly checking to make sure that the document conforms to the schema.

4.3.1 *Schema rules*

Rules that a schema can specify include:

- The allowed children of an element. For example, according to the `article` schema, there can be only one `article` element, which can contain `title`, `author`, `date` and `body` elements.
- The order of the children. The children of the `article` element must appear in the order specified in the schema.
- The number of occurrences of each child. A `section` element must contain one and only one `header` element, but it may contain one or more `para` elements.
- The presence or absence of character data content in an element. The `title` element can contain character data, but a `section` element cannot.
- The datatype of an element or attribute. The `id` attribute of the `article` element must contain a valid ID.

Using datatypes, you can specify additional rules that limit the length of a string, require that a string match a particular pattern, limit a number to a particular range, specify a list of valid values, and apply various other constraints. For more information on the capabilities of datatypes, see Chapter 21, "Datatypes", on page 442.

4.3.2 *Validity errors*

When a document (or part of a document) you are editing is invalid according to the schema, Word shows this in two ways:

- A purple wavy line (similar to the one that shows spelling and grammatical errors). For errors that span multiple lines, it appears down the left side of the document. Otherwise, it underlines the error.
- The top part of the XML Structure task pane shows icons next to invalid elements, as described in the next section.

Some of the possible errors that could be found are:

- The element has invalid content. For example, character data appears where it should not, or the character data it contains is invalid according to its datatype.
- The element is not expected to appear here. This could be because it is not a valid child, it does not appear in the correct sequence, or a required element that should appear before it is missing.
- The element is empty, but according to the schema, it should have children, or some required content is missing.
- One or more of the element's attributes is missing or invalid.

4.4 | The XML Structure task pane

Now that we have marked up the elements, let's take a closer look at the XML Structure pane.

4.4.1 *Document structure*

The top part of the XML Structure pane shows the structure of your XML document. When you select an element in the task pane, it selects the contents of that element in the document itself. This provides an easy way to navigate the document. In addition, when you position the cursor in the document, the appropriate element is selected on the task pane.

4.4.2 *Error signals*

When there are errors in the document, a diamond-shaped yellow icon appears next to the element in the task pane. Hovering over the icon will reveal an explanation of the problem.

4.4.3 *Available element types*

The bottom part of the XML Structure task pane normally lists the element types available for children of the current element. You can see *all* element-type names in the vocabulary by unchecking the **List only child elements of current element** box. [5]

Despite the list, you can still add an element that is not valid. That is because the list does not take into account any required sequence of child elements, nor the number of times child elements are allowed to occur. Fortunately, such errors *do* appear in the top part of the task pane.

4.4.4 *Viewing tag icons*

There is an alternative view in Word that does not show the tag icons in the document pane. You can switch to this view by unchecking the **Show XML tags in the document** box on the XML Structure pane. The document will then look like a typical Word document, although the XML Structure pane will still be usable to identify and tag elements shown in the document pane.

4.5 | Working with attributes

So far, our discussion has focused on elements. XML attributes are less visible in Word. You must go to a separate **Attributes** dialog to assign, edit or remove values for the attributes of an element.

To assign a value to an attribute:

1. Right-click the `article` element, either in its start-tag icon or in the top part of the XML Structure task pane.
2. Click **Attributes**. This will bring up the **Attributes** dialog as shown in Figure 4-8.
3. In the top part of the dialog, select the attribute for which you want to specify a value. Only the attributes that are declared for the element type are listed. If no schema is associated, the individual element's actual attributes are shown.

---

5. This dialog can be confusing because it mixes *element* with *element type*. For example, the first and third occurrences of "element" are correct while the second should be "element type". See 20.2, "Tag vs. element", on page 431.

4. The dialog then displays the type of the attribute. Specify a value in the **Value** box.

5. Once you have entered a value, click **Add**. The button text now turns to **Modify**, which is the way it is shown in the dialog.

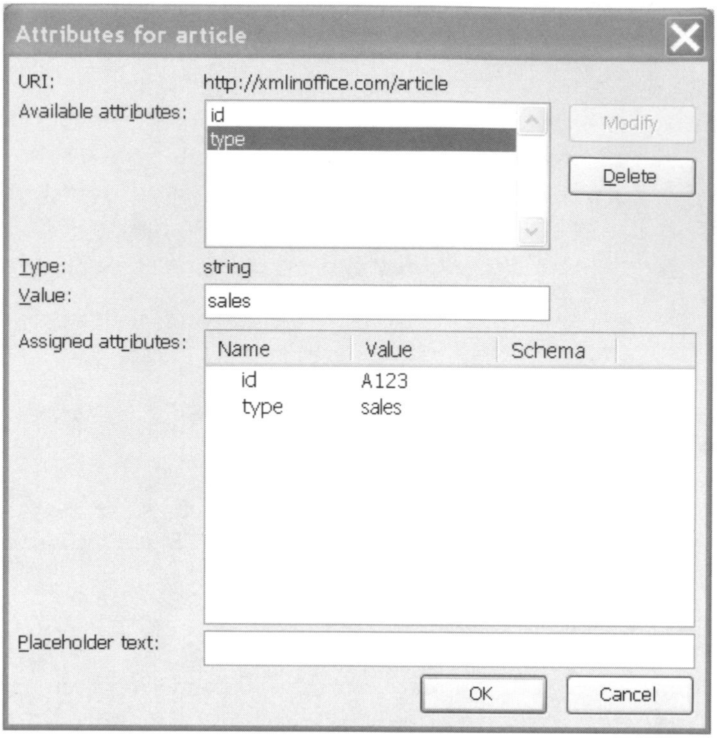

Figure 4-8   The Attributes dialog

If you enter a value that is invalid for that type, you will receive the message "This attribute value is not allowed." In our example, the value of the id attribute must conform to the type ID. This means that it must start with a letter or underscore and contain only letters, digits, underscores and periods.

You can also modify or delete the value for an attribute by selecting it in the bottom section of the dialog and clicking the appropriate button.

4.6 | Saving a document

To save a document as XML:

1. On the **File** menu, click **Save As**.
2. Select **XML Document (*.xml)** from the **Save as type** list.
3. Click **Save**.

There are two options, depending on whether you check the **Save data only** box on the **Save As** dialog.[6]

Caution   The **Save data only** box is confusingly named since you will be saving markup even if you check it. Think of it as "Save without WordML" or "Save custom XML only".

4.6.1 *Saving XML without WordML*

When the **Save data only** box is checked, none of the Word formatting information is saved. In the case of Doug's article document, the result is identical to Example 4-1. It contains only the `article` tags and is valid according to the `article.xsd` schema.

Any other information has been lost; when you reopen the document in Word, there will be no styles or formatting applied to the text, and the settings such as page margins and tracked changes will be wiped out.

4.6.2 *Saving mixed vocabularies*

If the **Save data only** box is *not* checked, the resulting XML document contains elements from both the WordML and `article` schemas, mixed

---

6. The **Apply transform** check box on the **Save as** dialog offers another option: to specify a transformation to execute upon saving. It is discussed in 5.3.2.3, "Saving a document using a transformation", on page 112.

together. Namespaces are used to distinguish between the two vocabularies. This option is discussed further in 5.2, "Mixing WordML with other vocabularies", on page 102.

The marked up `article` document could also be saved as a Word document in the `.doc` binary format. As with WordML, the `.doc` representation retains all the `article` markup. However, it is less useful than WordML because it is not easily processable by other products.

4.7 | Combining documents

In Chapter 1, "Desktop XML: The reason why", on page 4, we learned about Denise, who is responsible for putting the newsletter together from many articles. One of the nice things about using XML is that all the articles Denise receives have the same XML markup, making her compilation job easier. Simply by opening the incoming articles in Word, she can validate them against the `article` schema to ensure that they meet her standards; for example, that they all have a title.

4.7.1 *Combining elements from multiple namespaces*

Denise has a `newsletter` skeleton document, shown in Example 4-3, that she uses when creating a newsletter. As we saw in 4.2.3, "Opening a skeleton document", on page 73, a skeleton is simply an XML document without the data content. Because Denise is the only user, and prefers to see the tag icons so that she knows what is going on with the XML representation, she did not bother with placeholder text for the skeleton.

Example 4-3. Newsletter skeleton document (newsletter temp.xml)

```
<?xml version="1.0" encoding="UTF-8" standalone="yes"?>
<newsletter xmlns="http://xmlinoffice.com/newsletter">
  <volume></volume>
  <number></number>
  <date></date>
  <body> <!--body must contain one or more article elements -->
  </body>
</newsletter>
```

She also has a newsletter schema, shown in Example 4-4, whose target namespace is `http://xmlinoffice.com/newsletter`. According to the `BodyType` definition, the `body` element of a `newsletter` can contain one or more `article` elements.

Example 4-4. Newsletter schema (newsletter.xsd)

```
<?xml version="1.0" encoding="UTF-8" standalone="yes"?>
<xs:schema targetNamespace="http://xmlinoffice.com/newsletter"
           xmlns="http://xmlinoffice.com/newsletter"
           xmlns:art="http://xmlinoffice.com/article"
           xmlns:xs="http://www.w3.org/2001/XMLSchema"
           elementFormDefault="qualified">
  <xs:import namespace="http://xmlinoffice.com/article"
             schemaLocation="article.xsd"/>
  <xs:element name="newsletter" type="NewsletterType"/>

  <xs:complexType name="NewsletterType">
    <xs:sequence>
      <xs:element name="volume" type="xs:integer"/>
      <xs:element name="number" type="xs:integer"/>
      <xs:element name="date" type="xs:string"/>
      <xs:element name="body" type="BodyType"/>
    </xs:sequence>
  </xs:complexType>

  <xs:complexType name="BodyType">
    <xs:sequence>
      <xs:element ref="art:article" maxOccurs="unbounded"/>
    </xs:sequence>
  </xs:complexType>
</xs:schema>
```

This combining of elements from more than one namespace is not unusual, and Word supports it. When Word opens a `newsletter` document, it knows it must also use the `article` schema, because of the `import` element in the `newsletter` schema.

4.7.2 *Compiling document fragments*

Denise has three choices for compiling the articles: cutting and pasting elements, copying and inserting documents, and linking to documents.

4.7.2.1   Cutting and pasting elements

One straightforward way to put the newsletter together is to cut and paste `article` elements into the newsletter document. Word supports the cutting and pasting of XML fragments to and from documents.

When Denise opens her newsletter skeleton in Word, it looks something like Figure 4-9. She can then cut the `article` elements from the various article XML documents that were submitted to her, and paste them into the newsletter document.

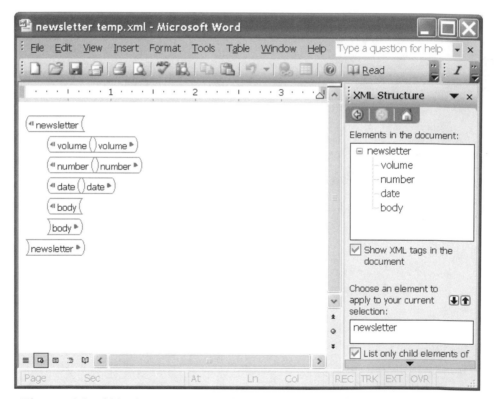

Figure 4-9   Word presentation of the `newsletter` skeleton

Because the `newsletter` schema requires the children of `body` to be `article` elements (i.e. root elements from the `article` schema), inserting the articles will not cause any errors to be raised. If the elements had been from any other vocabulary, she would still be able to paste them, but errors would be flagged in the XML Structure task pane.

4.7.2.2 Copying and inserting documents

Another method is to insert entire `article` documents into the `newsletter` document. To do this:

1. Position your cursor in the desired insert location.
2. On the **Insert** menu, click **File**.
3. Select an `article` XML file, such as `article.xml`.
4. Click **Insert**.

Word will insert the entire document as a child of the current element. If a default solution stylesheet is specified (in the Schema Library) for the article document, it is applied automatically when the article is inserted into the newsletter.

4.7.2.3 Linking to documents

Another possibility is to insert links to the article files, so that if the articles are updated in the future, the newsletter will be updated as well. This method is useful if Denise needs to begin compiling the newsletter before the articles are finished. To do this:

1. Position your cursor in the desired insert location.
2. On the **Insert** menu, click **File**.
3. Select an `article` XML file, such as `article.xml`.
4. Click the down arrow just to the right of the **Insert** button.
5. Click **Insert as Link**.

To refresh the newsletter after an article file has been updated, you can select the linked `article` elements and press **F9**. Alternatively, you can right-click an `article` start-tag and click **Update Field**, as shown in Figure 4-10.

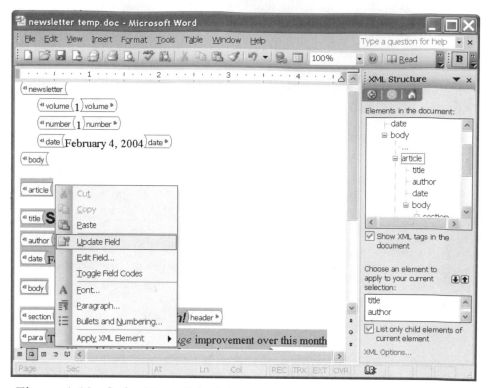

Figure 4-10   Refreshing a linked document

Rendering and presenting XML documents

- Word Markup Language (WordML)
- Mixing WordML with other vocabularies
- Creating WordML with stylesheets

Chapter

5

In the previous chapter we learned how to use Word to create and edit XML documents as unrendered abstractions. We also learned how to convert a rendered Word document to XML. We did these things using Word's default schema-independent presentation of XML documents: pink icons that represent tags.

In this chapter, we do the opposite. We learn how to transform an abstract XML document into a WordML rendition, both manually and with XSLT stylesheets. Doing so allows us to use Word's WYSIWYG interface to view and print the documents, and even to edit the abstract XML data.

These presentations can include any formatting available in Word, such as styles and page numbers. The transformations can also filter out unwanted information, or summarize or reorganize it.

Skills required   In addition to general Word end user skills, it is helpful to understand the basics of XSLT, which can be found in Chapter 18, "XSL Transformations (XSLT)", on page 392.

5.1 | Word Markup Language (WordML)

The *Word Markup Language (WordML)* is the native XML representation for Microsoft Word. It captures everything that might be known about a Word document. It covers not just the text of the document itself, but also all the formatting, all the styles associated with that document (whether they are used or not), and all of the various settings (such as page margins and tabs). Since it covers so many things, it is very verbose, and it is somewhat difficult to understand just by reading it.

Nevertheless, WordML has a significant benefit over the equivalent `.doc` binary format of Word documents: Any tool that can parse XML can make use of the Word document. This includes tools that transform, display, search, validate, store, index and query XML documents.

As Office 2003 increases in popularity, we expect third-party tools to be released that will use WordML to process Word documents in new ways and to generate Word documents from other data sources.

Caution   Because WordML is a native Word document representation, Word treats it quite differently from other uses of XML. To avoid the constant interjection of "except for WordML", we normally do not include WordML when we discuss Word's treatment of XML documents. If we do mean to include it, that will be clear from the context.

5.1.1 *The WordML vocabulary*

WordML is a large, complex vocabulary with over 400 different element types. Fortunately, in order to create, or even parse, WordML documents, you only need to be familiar with a small fraction of the vocabulary.[1] In fact, the first WordML document you write can be quite small and simple. It is shown in Example 5-1.

---

1. A reference guide that covers the entire WordML vocabulary is included with the *Microsoft Word XML Content Development Kit* that can be downloaded from the MSDN library at: `http://msdn.microsoft.com`

Example 5-1. Your first WordML document (minimal WordML.xml)

```
<?xml version="1.0" encoding="UTF-8" standalone="yes"?>
<?mso-application progid="Word.Document"?>
<w:wordDocument
 xmlns:w="http://schemas.microsoft.com/office/word/2003/wordml">
  <w:body>
    <w:p>
      <w:r><w:t>hello, Word</w:t></w:r>
    </w:p>
  </w:body>
</w:wordDocument>
```

5.1.2 *Saving a Word document as WordML*

Recall Doug's article for Worldwide Widget's newsletter. It started life as an ordinary Word document. We repeat it here in Figure 5-1 for your convenience.

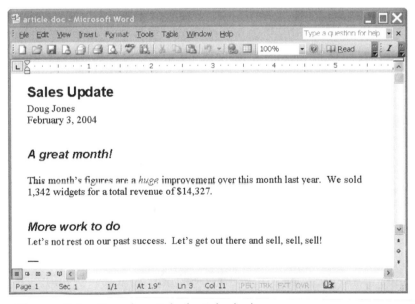

Figure 5-1   Doug's article (article.doc)

The default format when you save a Word document is still the binary .doc format. However, if you choose to save a document as XML and

Word cannot associate that document with a schema, it will be saved as WordML.[2]

Let's save Doug's article as WordML and see what we get. To do so:

1. On the **File** menu, click **Save As**.
2. Select **XML Document (*.xml)** from the **Save as type** list.
3. Click **Save**.

We'll look at the actual WordML representation, as a Word rendition would be identical to Figure 5-1. Because the WordML document is extremely long, we will excerpt pieces as examples as we go along.

5.1.3 *Structure of a WordML document*

The basic structure of a WordML document is shown in Model 5-1.

Model 5-1. WordML document structure

```
[Document (wordDocument)
  [0..1]Document Properties -- General (DocumentProperties)
  [0..1]Lists (lists)
  [0..1]Styles(styles)
  [0..1]Document Properties -- Word-specific (docPr)
  [1..1]Body (body)
```

The root of a WordML document is always a wordDocument element. The most commonly used children of a wordDocument element are:

- an optional DocumentProperties element, which contains general information about the document such as the date it was created and last updated, the author name, and the revision number
- an optional lists element contains information about the formatting of lists, such as the type of bullet or number, and the indentation used

---

2. We saw in 4.6, "Saving a document", on page 79 how to save a document that *is* associated with a schema, using that schema alone. Later we will see how to save it using a combination of its own schema and WordML.

- an optional `styles` element contains the information about the styles used in the document, such as the font and size, language, and paragraph formatting
- an optional `docPr` element, which contains Word-specific information on the settings for the document, such as margins and header and footer properties
- a required `body` element that contains the bulk of the document

As you can see, most of these elements can be left out. If you omit an optional element, it defaults to the settings for new documents in Word.

5.1.4   *In the beginning*

Example 5-2 shows the very beginning of the WordML document.[3]

Example 5-2. Beginning of WordML document (article WordML.xml)

```
<?xml version="1.0" encoding="UTF-8" standalone="yes"?>
<?mso-application progid="Word.Document"?>
<w:wordDocument
 xmlns:w="http://schemas.microsoft.com/office/word/2003/wordml"
 xmlns:v="urn:schemas-microsoft-com:vml"
 xmlns:w10="urn:schemas-microsoft-com:office:word"
 xmlns:SL="http://schemas.microsoft.com/schemaLibrary/2003/core"
 xmlns:xsi="http://www.w3.org/2001/XMLSchema-instance"
 xmlns:aml="http://schemas.microsoft.com/aml/2001/core"
 xmlns:wx="http://schemas.microsoft.com/office/word/2003/auxHint"
 xmlns:o="urn:schemas-microsoft-com:office:office"
 xml:space="preserve">
 <o:DocumentProperties>
   <o:Title>Heading 1</o:Title>
   <o:Author>Priscilla Walmsley</o:Author>
   <o:LastAuthor>Priscilla Walmsley</o:LastAuthor>
   <o:Revision>2</o:Revision>
```

---

3. Some whitespace was added to all examples to make them more readable.

line 1

> The document starts out on line 1 with an XML declaration, which identifies the document as XML and indicates the encoding used in the document.

line 2

> On line 2, a processing instruction appears which identifies the document as a Word document. The purpose of this processing instruction is to tell Windows to open this file in Word, rather than in Internet Explorer, which is often the application associated with the `.xml` extension.

line 3

> The root element is `w:wordDocument`, whose start-tag has a number of namespace declarations.

line 4

> The namespace of the WordML vocabulary is:`http://schemas.microsoft.com/office/word/2003/wordml` This namespace is commonly mapped to the `w` prefix, although there is no requirement that this prefix be used.

line 13

> The first child of `w:wordDocument` is a `o:DocumentProperties` element that contains general information about the document. It is followed by a huge number of elements representing style information, which is not shown.

5.1.5 *The body*

The body of the WordML document, represented by the `body` element, contains all the text of the document. Its structure is shown in Model 5-2.

The body can contain sections that contain paragraphs, or it can contain paragraphs directly. Paragraphs, in turn, contain text runs, which contain text elements, which contain data characters. There is a separate text run for every data character string that has a distinct style or other properties. A paragraph can also contain images, hyperlinks and other components.

Model 5-2. WordML body structure

```
Body (body)
  [0..*]Section (sect)
        [0..*]Paragraph (p)
                [0..*]Text Run (r)
                        [0..*]Text (t)
  [0..*]Paragraph (p)
        ...
```

5.1.5.1   Paragraphs and text

Each paragraph is represented by a p element. The paragraph has a style (and possibly other settings) associated with it in its properties child, pPr. If no style is associated with the paragraph, it defaults to "Normal" style.

A text run (r) can contain multiple text elements, as well as pictures, footnotes, fields and other Word objects. A text element (t), on the other hand, can only contain data characters, with no child elements. Every data character in the document text is contained directly in a t element.

An excerpt from the body of the WordML representation of Figure 5-1 is shown in Example 5-3. It contains two paragraphs (p elements). The first paragraph has a pPr child that identifies properties of the paragraph, namely that the style is "Heading2". It then contains a text run (r element), which contains a single text element (t).

The second paragraph contains three text runs (w:r elements). As the word "huge" is in italics, it must have its own text run with its own properties (the w:rPr element) that specify the italics (the w:i element).

5.1.5.2   Lists

Bulleted and numbered lists are common in Word documents. In WordML, list items are simply paragraphs that refer to a list ID in their properties. The list ID corresponds to a list defined in the lists section of the document.

For example, suppose Doug wanted to list the identifying elements of his article in a bulleted list, as shown in Figure 5-2. The corresponding WordML would look like Example 5-4.

Each paragraph properties (pPr) element contains a list properties (listPr) element which in turn has two children:

Example 5-3. WordML paragraphs (article WordML.xml)

```
<w:p>
  <w:pPr>
    <w:pStyle w:val="Heading2"/>
  </w:pPr>
  <w:r><w:t>A great month!</w:t></w:r>
</w:p>
<w:p>
  <w:r><w:t>This month's figures are a </w:t></w:r>
  <w:r>
    <w:rPr>
      <w:i/>
    </w:rPr>
    <w:t>huge</w:t>
  </w:r>
  <w:r>
    <w:t> improvement over this month last year. We sold
1,342 widgets for a total revenue of $14,327.</w:t>
  </w:r>
</w:p>
```

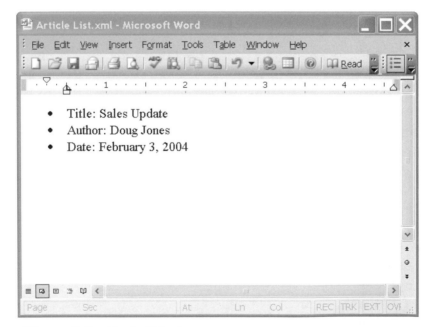

Figure 5-2   List in Word

Example 5-4. WordML list

```
<w:p>
  <w:pPr>
    <w:listPr><w:ilvl w:val="0"/><w:ilfo w:val="2"/></w:listPr>
  </w:pPr>
  <w:r><w:t>Title: Sales Update</w:t></w:r>
</w:p>
<w:p>
  <w:pPr>
    <w:listPr><w:ilvl w:val="0"/><w:ilfo w:val="2"/></w:listPr>
  </w:pPr>
  <w:r><w:t>Author: Doug Jones</w:t></w:r>
</w:p>
<w:p>
  <w:pPr>
    <w:listPr><w:ilvl w:val="0"/><w:ilfo w:val="2"/></w:listPr>
  </w:pPr>
  <w:r><w:t>Date: February 3, 2004</w:t></w:r>
</w:p>
```

- The `ilvl` element indicates the level of the item in the list, starting with zero. If a list contains items at different outline levels, this property indicates this.
- The `ilfo` element associates the paragraph with a specific list. The number specified in its `val` attribute is an ID that corresponds to the `ilfo` attribute of a `list` element in the `lists` section.

The `lists` element of the same document appears in Example 5-5. Notice that it has two types of children. The `listDef` element defines various properties of the list, such as the style used and a unique identifier. The `list` element has only a unique identifier and the link to a `listDef` element through its `ilst` child. The many levels of definitions for lists are due to the complexity of starting and stopping the numbering for numbered lists.

5.1.5.3 Tables

The structure of WordML tables (Model 5-3) is very similar to XHTML tables, so if you are familiar with HTML you have a head start. A table ele-

Example 5-5. The WordML `lists` element

```
<w:lists>

  <w:listDef w:listDefId="0">
    <w:lsid w:val="1E525C74"/>
    <w:listStyleLink w:val="Style1bulletpw"/>
  </w:listDef>

  <w:list w:ilfo="1">
    <w:ilst w:val="0"/>
  </w:list>

</w:lists>
```

ment (tbl) can appear anywhere a paragraph can appear, namely as a child of body.

Model 5-3. WordML table structure

```
Table (tbl)
  [1..1]Table Properties (tblPr)
  [1..1]Table Grid (tblGrid)
        [1..*]Table Grid Column (tblGridCol)
  [0..*]Row (tr)
        [0..1]Row Properties (trPr)
        [1..*]Cell (tc)
                [1..1]Cell Properties (tcPr)
                [0..*]Tables (tbl)
                [1..*]Paragraphs (p)
```

The table properties element (`tblPr`) is used to specify the properties of the table, such as the style used, the cell spacing, and the borders. The element is required, but none of its children (which set the individual properties) is required, so it is possible to have an empty `tblPr` element. All of the settings have defaults, which are used in case they are not specified.

The table grid element (`tblGrid`) is used to set the column widths. For each column in the table it contains a `tblGridCol` with a `w` attribute that specifies the column width in twips (twentieths of a point). The `tblGrid` element and its `tblGridCol` children are required.

Each row in the table is represented by a `tr` element. Each `tr` element has an optional properties child, `trPr`, and one or more cells, represented by `tc` elements. Each `tc` may itself have a properties child, `tcPr`, and must have one or more other tables (tbl) or paragraphs (p). The last child of the tc must always be a paragraph rather than another table.

Suppose that Doug wants to display sales data in a table. The table shown in Example 5-6 will look like Figure 5-3 when shown in Word.

Sales Table.xml - Microsoft Word

File   Edit   View   Insert   Format   Tools   Table   Window   Help

The sales figures from 2003 are as follows:

Q	Revenue	Profit
1	$14,332.35	$2,115.12
2	$13,224.22	$1,655.51
3	$14,778.26	$2,243.98
4	$17,455.15	$2,988.22

Page 1   Sec 1   1/1   At 1"   Ln 1   Col 1   REC TRK EXT

Figure 5-3   Sales table displayed in Word

For more complex tables, you can use the many table formatting features of Word, such as vertical and horizontal merge, and borders and shading. You can even include tables within other tables, as we saw.

Tip   When designing a complex table, the best approach is to create an example of the table in Word and save it as WordML. This will give you a model to work from, and will save you the effort of learning every single relevant WordML element.

Example 5-6. WordML table

```
<w:tbl>
  <w:tblGrid>
    <w:gridCol w:w="828"/>
    <w:gridCol w:w="1620"/>
    <w:gridCol w:w="1440"/>
  </w:tblGrid>
  <w:tr>
    <w:tc>
      <w:p>
        <w:pPr><w:pStyle w:val="Heading3"/></w:pPr>
        <w:r><w:t>Q</w:t></w:r>
      </w:p>
    </w:tc>
    <w:tc>
      <w:p>
        <w:pPr><w:pStyle w:val="Heading3"/></w:pPr>
        <w:r><w:t>Revenue</w:t></w:r>
      </w:p>
    </w:tc>
    <w:tc>
      <w:p>
        <w:pPr><w:pStyle w:val="Heading3"/></w:pPr>
        <w:r><w:t>Profit</w:t></w:r>
      </w:p>
    </w:tc>
  </w:tr>
  <w:tr>
    <w:tc><w:p><w:r><w:t>1</w:t></w:r></w:p></w:tc>
    <w:tc><w:p><w:r><w:t>$14,332.35</w:t></w:r></w:p></w:tc>
    <w:tc><w:p><w:r><w:t>$2,115.12</w:t></w:r></w:p></w:tc>
  </w:tr>
  <w:tr>
    <w:tc><w:p><w:r><w:t>2</w:t></w:r></w:p></w:tc>
    <w:tc><w:p><w:r><w:t>$13,224.22</w:t></w:r></w:p></w:tc>
    <w:tc><w:p><w:r><w:t>$1,655.51</w:t></w:r></w:p></w:tc>
  </w:tr>
  <w:tr>
    <w:tc><w:p><w:r><w:t>3</w:t></w:r></w:p></w:tc>
    <w:tc>
    <w:p><w:r><w:t>$14,778.26</w:t></w:r></w:p></w:tc><w:tc>
    <w:p><w:r><w:t>$2,243.98</w:t></w:r></w:p></w:tc>
  </w:tr>
  <w:tr>
    <w:tc><w:p><w:r><w:t>4</w:t></w:r></w:p></w:tc>
    <w:tc><w:p><w:r><w:t>$17,455.15</w:t></w:r></w:p></w:tc>
    <w:tc><w:p><w:r><w:t>$2,988.22</w:t></w:r></w:p></w:tc>
  </w:tr>
</w:tbl>
```

5.1.5.4 Images

An image embedded in a Word document is represented in WordML by a `pict` element. Each `pict` element contains a Vector Markup Language (VML) description of the shape, location and size of the image, and the image data itself in `base64Binary` datatype format.

Tip   *As with other Word components, the best way to include an image in a generated WordML document is to create a Word document that contains the image in the desired location and size, and save it as WordML. You can then copy the* `pict` *element from the saved WordML document and place it in your XSLT stylesheet.*

5.1.5.5 Hyperlinks

A hyperlink is represented in WordML by an `hlink` element. Example 5-7 shows a paragraph that has an embedded hyperlink.

Example 5-7. Hyperlink in WordML

```
<w:p>
  <w:r>
    <w:t>More information on the new marketing
         plan be found at </w:t>
  </w:r>
  <w:hlink w:dest="http://www.xmlinoffice.com/mkplan">
    <w:r>
      <w:rPr><w:rStyle w:val="Hyperlink"/></w:rPr>
      <w:t>http://www.xmlinoffice.com/mkplan</w:t>
    </w:r>
  </w:hlink>
  <w:r>
    <w:t>. </w:t>
  </w:r>
</w:p>
```

The `hlink` element is contained directly within the p element, rather than within a text run. In fact, it contains its own text run for the hyperlink text that appears when the document is presented, as in Figure 5-4. The `dest` attribute of the `hlink` element specifies the linked URL.

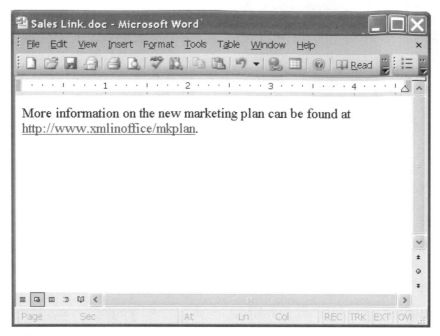

Figure 5-4   Hyperlink displayed in Word

5.1.6 *Using Word styles*

There are four kinds of style in Word:

- A *character style* applies to a data character string within a paragraph.
- A *paragraph style* applies to an entire paragraph.
- A *table style* has special settings relating to tables, such as background color and justification.
- A *list style* has special settings related to lists, such as the bullet or numbering used.

There are quite a few different properties of a style, ranging from character properties, such as font and size, to paragraph properties, such as indentation and tab settings. Any style setting that can be specified in Word can also be expressed in WordML.

5.1.6.1   A style example

The `styles` element that appears before the body contains all the information about the styles used in the document. Each `style` element has a unique name that is specified in its `styleId` attribute. The text in the body of the document then refers to these styles by name.

In Example 5-3, the first paragraph refers to the style whose name is "Heading2". The `style` element for Heading2 is shown in Example 5-8.

Example 5-8. WordML style (article WordML.xml)

```
<w:style w:type="paragraph" w:styleId="Heading2">
  <w:name w:val="heading 2"/>
  <w:basedOn w:val="Normal"/>
  <w:next w:val="Normal"/>
  <w:rsid w:val="CF4316"/>
  <w:pPr>
    <w:pStyle w:val="Heading2"/>
    <w:spacing w:before="240" w:after="60"/>
  </w:pPr>
  <w:rPr>
    <w:rFonts w:ascii="Arial" w:h-ansi="Arial" w:cs="Arial"/>
    <w:b/>
    <w:b-cs/>
    <w:kern w:val="48"/>
    <w:sz w:val="48"/>
    <w:sz-cs w:val="48"/>
  </w:rPr>
</w:style>
```

5.1.6.2   Generating WordML style definitions

Fortunately, there is no need to learn all the WordML elements for the style settings you need. Attempting to construct WordML style definitions by hand would be a tedious, trial-and-error process. Because Word already provides a user-friendly front-end for defining styles, you should use Word itself to create a document that has all the styles you want to use.

You can save that document as WordML using the procedure described in 5.1.2, "Saving a Word document as WordML", on page 89. The result is a WordML document that contains all the styles you need. You can then copy the `styles` section of that document (and the `lists` section if needed).

This is a good approach not just for paragraph styles, but also for character styles. For example, if you wish to italicize a word in the middle of a sentence, you could do this using the `i` property for the text run, as shown in Example 5-3. However, it is sometimes difficult to remember the names of all the different properties that can be applied to text.

Using Word, you can create a character style for italics named, for example, "emphasis". Any text that should be italicized because it should be emphasized can then refer to that style, rather than using the `i` property. In effect you are using the principles of generalized markup for style names, just as you do for XML element-type names.

As with XML, this approach to style definitions has the added benefit of making it easy to apply a change to all text of that type. For example, if you use italics for both emphasized words and citations, you can create two styles: "emphasis" and "citation". If later, you decide you want to put citations in a different font, you can simply change the "citation" style rather than having to change the font of some but not all of the italicized text.

5.2 | Mixing WordML with other vocabularies

As we saw in 4.6, "Saving a document", on page 79, WordML can be interspersed with other vocabularies. When a Word document associated with a schema is saved as XML, by default the saved file contains both WordML elements and elements of the associated schema.

For example, saving an article document as XML results in a document that contains elements from the `article` schema interspersed with WordML elements, as shown in Example 5-9.

Namespaces are used to distinguish between the two vocabularies. The WordML elements use the `w` prefix, as in `w:p` and `w:t`. The `article` vocabulary uses the `ns0` prefix, as in `ns0:section` and `ns0:header`.

Because of the hierarchical structure of XML, an element from the `article` schema must always contain one or more entire WordML paragraphs, or be contained in a WordML paragraph. It is not possible for it to span part of one WordML paragraph plus part of the next paragraph.

In addition, each element from the `article` schema must contain its own text run. It cannot be included as a child of a text run element (`r`), nor as a child of a text element (`t`). For example, the following text run is illegal:

Example 5-9. `article`/WordML mixture (article data and WordML.xml)

```
<ns0:section>
  <ns0:header>
    <w:p>
      <w:pPr>
        <w:pStyle w:val="Heading2"/>
      </w:pPr>
      <w:r>
        <w:t>A great month!</w:t>
      </w:r>
    </w:p>
  </ns0:header>
  <ns0:para>
    <w:p>
      <w:r>
        <w:t>This month's figures are a</w:t>
      </w:r>
      <ns0:em>
        <w:r>
          <w:rPr>
            <w:i/>
          </w:rPr>
          <w:t>huge</w:t>
        </w:r>
      </ns0:em>
      <w:r>
        <w:t> improvement over this month last year. We sold  1,342
widgets for a total revenue of 14,327.</w:t>
      </w:r>
    </w:p>
  </ns0:para>
</ns0:section>
```

```
<w:r><w:t><ns0:title>Sales Update</ns0:title></w:t></w:r>
```

Instead, the `ns0:title` element should be moved out to contain the `w:r` element, as in:

```
<ns0:title><w:r><w:t>Sales Update</w:t></w:r></ns0:title>
```

Combining WordML with other vocabularies allows all of the Word formatting and other information to be retained, so that the document can be reopened in Word and the styles and settings will be intact. This is useful if you or other users will continue to edit the document in Word.

However, a mixed document is not valid according to the `article` schema. If you need an `article` document to pass to an application that is expecting it, just save the document as XML with the **Save data only** box checked.

5.3 | Creating WordML with stylesheets

WordML is very rarely created by hand, because it is much easier for a person to format a document with Word than to compose the equivalent WordML representation. But that approach is most useful for one-off tasks.

If you want to create Word renditions of multiple XML documents of the same document type, it is more efficient to generate WordML using XSLT. This technique also allows data from other sources to be incorporated into the Word documents. Moreover, multiple views of the same data (e.g. for different classes of user) can be created using several different transformations.

This section provides an overview of the creation and use of stylesheets for Microsoft Word. For more information on XSLT stylesheets, please see Chapter 18, "XSL Transformations (XSLT)", on page 392.

5.3.1 *Creating an XSLT stylesheet*

Each desired rendition is expressed as an XSLT stylesheet that is associated with a particular schema in the Word Schema Library. An XSLT stylesheet contains XSLT instruction elements (usually prefixed with `xsl:`) that select elements and attributes from the source document. The instructions are interleaved with elements from other namespaces that are to appear in the result document.

For use with Word, a stylesheet must transform documents from your source vocabulary (e.g. `article`) to WordML. As we have seen, this can be a challenging task, since WordML is quite complex and not entirely intuitive. But fortunately, as we have also seen, you can copy most of the complex parts from an existing WordML document.

If you have (or create) a Word document that has the settings you want to use – for example the styles and page margins – you can simply save that document as WordML. You can then paste the beginning of the document, which contains all the settings, into your stylesheet.

5.3.1.1 Stylesheet structure

Worldwide Widget maintains an archive of its newsletter articles in XML so they can easily be reused. Authors frequently access the archive to rework old articles for new issues of the newsletter. The company has implemented a stylesheet that will transform an XML `article` (the *source document*) into a WordML/`article` combination (the *result document*).

Example 5-10 shows the general structure of the stylesheet (named `article_view.xsl`) that accomplishes this.

Example 5-10. Article stylesheet general structure (article_view.xsl)

```
<xsl:stylesheet version="1.0" xml:space="preserve"
  xmlns:w="http://schemas.microsoft.com/office/word/2003/wordml"
  xmlns:art="http://xmlinoffice.com/article"
  xmlns:xsl="http://www.w3.org/1999/XSL/Transform">
  <xsl:template match="/">
  <w:wordDocument xml:space="preserve">
     <w:lists>  <!--taken from Word-->  </w:lists>
     <w:styles> <!--taken from Word-->  </w:styles>
     <w:docPr>  <!--taken from Word-->  </w:docPr>
     <w:body>
        <xsl:apply-templates select="/art:article"/>
     </w:body>
  </w:wordDocument>
  </xsl:template>

<!--rest of template rules here-->

</xsl:stylesheet>
```

Rather than start from scratch with the styles, we took the `lists` and `styles` elements from a Word document that had styles defined to our liking, as was recommended in 5.1.6.2, "Generating WordML style definitions", on page 101. [4]

The `body` element contains the `xsl:apply-templates` instruction to apply the correct template rule to the source elements whose element-type name is `article`. (Only one such element is allowed by the `article` schema.)[5]

---

4. The comment `<!--taken from Word-->` appears instead of the actual definitions to reduce the size of the example; for a full listing, see `article_view.xsl`.
5. The `xsl:template` instruction element is actually a *template rule*; its content is the template. The `xsl:apply-templates` instruction actually applies template rules, which include match patterns as well as templates.

5.3.1.2   Template rules

The `article_view.xsl` stylesheet has a template rule for every `article` schema element type. The template rule that matches the root element, `article`, is shown in Example 5-11. It inserts WordML paragraphs (`p` elements) for the title, author and date. It also applies other template rules that transform the `article` element's children.

Example 5-11. Template rule for `article` schema element type (article_view.xsl)

```
<xsl:template match="art:article">
 <xsl:copy>
  <w:p>
   <w:pPr>
    <w:pStyle w:val="Heading1"/>
   </w:pPr>
   <xsl:apply-templates select="art:title"/>
  </w:p>
  <w:p>
   <xsl:apply-templates select="art:author"/>
  </w:p>
  <w:p>
   <w:pPr>
    <w:pBdr>
     <w:bottom w:val="single" w:sz="6" w:space="22" w:color="auto"/>
    </w:pBdr>
   </w:pPr>
   <xsl:apply-templates select="art:date"/>
  </w:p>
  <xsl:apply-templates select="art:body"/>
 </xsl:copy>
</xsl:template>
```

The `xsl:copy` instruction copies a source element so that it also appears in the resulting WordML; it does not copy child elements or attributes. If you want a pure WordML document with no elements from the `article` vocabulary, you can leave out the `xsl:copy` instructions in the templates.

The template rule shown in Example 5-12 is used to transform both `author` and `date` elements, since they are processed similarly. Their contents are simply included unchanged in a text element contained within a text run.

A third template rule, for the `section` element type, is shown in Example 5-13. It includes a paragraph (`p`) for the header, then uses an XSLT

Example 5-12. Template rule for author and date element types (article_view.xsl)

```
<xsl:template match="art:author|art:date">
  <xsl:copy>
    <w:r>
      <w:rPr>
        <w:b/>
      </w:rPr>
      <w:t><xsl:value-of select="."/></w:t>
    </w:r>
  </xsl:copy>
</xsl:template>
```

for-each element to loop through the child paragraphs and process them individually.

Example 5-13. Template rule for section element type (article_view.xsl)

```
<xsl:template match="art:section">
  <xsl:copy>
    <w:p>
      <w:pPr>
        <w:pStyle w:val="Heading2"/>
      </w:pPr>
      <xsl:apply-templates select="art:header"/>
    </w:p>
    <xsl:for-each select="art:para">
      <xsl:apply-templates select="."/>
    </xsl:for-each>
  </xsl:copy>
</xsl:template>
```

The result of applying the stylesheet is a WordML/article combination that can be displayed in Word with or without the article tag icons, as shown in Figure 5-5.

5.3.2 *Using stylesheets*

This section explains how to use our newly-created stylesheet (article_view.xsl) with Word.

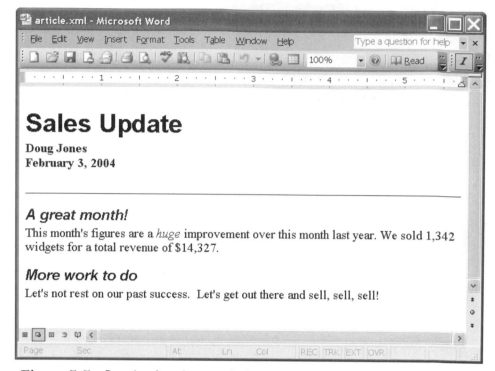

Figure 5-5   Result of applying stylesheet to an `article`

5.3.2.1   Associating stylesheets with schemas

Stylesheets are associated with schemas using the Schema Library, where they are known as *solutions*. Multiple stylesheets can be associated with the same schema. First, let's associate the `article_view.xsl` stylesheet with the `article` schema. To do this:

1. On the **Tools** menu, click **Templates and Add-Ins**.
2. Click the **XML Schema** tab.
3. Click **Schema Library**.
4. Select the `article` schema.
5. Click **Add Solution**.
6. Browse to the location of the `article_view.xsl` document and select it.
7. This will bring up the **Solution Settings** dialog shown in Figure 5-6.

8. The default type is **XSL Transformation**, which is what we want in this case.
9. In the **Alias** box, enter a nickname for the solution, such as "Article View", and click **OK**.
10. The solution (stylesheet) now appears in the bottom half of the **Schema Library** dialog, as shown in Figure 5-7.

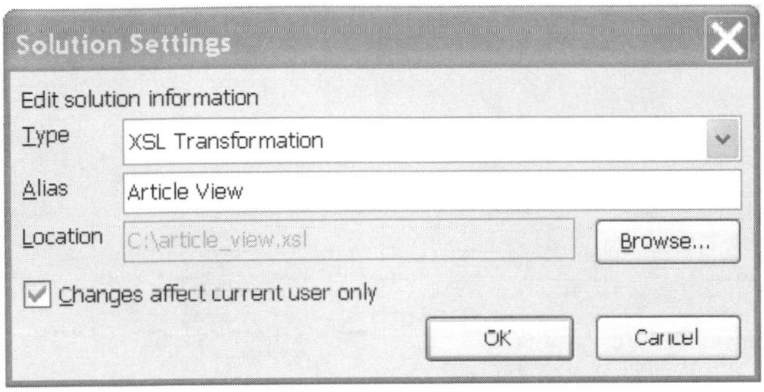

Figure 5-6 The Solution Settings dialog

It is possible in the **Schema Library** dialog to specify a particular solution as the default. To do this, select a solution from the **Default solution** list. The default stylesheet is applied whenever a document associated with that schema is opened.

5.3.2.2   Opening a document with a stylesheet

There are three ways to choose a stylesheet to apply while opening a document: by default, while opening the document, and after opening the document but before editing it.

5.3.2.2.1 *Default stylesheet*

Opening a document whose schema is associated with a default stylesheet will result in that stylesheet being applied automatically. For example, now, when we open `article.xml`, the `article_view.xsl` stylesheet is automatically applied, as shown in Figure 5-8.

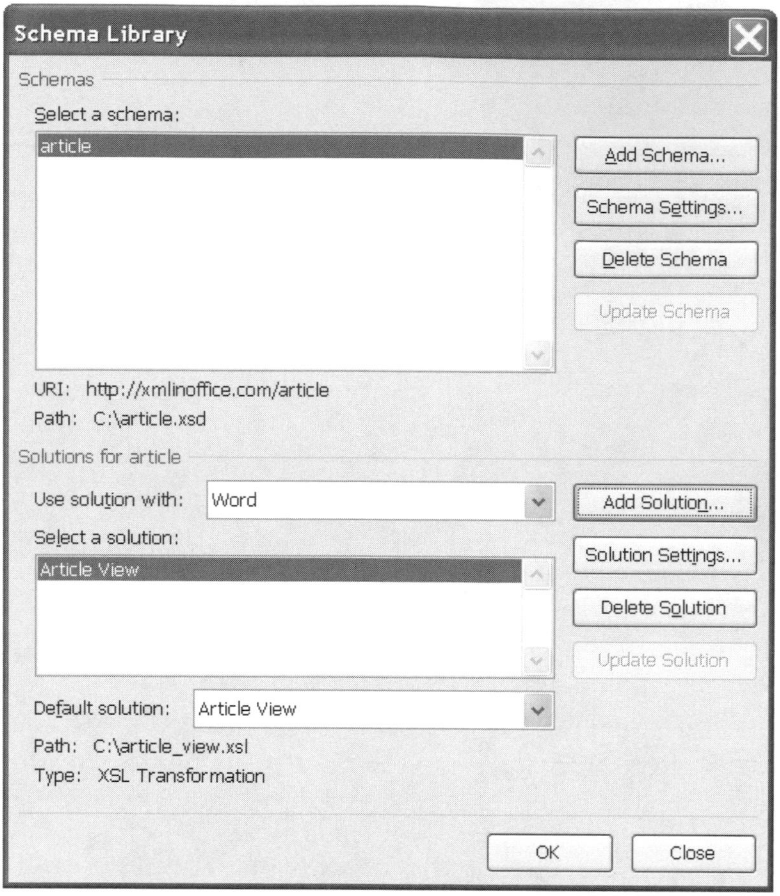

Figure 5-7   Solution listed in the Schema Library dialog

If you previously had the **Show XML tags in document** box checked, you will have to uncheck it in order to see the document rendered according to the stylesheet. You can do this on the **XML Structure** task pane.

5.3.2.2.2 *Choose while opening*

If there is no default stylesheet for a schema, or if you wish to use a different style, you can choose a stylesheet while opening a document. To do this:

1. On the **File** menu, click **Open**.
2. Select the file you wish to open.

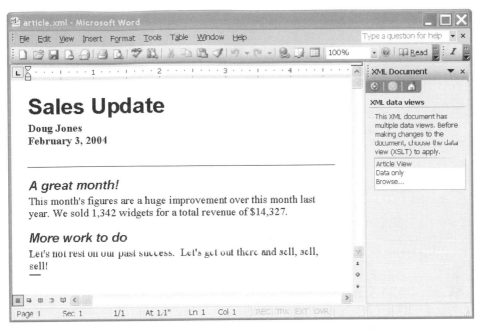

Figure 5-8 Article with `article_view` stylesheet applied

3. Click the down arrow on the right side of the **Open** button, and select **Open with Transform** from the list.
4. Select the file name of the stylesheet you wish to use. The document will open using the specified transformation.

5.3.2.2.3 *Choose before editing*

The XML Document task pane lists all the associated stylesheets, as well as the generic **Data only** rendition that is used as a default when no other stylesheet is available. You can check out the different renditions of the document simply by selecting them from this list.

You can also click **Browse** to look for an additional XSLT stylesheet to apply.

You can choose between stylesheets only until you have begun editing the document. Once you change the document in any way, the XML Document task pane closes and you lose the ability to change to a different rendition of the document.

Tip   *Styles are not necessarily applied to newly added elements. For example, if you insert a new* `section` *in your article, its* `header` *element will not automatically be given the Heading2 style like the original section headers. However, if you save the document using* **Save data only***, then reopen it, the stylesheet will format it appropriately.*

5.3.2.3   Saving a document using a transformation

You can apply a stylesheet when you are saving a document. This may seem confusing, since styles are generally associated with the way a document is formatted and presented rather than the way it is stored.

However, XSLT stylesheets are not just for formatting; you can also use them to transform XML documents from one vocabulary to another. This feature is useful if, for example, you want to allow the user to work with a small, simple vocabulary, but the documents need to be transformed into a more complex vocabulary to be used by another process.

To specify a stylesheet when saving a document:

1. On the **File** menu, click **Save As**.
2. Select **XML Document (*.xml)** from the **Save as type** list.
3. Check the **Apply transform** box.
4. Click the **Transform...** button to select a stylesheet.
5. Select the stylesheet you wish to apply and click **Open**.
6. Click **Save**.

Using external XML data in documents

- Complete XML documents

- XML search results

- Web services

- Automatic event-based updates

Chapter

6

W ord can access external data and insert it in your XML documents. You can accomplish tasks such as looking up an address in an external XML document, importing canned text, or getting information about a ZIP code from a Web service.

This chapter will show you how to:

- Access XML document sources from a file system or with a URL.
- Get data from Web services using a SOAP interface

We'll also explain how to refresh external data automatically when changes are made to the document.

Skills required   Some knowledge of Visual Basic for Applications (VBA) and the Word object model. The section on Web services assumes a basic knowledge of Web services. For more information on Web services, see Chapter 19, "Web services introduction", on page 414 and Chapter 23, "Web services technologies", on page 484.

6.1 | External XML documents

Worldwide Widget Corporation is known for its award-winning customer service. It responds to all customer complaints with a sincere personalized form letter. Thanks to XML, the letter is largely computer-generated.

Figure 6-1 shows how a typical letter looks when rendered by Word.

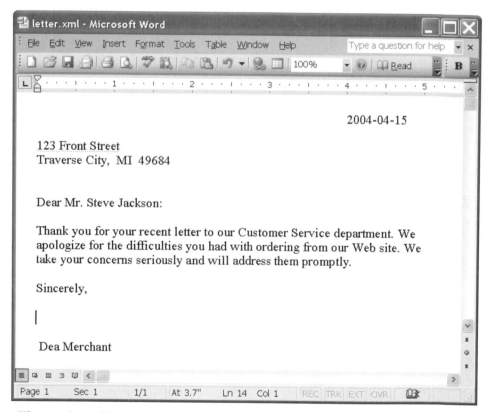

Figure 6-1   Typical customer letter, rendered by Word

The XML representation is shown in Example 6-1 and its schema in Example 6-2.

The letter has XML elements representing the customer's name and address, the nature of the problem, the name of the employee who generated the letter, and so on. Because of the self-describing markup, these data

Example 6-1. Typical customer letter (letter.xml)

```
<?xml version="1.0" encoding="UTF-8"?>
<customerLetter xmlns="http://xmlinoffice.com/letter">
  <date>2004-04-15</date>
  <address>
    <line>123 Front Street</line>
    <city>Traverse City</city>
    <state>Michigan</state>
    <zip>49684</zip>
  </address>
  <greeting> Dear <salutation>Mr.</salutation> <customer id=
    "C12266">Steve Jackson</customer>:</greeting>
  <body type="problem">
<p>Thank you for your recent <format>letter</format> to our
Customer Service department. We apologize for the difficulties
you had with <problem>ordering from our Web site</problem>.
We take your concerns seriously and will address them
promptly.</p>
<p>We appreciate your business and hope to retain you as a
customer.</p>
  </body>
  <footer>Sincerely,
    <emp id="E18234">Denise Dorning</emp>
  </footer>
</customerLetter>
```

elements can easily be manipulated, validated or completed from an external data source.

For example, Worldwide's system automatically fills in a customer's address based on its name, imports canned text from an external document, and automatically fills in the city and state based on the ZIP code.

6.1.1 *Importing an external XML document*

Note from Example 6-1 that the body element has a type attribute:

```
<body type="problem">
```

The plan is that the letter reply system will eventually support a variety of body types. For each type there would be a separate XML file with appropriate canned text.

For now there is just the XML document shown in Example 6-3, which is to be included in every customer "problem" letter. It contains a paragraph to be embedded directly in the body of the letter, with placeholder text for

Example 6-2. Customer letter schema (letter.xsd)

```xml
<?xml version="1.0"?>
<xs:schema targetNamespace="http://xmlinoffice.com/letter"
           xmlns="http://xmlinoffice.com/letter"
           xmlns:xs="http://www.w3.org/2001/XMLSchema"
           elementFormDefault="qualified">
 <xs:element name="letter" type="LetterType"/>
 <xs:complexType name="LetterType">
  <xs:sequence>
   <xs:element name="date" type="xs:date"/>
   <xs:element name="address" type="AddressType"/>
   <xs:element name="greeting" type="GreetingType"/>
   <xs:element name="body" type="BodyType"/>
   <xs:element name="footer" type="FooterType"/>
  </xs:sequence>
  <xs:attribute name="id" type="xs:ID"/>
  <xs:attribute name="type" type="xs:string"/>
 </xs:complexType>
 <xs:complexType name="AddressType"><xs:sequence>
   <xs:element name="line" type="xs:string" maxOccurs="unbounded"/>
   <xs:element name="city" type="xs:string"/>
   <xs:element name="state" type="xs:string"/>
   <xs:element name="zip" type="xs:string"/>
 </xs:sequence></xs:complexType>
 <xs:complexType name="GreetingType" mixed="true"><xs:sequence>
   <xs:element name="salutation" type="xs:string"/>
   <xs:element name="customer" type="IdentifiedType"/>
 </xs:sequencc></xs:complexType>
 <xs:complexType name="BodyType">
  <xs:sequence>
   <xs:element name="p" type="ParaType" maxOccurs="unbounded"/>
  </xs:sequence>
  <xs:attribute name="type" type="xs:string"/>
 </xs:complexType>
 <xs:complexType name="ParaType" mixed="true">
  <xs:choice minOccurs="0" maxOccurs="unbounded">
   <xs:element name="format" type="xs:string"/>
   <xs:element name="problem" type="xs:string"/>
  </xs:choice>
 </xs:complexType>
 <xs:complexType name="FooterType" mixed="true"><xs:sequence>
   <xs:element name="emp" type="IdentifiedType"/>
 </xs:sequence></xs:complexType>
 <xs:complexType name="IdentifiedType">
  <xs:simpleContent><xs:extension base="xs:string">
   <xs:attribute name="id" type="xs:string"/>
  </xs:extension></xs:simpleContent>
 </xs:complexType>
</xs:schema>
```

the `format` and `problem` elements to be replaced by the human sending the letter.

Example 6-3. Canned letter paragraph (problem_para.xml)

```
<?xml version="1.0" encoding="UTF-8" standalone="yes"?>
<p xmlns="http://xmlinoffice.com/letter">Thank you for your recent
<format>ENTER FORMAT</format> to our Customer Service department.
We apologize for the difficulties you had with <problem>ENTER
PROBLEM</problem>. We take your concerns seriously and will
address them promptly.</p>
```

You can set up your Word document so that when a `body` element is inserted, it is automatically populated with the contents of the `problem_para.xml` document. The VBA function shown in Example 6-4 accomplishes this.[1]

Example 6-4. Function to automatically insert external XML document

```
Private Sub Document_XMLAfterInsert(ByVal NewXMLNode
As XMLNode, ByVal InUndoRedo As Boolean)
    If NewXMLNode Is Nothing Then
        'do nothing
    ElseIf NewXMLNode.BaseName = "body" Then
        Dim theRange As Word.Range
        Set theRange = NewXMLNode.Range
        theRange.InsertFile "C:\problem_para.xml"
    End If

End Sub
```

This function is automatically executed in response to the event `XMLAfterInsert`, which occurs every time an XML element is added to the letter document. On line 5 it checks whether the newly inserted element is of type `body`. If so, it creates a range variable `theRange` and assigns it the range of the newly inserted `body` element. It then inserts the contents of `problem_para.xml` into the range. (In the future, it will test the value of the `type` attribute to determine which external XML document to insert.)

---

1. All of the examples in this chapter are written in Visual Basic for Applications (VBA).

A working version of this code can be found in the example file `letter insert.doc`.

> *Tip*   The inserted canned text need not be an XML document in a file system. It could also be returned from a URL reference. For example, Worldwide Widget has a customer information application that returns a customer's address from, for example: `http://xmlinoffice.com/customerlookup?id=123456`. The returned XML can be inserted exactly as if it was a local file. The important thing is the XML; any means of addressing it will work the same way.

6.1.2 *Querying an external XML document*

On the other hand, suppose you do not want to insert an entire XML document, but want to look up a value in an external XML document. For example, you might have some customer names and addresses stored in an XML document that looks like the one in Example 6-5.

Example 6-5. External customer address file (`customers.xml`)

```xml
<?xml version="1.0" encoding="UTF-8"?>
<customers>
  <customer>
    <name>Steve Jackson</name>
    <salutation>Mr.</salutation>
    <address>123 Front Street</address>
    <city>Traverse City</city>
    <state>Michigan</state>
    <zip>49684</zip>
  </customer>
  <customer>
    <name>Brenda Smith</name>
    <salutation>Ms.</salutation>
    <address>5 Wilson Boulevard</address>
    <city>Arlington</city>
    <state>Virginia</state>
    <zip>22203</zip>
  </customer>
  <!-- etc. -->
</customers>
```

When a document author enters the customer name in the customer element, the document should automatically look up the customer's address in the customers.xml file and complete it in the letter. The function shown in Example 6-6 will do this.

- Lines 9 through 16 assign the relevant nodes of the letter document to variables.
- Lines 19 through 22 then access the customers.xml document and assign it to the variable custXML.
- Lines 25 to 28 retrieve the customer name from the letter document and attempt to find a match in the customer document.
- If the customer node is found, lines 38 through 41 assign the selected values to the relevant nodes in the letter document.

This function assumes that the line, city, state and zip elements already exist in the document. A more sophisticated function could be written to check for their existence and insert them if necessary.

6.1.3 Responding to an event

Rather than requiring the user to take some action to update the address, perhaps you want this function to be executed every time the user changes the customer name. To do this, you need to write a function that responds to the XMLSelectionChange event, which occurs every time the user changes the selection to a different element.

The desired function is shown in Example 6-7. It determines whether the changed XML is the content of the customer element and, if so, it calls the GetAddress function.

A working version of this code can be found in the example file letter query.doc.

6.2 | SOAP Web services

In this section, we will see how the letter document utilizes a Web service that, given a U.S. ZIP code, returns the city and state. To do this, we will

Example 6-6. Function to automatically update address based on customer name

```
Sub GetAddress()

    Const xmlnsLetter = "xmlns:let='http://xmlinoffice.com/letter'"
    Dim str_customer, str_line, str_city, str_state, str_zip
      As String
    Dim cust_node, line_node, city_node, state_node, zip_node
      As XMLNode

    Set line_node =
      ActiveDocument.SelectSingleNode("//let:line", xmlnsLetter)
    Set city_node =
      ActiveDocument.SelectSingleNode("//let:city", xmlnsLetter)
    Set state_node =
      ActiveDocument.SelectSingleNode("//let:state", xmlnsLetter)
    Set zip_node =
      ActiveDocument.SelectSingleNode("//let:zip", xmlnsLetter)

    'Open the customers document
    Dim custXML As MSXML2.DOMDocument50
    Set custXML = New MSXML2.DOMDocument50
    custXML.async = False
    custXML.Load ("c:\customers.xml")

    'Find the appropriate customer element
    str_customer = ActiveDocument.
      SelectSingleNode("//let:customer", xmlnsLetter).Text
    Set cust_node = custXML.
      SelectSingleNode("//customer[name='" & str_customer & "']")

    'Assign values from customer.xml to letter.xml
    If cust_node Is Nothing Then
        MsgBox ("Invalid customer name " + str_customer)
        line_node.Text = "UNKNOWN"
        city_node.Text = "UNKNOWN"
        state_node.Text = "UNKNOWN"
        zip_node.Text = "UNKNOWN"
    Else
        line_node.Text = cust_node.SelectSingleNode("address").Text
        city_node.Text = cust_node.SelectSingleNode("city").Text
        state_node.Text = cust_node.SelectSingleNode("state").Text
        zip_node.Text = cust_node.SelectSingleNode("zip").Text
    End If

End Sub
```

make use of a separate toolkit provided by Microsoft for dealing with the SOAP interface.

Example 6-7. Responding to the `XMLSelectionChange` event

```
Dim WithEvents oApp As Word.Application
Private Sub Document_Open()
    Set oApp = Application
End Sub
Private Sub oApp_XMLSelectionChange
  (ByVal Sel As Word.Selection,
   ByVal OldXMLNode As Word.XMLNode,
   ByVal NewXMLNode As Word.XMLNode,
   Reason As Long)

   If OldXMLNode Is Nothing Then
       'do nothing
   ElseIf OldXMLNode.BaseName = "customer" Then
       GetAddress
   End If

End Sub
```

6.2.1 *The ZIP code Web service*

First, let's take a look at the Web service we will be using for this example. This Web service has several operations related to United States ZIP codes. The one we are going to use is called `GetInfoByZIP`. Given a ZIP code, this operation returns the city, state, area code and time zone.

The WSDL description of this Web service can be found at:

`http://www.webservicex.net/uszip.asmx?WSDL`

Within the WSDL document, we can see the operation we want. It is shown in Example 6-8.

Example 6-8. WSDL description of a Web service operation

```
<operation name="GetInfoByZIP">
  <documentation>Get State Code,City,Area Code,Time Zone,
Zip Code by Zip Code</documentation>
  <input message="s0:GetInfoByZIPSoapIn" />
  <output message="s0:GetInfoByZIPSoapOut" />
</operation>
```

The operation definition references the input and output messages that are shown in Example 6-9.

Example 6-9. Web service input and output messages

```
<message name="GetInfoByZIPSoapIn">
  <part name="parameters" element="s0:GetInfoByZIP" />
</message>
<message name="GetInfoByZIPSoapOut">
  <part name="parameters" element="s0:GetInfoByZIPResponse" />
</message>
```

The input and output messages, in turn, refer to the types of element that are sent to and returned from the Web service. An excerpt from the schema definition that declares them is shown in Example 6-10.

Example 6-10. Declarations of message element types

```
<s:element name="GetInfoByZIP">
  <s:complexType>
    <s:sequence>
      <s:element minOccurs="0" maxOccurs="1"
                 name="USZip" type="s:string" />
    </s:sequence>
  </s:complexType>
</s:element>
<s:element name="GetInfoByZIPResponse">
  <s:complexType>
    <s:sequence>
      <s:element minOccurs="0" maxOccurs="1"
                 name="GetInfoByZIPResult">
        <s:complexType mixed="true">
          <s:sequence>
            <s:any />
          </s:sequence>
        </s:complexType>
      </s:element>
    </s:sequence>
  </s:complexType>
</s:element>
```

According to the schema for the input message, the operation expects to receive a GetInfoByZIP element, which in turn contains a USZip element that contains a string: the ZIP code.

The structure of the output message is unknown, since the schema for the output message does not constrain the content of the GetInfoByZIPResult element. However, by running a test we find that the output looks like Example 6-11.

Example 6-11. XML document returned by ZIP code Web service

```
<ws:GetInfoByZIPResponse xmlns:ws="http://www.webserviceX.NET">
  <ws:GetInfoByZIPResult>
    <NewDataSet>
      <Table>
        <CITY>Traverse City</CITY>
        <STATE>MI</STATE>
        <ZIP>49684</ZIP>
        <AREA_CODE>616</AREA_CODE>
        <TIME_ZONE>E</TIME_ZONE>
      </Table>
    </NewDataSet>
  </ws:GetInfoByZIPResult>
</ws:GetInfoByZIPResponse>
```

Both the input and output messages are contained in SOAP wrappers when transmitted. Parsing and generating SOAP is best left to specialized software, which is available for the Office products.

6.2.2 *The Office Web Services Toolkit*

To simplify the use of SOAP Web services with Office, Microsoft provides a separate, downloadable toolkit. The Office Web Services Toolkit frees the developer from generating and parsing SOAP messages, and even from constructing the XML fragments that contain the data sent to and received from the Web service.

For each service, the toolkit generates a class (or classes) that has a method for each of the service's operations. Application code can then be written to access these simplified classes.

At the time of writing, the current version of the toolkit is called Office XP Web Services Toolkit 2.0. It can be downloaded from

http://msdn.microsoft.com/library/default.asp?url=/library/en-us/dnxpwst/html/odc_wstoolkitoverview.asp.[2]

The toolkit contains documentation and examples, and a tool called the Web Services Reference Tool that is integrated with the Visual Basic Editor.[3]

---

2. Although the name of the toolkit implies that it is only for Office XP, it also works with Office 2003 and its name may be changed to reflect this fact.

6.2.3 *Using the Web Services Reference Tool*

The Web Services Reference Tool allows you to generate classes that you can use to access a particular Web service. You can search for a Web service based on keywords, or specify a Web service by its URL.

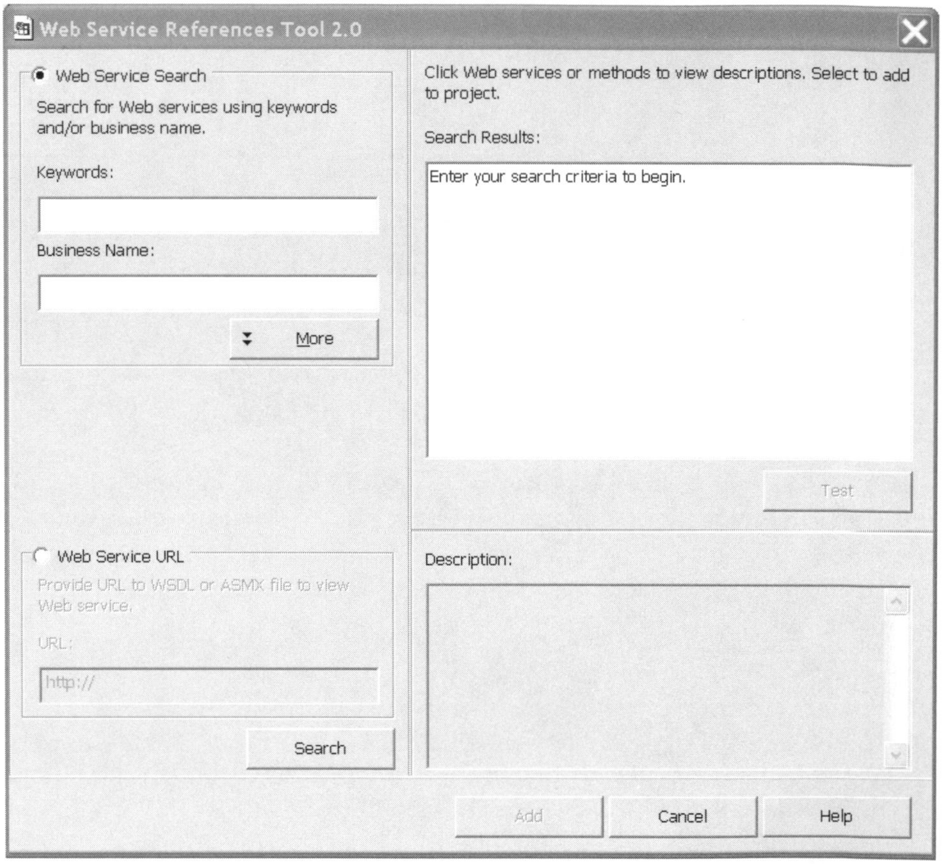

Figure 6-2   The Web Services Reference Tool

3. Installation of the toolkit is in two parts. You must first install the toolkit itself, from the downloaded compressed file. The Web Services Reference Tool is then installed separately from the setup.exe executable file in the directory where you installed the toolkit.

To launch the Web Services Reference Tool, first open the document from which you will be calling the Web service. To use our form letter example:

1. Open the document `letter.xml`.
2. On the **Tools** menu, point to **Macro**, then click **Visual Basic Editor**. This will open the Visual Basic Editor.
3. Launch the Web Services Reference Tool by clicking **Web Services References** on the **Tools** menu. This brings up the main dialog shown in Figure 6-2.
4. In our case, we already know the particular Web service we want to use, so we can go directly to it. Click **Web Service URL** on the left side of the dialog.
5. Type the Web service location `http://www.webservicex.net/uszip.asmx?WSDL` into the **URL** box and click **Search**.
6. This will bring up the name of the Web service and its operations on the right side of the dialog, as shown in Figure 6-3.
7. Select the `USZip` service by checking the box next to it and click **Add**. This will generate the necessary class in the Visual Basic Editor.

6.2.4 *Working with the generated Web service class*

The generated class named `clsws_USZip` represents the Web service. It has a method called `wsm_GetInfoByZIP`, which corresponds to the `GetInfoByZIP` operation of the Web service. You can write a `GetCityState` method that calls the `wsm_GetInfoByZIP` method, as shown in Example 6-12.

- Lines 3 through 12 define all the constants and variables used.
- Lines 14 through 19 locate the city, state and ZIP nodes in our letter document, which are relevant to the Web service.
- Line 21 calls the `wsm_GetInfoByZIP` method, passing it the ZIP code. Rather than returning the whole SOAP message that contains the document shown in Example 6-11, the method extracts the relevant returned data, namely the

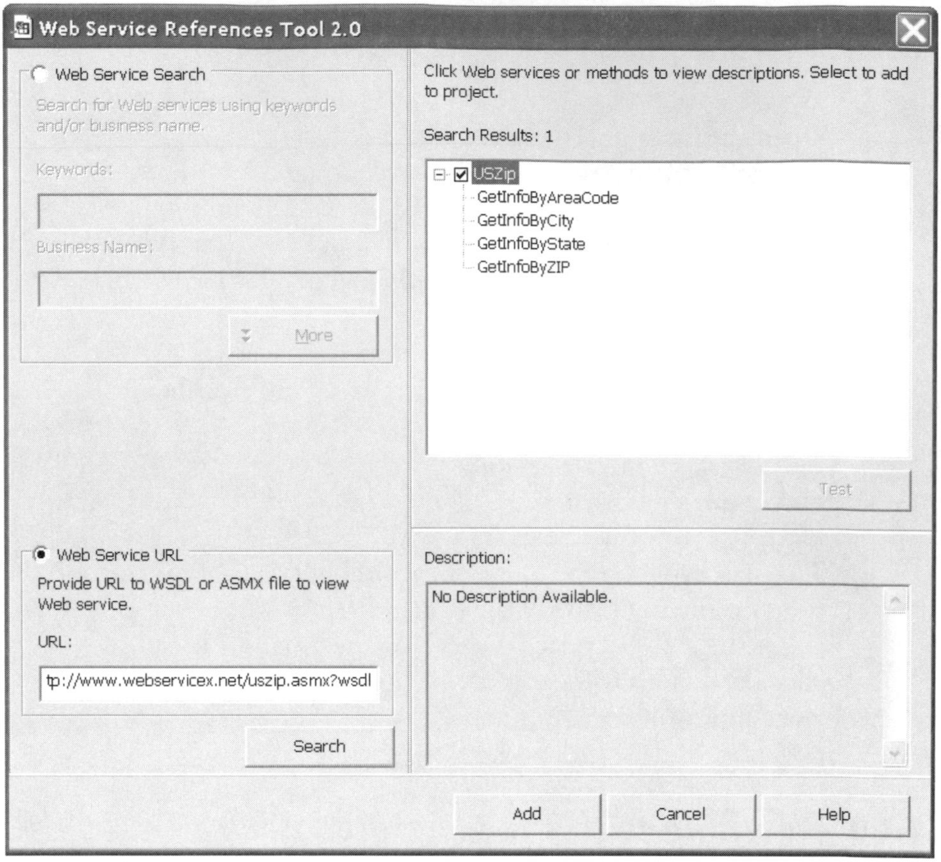

Figure 6-3   The Web Services Reference Tool showing available services and operations

NewDataSet element. This is represented as a variable called returnedNodes, which is a list of nodes of type IXMLDOMNodeList.

- Lines 23 and 24 assign the values of the CITY and STATE elements to two string variables.

Example 6-12. `GetCityState` method

```
Sub GetCityState()

Const xmlnsLetter =
  "xmlns:let='http://xmlinoffice.com/letter'"
Dim objResolver As clsws_USZip
Set objResolver = New clsws_USZip
Dim returnedNodes As MSXML2.IXMLDOMNodeList
Dim str_city As String
Dim str_state As String
Dim city_node As XMLNode
Dim state_node As XMLNode
Dim zip_node As XMLNode

Set city_node =
  ActiveDocument.SelectSingleNode("//let:city", xmlnsLetter)
Set state_node =
  ActiveDocument.SelectSingleNode("//let:state", xmlnsLetter)
Set zip_node =
  ActiveDocument.SelectSingleNode("//let:zip", xmlnsLetter)

Set returnedNodes = objResolver.wsm_GetInfoByZIP(zip_node.Text)

str_city = returnedNodes.Item(0).SelectSingleNode("//CITY").Text
str_state = returnedNodes.Item(0).SelectSingleNode("//STATE").Text
city_node.Text = str_city
state_node.Text = str_state

End Sub
```

- Lines 25 and 26 then assign these string values to the appropriate nodes in our letter document.

Warning   The Office Web Services toolkit is very useful for simple examples like this one. It has a number of limitations that prevent it from working without modifications on all Web services. For example, it can't handle element-type names that are also Visual Basic reserved words, and it doesn't support extensions in the XML Schema types defined in the WSDL. However, it can generate a starting point, which you can tweak for your Web service.

6.2.5 *Responding to two variations of an event*

In 6.1.3, "Responding to an event", on page 121 we saw how external data could be updated automatically when a corresponding field in the document was changed. The technique works the same way when the external data is provided by a Web service.

In fact, you can use the same code as we did in Example 6-15. The only difference is that you would replace:

Example 6-13. Test for change in customer

```
ElseIf OldXMLNode.BaseName = "customer" Then
    GetAddress
```

with:

Example 6-14. Test for change in zip

```
ElseIf OldXMLNode.BaseName = "zip" Then
    GetCityState
```

If you wanted automatic updates for both situations, you could use both tests at once, as shown in Example 6-15.

After saving this project and closing and reopening the letter.xml document, you will find that every time you change the ZIP code, the city and state will automatically be updated. Similarly, every time you change the customer its address will be updated.

Example 6-15. Responding to two kinds of `XMLSelectionChange` event

```
Dim WithEvents oApp As Word.Application

Private Sub Document_Open()
    Set oApp = Application
End Sub

Private Sub oApp_XMLSelectionChange
  (ByVal Sel As Word.Selection,
   ByVal OldXMLNode As Word.XMLNode,
   ByVal NewXMLNode As Word.XMLNode,
   Reason As Long)

    If OldXMLNode Is Nothing Then
        'do nothing
    ElseIf OldXMLNode.baseName = "customer" Then
        GetAddress
    ElseIf OldXMLNode.BaseName = "zip" Then
        GetCityState
    End If

End Sub
```

Using XML data in spreadsheets

- ▌ Mapping between XML and worksheets
- ▌ Flattening structure for data analysis
- ▌ XMLSS: The Excel XML vocabulary

Chapter

7

Narrative text may be the most flexible way to communicate data, but when you want to see how it all lines up, there is nothing quite like a spreadsheet. It was the original "killer app" for the PC, and now, with a strong shot of XML, it is more powerful and useful than ever.

This chapter teaches you how to create worksheets that import and export XML data. Excel makes it easy: you don't have to write scripts or code to work with XML.

And XML import means you can use Excel's advanced capabilities for data analysis on almost any data, whether it comes from a database, Web service, or an XML file.

Skills required   Experience using Microsoft Excel to perform basic tasks, such as creating and editing worksheets. Sharing data with some kinds of XML documents requires knowledge of XSLT (see Chapter 18, "XSL Transformations (XSLT)", on page 392).

7.1 | Why use XML with Excel?

Excel is a powerful tool for tabular, especially numeric, data. It allows you to analyze that data using charts and graphs, and perform calculations based on that data. In previous versions of Excel, the sources of that data were limited. Importing data into Excel either required programming, or it involved a lot of manual shuffling of data once it was imported.

Excel 2003 allows you to specify a particular area of a worksheet into which you can import XML data. Once you set up the map between the schema and the worksheet, you can import new data at any time without having to do any reformatting or shuffling around of data. Excel simply knows where each item of imported data should appear in the worksheet. Because most data is now available as XML, either in its native form or through a tool export, this opens up a much broader set of source data for Excel analysis. You can:

- use all of Excel's data analysis features (charts, graphs, calculations) on almost any data
- save the worksheets that contain this analyzed data to use as reports
- calculate new data from this analysis and save it as XML for use by other applications

7.2 | The Worldwide Widget expense report

Figure 7-1 shows the Worldwide Widget Corporation expense report.[1]

Excel, like the other Office products, has no restricted list of "supported XML vocabularies". Accordingly, Worldwide has developed its own vocabulary for expense reporting. The XML representation of a report is shown in Example 7-1.

The report conforms to the schema shown in Example 7-2. As we'll see in 7.5.2, "Inferring a schema", on page 150, Excel doesn't require a schema,

---

1. You can find the worksheets used in this chapter among the book's example files.

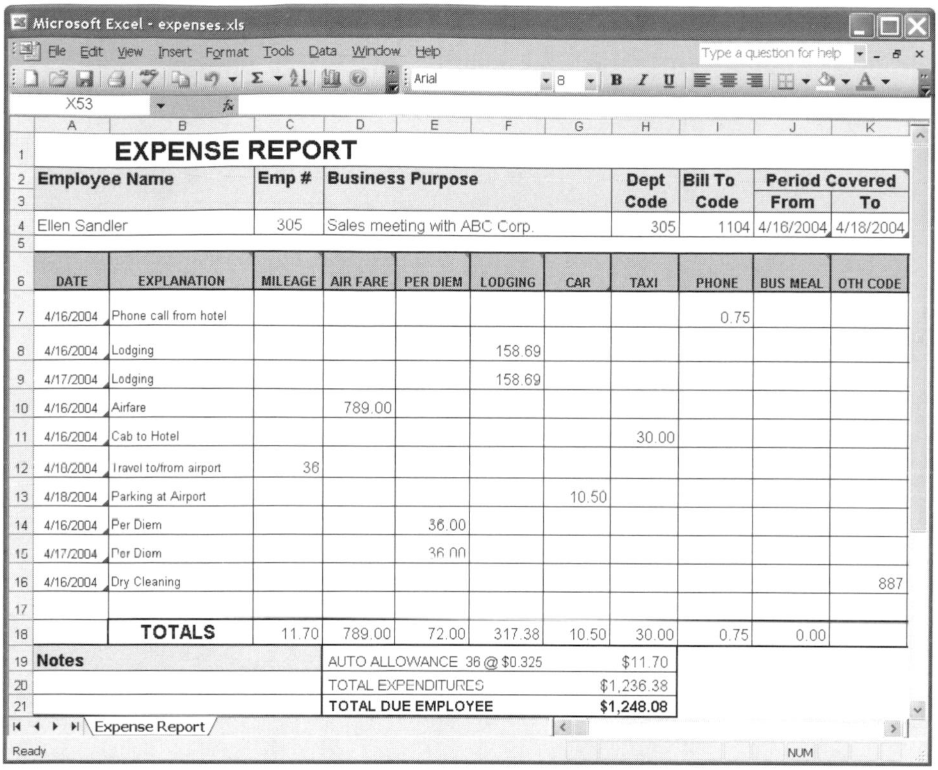

Microsoft Excel - expenses.xls

EXPENSE REPORT

Employee Name	Emp #	Business Purpose	Dept Code	Bill To Code	Period Covered From	To
Ellen Sandler	305	Sales meeting with ABC Corp.	305	1104	4/16/2004	4/18/2004

DATE	EXPLANATION	MILEAGE	AIR FARE	PER DIEM	LODGING	CAR	TAXI	PHONE	BUS MEAL	OTH CODE
4/16/2004	Phone call from hotel							0.75		
4/16/2004	Lodging				158.69					
4/17/2004	Lodging				158.69					
4/16/2004	Airfare		789.00							
4/16/2004	Cab to Hotel						30.00			
4/18/2004	Travel to/from airport	36								
4/18/2004	Parking at Airport					10.50				
4/16/2004	Per Diem			36.00						
4/17/2004	Per Diem			36.00						
4/16/2004	Dry Cleaning									887
	TOTALS	11.70	789.00	72.00	317.38	10.50	30.00	0.75	0.00	

Notes		
	AUTO ALLOWANCE 36 @ $0.325	$11.70
	TOTAL EXPENDITURES	$1,236.38
	TOTAL DUE EMPLOYEE	$1,248.08

Figure 7-1 The expense worksheet (expenses.xls)

but Worldwide has one as part of its comprehensive XML-based information management plan.

7.3 | Worksheets, maps and schemas

Excel handles the relationship between schemas, XML documents and their presentation somewhat differently from Word. A worksheet should be considered as a reporting template that you can reuse for various different sets of data, rather than a container for the data itself.

You create a *map* that causes the items of XML data to be connected with the cells where they will appear in the worksheet. Each cell may only be mapped once.

Example 7-1. Expense report in XML (expenses.xml)

```xml
<?xml version="1.0" encoding="UTF-8" standalone="yes"?>
<expenseReport xmlns="http://xmlinoffice.com/expenses"
  xmlns:xsi="http://www.w3.org/2001/XMLSchema-instance"
  xsi:schemaLocation="http://xmlinoffice.com/expenses
                      expenses.xsd">
  <empName>Ellen Sandler</empName>
  <empNum>305</empNum>
  <purpose>Sales meeting with ABC Corp.</purpose>
  <deptCode>305</deptCode>
  <billToCode>1104</billToCode>
  <periodFrom>2004-04-16</periodFrom>
  <periodTo>2004-04-18</periodTo>
  <expense>
    <date>2004-04-16</date>
    <explanation>Phone call from the hotel</explanation>
    <phone>.75</phone>
  </expense>
  <!-- ... -->
  <expense>
    <date>2004-04-16</date>
    <explanation>Dry Cleaning</explanation>
    <other>
      <code>883</code>
      <amount>16.75</amount>
    </other>
  </expense>
</expenseReport>
```

Each map is associated with one schema. Excel allows you to map your schema to a worksheet using a drag-and-drop facility. It is possible to have more than one map associated with a worksheet. This is useful if data is coming from two or more different sources, using different schemas.

Both the map and the schema are stored in the .xls file along with the worksheet. In the case of the schema, it is a copy of the schema file that you

Example 7-2. Expense report schema (expenses.xsd)

```xml
<?xml version="1.0" encoding="UTF-8" standalone="yes"?>
<xs:schema targetNamespace="http://xmlinoffice.com/expenses"
           xmlns="http://xmlinoffice.com/expenses"
           xmlns:xs="http://www.w3.org/2001/XMLSchema"
           elementFormDefault="qualified">
  <xs:element name="expenseReport" type="ExpenseReportType"/>

  <xs:complexType name="ExpenseReportType">
    <xs:sequence>
      <xs:element name="empName" type="xs:string"/>
      <xs:element name="empNum" type="xs:integer"/>
      <xs:element name="purpose" type="xs:string"/>
      <xs:element name="deptCode" type="xs:integer"/>
      <xs:element name="billToCode" type="xs:integer"/>
      <xs:element name="periodFrom" type="xs:date"/>
      <xs:element name="periodTo" type="xs:date"/>
      <xs:element name="expense" type="ExpenseType"
                  maxOccurs="unbounded"/>
    </xs:sequence>
  </xs:complexType>

  <xs:complexType name="ExpenseType">
    <xs:sequence>
      <xs:element name="date" type="xs:date"/>
      <xs:element name="explanation" type="xs:string"/>
      <xs:element name="mileage" type="xs:integer" minOccurs="0"/>
      <xs:element name="airFare" type="xs:decimal" minOccurs="0"/>
      <xs:element name="perDiem" type="xs:decimal" minOccurs="0"/>
      <xs:element name="lodging" type="xs:decimal" minOccurs="0"/>
      <xs:element name="auto" type="xs:decimal" minOccurs="0"/>
      <xs:element name="taxi" type="xs:decimal" minOccurs="0"/>
      <xs:element name="phone" type="xs:decimal" minOccurs="0"/>
      <xs:element name="businessMeals" type="xs:decimal"
                  minOccurs="0"/>
      <xs:element name="other" type="OtherExpenseType"
                  minOccurs="0"/>
    </xs:sequence>
  </xs:complexType>

  <xs:complexType name="OtherExpenseType">
    <xs:sequence>
      <xs:element name="code" type="xs:integer"/>
      <xs:element name="amount" type="xs:decimal"/>
    </xs:sequence>
  </xs:complexType>
</xs:schema>
```

selected for mapping. Therefore, changing or deleting the schema file after you have selected it has no effect on the worksheet.

Caution   *Excel makes it very difficult to change the map, and almost impossible to change the schema once you have created the map. Make sure your schema is the way you want it before you start mapping it.*

A map causes a worksheet to be linked to the source of its data. If you import XML into a worksheet, the map maintains a link to that source. However, when you save a worksheet, Excel will save the data that is currently in the cells. If you reopen the worksheet and the source data has changed, Excel will not refresh the data automatically. You have to refresh the data explicitly to get the changes.

7.3.1 *Creating a map*

Let's see how Ellen created the map for the expenses.xls worksheet, using the expenses.xsd schema. She might have started from scratch, defining a map between the schema and a blank worksheet. However, since Worldwide already had a worksheet design, she started with that.

To associate the worksheet with the schema:

1. Open expenses.xls in Excel.
2. On the **Data** menu, point to **XML**, then click **XML Source**. This brings up the XML Source task pane.
3. At the bottom of the XML Source task pane, click **XML Maps**. This brings up the **XML Maps** dialog, shown in Figure 7-2.
4. Click **Add** to add a map.
5. Browse to the location of expenses.xsd, select it from the list, and click **Open**. The **XML Maps** dialog will now list the new map.

6. Click **OK** to return to the main window. The **XML Source** task pane will now show the expense report structure from the schema.

Figure 7-2   The XML Maps dialog

7.3.2 *The XML Source task pane*

The XML Source task pane is used during the mapping process to create the links between the XML element types and the worksheet cells. The top part of the XML Source task pane shows the general structure allowed by the schema, as shown in Figure 7-3.[2]

The task pane shows all the XML element types and attributes, organized into the hierarchical structure allowed by the schema. There are several things to notice about the way element types and attributes are displayed:

- Required element types and attributes, such as empName and explanation, are displayed with a red asterisk.
- Element types that can have children have a folder icon, while element types that can only have character data content have a document icon. Attributes have a slightly darker icon.

---

2. The XML Source pane is different from the top part of the XML Structure pane in Word. Word only shows the *individual elements* of the current document, while Excel shows the *element types allowed* by the document's schema.

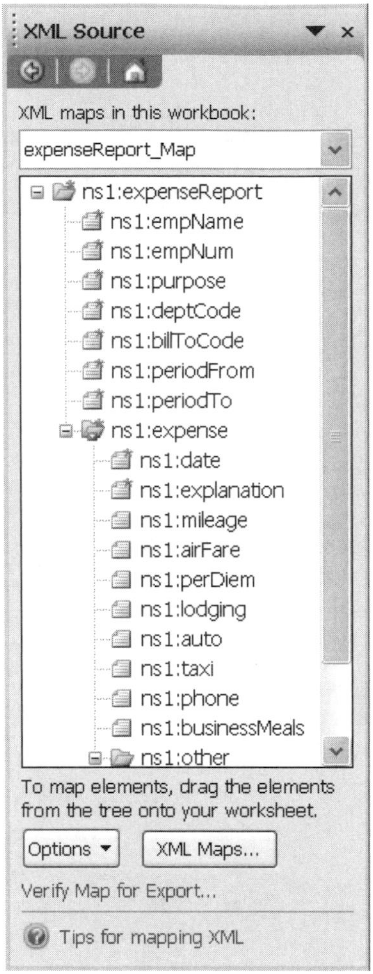

Figure 7-3   The XML Source task pane

Repeating element types have a blue rectangle at the base of the folder or document icon.

■ Bold font indicates element types that have already been mapped to the worksheet.

Once an element type or attribute is mapped, selecting it in the XML Structure task pane causes Excel to select its mapped cell(s) in the worksheet. Likewise, when you select a mapped cell in the worksheet, Excel selects the element type or attribute to which it is mapped in the task pane.

7.3.3 *The mapping process*

Element types and attributes can be mapped to cells by dragging them from the task pane to the worksheet. It is also possible to right-click the element type or attribute in the task pane. From the resulting context menu, click **Map element**.

During the mapping process, Excel makes a distinction between repeating and non-repeating element types. The latter only occur once within the XML structure, according to the schema. In our example, they include the element types that make up the header of the expense report, such as empName, empNum, and billToCode.

Repeating element types may appear more than once. In our example, the expense items, such as explanation and mileage, are repeating. Even though they may only appear once in their parent element, expense, the parent may appear more than once, so the children are therefore considered repeating.

Excel looks at the maxOccurs attributes in the schema to determine whether an element type is repeating. The default for this attribute is 1. If an element type, *or any of its ancestors*, is declared with a maxOccurs value of more than 1 (including "unbounded"), it is considered to be repeating.

Attributes are considered repeating if they belong to repeating element types; otherwise they are non-repeating.

The mapping process differs depending on whether the element type or attribute is repeating or non-repeating, so we will discuss each separately.

7.3.3.1 Mapping non-repeating element types and attributes

You generally map a non-repeating element type or attribute to a single cell in the worksheet.[3]

---

3. Sometimes you may want it to appear in a list; we describe that later in the chapter.

Let's map the non-repeating element types of the schema to our expense report worksheet. To do this, drag each one to the cell that is to contain the data. For example, drag the `empName` element type onto cell A4.

This will cause a smart tag to appear next to the cell. Clicking it reveals three options, as shown in Figure 7-4:

- My Data Already Has a Heading
- Place XML Heading to the Left
- Place XML Heading Above

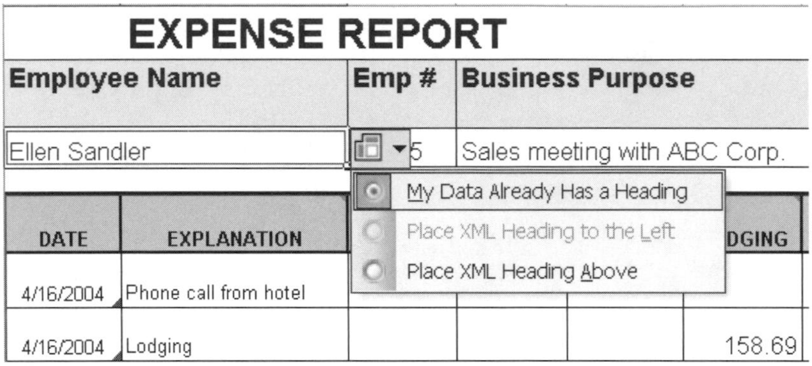

Figure 7-4   Heading-related options

These choices allow you to insert a heading for your cell. Since we already have column headers in our worksheet, we can choose the first option (the default). If you choose either of the other two options, the XML name will be placed in the cell to the left of or above the chosen cell.

Notice that the cell that we have mapped now has a blue border around it. Continue to map the rest of the non-repeating element types and attributes.

To change the map, you can right-click the name in the XML Structure task pane, and click **Remove element**. This will remove the link between that element type or attribute and the cell. You can then remap the element type or attribute to another cell.

7.3.3.2   Mapping repeating element types and attributes

Dragging a repeating element type to the worksheet has a somewhat different result. Instead of associating the element type with a single cell, Excel creates a *list range*. A list range is a vertical column (or columns) of data that can be manipulated and sorted as a group.

The element type should be dragged to the cell that contains the header for the column. In our example, you simply drag the element types to the existing header cells. If you drag the element type to an empty cell, for example in a blank worksheet, Excel will insert the XML name as the header in the empty cell you selected, and assume that the actual data starts in the cell below the header.

For example, drag the date element type to cell A6, which contains the word **DATE**. Excel will create a list range and outline it in blue. Excel makes an assumption about where the list range ends based on the data that is currently in the worksheet (if any). In our example, it takes the list range all the way to the last expense item. If Excel assumes the size of the list range incorrectly, you can adjust the size by selecting a cell in the list, clicking **List** on the **Data** menu, and clicking **Resize List** on the **List** menu.

Drag the rest of the repeating element types to the appropriate header cells. When the columns are adjacent, as they are in our case, Excel expands the list range to add the additional columns.

List ranges are a handy tool for analyzing data. The drop-down menus on each of the column headers allow you to perform operations on the range quickly. You can sort the rows by any of the columns, or filter the data to include only rows matching a particular value. You can also select the "top 10" values or write custom queries to filter out other rows.

7.4 | Importing and exporting XML data

Once you have set up the map, you can import and export XML data from the worksheet. In this scenario, the Excel worksheet serves as a report template that you can regularly update with new data. You can also use Excel as a tool for entering data that you can then export in a format that is reusable and accessible to other applications.

7.4.1 *Exporting XML*

You can export the data that is currently in the worksheet as an XML document by clicking **Export** on the **XML** submenu. This will save a document that conforms to the `expenses.xsd` schema.

Unlike Word, Excel is not constantly validating your data against the schema as you edit it. When you export it, though, it does validate it and it reports any errors it finds. These errors might include:

- required elements that are missing, because they were not mapped
- values that do not conform to the datatypes declared in the schema
- elements that appear more times than allowed by the schema

Excel will inform you about the first of the validation errors it encounters (not all of them), but it will save the exported XML anyway. An example of what is saved is shown in Example 7-3.

Notice that all possible elements are included in the exported XML. If a cell is empty, an empty element appears, rather than the element simply being omitted. This can sometimes cause a problem for elements with numeric or date types, for which an empty element is not valid.

7.4.2 *Importing XML data*

New XML data can also be imported into the worksheet. This is accomplished by clicking **Import** on the **XML** submenu, and selecting the name of the XML file to import.

Importing XML data into an existing worksheet is quite different from simply opening an XML document in Excel, as we will see in 7.5.1, "Using a schema", on page 148. When XML data is imported, Excel will place all the data from the XML document into the correct cells based on the maps.

For example, we can import a new expense file called `new expenses.xml` to see how the import works. To do this:

1. Click **Import** from the **XML** submenu.
2. Select the file `new expenses.xml` and click **Import**.

Example 7-3. Exported XML fragment (expenses exported.xml)

```xml
<?xml version="1.0" encoding="UTF-8"?>
<ns1:expenseReport xmlns:ns1="http://xmlinoffice.com/expenses">
  <ns1:empName>Ellen Sandler</ns1:empName>
  <ns1:empNum>305</ns1:empNum>
  <ns1:purpose>Sales meeting with ABC Corp.</ns1:purpose>
  <ns1:deptCode>305</ns1:deptCode>
  <ns1:billToCode>1104</ns1:billToCode>
  <ns1:periodFrom>2004-04-16</ns1:periodFrom>
  <ns1:periodTo>2004-04-18</ns1:periodTo>
  <ns1:expense>
    <ns1:date>2004-04-16</ns1:date>
    <ns1:explanation>Phone call from hotel</ns1:explanation>
    <ns1:mileage/>
    <ns1:airFare/>
    <ns1:perDiem/>
    <ns1:lodging/>
    <ns1:auto/>
    <ns1:taxi/>
    <ns1:phone>0.75</ns1:phone>
    <ns1:businessMeals/>
    <ns1:other>
      <ns1:code/>
      <ns1:amount/>
    </ns1:other>
  </ns1:expense>
        ...
  <ns1:expense>
    <ns1:date>2004-04-16</ns1:date>
    <ns1:explanation>Dry Cleaning</ns1:explanation>
    <ns1:mileage/>
    <ns1:airFare/>
    <ns1:perDiem/>
    <ns1:lodging/>
    <ns1:auto/>
    <ns1:taxi/>
    <ns1:phone/>
    <ns1:businessMeals/>
    <ns1:other>
      <ns1:code>887</ns1:code>
      <ns1:amount>16.75</ns1:amount>
    </ns1:other>
  </ns1:expense>
</ns1:expenseReport>
```

You will now see the new data in the worksheet. Note that the number of lines in the list range has been reduced, as shown in Figure 7-5.

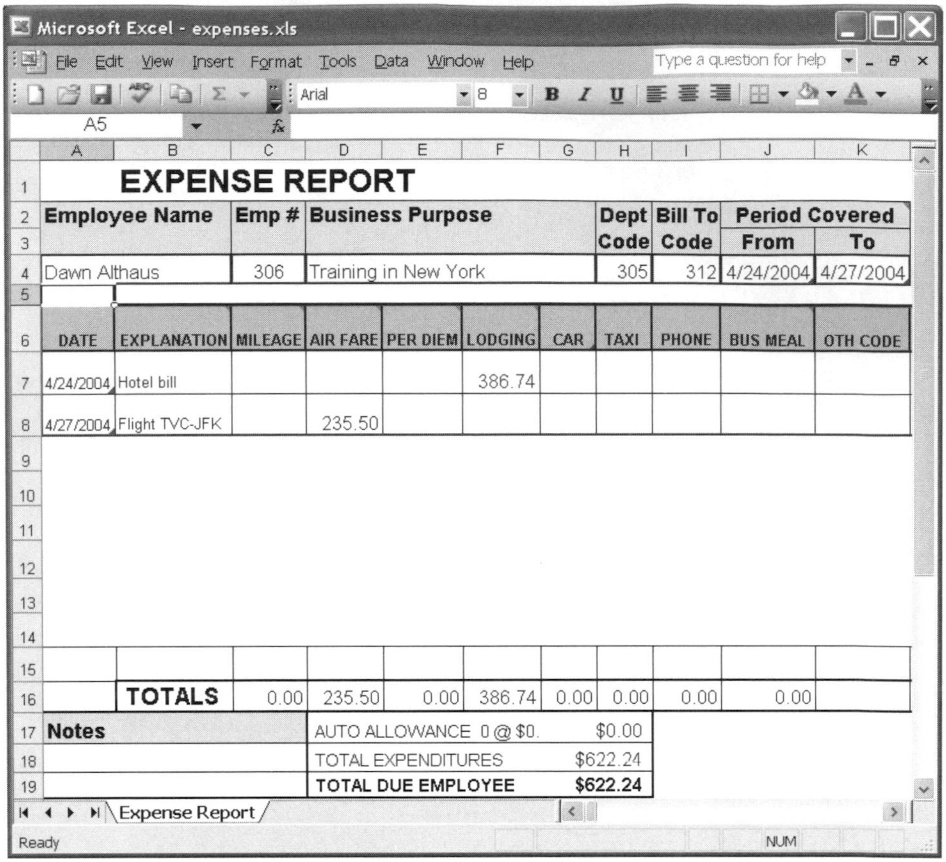

Figure 7-5   Imported data

7.4.2.1   Preserving data and formatting

By default, importing XML data will overwrite the data that is currently in the cells, and it will alter the size of the list range (by adding or deleting rows) to accommodate the new data. It is also possible to append repeating data to what already exists, adding new rows to the list range while preserving the existing ones. This process can be controlled by a number of options that are available by clicking **XML Map Properties** from the **XML** submenu. The resulting dialog is shown in Figure 7-6.

The following options are available from this dialog:

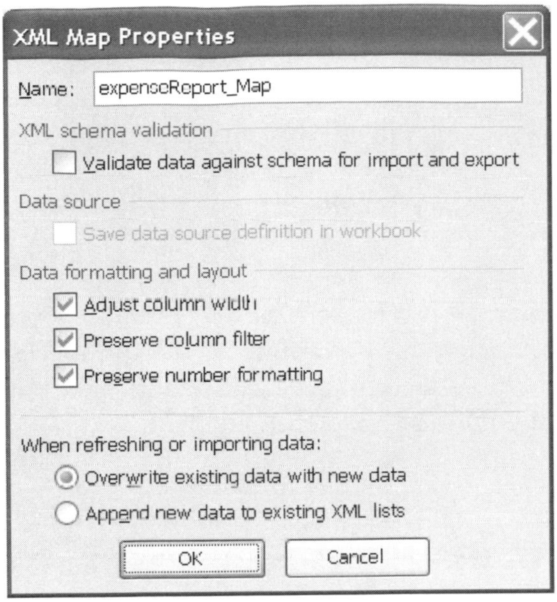

Figure 7-6 The XML Map Properties dialog

- **Validate data against schema for import and export.** If this box is checked, Excel will validate imported and exported XML documents against the schema.
- **Adjust column width.** The column widths will be automatically updated to accommodate the width of the data that is imported. If you have carefully formatted your worksheet, you may wish to uncheck this box.
- **Preserve column filter.** The current options specified for the list range will not be overwritten on import.
- **Preserve number formatting.** The formatting of the numbers in cells will not be overwritten on import.
- **Overwrite existing data with new data.** All existing data will be deleted and new data inserted.
- **Append new data to existing XML lists.** New data will be appended to the existing data in the list range. This does not affect non-repeating elements, which will be overwritten.

7.4.2.2   Importing and validation

The imported XML file must be well-formed XML. If you have checked the **Validate data against schema for import and export** box on the **XML Map Properties** dialog, Excel will validate the document upon import. The imported document must have the same namespace as the target namespace of the schema. If not, Excel will prompt you to indicate where you want the data imported, and it will not import it according to the map.

Otherwise, Excel will report any errors it finds in the document. It is very forgiving if the document is not valid and it will import the invalid data into the worksheet. Missing elements are represented as empty cells, and invalid values are simply shown as they appear in the document.

7.5 | Mapping from an existing XML document

In our previous example, we started with an Excel worksheet and mapped a schema to it. There is another alternative: You can open an XML document in Excel and it will bring up a blank worksheet. You can then map to that using either the schema of the XML document, or an inferred schema.

The advantage to this approach is that you can refresh the data during the mapping process to ensure that it is being imported correctly from the XML document. The disadvantage is that you have to start from scratch with the formatting and layout of the worksheet.

7.5.1   Using a schema

Some XML documents, such as the `expenses.xml` document, shown in Example 7-1, use the `xsi:schemaLocation` attribute to specify the location of the schema. When you open such a document, Excel knows about the schema and it automatically brings it up in the XML Source task pane.

To open an XML document with a schema in Excel:

1. Click **Open** on the **File** menu.
2. Select **XML Files (*.xml)** from the **Files of type:** list.

3. Select the `expenses.xml` file and click **Open**. You are given a dialog with three options, as shown in Figure 7-7.

4. Choose the third option, **Use the XML Source task pane**. The first two options bring in the XML data in a less useful way.

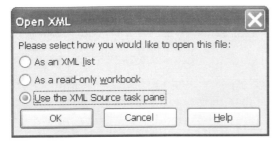

Figure 7-7   The Open XML dialog

The schema structure automatically appears. The worksheet is a completely blank slate, and you can begin mapping to it.

For non-repeating element types, you can use the smart tag that appears to the right of a recently mapped cell to add a label for the data, namely the element-type name. For repeating element types, the list column headers are automatically populated with the element-type names.

You can map a parent element type and all its children in one step by selecting the parent and dragging it to the worksheet. For example, select `expense` and drag it to cell B2. This will create a list range starting at B2 which has a column for each child of `expense`. You can remove any unwanted columns from the list range by selecting a column (for example `phone`), right-clicking it, and clicking **Remove element**.

Once you have mapped some element types, you can populate the data to ensure that the map is correct. To do this, position your cursor in a mapped cell and click **Refresh** on the **XML** submenu. You can refresh as often as you like during the mapping process.

7.5.2 *Inferring a schema*

If you don't have a schema, Excel will infer a schema from an XML document. If you attempt to open an XML document that does not make use of the `xsi:schemaLocation` attribute to indicate a schema, Excel will prompt you with a dialog saying "The specified XML source does not refer to a schema. Excel will create a schema based on the XML Source data." It will then infer a schema from the XML document.

We do not recommend this approach. The problem is that Excel may not get the schema 100% right, because it has limited information. That is understandable, but there is no way to change the schema once it is inferred. It is embedded in the Excel workbook and you cannot edit it. One of the most common problems is that the schema inference tool assumes that some non-repeating element types are actually repeating. This wreaks havoc on the ability to map them to the worksheet.

To avoid writing a schema from scratch, you can use a separate tool to infer a schema from an XML document. Microsoft provides a free schema inference tool at:

`http://apps.gotdotnet.com/xmltools/xsdinference`.

Once you have generated a schema, you will have the ability to fine-tune it before you begin mapping.

7.6 | Data analysis

Dawn, the Worldwide Widget accountant, finds that XML has added benefits when she wants to analyze all the expense reports that were submitted to her.

In the past, when all the employees submitted their Excel expense reports to her, Dawn had to do a lot of cutting and pasting to get any kind of summary reports. Now that they are submitting XML documents, she can create her own workbook to utilize a whole set of analysis tools.

Employees submit their expense reports by e-mail. They attach XML documents named `EXP_nnn_YYYYMMDD.xml`, where `nnn` is their employee number, and `YYYYMMDD` is the end date of the expense report.

Dawn creates an Excel workbook that consists of several worksheets. The first worksheet, entitled Raw Data, contains the map to import all the data from the expense reports.

7.6.1 *Flattening XML data*

Dawn wants to import expense reports from several different employees into the same worksheet. The worksheet we created earlier in this chapter would not work, because it would overwrite all the non-repeating elements every time a new expense report was imported. Instead, Dawn needs a worksheet that will repeat all the normally non-repeating "header" information in each row, alongside the repeating expense item elements.

You can think of this as flattening the hierarchy. We are extracting the elements with data content, regardless of the level they are at, and presenting them in adjacent cells in the same rows of the spreadsheet.[4]

To do this:

1. Open a new, blank worksheet.
2. Create a new map based on the **expenses.xsd** schema, as described in 7.3.1, "Creating a map", on page 138.
3. This time, instead of dragging each element type onto the worksheet individually, select the `expenseReport` element type and drag it to the worksheet.

You now have a large list range with a column for each element type that can contain only data (i.e. that cannot contain elements). The column headings (element-type names) are shown in Table 7-1.

During import, the data in the non-repeating element types is repeated in each expense item row.

To import several expense reports at once:

1. Click **Import** on the **XML** submenu.
2. Select all the files in the `raw data` directory at once, using Shift+click or Ctrl+click.
3. Click **Open**.

---

4. In the punched card data processing days, this was called a *unit record* because it was a self-contained complete record of a transaction and therefore could be sorted and tabulated.

Table 7-1   Column headings for flattened structure

empName
empNum
purpose
deptCode
billToCode
periodFrom
periodTo
date
explanation
mileage
airFare
perDiem
lodging
auto
taxi
phone
businessMeals
code
amount

	A	B	C	H	I	J	K	L	M
1	Name	Num	Purpose	Date	Explanation	Miles	Air	Per Diem	Lodgir
2	Steve Smith	208	Dev. meeting Atlanta	4/18/2004	Dev meeting atlanta		325	35	11￡
3	Steve Smith	208	Dev. meeting Atlanta	4/19/2004	Dev meeting atlanta			35	11￡
4	Jerry Addison	305	Consulting for MNOP Corp.	4/16/2004	Phone call from hotel				
5	Jerry Addison	305	Consulting for MNOP Corp.	4/16/2004	Lodging				158.
6	Jerry Addison	305	Consulting for MNOP Corp.	4/17/2004	Lodging				158.
7	Jerry Addison	305	Consulting for MNOP Corp.	4/16/2004	Airfare		789		
8	Jerry Addison	305	Consulting for MNOP Corp.	4/16/2004	Cab to Hotel				
9	Jerry Addison	305	Consulting for MNOP Corp.	4/18/2004	Travel to/from airport	36			
10	Jerry Addison	305	Consulting for MNOP Corp.	4/18/2004	Parking at Airport				
11	Jerry Addison	305	Consulting for MNOP Corp.	4/16/2004	Per Diem			36	
12	Jerry Addison	305	Consulting for MNOP Corp.	4/17/2004	Per Diem			36	
13	Jerry Addison	305	Consulting for MNOP Corp.	4/16/2004	Dry Cleaning				
14	Monica Lyle	312	RRC Partnership Meeting	4/25/2004	Airfare TVC-DTM		325		
15	Monica Lyle	312	RRC Partnership Meeting	4/25/2004	Cab to airport				
16	Monica Lyle	312	RRC Partnership Meeting	4/25/2004	Parking airport				
17	Marla Worthington	318	XML Conference	4/22/2004	Lodging				1
18	Marla Worthington	318	XML Conference	4/23/2004	Lodging				1
19	Marla Worthington	318	XML Conference	4/24/2004	Lodging				1
20	Marla Worthington	318	XML Conference	4/22/2004	Telephone				
21	Marla Worthington	318	XML Conference	4/22/2004	Per Diem			35	
22	Marla Worthington	318	XML Conference	4/23/2004	Per Diem			35	
23	Marla Worthington	318	XML Conference	4/24/2004	Per Diem			35	

Figure 7-8 Flattened data from multiple expense reports (expense data analysis.xls)

This will import all the data from all of the expense reports, as shown in Figure 7-8.

Caution   The flattened data cannot be exported using the map with which you imported it. Excel will warn that the map is not exportable because it contains denormalized data. However, you can export the data – or calculations based on the data – by creating a separate range of cells that reference the data using cell equations. This second range of cells can be mapped to a separate schema and exported.

7.6.2 *Reports and charts*

Now that the data is combined, Dawn can use summary reports and charts to analyze it, as shown in Figure 7-9 and Figure 7-10. When she wants to update the analysis, she can simply import new XML data (or refresh the current data) and the summary report and charts will automatically be updated. A working version of this worksheet is in `expense data analysis.xls`.

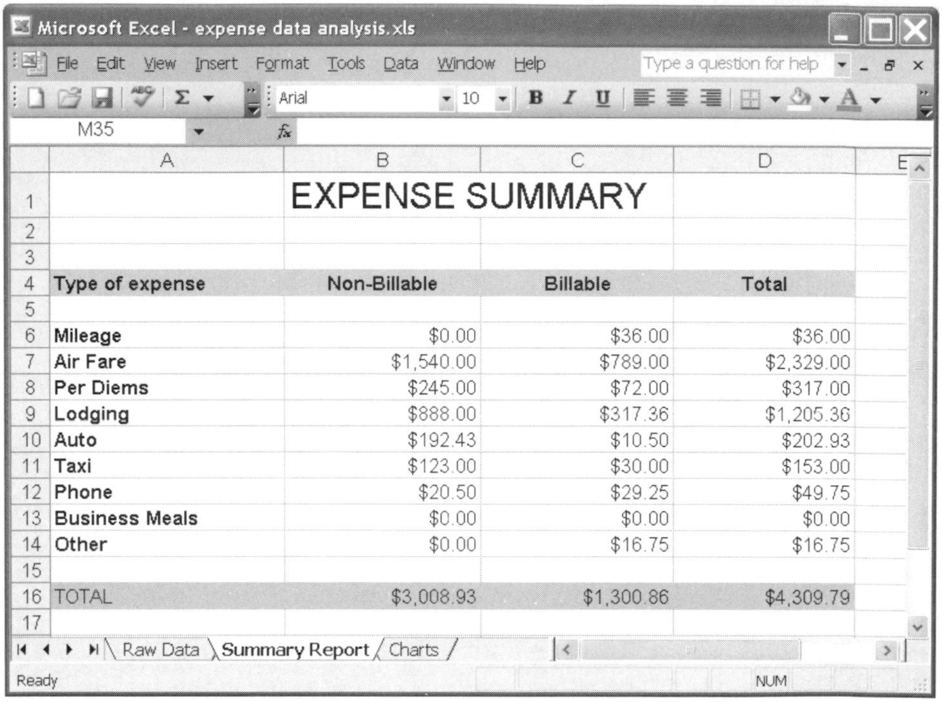

Type of expense	Non-Billable	Billable	Total
Mileage	$0.00	$36.00	$36.00
Air Fare	$1,540.00	$789.00	$2,329.00
Per Diems	$245.00	$72.00	$317.00
Lodging	$888.00	$317.36	$1,205.36
Auto	$192.43	$10.50	$202.93
Taxi	$123.00	$30.00	$153.00
Phone	$20.50	$29.25	$49.75
Business Meals	$0.00	$0.00	$0.00
Other	$0.00	$16.75	$16.75
TOTAL	$3,008.93	$1,300.86	$4,309.79

Figure 7-9 Summary report

7.7 | More complex XML documents

Excel works best with tabular data that naturally fits into rows and columns. XML documents, on the other hand, can have virtually any structure. This can make it challenging to map some XML document types to a

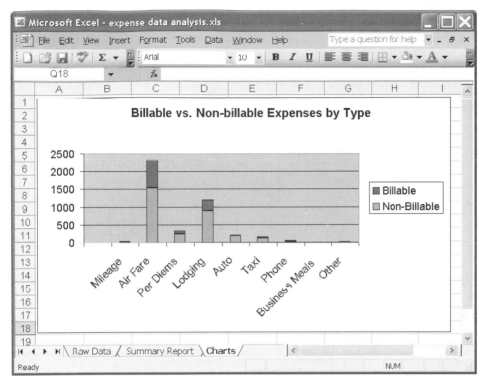

Figure 7-10   Data analysis using charts

worksheet. In our prior example, we had a simple XML document with some header information and some repeating element types that fit conveniently into one column each.

7.7.1 *Different structures*

Worldwide accumulates all of its expense reports in a database for long-term analysis of trends. The database format has a slightly different structure. Instead of individual mileage, airFare, etc. elements, it has a single repeating amount element with an expenseTypeCode attribute indicating the type of expense.

The corresponding XML document is shown in Example 7-4.

The schema for this document does not map directly to the expense report worksheet because the data that belongs in the various expense type

Example 7-4. Modified expense report (expenses modified.xml)

```
<?xml version="1.0" encoding="UTF-8" standalone="yes"?>
<expenseReport xmlns="http://xmlinoffice.com/expenses">
  <empName>Ellen Sandler</empName>
  <empNum>305</empNum>
  <purpose>Sales meeting with ABC Corp.</purpose>
  <deptCode>305</deptCode>
  <billToCode>1104</billToCode>
  <periodFrom>2004-04-16</periodFrom>
  <periodTo>2004-04-18</periodTo>
  <expense>
    <date>2004-04-16</date>
    <explanation>Phone call from the hotel</explanation>
    <amount expenseTypeCode="801">.75</amount>
  </expense>
  <!-- ... -->
  <expense>
    <date>2004-04-16</date>
    <explanation>Dry Cleaning</explanation>
    <amount expenseTypeCode="883">16.75</amount>
  </expense>
</expenseReport>
```

columns comes from the same amount element. Excel does not allow you to map, say, the "Phone" column to "all amount elements with an expenseTypeCode attribute whose value is 801".

XSLT stylesheets can be used to create compatibility between the worksheet-friendly XML and the database-compatible alternative.

from worksheet to database

Export the data to XML in the usual way. A stylesheet will then transform the XML data from its exported structure, shown in Example 7-3, to the database structure shown in Example 7-4.

from database to worksheet

For analysis of the historical data, you can create an XSLT stylesheet that works in the opposite direction. It transforms the database-compatible document structure into a structure that can be mapped directly to Excel.

Paired transforms can also be used with other document types that don't naturally fit into a tabular structure. For example, those with multiple levels of hierarchy, or that contain element types whose content must be combined or split apart for use in the worksheet.

7.8 | XMLSS: The Excel XML vocabulary

Like Word, Excel has an XML vocabulary that can be used to save entire Excel workbooks as XML documents. It is known as *XML Spreadsheet (XMLSS)*. You can save any workbook as XMLSS, and you can open any XMLSS document as a workbook.

An XMLSS document contains the contents of each cell, as well as formatting and datatype information. Like WordML, XMLSS is very verbose. Example 7-5 shows the XMLSS representation of two rows of our expense report.

Caution   Unlike a WordML document, an XMLSS document does not contain everything there is to know about an Excel worksheet. Saving a document as XMLSS and then reopening that document in Excel may result in some missing information, in particular the macros and charts associated with that worksheet.

To save a worksheet as XMLSS:

1. On the **File** menu, click **Save As**.
2. Select **XML Spreadsheet (*.xml)** in the **Save as type** list.
3. Type the name of the file and click **Save**.

If you save a mapped document as XMLSS, it does not intertwine the custom tags (for example, <empName>) with the XMLSS tags, the way Word does with WordML. However, it does save a copy of the schema, as well as the XPath expressions that map between the cells and the element types.

XMLSS is potentially useful for software that converts Excel worksheets to and from other spreadsheet representations. However, it is of limited utility for general applications because:

Example 7-5. XMLSS document fragment (expenses XMLSS.xml)

```
<Row ss:AutoFitHeight="0" ss:Height="22.125">
  <Cell ss:StyleID="s114">
    <Data ss:Type="DateTime">2004-04-16T00:00:00.000</Data>
  </Cell>
  <Cell ss:StyleID="s115">
    <Data ss:Type="String">Phone call from hotel</Data>
  </Cell>
  <Cell ss:StyleID="s187"/><Cell ss:StyleID="s75"/>
  <Cell ss:StyleID="s75"/><Cell ss:StyleID="s75"/>
  <Cell ss:StyleID="s75"/><Cell ss:StyleID="s75"/>
  <Cell ss:StyleID="s75">
    <Data ss:Type="Number">0.75</Data>
  </Cell>
  <Cell ss:StyleID="s75"/><Cell ss:StyleID="s187"/>
  <Cell ss:StyleID="s75"/>
</Row>
<Row ss:AutoFitHeight="0" ss:Height="21.5625">
  <Cell ss:StyleID="s114">
    <Data ss:Type="DateTime">2004-04-16T00:00:00.000</Data>
  </Cell>
  <Cell ss:StyleID="s115">
    <Data ss:Type="String">Lodging</Data>
  </Cell>
  <Cell ss:StyleID="s186"/><Cell ss:StyleID="s77"/>
  <Cell ss:StyleID="s77"/>
  <Cell ss:StyleID="s75">
    <Data ss:Type="Number">158.69</Data>
  </Cell>
  <Cell ss:StyleID="s77"/><Cell ss:StyleID="s77"/>
  <Cell ss:StyleID="s77"/><Cell ss:StyleID="s77"/>
  <Cell ss:StyleID="s186"/><Cell ss:StyleID="s77"/>
</Row>
```

- It does not contain any information about the meaning of the data.
- It is rather verbose and difficult to understand.
- It is difficult to write a stylesheet to extract information from XMLSS because most data items are not in fixed cells; their position varies from one worksheet to the next, depending on the amount of data.

Using Web services with spreadsheets

- REST Web services
- SOAP Web services
- Excel Object Model

Chapter

8

I n Chapter 7, "Using XML data in spreadsheets", on page 132, we learned how to share XML data between Excel worksheets and local files. But there are other sources for XML data and one of the most important is Web services. Not just public services offered to all Web users, but services your company might deploy to facilitate sharing of its own data among its employees.

In this chapter we'll show you how to share data between Excel worksheets and Web services by writing macros or Excel-based code. SOAP Web services are accessed with essentially the same techniques that we employed for Word in 6.2, "SOAP Web services", on page 121, but incorporating the results is somewhat different.

Skills required   What we covered in the previous chapter *on Excel, plus the above-mentioned material in the Word chapter, and the basics of Web services (Chapter 19, "Web services introduction", on page 414 and Chapter 23, "Web services technologies", on page 484).*

8.1 | Analyzing stock quotes with a REST Web service

Worldwide Widget Corporation is known for its award-winning pension plan. Each month, N. Ron Ponzi, the plan's investment advisor, analyzes dozens of securities before investing 100% of the pension fund in Worldwide's own stock.

Ron would like us to create an Excel worksheet to help him analyze stock price information. He wants to be able to enter a stock symbol, month and year, and retrieve the quotes for that month into the worksheet. These quotes can easily be retrieved from a Web service.

An example of the stock quote worksheet is shown in Figure 8-1.

Importing the quote data into Excel allows Ron to take advantage of Excel's data analysis features, creating charts and graphs of the data such as the one shown in Figure 8-2.

Our solution requires several steps:

1. Save a sample of the Web service output as a local XML file.
2. Create a worksheet that is mapped to the schema that Excel infers from the sample service output.
3. Write some Visual Basic for Applications (VBA) code that accesses the Web service and reimports the map with the XML data returned by the Web service. This code will be executed every time the user clicks a "Refresh" button that we will add to the worksheet.

8.1.1 *The stock quote Web service*

To access the data, we will use the Web service located at `http://www.xignite.com/xquotes.asmx`.

This Web service consists of a set of operations that retrieve stock quote data. If you browse the above URL, you will see a list of those operations. We will use one called `GetQuotesHistorical`.

Selecting that operation will bring up a page that describes the operation and provides examples. About half way down the page is the syntax for call-

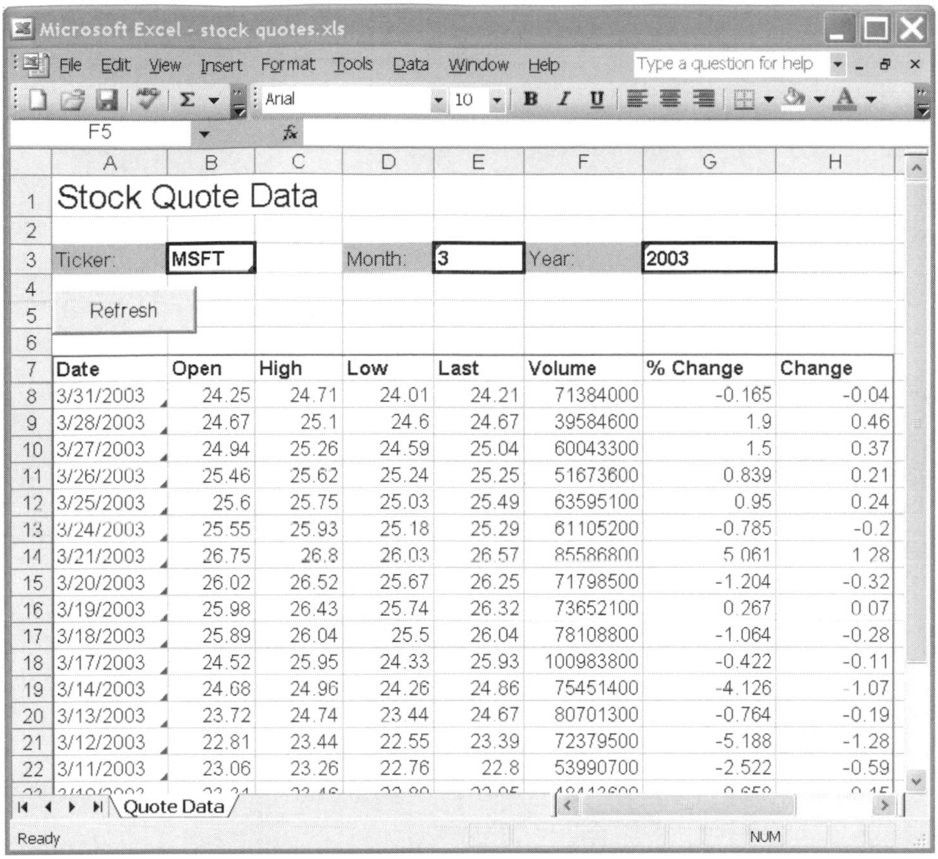

	A	B	C	D	E	F	G	H
1	Stock Quote Data							
2								
3	Ticker:	MSFT		Month:	3	Year:	2003	
4								
5	Refresh							
6								
7	Date	Open	High	Low	Last	Volume	% Change	Change
8	3/31/2003	24.25	24.71	24.01	24.21	71384000	-0.165	-0.04
9	3/28/2003	24.67	25.1	24.6	24.67	39584600	1.9	0.46
10	3/27/2003	24.94	25.26	24.59	25.04	60043300	1.5	0.37
11	3/26/2003	25.46	25.62	25.24	25.25	51673600	0.839	0.21
12	3/25/2003	25.6	25.75	25.03	25.49	63595100	0.95	0.24
13	3/24/2003	25.55	25.93	25.18	25.29	61105200	-0.785	-0.2
14	3/21/2003	26.75	26.8	26.03	26.57	85586800	5.061	1.28
15	3/20/2003	26.02	26.52	25.67	26.25	71798500	-1.204	-0.32
16	3/19/2003	25.98	26.43	25.74	26.32	73652100	0.267	0.07
17	3/18/2003	25.89	26.04	25.5	26.04	78108800	-1.064	-0.28
18	3/17/2003	24.52	25.95	24.33	25.93	100983800	-0.422	-0.11
19	3/14/2003	24.68	24.96	24.26	24.86	75451400	-4.126	-1.07
20	3/13/2003	23.72	24.74	23.44	24.67	80701300	-0.764	-0.19
21	3/12/2003	22.81	23.44	22.55	23.39	72379500	-5.188	-1.28
22	3/11/2003	23.06	23.26	22.76	22.8	53990700	-2.522	-0.59

Figure 8-1 Stock quote worksheet

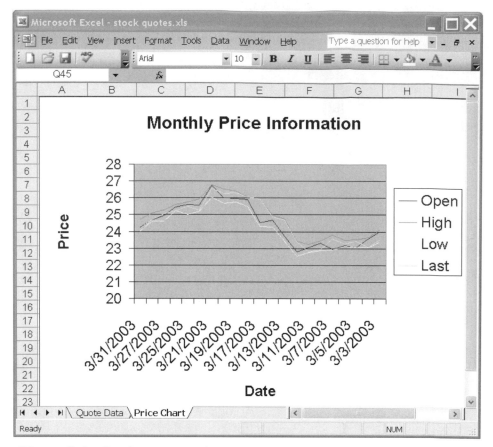

Figure 8-2   Stock quote graph

ing the service using the HTTP GET method, which is a REST interface. It says:

Example 8-1. Syntax for Web service request

```
GET http://www.xignite.com/xquotes.asmx/GetQuotesHistorical?
    Symbol=string&Month=string&Year=string HTTP/1.1
Host: www.xignite.com
```

As we are using a REST interface to this Web service, rather than its SOAP interface, we can invoke the service simply by specifying a URL that includes the necessary parameters. For example, if we want the quotes for

Microsoft Corporation, for March of 2003, we can specify the following URL:

Example 8-2. Web service request URL for MSFT data

```
http://www.xignite.com/xquotes.asmx/GetQuotesHistorical?
Symbol=MSFT&Month=3&Year=2003
```

The result will be returned as an XML document, as shown on that page. An example is shown in Example 8-3.

Example 8-3. Sample output of the stock quote Web service

```
<?xml version="1.0" encoding="utf-8"?>
<ArrayOfHistoricalQuote
  xmlns:xsd="http://www.w3.org/2001/XMLSchema"
  xmlns:xsi="http://www.w3.org/2001/XMLSchema-instance"
  xmlns="http://www.xignite.com/services/">
  <HistoricalQuote>
    <Outcome>Success</Outcome>
    <Date>3/31/2003</Date>
    <Open>24.25</Open>
    <High>24.71</High>
    <Low>24.01</Low>
    <Last>24.21</Last>
    <Volume>71384000</Volume>
    <PercentChange>-0.165</PercentChange>
    <SplitRatio>1</SplitRatio>
    <OpenAdjusted>24.25</OpenAdjusted>
    <HighAdjusted>24.71</HighAdjusted>
    <LowAdjusted>24.01</LowAdjusted>
    <LastAdjusted>24.21</LastAdjusted>
    <ChangeAdjusted>-0.04</ChangeAdjusted>
    <VolumeAdjusted>71384000</VolumeAdjusted>
    <Change>-0.04</Change>
  </HistoricalQuote>
  <HistoricalQuote>
    <Outcome>Success</Outcome>
    <Date>3/28/2003</Date>
    <Open>24.67</Open>
    <!-- ... -->
  </HistoricalQuote>
</ArrayOfHistoricalQuote>
```

You can test this out yourself by entering the URL in Example 8-2 into your browser and viewing the source.

8.1.2 *Setting up the XML map*

To create the XML map in the worksheet, we will need a sample of the XML data that will be returned from the Web service. This can be obtained by executing the Web service in a browser and copying the result, or by copying the sample output from the page describing the Web service. We have provided sample output in the file `sampledata.xml`. It does not matter which ticker symbol or month you choose right now; we simply care about the structure.

To set up the map:

- Open the worksheet `stock quotes start.xls`. This is a mostly empty worksheet.
- On the **Data** menu, point to **XML**, then click **XML Source**. This brings up the **XML Source** task pane.
- Click **XML Maps** to bring up a list of XML maps in the worksheet (currently there are none).
- Click **Add** and select `sampledata.xml` from the list. Alternatively, you can enter a URL request to execute the Web service and return a result; e.g. the URL in Example 8-2.
- Click **Open**.
- Click **OK** when Excel warns you that it will infer a schema, then **OK** again to return to the main dialog.
- This brings up the **XML Source** task pane. From it, drag the `ns1:HistoricalQuote` element type to the top left corner of the location where you want to put the quote data in the worksheet; for example, cell A7.

You can customize the map to meet your needs. For example, you can change the column headers, or delete columns that contain data that you do not need (for example, `Outcome`). You now have a map that will import the data returned by the `GetQuotesHistorical` operation of the Web service.

8.1.3 *Refreshing the data*

Because the user wants to pass different parameters to the Web service each time he refreshes the data in the map, he cannot simply use the **Refresh XML Data** command on the **XML** submenu. He could use the Import command on the XML submenu, but only if he were willing to enter a new URL (with different parameters) for each import. However, N. Ron Ponzi felt (not unreasonably) that constructing a URL would be cumbersome and error-prone.

Instead, we decided to write a macro that constructed the URL from parameters entered in the worksheet. Clicking a "Refresh" button would call the macro, which would invoke the Web service with the constructed URL and refresh the data.

To create the button and macro:

- Right-click the toolbar at the top of the window and click **Control Toolbox**. This will display the small **Control Toolbox** toolbar shown in Figure 8-3.
- Click the picture that looks like a button.
- Click the location in the worksheet where you want the button placed.
- Select the button and right-click. On the shortcut menu, click **Properties**.
- Change *both* the **(Name)** and the **Caption** properties to Refresh.
- Close the **Properties** dialog.
- Right-click the button again. On the context menu, click **View Code**. This will bring up the Visual Basic Editor with the cursor positioned in a function that will be executed each time the button is clicked. This is shown in Figure 8-4.

Figure 8-3 The Control Toolbox toolbar

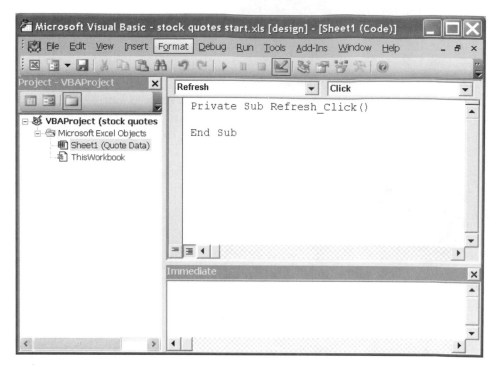

Figure 8-4   Visual Basic Editor

The code entered into the Visual Basic Editor should look like that shown in Example 8-4. You can either type it in or insert it from the example file `refresh_quotes.txt`.

The code takes the parameters entered by the user from the worksheet, strings them together to construct the URL, and then refreshes the data in the map with the results.

- Lines 3-5 of the example declare the variables and assign the appropriate (first and only) map to the variable `theMap`.
- Lines 7 to 12 concatenate the various parts of the URL based on the contents of the cells that contain the parameters.
- Line 14 performs the actual import, using the constructed URL.

To test your solution, you must first exit design mode by clicking the top left icon on the **Control Toolbox** toolbar.

Example 8-4. Function to import from a constructed URL

```
Private Sub Refresh_Click()

Dim theURL, ticker, month, year, beginningOFURL As String
Dim theMap As XmlMap
Set theMap = ActiveWorkbook.XmlMaps(1)

beginningOFURL =
"http://www.xignite.com/xquotes.asmx/GetQuoteHistorical?Symbol="
ticker = Range("B3").Text
month = Range("F3").Text
year = Range("G3").Text
theURL = beginningOFURL+ticker+"&Month="+month+"&Year="+year

theMap.Import (theURL)

End Sub
```

A complete working version of this example can be found in the sample file stock quotes.xls.

8.2 | Currency conversion with a SOAP Web service

Ellen would like to extend the XML expense report system for foreign travel and thinks that automatic capture of currency conversion rates would be a requirement. Fortunately, there is a Web service available for the purpose.

We will create a simple worksheet to develop and test the use of the Web service. Eventually, we can move the code to the expense report worksheet.

For pedagogical reasons we will use the SOAP interface to the service (it has REST interfaces as well) and we will again use the Office Web Services Toolkit to hide the complexity of SOAP (as we did in 6.2, "SOAP Web services", on page 121).

Also for pedagogical reasons we will use code to update individual cells instead of simply creating an XML map and importing the Web service output. Using code will allow us to see how the toolkit returns the data.[1]

The worksheet is shown in Figure 8-5. It has cells for the parameters – the "from" currency ("Expense Currency") and the "to" currency ("Expense

Report Currency") – and a **Refresh** button that retrieves the exchange rate from the Web service.

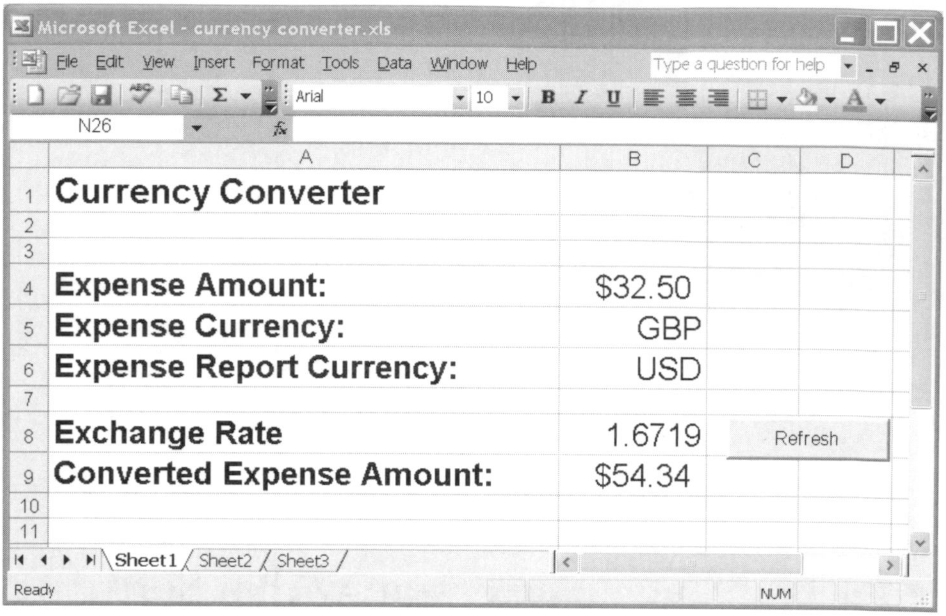

Figure 8-5   The currency converter worksheet

To create this example, open the worksheet `currency converter start.xls`. It is a skeleton worksheet to which we will add the currency lookup capability.

8.2.1   *The currency converter Web service*

The Web service is located at:
`http://www.webservicex.net/CurrencyConvertor.asmx`. It has one operation, named `ConversionRate`, that will provide the current exchange rate, given a "from" currency and a "to" currency.

---

1. In real life we would only use code if we needed more control over the placement of the data in the worksheet; for example, for complex structures that we needed to flatten or rearrange in some way.

If you browse the above URL, you will see a brief description of the operation. Clicking on ConversionRate will bring up a page that describes the operation fully and provides examples. Although the page shows the input and output messages, we do not need to concern ourselves with them because of our use of the Office Web Services Toolkit.

8.2.2 *The Office Web Services Toolkit*

Generating the necessary classes in Excel is identical to the process described in 6.2.3, "Using the Web Services Reference Tool", on page 126. We execute that process, this time using the URL:

http://www.webservicex.net/CurrencyConvertor.asmx?wsdl

The name of the Web service and its methods is shown on the right side of the dialog in Figure 8-6.

The procedure generates a single class named clsws_CurrencyConvertor which allows access to the ConversionRate operation.

8.2.3 *Refreshing the data*

As in the previous example, we will use a **Refresh** button to update the data in the worksheet. Follow the instructions in 8.1.3, "Refreshing the data", on page 167 to create the Refresh button. This time, use the code shown in Example 8-5, which can be copied from the example file refresh_currency.txt.

- Line 3 creates a new instance of the generated class clsws_CurrencyConvertor.
- Lines 5 through 7 declare the other variables used.
- Lines 8 and 9 assign the text entered by the user in cells B5 and B6 to the variables fromCurrency and toCurrency.
- Line 10 sets the range to be filled in, namely cell B8.
- Line 12 calls the method wsm_ConversionRate and assigns the result to the variable rate. If rate is not null, the value is assigned to the appropriate cell.

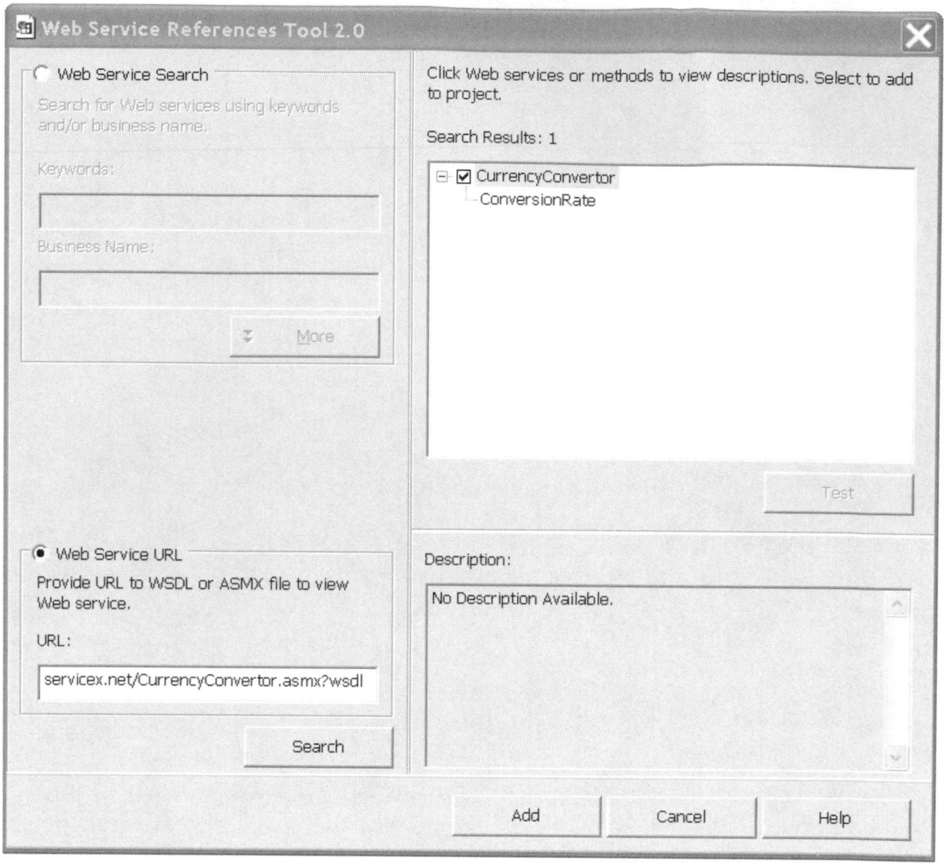

Figure 8-6   The Web Services Reference Tool

Note that, unlike the previous example, there is no XML Map involved. The data returned from the Web service is placed into the cells by the code, rather than through XML import. This technique allows more control over which data is mapped and where it is placed in the worksheet.

A complete working version of this example can be found in the sample file currency converter.xls.

Example 8-5. Refresh code for symbol lookup example

```
Private Sub Refresh_Click()

Dim objLookup As New clsws_CurrencyConvertor

Dim fromCurrency As String
Dim toCurrency As String
Dim rate As Double
fromCurrency = Range("B5").Text
toCurrency = Range("B6").Text
Set rateRange = Range("B8")

rate = objLookup.wsm_ConversionRate(fromCurrency, toCurrency)
If (rate) Then
    rateRange.Value = rate
Else
    rateRange.Value = 0
End If

End Sub
```

8.3 | Other approaches

There are several approaches to accessing Web services with Excel. The two scenarios in this chapter are just examples of what is possible. You could, for example, combine those two, using the Office Web Services toolkit with an XML Map, or using REST and manually parsing the XML result and placing the contents into the worksheet.

If you will be calling the Web service with no parameters, or with the same parameters every time, your task is simplified. You can simply create an XML map for the output from the appropriate URL and use the Refresh XML Data command on the XML submenu to refresh the data.

For example, if the Web service is designed to return current information on a fixed set of market indices, you can create a map to the URL:

`http://www.xignite.com/xquotes.asmx?GetIndices.`

This approach does not require any code to be written.

You can write an application outside Excel that retrieves information from a Web service and writes it to an XML document on the file system. This application could be run on a daily basis, for example. The map in the Excel worksheet could then be set up to retrieve data from the local document.

Finally, you can also use an XML Map in a worksheet to *post* an XML document to a Web service. For example a Web service could be created for accepting expense report submissions, and users could create their expense reports in Excel and submit them to the Web service for approval.

The ability to write code that is integrated with Excel means that the possibilities are almost endless. In this chapter, we used examples written in Visual Basic for Applications (VBA). However, you can also write separate applications in Visual Basic, C# or C++ that are integrated with Excel.

8.4 | The Excel Object Model

The Excel Object Model exists to allow programmers to write code to perform Excel-related functions. The Object Model includes classes for such things as worksheets, cells, cell ranges, charts, and many other Excel constructs. These classes allow you to write code that inserts, modifies, formats or deletes data in the cells, creates new worksheets, adds charts, and performs almost any other function that can be performed by an Excel user.

In Office 2003 the Excel Object Model was extended to support XML. It now has classes for things like the `XmlMap` object.

Complete coverage of the Excel Object Model is outside the scope of this book, but this section will provide some pointers on understanding the XML-specific aspects of it.

8.4.1 *XML-related concepts*

Unlike the Word or InfoPath object models, which represent the underlying document as XML, the Excel object model does not treat the underlying worksheet as an XML document. Instead, it keeps track, by means of XPath expressions, of the relationship between cells and their locations in the mapped schema. When the map is imported or exported, Excel performs the appropriate transformation based on the XPath expressions.

Two terms are important to understanding the XML Object Model: maps and lists. *Maps* were introduced in Chapter 7, "Using XML data in spreadsheets", on page 132. A map is the relationship between an Excel workbook and a schema. Our stock quote example has a single map, which ties `stock quotes.xls` to the schema of the documents returned by the stock quote Web service. It is possible for a single workbook to have multiple maps, with different schema definitions. It is also possible for a single map to have multiple schemas associated with it, if the "main" schema document includes others.

Lists represent the repeating element types of the map. For example, our stock quote example has one list, which represents the repeating set of stock quotes. This list has multiple columns associated with it.

8.4.2 *Maps*

Maps in the object model are represented by the XmlMap class. You can retrieve the maps associated with a workbook through the XmlMaps collection. For example, the following code will return the first map of the active workbook:

Example 8-6. Return the first map

```
Dim firstMap As XmlMap
Set firstMap = ActiveWorkbook.XmlMaps(1)
```

You can then use the XmlMap object to import or export the XML data. For example, you can export the data to the XML file C:\expenses.xml with:

Example 8-7. Export to XML file

```
firstMap.Export("C:\expenses.xml")
```

You can also use the ExportXML method to export the XML data as a string. For example, you can assign a string containing the XML data to the variable xmlString with:

Example 8-8. Assign XML data string to variable

```
Dim xmlString as String
firstMap.ExportXML(xmlString)
```

To import, you can use the `Import` method. For example, to import the XML data from the file `C:\expenses.xml`:

Example 8-9. Import XML data from a file

```
firstMap.Import("C:\expenses.xml")
```

In addition to these methods, the `XmlMap` class has a number of properties that allow you to set various options on the map; for example:

`AdjustColumnWidth`
indicates whether to adjust column widths to fit the data when importing.

`AppendOnImport`
specifies whether to append to the existing data in the map or overwrite it.

8.4.3   *Lists, cells and XPath expressions*

Lists, which represent repeating XML data, arc represented by the `ListObject` class. For example, our stock quotes example has one list that represents all the repeating stock quote information. The relationship between lists, columns and their maps and XPath expressions is depicted in Figure 8-7.

You can retrieve the lists associated with a worksheet through the `ListObjects` collection. A `ListObject` may be associated with one or more `ListColumn` objects. In our stock quote example, the `ListObject` is associated with eight `ListColumn` objects, one for each column of data.

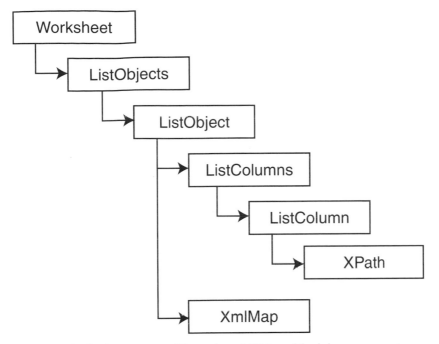

Figure 8-7   Structure of list-related Object Model components

Each list column has an XPath expression associated with it. In our stock quotes example, the first column in the list is associated with the XPath expression:

Example 8-10. XPath expression

```
ArrayOfHistoricalQuote/HistoricalQuote/Date
```

Individual cells can have XPath expressions associated with them as well. In our expense report example in Chapter 7, "Using XML data in spreadsheets", on page 132, there were several cells that contained non-repeating data, such as the employee name and the charge code. These cells have their own XPath expressions associated with them to locate their data. For example, the following code will display a dialog containing the XPath expression associated with cell E5:

Example 8-11. Display associated with XPath expression

```
Set myCell = Range("E5")
MsgBox (myCell.XPath)
```

It is also possible to determine which range of cells is mapped to the data located by a given XPath. This is accomplished using the `XmlDataQuery` method of the `Worksheet` class. For example, the following code will return a range representing the first column of the stock quotes worksheet.

Example 8-12. Return cells mapped to located data

```
Set myRange=myWorkSheet.XmlDataQuery(
    "ArrayOfHistoricalQuote/HistoricalQuote/Date")
```

This section has given you a taste of the capabilities of the Excel Object Model. Basically, any XML-related task that can be performed manually in Excel can also be performed using the object model, and then some. This includes creating, modifying and deleting maps, setting all the XML-related options, and performing imports and exports.

The Excel Object Model can be viewed and navigated using Object Browser in the Visual Basic Editor.

Designing and using forms

▌ Forms on steroids

▌ Using a form

▌ Designing a form

nfoPath, a new addition to the Office suite, is at heart a forms processor, although with novel features that transcend the category. Nevertheless, we pragmatic authors would have named it "Microsoft Forms".

But Jean Paoli, who conceived the product, has a philosophic bent. Jean says the name InfoPath was chosen to connote the idea of "providing a path for information to travel among the disconnected islands of a business".

In this chapter we'll help you get your information traveling. We'll teach you how to design forms and how end users go about completing them.

Skills required   No special skills are required for this chapter. However, general familiarity with Office products will be helpful as InfoPath uses some Office functions and provides a similar interface and environment.

9.1 | Forms on steroids

Whether on paper or electronic, forms are the dominant form of business transaction record where humans are involved. That's because a well-designed form provides the guidance and constraints that help you get the data entry right.

guidance

    A form guides you by providing a separate space for each piece of information, with the appropriate granularity (e.g. one address field, or separate fields for street, city, and state).

constraints

    A form can constrain the length of each field (perhaps with a box for each character), or limit data values to items checked off from a printed list.

But these strengths of traditional forms – guided entry and constrained data values – can be weaknesses as well. InfoPath improves on conventional forms software in several ways:

- InfoPath guides data entry based on a schema of the form designer's choosing. It will even help you create a schema.
- InfoPath enforces the constraints of the schema, plus additional constraints that the form designer can specify.
- The user is actually creating an abstract XML document while completing the form, although he only sees the rendered form view. The experience is similar to other Office products.
- The user can add and delete repeating elements, or even groups of repeating elements. The form view expands and contracts as needed.
- There can be multiple form views for a single document type. The layout of the fields in the form views does not have to follow the order in the underlying XML document.
- The form can have XHTML rich text elements, with lists, highlighted phrases, etc.

9.2 | Using a form

Worldwide Widget Corporation has an award-winning logo merchandising program. Although its widgets have lost money from the beginning, the company makes a healthy profit from its popular line of "Widget Wear", emblazoned with its distinctive "W2C" logo.

Worldwide's order clerks have quickly become comfortable with Info-Path because of its similarity to their other Office tools. With most forms software, end users operate in "form completion" mode, filling in the blanks. The InfoPath end user environment offers much more flexibility than a typical forms package, with many familiar features from the other Office products.

For this reason, Microsoft refers to the forms completion process as *forms editing*.

Just as when working with XML in Word, the document on the screen is a rendition of an underlying abstract XML document. However, users normally do not need to know that they are editing an XML document, let alone understand its structure. They simply enter data into the form with help from the various features of InfoPath.

This is known as working in *edit mode*. Edit mode allows users to enter and modify data, and to open and save documents. The users cannot affect the design of the form.

9.2.1 *Opening an empty form*

Upon launching InfoPath, the **Fill Out a Form** task pane appears on the right side of the window. There are several ways to bring up an empty form to begin entering data:

- You can select a form in the **Fill out a form** section of the task pane. This will immediately bring up the form associated with that name.
- You can click **On My Computer** or **On My Web Sites** from the **Open a form** section of the task pane. This will allow you to browse for form files on your computer or on the Web.
- You can click **Open** on the **File** menu, then select a file and click **Open**. If you choose a form file (with a .xsn extension),

InfoPath will open a blank form of that kind. If you choose an XML document, InfoPath will open that document as a form.

To use the Worldwide example, choose either of the last two options. Select the `order.xsn` file and click **Open**. This will bring up an order form, shown in Figure 9-1.

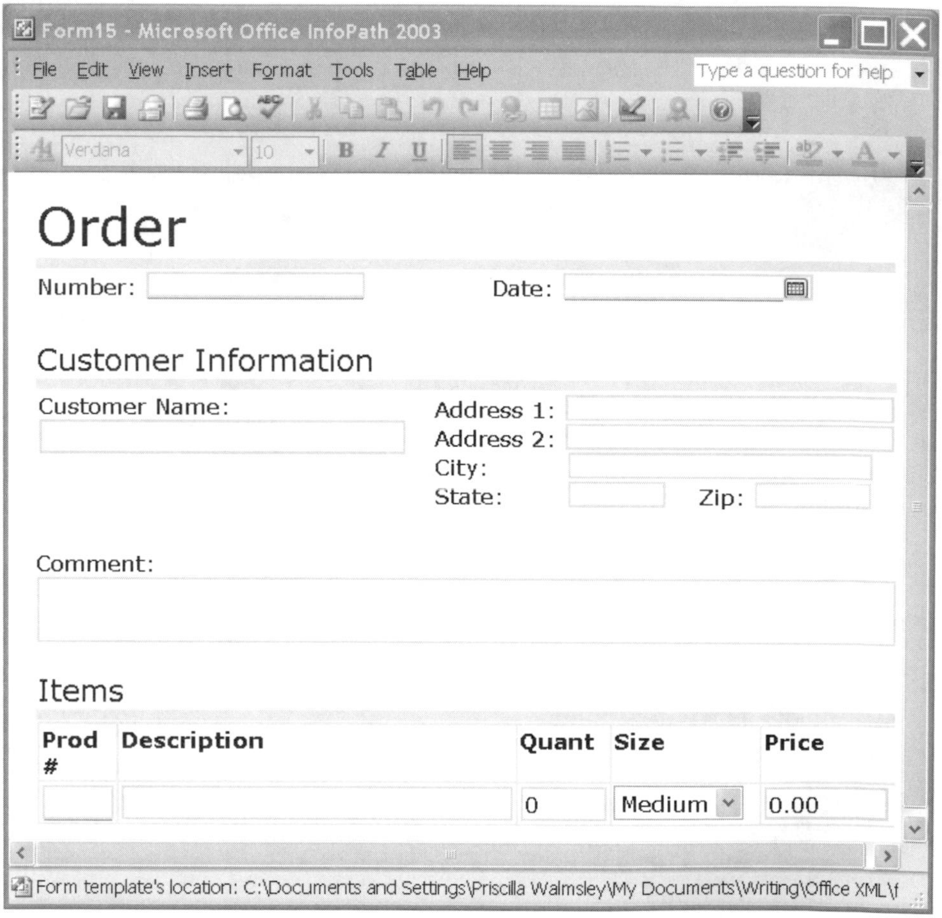

Figure 9-1   The order form (order.xsn)

9.2.2 *The InfoPath environment*

InfoPath offers a familiar environment that is consistent with the rest of the Microsoft Office products. It has many of the same features as other Office products, including:

- Cut, copy and paste
- Spell check
- Find and replace
- Undo and redo
- Select all
- Print, print preview and page setup

Just as a spreadsheet mapped to an XML document has repeating and non-repeating cells, a form has repeating and non-repeating fields. In our example, Items is a *repeating table*. Its rows repeat for each item ordered, which means the five fields in a row are repeating fields.

9.2.3 *Fields*

Filling out the form is simply a matter of filling in the blanks. As you position the cursor over an editable field, its border becomes a dark gray. The **Tab** key can be used to move between fields. Fields that are required to contain data are underlined in red. In our example, the Number, Date and Product Number fields are required.

Every field has an associated datatype. Some, such as Customer Name, are simply strings, which allow any data to be entered. Others have specific types, such as `dateTime` for the Date field, and `integer` for the Quant field. Additional constraints can be placed on the contents of a field, as discussed in 9.3.4.2, "Field-based constraints", on page 199.

If you enter a value in a field that is invalid for the field's datatype, or violates a constraint, a red-dashed border will appear around the field. Right-clicking the field will bring up a description of the violation.

Controls can be used to change the appearance and/or capabilities of a field. Most fields in our form have ordinary text boxes for controls, but three fields are associated with other kinds of controls:

- The Date field has a calendar control, which allows the user to select the date from a calendar.
- The Comment field has a rich text box control, which allows the user to format the text of the comment by using fonts, sizes, colors, lists and styles.
- The Size field has a drop-down list associated with it, allowing the user to select from the values Small, Medium or Large.

9.2.4 *Tables*

The last part of the order form is a table, which allows repeating items for the order. Only one row is initially displayed in the empty form. When the cursor is positioned in any field on the row, you can click the down arrow at the left of the row to bring up the table menu, shown in Figure 9-2. This menu allows you to insert and remove rows.

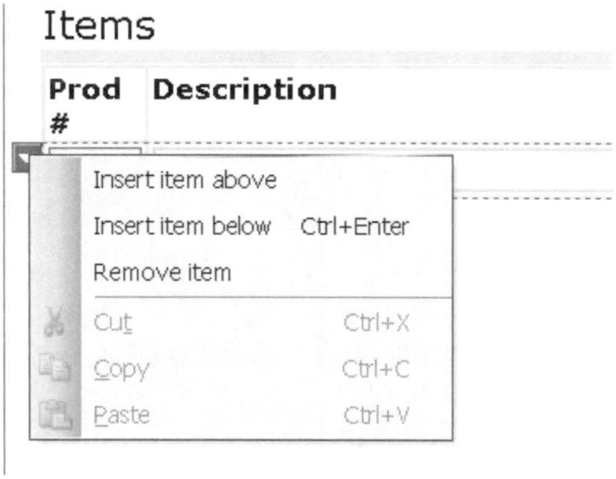

Figure 9-2   The table menu

As an exercise, fill in the order form with data, including more than one item in the table. The completed form will look something like Figure 9-3.

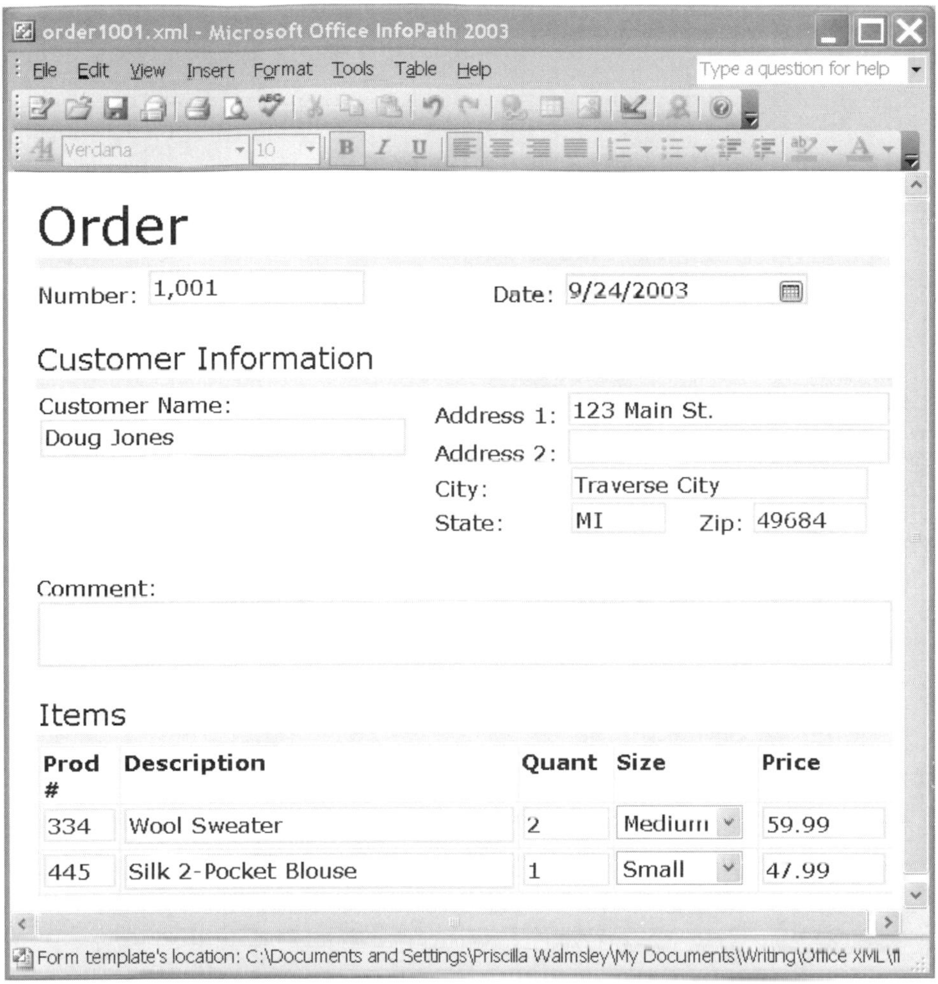

Figure 9-3   The completed order form

9.2.5 *Saving and opening documents*

Once the form is completed, you can save the data as an XML document. To do this, simply click **Save** on the **File** menu and specify a file name. Note that it is possible to save a document that contains errors; the resulting document simply won't be valid according to its associated schema.

The generated document is shown in Example 9-1. An end user will probably never have to look at it, but as we are going to be designing forms, it may be helpful to know what InfoPath is generating.

Example 9-1. Saved XML document (order1001.xml)

```
<?xml version="1.0" encoding="UTF-8"?>
<?mso-infoPathSolution productVersion="11.0.5531"
                       PIVersion="1.0.0.0" href="order.xsn"
                       language="en-us"
                       solutionVersion="1.0.0.197" ?>
<?mso-application progid="InfoPath.Document"?>
<ns1:order number="1001"
           xmlns:ns1="http://xmlinoffice.com/orders">
  <ns1:date>2003-09-24T00:00:00</ns1:date>
  <ns1:comment></ns1:comment>
  <ns1:customer>Doug Jones</ns1:customer>
  <ns1:shipTo>
    <ns1:addr>123 Main St.</ns1:addr>
    <ns1:addr2></ns1:addr2>
    <ns1:city>Traverse City</ns1:city>
    <ns1:state>MI</ns1:state>
    <ns1:postal_code>49684</ns1:postal_code>
  </ns1:shipTo>
  <ns1:items>
    <ns1:item number="334">
      <ns1:desc>Wool Sweater</ns1:desc>
      <ns1:quant>2</ns1:quant>
      <ns1:size>M</ns1:size>
      <ns1:price>59.99</ns1:price>
    </ns1:item>
    <ns1:item number="445">
      <ns1:desc>Silk 2-Pocket Blouse</ns1:desc>
      <ns1:quant>1</ns1:quant>
      <ns1:size>S</ns1:size>
      <ns1:price>47.99</ns1:price>
    </ns1:item>
  </ns1:items>
</ns1:order>
```

Note that there are two processing instructions at the beginning of the document. The first, labeled mso-infoPathSolution, indicates the form associated with this document, namely `order.xsn`.[1] This allows InfoPath to associate the document with the form when it is opened.

The second processing instruction, labeled `mso-application`, indicates that the program used to open this document should be InfoPath. Documents with a `.xml` extension that do not contain such a processing instruction are usually opened in a Web browser.

Instead of starting out with an empty form, you can open an existing XML document, edit it, and resave it. However, in order to open a document in InfoPath it must have the two processing instructions shown in Example 9-1. Otherwise, InfoPath will not know what form to associate with the document. This means that if the XML document was generated by some other process, those two instructions must be added before it can be used in InfoPath.

There are two ways to open an existing XML document in InfoPath:

- You can click **On My Computer** or **On My Web Sites** from the **Open a form** section of the **Fill Out a Form** task pane.
- You can click **Open** on the **File** menu, then select the file and click **Open**.

In either case, this will allow you to browse for files on your computer or on the Web. If you choose an XML document that has the appropriate processing instructions, it will be opened in InfoPath.

You can save your completed form as an XML document. In addition, you can export it to either an HTML page, or to Microsoft Excel. To export a completed form, click **Export** on the **File** menu.

9.3 | Designing a form

InfoPath's *design mode* allows us to create or modify the layout of the form. Just as with Word, we will be creating a rendition of the XML document we want the end user to complete. Unlike Word, however, InfoPath can create

---

1. Normally, the entire path is included; we have shortened it to simplify the example.

the necessary XSLT stylesheet – and other information needed to render the form from the XML document – entirely from the design mode interface.[2]

To enter design mode, when the order form is open in edit mode, click **Design this Form** on the **Tools** menu.

This brings up the form in design mode, along with the **Design Tasks** task pane. This is shown in Figure 9-4. There is a lot there to experiment with and you are encouraged to do so as we move ahead with the design.

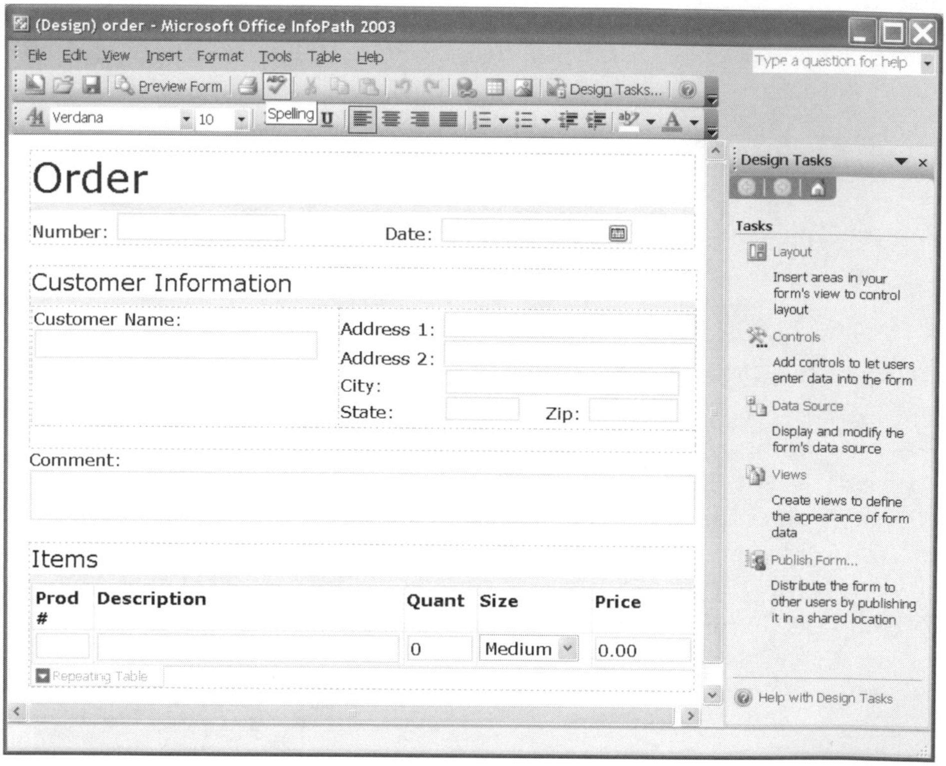

Figure 9-4   Design mode

Designing a form in InfoPath involves heavy use of the task panes as well as the main window. Individual fields and parts of the form layout can be

---

2. And if you need to do more than the interface supports, you can supplement it with scripting, as we'll show you in Chapter 10, "Using scripts with forms", on page 226.

dragged from the task pane onto the form. The form is displayed roughly as it will appear to the user.

The **Design Tasks** task pane provides links to the four other task panes that are relevant to designing forms, namely:

- The **Layout** task pane allows you to manage the layout of the form using layout tables. It is discussed in 9.3.2, "Laying out the form", on page 193.
- The **Controls** task pane allows you to add controls to fields. It is discussed in 9.3.3, "Fields and controls", on page 196.
- The **Data Source** task pane shows the structure allowed by a schema, and allows you to add fields to the form. It is discussed in 9.3.1, "Working with the data source", on page 191.
- The **Views** task pane allows you to create more than one view of the data, and manage the views. It is discussed in 9.3.7, "Views", on page 218.

Each of these four task panes can also be selected from the task pane menu, which is displayed by clicking the name of the currently displayed task pane.

9.3.1 *Working with the data source*

The **Data Source** task pane, shown in Figure 9-5, displays the structure allowed by the schema of the underlying XML document. It displays the element types and attributes (preceded by a colon) in a tree structure. Element types and attributes that are required are displayed with a red asterisk.

Tip   Some element types that are in fact required by the schema are not marked as required in the data source structure. This is because they have datatypes (for example, string) that allow empty values.

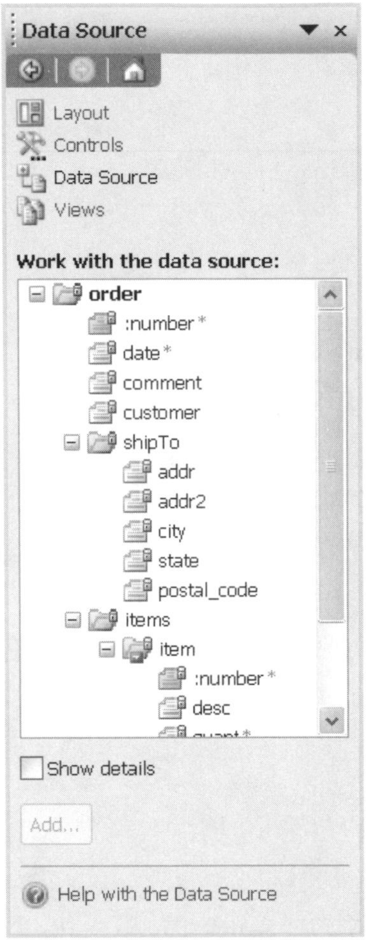

Figure 9-5   The Data Source task pane

If you check the **Show details** box, InfoPath will show you the datatypes of each of the element types and attributes.

Element types and attributes can be added to the form by dragging them from the **Data Source** task pane to the appropriate location in the form. They can be dragged into an empty area of the form, or dragged into a layout table, as we will see in 9.3.2, "Laying out the form", on page 193.

The structure shown in the task pane may have one of several origins. It may have been loaded from a schema definition, which it was in our case. It can also have been loaded from a schema inferred from a database or Web service. In any of these cases, the structure is static and cannot be changed by the form designer in InfoPath. That is because InfoPath assumes your intention is to create XML documents that are compatible with those schemas, databases, or Web services.

Alternatively, the structure may have been inferred from an example XML document, or constructed by the form designer from scratch. In either of these two cases, the form designer *can* modify the structure in the **Data Source** task pane. Modifying the XML structure is discussed further in 9.3.6.6, "Starting with a blank slate", on page 215.

Tip   So if you just want to use a database or Web service as a starting point for your design, save a sample of its output as a local XML document and start from that.

9.3.2 *Laying out the form*

The overall layout of a form can be modeled as one or more tables. The **Layout** task pane, which is shown in Figure 9-6, provides a set of design aids called *layout tables*. They can be added to the form by dragging them from the task pane.

Caution   Layout tables are used to organize fields on the form page. They should not be confused with **repeating tables**, such as the Items table in our order form, which are used to hold data.

The top half of the **Layout** task pane shows the types of layout tables that can be added to a form. The first choice, **Table with Title,** will add a one-column table that has a textual title associated with it. In fact, any layout table can have a title associated with it by inserting a row at the begin-

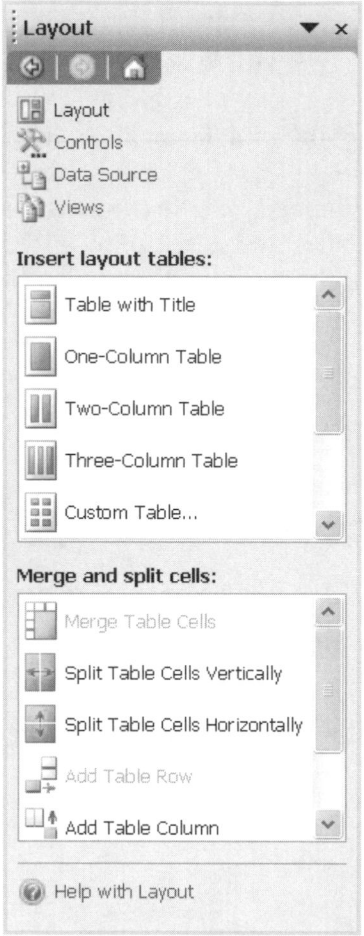

Figure 9-6   The Layout task pane

ning and placing text in it. The **Table with Title** option is simply a shortcut.

The next four choices allow you to insert tables with varying numbers of columns and rows. Layout tables can be inserted within other layout tables for more complex layouts.

The bottom half of the **Layout** task pane allows you to manipulate a layout table once it has been added to a form. It allows you to merge and split cells, and add rows and columns. All of the functions that can be performed from the **Layout** task pane are also commands on the **Table** menu on the main menu bar. The **Table** menu also allows you to delete columns and rows, select parts of tables, and specify formatting options such as borders and shading. These table-related functions are very similar to the table-related functions in Word.

Text and images can be added anywhere on the form, within any of the cells of a layout table or on the form background. The text can be formatted by changing its font, size or style.

9.3.2.1   Rendering repeating element types

In most business documents, some or all of the structure repeats itself. In our order example, a single order can contain multiple items, each of which has a product number, quantity and size. InfoPath allows you to render repeating elements using three different controls:

lists
> A *list* is a collection of text items that can be increased or decreased by the form user. Each item in the list is one field, a text string, which will be saved as the content of a single repeating element. Lists may be bulleted, numbered or plain (i.e. with no symbol preceding each item). A list might be used to represent repeating address lines or comments.

repeating tables
> For lists of items that are made up of multiple fields that can fit on a single line of the form, *repeating tables* can be used. In our example, the order items were represented by a repeating table because they have five fields: Prod #, Description, Quant, Size and Price. The table is shown on the form as a grid that allows the form user to add or delete rows. Don't let the name confuse you: the table itself doesn't repeat, it is the rows that repeat.

repeating sections
> A *section* is a grouping of controls in a form. Another way to represent repeating element types with multiple children is with *repeating sections*. Repeating sections don't have the restrictions of lists or repeating tables.

Repeating tables are a good choice when there are few enough fields that they fit easily on a single line. In other cases, repeating sections are used.

As repeating sections can contain repeating tables and/or other repeating sections, they can be used to render repeating element types that contain child repeating element types.

Each of these three controls for repeating element types can be added to the form from the **Controls** task pane, described in 9.3.3, "Fields and controls", on page 196.

Each of the controls must be associated with a specific element type that is allowed to repeat according to the data source. For example, our repeating table for order items is associated with the `item` element which is allowed to repeat within an `items` element. If the element type is not allowed to repeat according to the schema, InfoPath will not let you associate it with a list, repeating table, or repeating section.

9.3.2.2   Optional sections

An *Optional Section* is a section that may or may not appear in a completed form. A form user can delete the section, or add it if it is not displayed. If the section does not appear, no corresponding element will occur in the saved XML document. To render complex element types that are both repeating *and* optional, you can place a repeating section within an optional section.

9.3.3 *Fields and controls*

Each field in the form is the rendition of a particular element type in the schema. Certain aspects of a field are inherited from the element type, including the expected datatype (such as `string`, `integer` or `date`), the default value, whether or not it is required, and any additional validation constraints.

In addition, each field is associated with a particular control, which handles how the field appears to the user and in some cases what kind of data can be entered. For example, a date field might use a date picker control, which allows the user to select a date from a calendar. A complete list of the controls that can be related to individual fields is provided in Table 9-1.

Table 9-1   Types of field-related controls

Control type	Description
Text box	Plain text only, on one or more lines.
Rich text box	Text with formatting, such as fonts, sizes, bold and italics. It can also contain tables, images, and bulleted lists.
Drop-down list box	A drop-down list from which the user can choose one value.
List box	A scrollable menu of items that allows more than one value to be selected.
Date picker	A date/time box, with a displayable calendar that helps the user choose the date.
Check box	A box can either be checked or unchecked.
Option button	A set of radio buttons that can be used to select from a group of choices, with one selection being the default. Only one in the group can be selected.
Button	A button that is pushed to perform a particular action, such as resetting a value in the form, performing a calculation, or submitting the document to a SOAP Web service.
Hyperlink	A textual link to a resource (such as a Web page).
Picture	An image that links to a resource (such as a Web page).
Expression box	A read-only box that displays the result of a particular XPath expression. This is useful for displaying a calculation, such as a count or sum, or for numbering items in a repeating table.

When a simple element type is dragged from the Data Source task pane to the form, a field is created with the default control for its type, usually a text box. It is possible to change the control used by the field by right-clicking it, and clicking **Change To** from the resulting context menu. Alternatively, you can start out with the control you want by dragging it from the **Controls** task pane, shown in Figure 9-7.

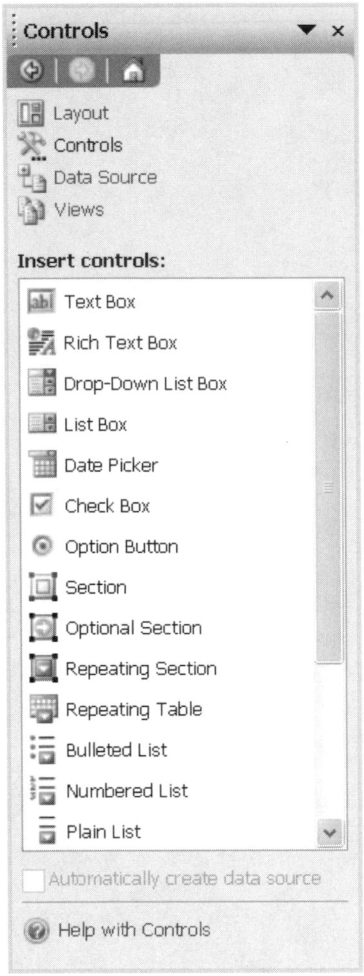

Figure 9-7   The Controls task pane

When a control is dragged to the form from the task pane, InfoPath will display a Binding dialog which asks you to specify the element type to which you want to bind the field.

It is possible to edit the properties of a field by double-clicking it. The properties differ depending on the control type, but many of them are associated with the way the data is validated or displayed. It is also possible to change the XML element type to which a field is bound. This is accomplished by right-clicking the field and clicking **Change Binding** on the resulting context menu.

9.3.4 *Validating the data*

InfoPath validates field values as the user enters them. Fields that contain errors are marked with a red dashed border. This allows the user to correct the error immediately rather than waiting until she saves the document.

There are three levels of validation in InfoPath: schema validation, declarative validation and script-based validation. Values entered into a field must be valid at all three levels in order to be accepted.

9.3.4.1   Schema-based constraints

XML Schema allows you to specify constraints on a document. Some are related to the document's structure, such as the number and order of child elements that may appear in the content of an element. Others are related to the content of an individual element. A schema can constrain:

- the datatype of a value (e.g. string, integer, date)
- whether a value is required
- the minimum and maximum value
- the minimum and maximum length of the value, or the number of digits
- the list of possible valid values

In addition, you can specify patterns (in the form of regular expressions) to which the values must conform.

9.3.4.2   Field-based constraints

InfoPath allows you to declare further constraints on data. It is not possible to override or loosen the constraints specified by the schema, but you may add new constraints. This is useful if the schema is not restrictive enough, or if you want to enforce constraints that cannot be expressed in a schema definition.

One common example is known as a *co-constraint*. In it, the validity of one field depends on the value (or presence) of another field.

To declare additional constraints on a field:

1. Right-click the field and click **Properties** on the resulting context menu.
2. On the **Data** tab, click **Data Validation**.
3. Click **Add**.

This brings up the **Data Validation** dialog shown in Figure 9-8. This dialog takes you through expressing these constraints in an intuitive way. A constraint can specify that a value must:

- be equal to, greater than or less than a specific value, or the value of another field
- be present or absent
- contain or begin with (or not) a specific string

You can specify multiple constraints and join them using either "and" or "or". You can also control the way the user is notified if there is an error, and provide an error message.

Note that a constraint is not limited to a single field. You can specify multiple constraints on multiple fields in the same data validation rule, even though that validation will be associated with a particular field.

For highly complex validation, InfoPath allows an Office developer to write custom scripts that can be run when the form user opens a document, places the cursor on a field, or leaves a field.

9.3.5 *Displaying and formatting the data*

InfoPath gives you quite a lot of control over the look and feel of the form. You can format any of the text in the form, such as the table titles and field labels. You can alter the color scheme or background color used in the form by clicking **Color Schemes** or **Background Color** on the **Format** menu.

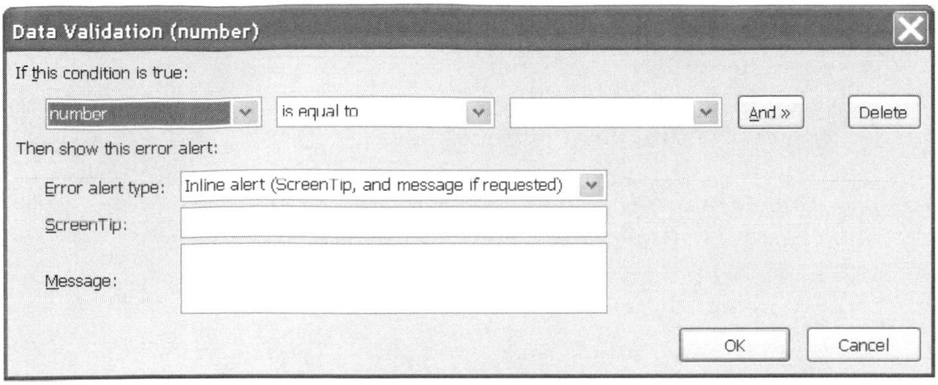

Figure 9-8   The Data Validation dialog

As for the data itself, there are several different ways to customize its formatting and appearance:

- You can change the font, size or style in which the data appears by clicking **Font** on the **Format** menu or using the task bar.
- You can change the way the data is formatted by right-clicking the field, clicking **Properties**, then **Format**. This allows options similar to those in Excel; for example, choosing to display a date as MM-DD-YYYY, or displaying a comma separator in a number.
- Right-click the field, click **Properties**, then **Display**. Here are other options related to displaying the data, such as placeholder text, whether text should be wrapped, and how the data should be aligned. The options available depend on the control type.

9.3.5.1   Conditional formatting

With some controls, you can use *conditional formatting* to specify that a data value should be displayed in a certain color or style if a condition is met. This is useful as a signal to the user that, for example:

- A financial number is negative rather than positive (often displayed in red).

- A data value is exceptionally high or low, indicating a possibly invalid value.
- An item is urgent and requires immediate attention.

To use conditional formatting:

1. Double-click the field to display its properties.
2. On the **Display** tab, click **Conditional Formatting**.
3. Click **Add**. This brings up the **Conditional Format** dialog shown in Figure 9-9.

This dialog is similar to the **Data Validation** dialog in that it allows you to specify one or more conditions. If the conditions, collectively, are true, the formatting designated in the dialog is applied. Multiple conditions can be added to a single field.

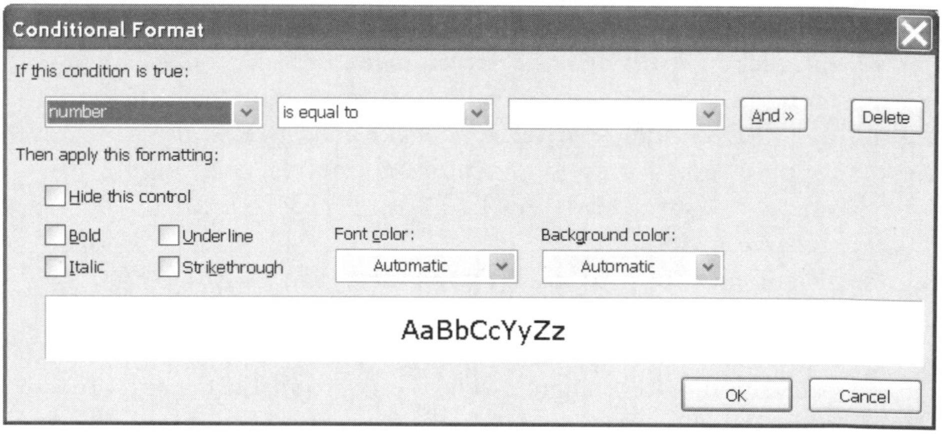

Figure 9-9   The Conditional Format dialog

9.3.6 *Creating a new form*

So far, we have worked with a form that already exists. When creating a new form, there are actually six ways to get started:

- Modify an existing form. You can adapt an existing form to your needs.

- Load a schema. If you already have a schema, you can load it and base the form design on it.
- Use an XML example. InfoPath will infer a schema from an example XML document.
- Start from a database. InfoPath will infer a schema from an Access or SQL Server database.
- Start from a Web service. InfoPath will infer a schema from the result of a call to a SOAP Web service.
- Start with a blank slate. You can start from scratch, creating the schema manually.

Each of these methods is discussed in the following sections.

9.3.6.1   Customizing an existing form

InfoPath comes with some excellent examples that exhibit all of the form design features. It is well worth looking through the examples to get a full appreciation for InfoPath's capabilities. It is possible to customize these examples as well. To do this:

1. Bring up the **Design a Form** task pane.
2. Click **Customize a Sample**.
3. Select a form of interest. This will open it in design mode.

Tip   If you want to use one of these examples, but want to change the structure of the XML document somewhat, you will have to save the form to a folder, as described in 9.3.9, "Saving form designs", on page 220, and edit the schema manually. You cannot modify the structure in the Data Source task pane, except to add new element types.

9.3.6.2   Loading a schema

InfoPath will accept a schema as input and fill in the data source pane with the structure allowed by the schema. This is a useful way to start if you already have a schema and want to design the form around it.

Warning   Once you have loaded a schema, modifying the schema file (`.xsd`) that you loaded has no effect on the structure in the form, and the schema cannot be modified using the **Data Source** task pane. You can, however, save the form to a folder and edit the schema manually as described in 9.3.9, "Saving form designs", on page 220.

To load a schema:

1. Bring up the **Design a Form** task pane.
2. Click **New from Data Source**.
3. Choose **XML Schema or XML data file** and click **Next**.
4. Type the location of the schema file and click **Finish**.

This will bring up a blank form, with the XML structure in the **Data Source** task pane.

Select Table			
Name	Description	Modified	Crea
ORDERS WITH MENS DEPT ITEMS		8/26/2003 6:29:45 PM	2/16,
ORDER_ITEMS		8/26/2003 4:49:58 PM	2/16,
ORDERS		8/26/2003 4:58:11 PM	2/16,
PRODUCTS		8/26/2003 4:48:18 PM	2/16,

OK	Cancel

Figure 9-10   The Select Table dialog

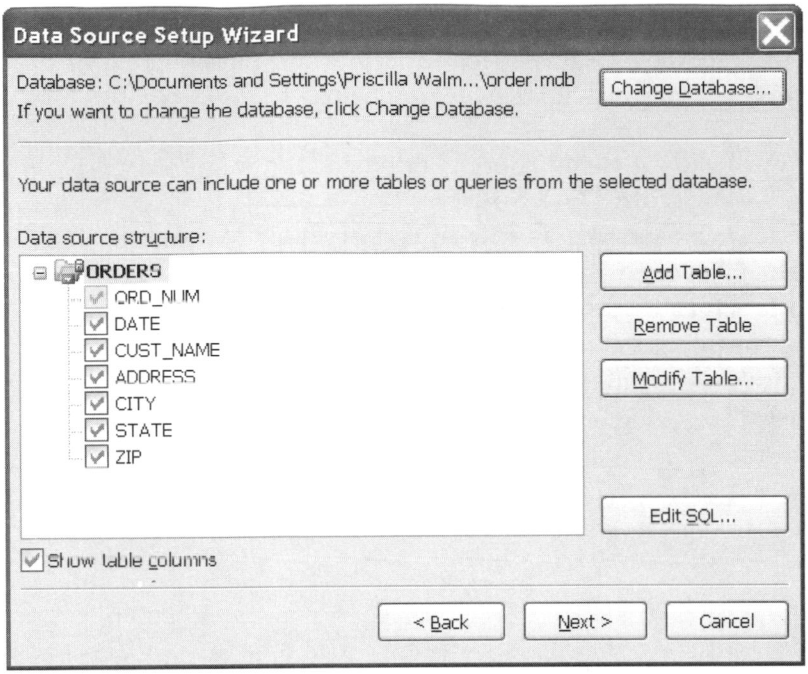

Figure 9-11   The data source structure

9.3.6.3   Using an XML example

InfoPath will infer a schema from an example XML document. It will make assumptions about the allowed children (and their order), the datatypes, and optionality based on the content of the example document. To use an XML example:

1. Bring up the **Design a Form** task pane.
2. Click **New from Data Source**.
3. Choose **XML Schema or XML data file** and click **Next**.
4. Type the location of the XML document and click **Finish**.

In this case, unlike when you load a schema, you will have an opportunity to edit the structure once it is loaded. Modifying the data source structure is discussed in 9.3.6.6, "Starting with a blank slate", on page 215.

9.3.6.4 Starting from a database

InfoPath will also allow you to specify the location of an Access or SQL Server database, from which it will infer a schema. To do this:

1. Click **Design a form** from the task pane list.
2. Click **New from Data Source**.
3. Click **Database (Microsoft SQL Server or Microsoft Office Access only)**, and click **Next**.
4. Click **Select Database** and choose a database file from the list. For this example, use order.mdb from the example files.
5. This will bring up the **Select Table** dialog shown in Figure 9-10. This dialog lists the tables, views and queries in that database.
6. Select ORDERS and click **OK**. This will display the structure of the data source, as shown in Figure 9-11.

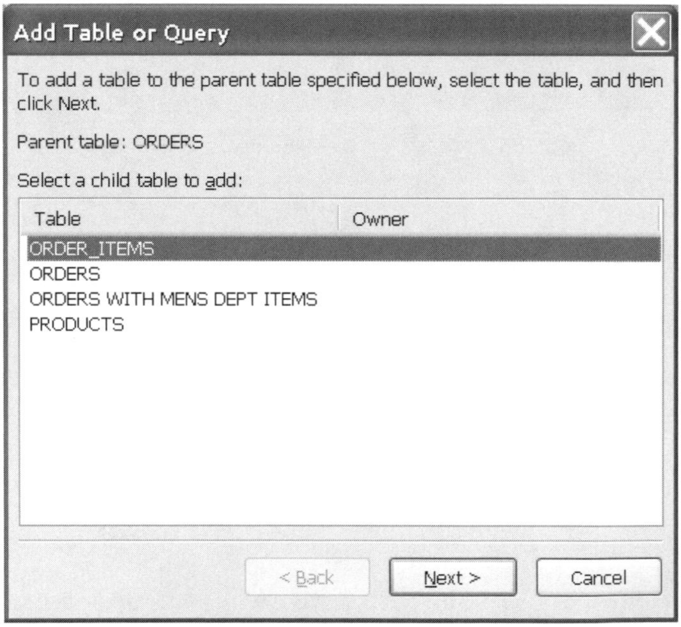

Figure 9-12 The Add Table or Query dialog

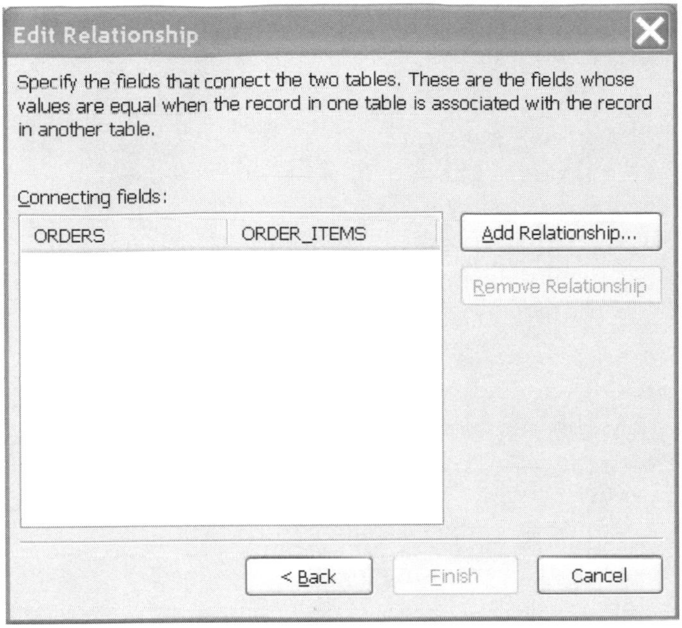

Figure 9-13   The Edit Relationship dialog

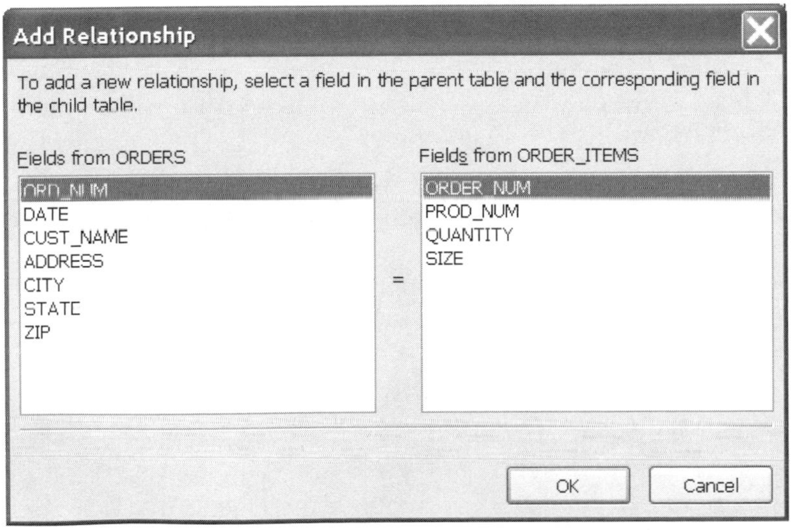

Figure 9-14   The Add Relationship dialog

The next order of business is to add the related ORDER_ITEMS table to the data source. To do this:

1. Click **Add Table**. This will bring up the **Add Table or Query** dialog shown in Figure 9-12.
2. Select ORDER_ITEMS and click **Next**. This will display the Edit Relationship dialog, shown in Figure 9-13.
3. Click **Add Relationship...**, which will in turn bring up the Add Relationship dialog, shown in Figure 9-14.
4. Select ORD_NUM from the ORDERS list, and ORDER_NUM from the ORDER_ITEMS list. This specifies the columns to be used to relate the two tables.
5. Click **OK**, which will return you to the Edit Relationship dialog, this time with the relationship between ORDERS and ORDER_ITEMS listed.
6. Click **Finish** to return to the Data Source Setup Wizard.
7. Repeat the above steps to create a relationship between ORDER_ITEMS and PRODUCTS. The PROD_NUM column of ORDER_ITEMS should be related to the NUM column of PRODUCTS.
8. Once you have returned to the Data Source Setup Wizard dialog, click **Next**. This will display a dialog like the one shown in Figure 9-15. Click **Finish**.

You now have a form with two views. One, called Query, will contain a field for each column in the main table (in this case, ORDERS), as shown in Figure 9-16. The other view, called Data Entry, will start out blank. You can switch between the two views by selecting Views on the task pane and selecting either one.

The Query view is designed for a user to specify criteria on which to search the database for records. When the user enters information into one of the fields and clicks Run Query, InfoPath will automatically switch to the Data Entry view, displaying the records that matched the criteria. The user can then edit the records and submit the changes to the database. The user can also insert a new record by clicking **New Record** on the Query view.

The Query view can be used as generated, but the Data Entry view starts out blank, so it needs to be designed. To do this:

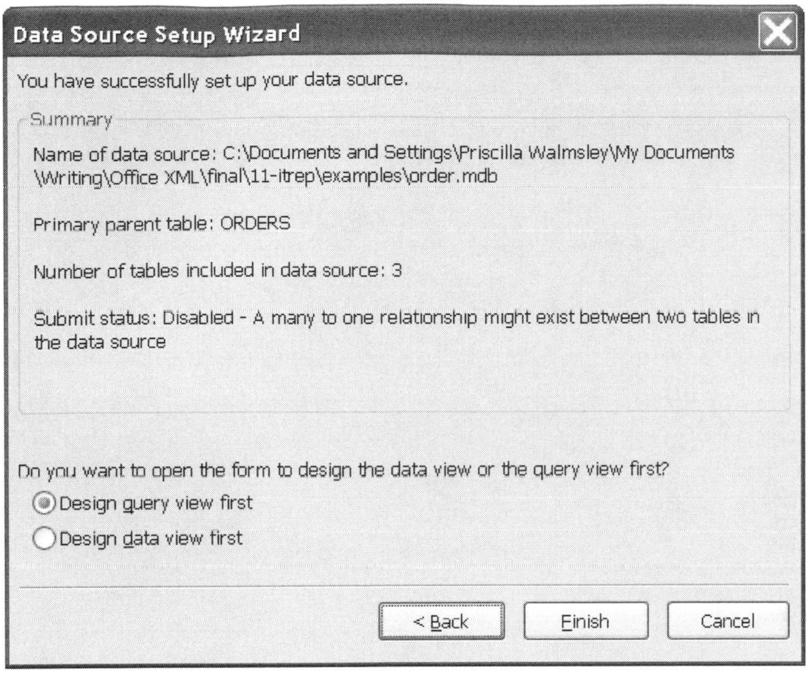

Figure 9-15   The success message

1. Switch to the Data Entry view by selecting it on the **Views** task pane.
2. Click **Data Source** on the task pane to bring up the database structure.
3. In the data source structure, the children of dataFields are intended to be used on the Data Entry view, while the children of queryFields are intended to be used on the Query view. The dataFields structure is shown in Figure 9-17.
4. Drag the d:ORDERS element type to the empty form. Click **Repeating Section** on the resulting menu.
5. Drag the individual element types under ORDERS (e.g. ORD_NUM and DATE) to the repeating section you just created.
6. Drag the ORDER_ITEMS element type to the repeating section. Click **Repeating Table** on the resulting menu.

After some reformatting and deletion of columns, you might have the form shown in Figure 9-18.

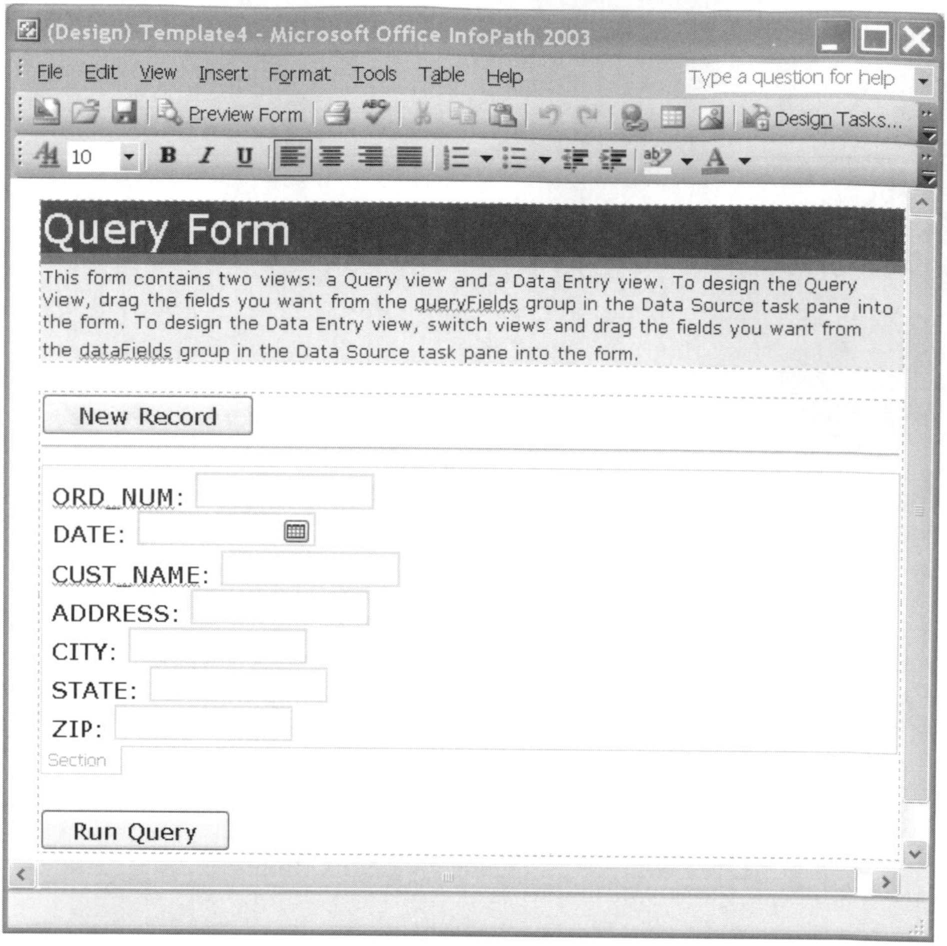

Figure 9-16   The Query view

As always, the form can be tested by clicking **Preview Form** on the toolbar. You can switch views by clicking the appropriate view name on the **View** menu. If, for example, you enter 1001 in the ORD_NUM field of the Query view and click Run Query, you will see the Data Entry view with the data for order 1001, as shown in Figure 9-19.

This particular Data Entry view does not allow the user to make changes and submit them to the database. This is because there is a many-to-one relationship between ORDER_ITEMS and PRODUCTS. If PRODUCTS were not

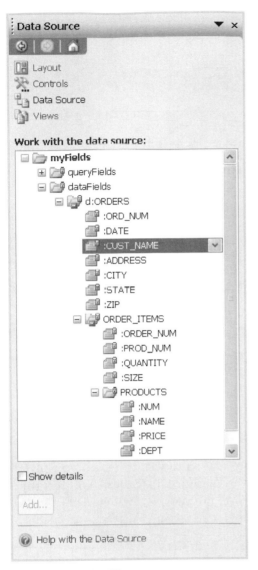

Figure 9-17 The `dataFields` structure

included in the list of tables in the data source, we would be able to add a `Submit` button that updates the database from the form.

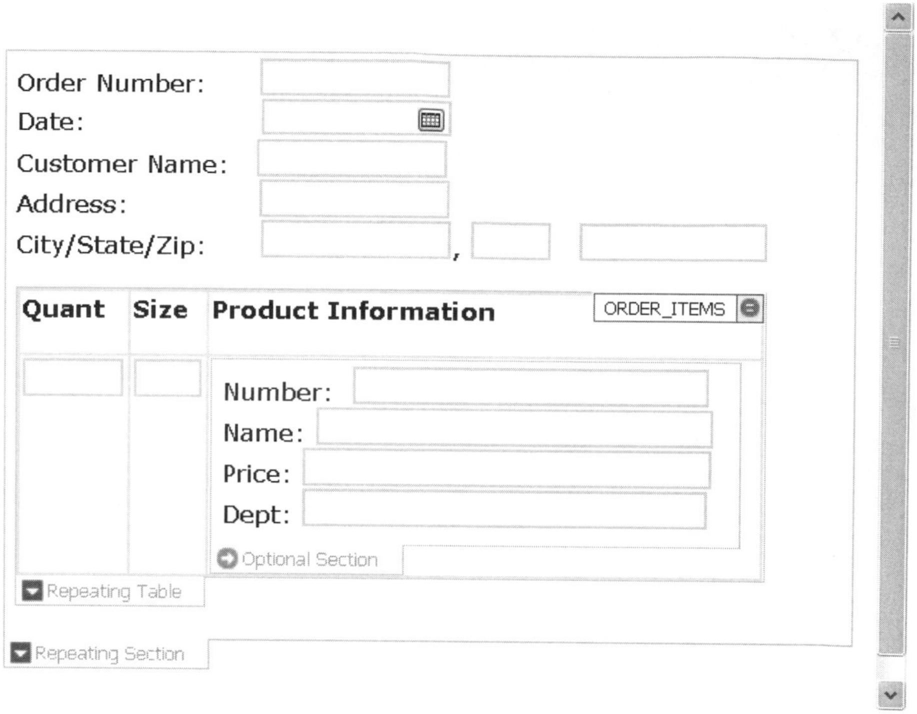

Figure 9-18   The Data Entry view

9.3.6.5   Starting from a SOAP Web service

InfoPath will also infer a schema from a Web service to which you plan to submit data, or from which you plan to receive data (or both). To do this:

1. Click **Design a form** on the task pane list.
2. Click **New from Data Source**.
3. Click **Web service**.
4. Indicate whether you plan to receive and submit data, submit data or just receive data. For this example, click **Receive data**.
5. Type the URI of the Web service. For this example, type in `http://www.xignite.com/xQuotes.asmx?wsdl`, as shown in Figure 9-20, and click **Next**.

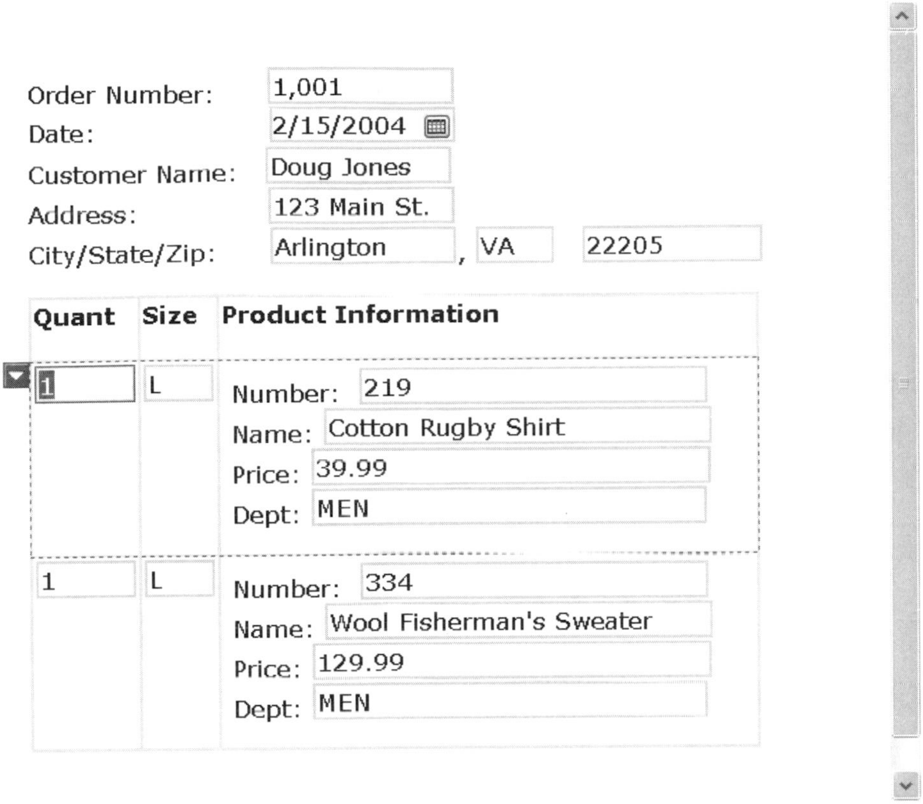

Order Number:	1,001		
Date:	2/15/2004		
Customer Name:	Doug Jones		
Address:	123 Main St.		
City/State/Zip:	Arlington	, VA	22205

Quant	Size	Product Information
1	L	Number: 219
		Name: Cotton Rugby Shirt
		Price: 39.99
		Dept: MEN
1	L	Number: 334
		Name: Wool Fisherman's Sweater
		Price: 129.99
		Dept: MEN

Figure 9-19   The Data Entry view with data

6. This will bring up a list of all the operations for that Web service. Select **GetMarketSummary**, as shown in Figure 9-21, and click **Next**.

7. InfoPath will then display a summary dialog, shown in Figure 9-22. Click **Finish**.

Starting from a Web service is similar to starting from a database, in that two views are generated: a Query view and a Data Entry view. If there are parameters to pass to the Web service, you can drag them to the Query view. In this case, no parameters are required.

You can then design the Data Entry form based on the results of the Web service. You do this by dragging element types from the dataFields data

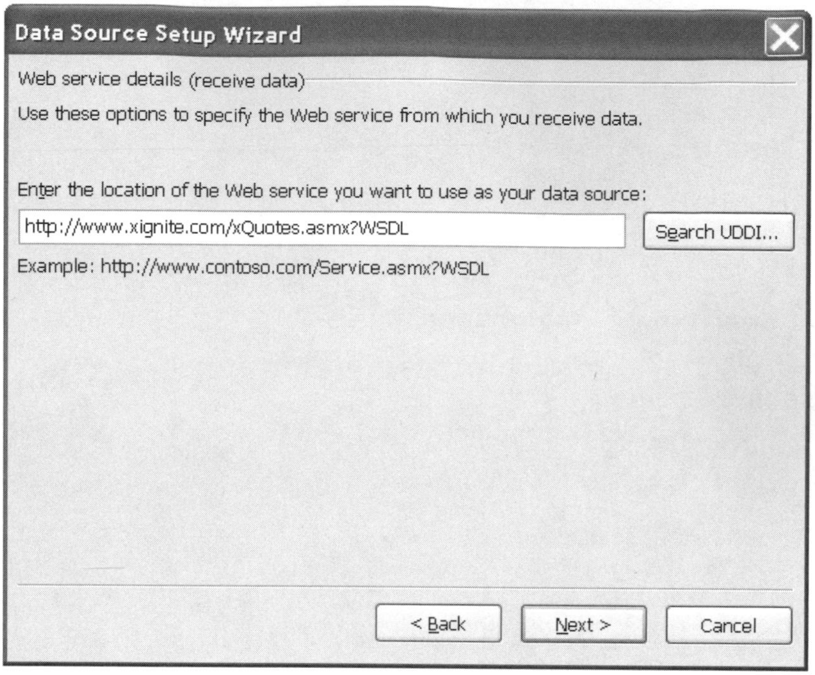

Figure 9-20   Entering the Web service location

source onto the form, just as in the database example in the previous section. The result might look like Figure 9-23.

This example simply receives data from a Web service and displays it. You can also allow users to fill out a form, then submit it to a Web service. For example, a purchase order might be filled in using InfoPath and then submitted to a Web service for processing by the ordering system. You can also receive data from one Web service, then submit it to another. In our

Data Source Setup Wizard ☒

The Web service that you selected has the following operations for providing the XML data that your form receives.

Select an operation:

GetIndices
GetTop
GetTopLosers
GetTopGainers
GetTopMovers
GetMarketChart
GetMarketSummary
GetQuotesHistoricalRange
GetQuotesHistoricalAsOf
GetQuotesHistorical
GetQuoteHistorical
GetFundQuote
GetQuote
GetQuotes
GetQuickQuotes

Description of operation:

This operation returns the current market level for the Dow, Nasdaq and S&P indices as well as the NYSE and NASDAQ volumes and the 10 Year Bond index.

[< Back] [Next >] [Cancel]

Figure 9-21   Choosing an operation

example, we might want to pass the retrieved market summary data to a Web service that updates our internal database with the statistics.

Caution   InfoPath does not support all Web services. It will not work with REST Web services or with SOAP Web services that use RPC-style processing rather than document-style processing. In addition, it will not work with Web services that return schema information with the result set.

9.3.6.6   Starting with a blank slate

If none of the above options is appropriate, you can start without a schema and construct it yourself. There are two ways to do this: you can manually create the structure in the data source task pane, or you can have InfoPath add the element types as you drag controls to the form. The advantage of

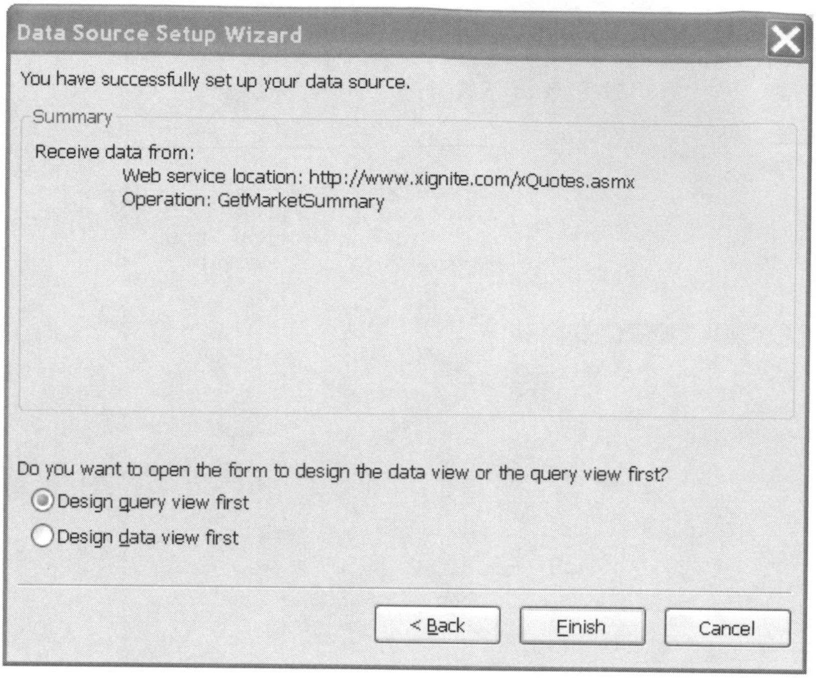

Figure 9-22   Summary dialog

either approach is that the structure is highly flexible; you can tweak it as you design the form.

To manually construct the schema:

1. Click **Design a form** on the task pane list.
2. Click **New Blank Form**.
3. Click **Data Source**.

The data source will be displayed with a root element type `myFields`. From there, you can add children to `myFields` using the **Add** button on the task pane or by right-clicking the desired parent and clicking **Add**. Adding a field brings up the **Add Field or Group** dialog shown in Figure 9-24.

The dialog allows you to specify the **Name** of the item to be added to the schema and its so-called **Type**, which is one of the following designations:

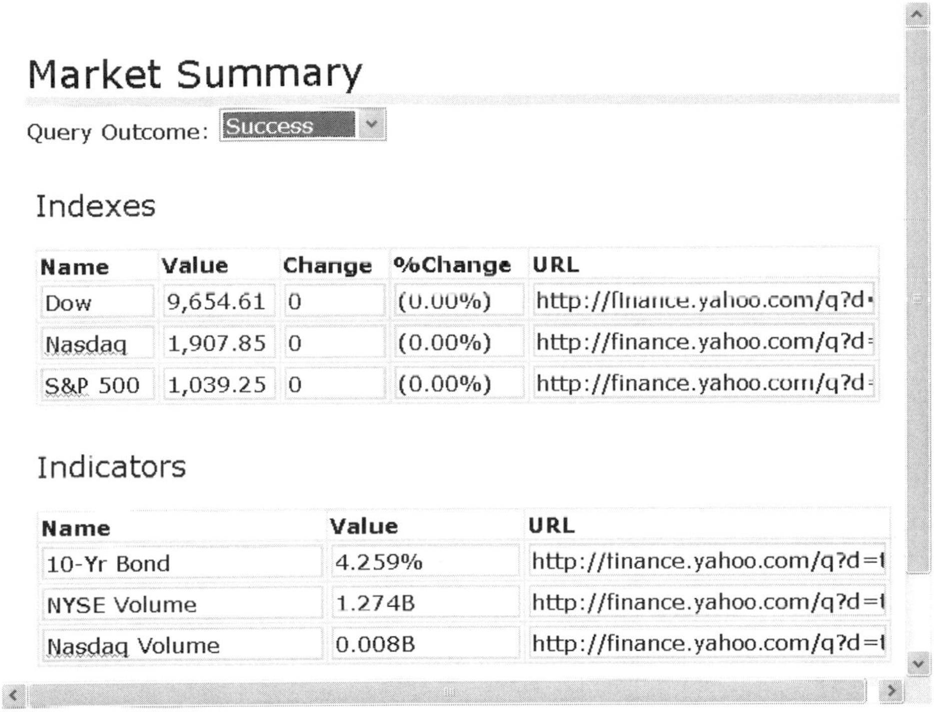

Market Summary

Query Outcome: Success

Indexes

Name	Value	Change	%Change	URL
Dow	9,654.61	0	(0.00%)	http://finance.yahoo.com/q?d▪
Nasdaq	1,907.85	0	(0.00%)	http://finance.yahoo.com/q?d▪
S&P 500	1,039.25	0	(0.00%)	http://finance.yahoo.com/q?d▪

Indicators

Name	Value	URL
10-Yr Bond	4.259%	http://finance.yahoo.com/q?d=t
NYSE Volume	1.274B	http://finance.yahoo.com/q?d=t
Nasdaq Volume	0.008B	http://finance.yahoo.com/q?d=t

Figure 9-23   A market summary form

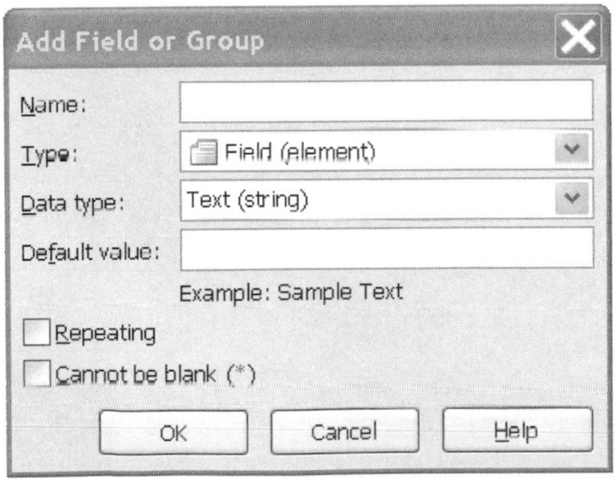

Add Field or Group

Name:

Type: Field (element)

Data type: Text (string)

Default value:

Example: Sample Text

☐ Repeating

☐ Cannot be blank (*)

OK   Cancel   Help

Figure 9-24   The **Add Field or Group** dialog

Attribute

Means that the added item is an attribute. If placed in the form it will be rendered as a field.

Field

Means that the added item is a child element type that can only contain data. If placed in the form it will be rendered as a field.

Group

Means that the added item is a child element type that could contain other elements (i.e. be a subtree). If placed in the form it will be rendered as a group of fields, either a section or a table.

You can also indicate whether an item is repeating. And for Attribute and Field you can also specify a **Data type** and **Default value** and whether the content or value can be empty (i.e. left blank in the form).

Caution   Despite its name, the **Add Field or Group** dialog does **not** add a field or group to the form. You can do that by dragging the added element type or attribute from the task pane.

From the **Data Source** task pane, you can also delete and move element types and attributes, and modify their properties.

The alternative is to have InfoPath create the structure based on the form you design. InfoPath will insert element types with generic names (field1, field2, etc.) as you drag controls to the form. If you add a repeating table or section, it will add an element type with child element types to the structure. You can modify the structure as desired, including changing properties such as the name and datatype.

9.3.1   *Views*

Multiple views can be created for the same form. For example, it may be useful to have one set of users edit some fields, while another set of users edits other fields. One view may present summary level data, while another allows editing of line item data. One view might be more appropriate for printing, while another is more appropriate for editing.

The views can be completely different, with different fields, and a different look and feel. The only connection is the underlying XML document. By default, InfoPath creates one view named View 1 when you begin form design. You can add views from the **Views** task pane, shown in Figure 9-25.

Figure 9-25 The Views task pane

The **Views** task pane allows you to add and delete views, as well as switch between them. You can also modify the properties of the view by double-clicking its name in the task pane. Properties of a view include its name, background color, default fonts, and print settings. You can designate one of the views as the default, which is brought up when the document is opened. In edit mode, the form user can switch between views by clicking the view name on the **View** main menu.

9.3.8 *Allowing users to submit forms*

Users can fill in forms and save them as XML documents on their file system. Those XML documents can then be emailed, moved to a server, or passed to an application for processing.

InfoPath can eliminate the extra step of passing the XML file around by allowing users to submit their documents directly from InfoPath. To set this up:

1. Click **Controls** on the task pane to bring up a list of controls.
2. Drag a **button** onto the form.
3. Right click the button, and click **Button Properties** on the resulting menu. This will bring up the **Button Properties** dialog shown in Figure 9-26.
4. Select **Submit** from the **Action** list. This will bring up the **Submitting Forms** dialog shown in Figure 9-27.

From here, you can choose to submit the form to a SOAP Web service or a database (if the original data source was a database), or you can write a custom script for submission. The custom script could be used, for example, to email the completed form to a specific person, or to place it at a specified location on a server.

9.3.9 *Saving form designs*

If you saved a form that you were designing in the previous section, you may have noticed that it was saved with a .xsn extension. That extension identifies a *form template*, a set of documents related to the form that is compressed and stored in a Microsoft cabinet archive.[3]

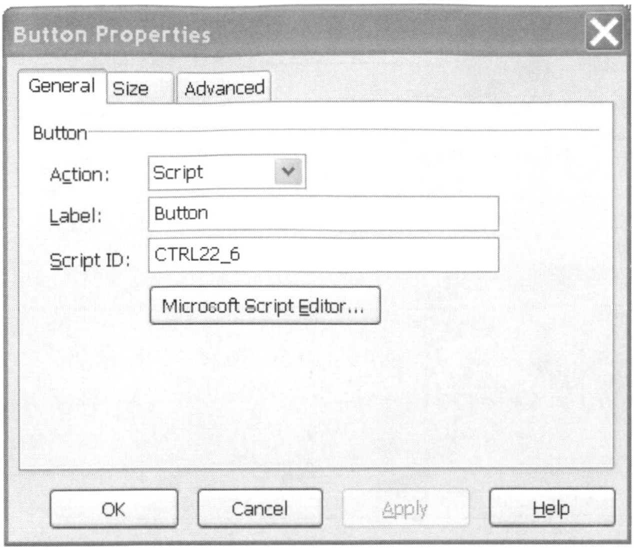

Figure 9-26 The Button Properties dialog

Table 9-2 describes the components of the form template for our order form example.

There are two ways to save a form and its related files. The default, when you create a new form or adapt a sample form, is to save all the components in the same cabinet (.xsn) archive. A file can be extracted from the .xsn file by opening it in InfoPath and resaving it, or by using cabinet archive utilities.

Another method of saving a form is by clicking **Extract Form Files** on the **File** menu. After you have chosen a folder, InfoPath will save all the component files, uncompressed, in that folder. You can reopen a form from

---

3. Cabinet archives normally have a .cab extension. However, cabinet software can also be used to process .xsn archives.

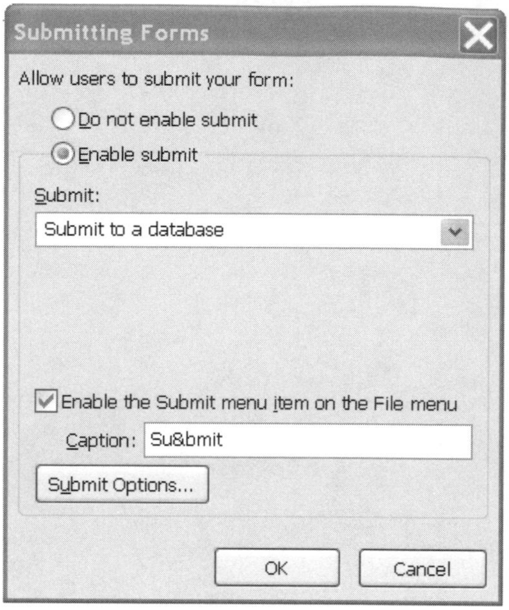

Figure 9-27 The Submitting Forms dialog

Table 9-2 Components of the order form template

Extension or fileid	Description
manifest.xsf	An XML directory of the form template. It identifies the files and contains supplementary information (beyond the stylesheets) for rendering views, validating input, and supporting structural changes during editing. (A schema for .xsf is available from Microsoft.)
*.xsd	The all-important schema definition, plus a common library of schema components. The schema defines a document type named order. There could be multiple schema documents if a schema definition included them.
*.xsl	Stylesheets: InfoPath provides one for each view.
*.gif	Graphics files for decorating the views.
*.js, .vbs, .dll, .exe	Scripts and program code written by the designer or provided by InfoPath.
template.xml	An empty order XML document.
sampledata.xml	An order XML document with initial placeholder data.

a folder, by opening the manifest (.xsf) file. When you resave it, it will save it to the folder rather than to a .xsn file.

Warning   *Create a separate folder for each form. Saving multiple forms in the same directory will cause some files to be overwritten.*

Tip   The advantage of saving the files to a folder rather than a form template file is that you can more easily view or edit the documents in a text editor or XML editor. For example, that is the only way to modify a schema once it has been loaded into a form.

9.3.10 *Publishing forms*

Once you have completed your form design, you may wish to roll it out to a number of users. To do this, you use the publishing feature of InfoPath. Clicking on **Publish** on the **File** menu will bring up the Publishing Wizard, which will guide you through the process.

You can choose to publish the form to a shared folder on a computer or network, a Web server, or a SharePoint form library. In the latter case, form users can open a form library and select the form from the **Fill out a form** task pane.

Tip   InfoPath has other uses besides the intended one that we described. For XML documents that are suitable for rendition as forms, it can serve as a data viewer and editor. It can also serve as a visual schema design tool for those kinds of documents.

Using scripts with forms

- Associating scripts with events
- Using Script Editor
- The InfoPath object model

Chapter

10

You can get more out of InfoPath by adding custom validation and calculations that aren't possible through the product's user interface. This chapter describes how to write scripts and associate them with InfoPath forms to add this extra functionality.

Skills required   *This chapter requires an understanding of XPath (see Chapter 17, "XPath primer", on page 384 and Chapter 24, "XML Path Language (XPath)", on page 498) and either VBScript or JScript.*

10.1 | Why use scripts?

Using a script, you can manipulate both the InfoPath user interface and the abstract XML document underlying the form. You can also call external code to add almost any functionality to a form. This can be useful in a broad range of situations, for example:

227

- More complex validation. The standard validation functionality of InfoPath is quite powerful, but sometimes there are constraints that cannot be expressed using the standard features. For example, constraints that involve more than two fields in the form, or ones that require a calculation to be performed.
- Calculations. Values, such as totals and averages, can be calculated based on other values specified by the user.
- Custom error messages. Custom error messages can be created that are more meaningful than the basic ones provided by InfoPath.
- Access to secondary data from a database, Web service or other XML document. A script is not required if you simply want to read and write an entire XML document from an external data source. However, a script *is* required if you want to use the secondary data source for validation, or to complete sections of the form. Because this is such a common use case, all of Chapter 11, "Using secondary data sources with forms", on page 250 is devoted to it.
- Custom user interface components. Using a script, you can add custom toolbars, menus and task panes, optimizing the InfoPath environment for a specific set of users.

Scripts can be executed when the user clicks a button on the form, when the user changes a value, when a form is first loaded, or in response to a number of other events. In this chapter we will provide a number of examples of InfoPath scripts, focusing mostly on the XML aspects rather than user interface customization.

10.2 | A simple sample script

Let's start with a very simple example to show the basics of script creation. To implement a simple script that displays a message for the user:

1. Start with a blank form, by clicking **New Blank Form** on the **Design a Form** task pane.
2. Click **Controls** on the **Design Tasks** task pane.

3. Drag a **Button** from the list of controls to the blank form.
4. Right-click the button in the form and click **Button Proper-ties**. This will bring up the **Button Properties** dialog shown in Figure 10-1. From this dialog, you can change the label displayed on the button, as well as the associated script ID, which is by default assigned a unique name like CTRL1_5.
5. Click **Microsoft Script Editor**. This will bring up Script Editor, which is the software used to create and edit script functions. Near the bottom of the script file (shown in Figure 10-2) is a function named something like CTRL1_5::OnClick, where CTRL1_5 is the button's name. The comment //Write your code here is displayed as a prompt.
6. Type the following line into the script body:
   ```
   XDocument.UI.Alert("This is your first script")
   ```
7. Save the script by clicking **Save** on the **File** menu in Script Editor, and exit Script Editor.
8. Save the form itself by clicking **Save** on the **File** menu in InfoPath.

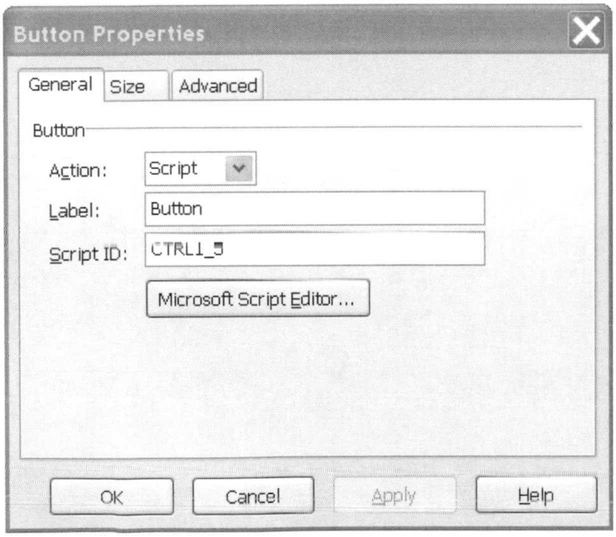

Figure 10-1   The Button Properties dialog

Now, test your script by filling out the form you just created. The easiest way to do this is to click **Preview Form** on the toolbar. When clicking the **Button** button, you should get a dialog saying "This is your first script", as shown in Figure 10-3.

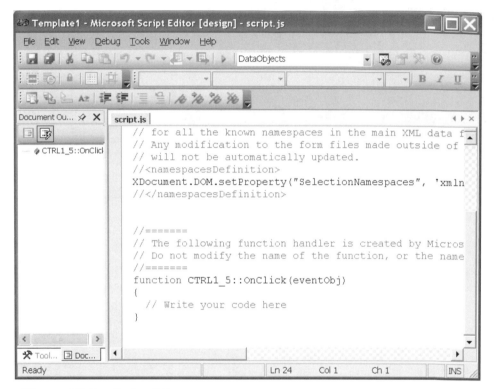

Figure 10-2   Script Editor

Figure 10-3   Output of the simple script

Let's take a closer look at the script in the example. The name of the function into which you inserted your code is something like `CTRL1_5::OnClick`. `CTRL1_5` is the script ID of the button, and `OnClick` is the name of the event that causes that function to be executed. We will look more closely at events in section 10.4, "Events", on page 232.

The single line of code refers to the object `XDocument`, which represents the current document that is displayed in the form. It then refers to the document's user interface via the property `UI`. Finally, it calls the `Alert` method of that `UI` object, passing it one parameter that is the string "This is your first script". The `Alert` method is used to display a message.

10.3 | Script files and forms

As you may have noticed, the script file that appears in Script Editor contains other functions in addition to the one you are editing at the moment. Each form has at least one script file associated with it that contains all the necessary functions for that form.

InfoPath scripts can be written in JScript or VBScript, the default being JScript. All of the examples in this chapter are written in JScript. These two languages are similar and are often embedded in HTML to enhance Web pages. To change the scripting language for a form, click **Options** on the **Tools** menu and click the **Design** tab. Under **Scripting**, choose whether you want to write scripts in JScript or VBScript.

Script files can contain a list of functions for that form, as well as variable definitions and comments. Some functions may be associated with a particular field or button, while others are associated with the form as a whole. In addition, you can create a library of added functions in the script file in order to reuse code.

When a form is saved, the script file is stored within the .xsn file. If you use the **Extract Form Files** command to extract the files associated with the form, the script file will appear as a separate file whose extension is .js. By default, it will be named `script.js`.

It is possible to create additional script files and associate them with the form using the **Resource Manager** which is accessible from the **Tools** menu. This is useful for sharing functions across multiple forms. However, you will not be able to edit the additional script files using Script Editor;

you will have to edit them in another tool such as a text editor or Visual Studio.

10.4 | Events

In our previous example, we associated a script function with a button, so that every time the button was clicked, the script function was executed. There are a number of different kinds of events that trigger script execution in addition to the clicking of a button. They include positioning the cursor on a field, changing a value, loading a form, switching views, and more. The InfoPath events are listed in Table 10-1.

Table 10-1   Types of events

Event type	Description
OnClick	The user clicks a button on the form.
OnBeforeChange	The user changes the value of a field (before the change is accepted).
OnValidate	The value in a field is validated, after it is changed.
OnAfterChange	The user changes the value of a field (after the change is accepted and validated).
OnLoad	A document is opened with the form.
OnSwitchView	The user switches views.
OnAfterImport	The user queries the data source to import new data.
OnSubmitRequest	The user submits the form.
OnVersionUpgrade	The user opens a document that was created using an older version of the form.

A script function may be associated with a particular event, and in some cases a particular field or button. In the script, the name of the function will indicate the event. For example:

- A function named CTRL1_5::OnClick will be executed when the CTRL1_5 button is clicked.
- A function named msoxd__item_number_attr::OnValidate will be executed when the item number field is validated.
- A function named XDocument::OnLoad will be executed when a new document is loaded.

You don't have to specify these function names yourself. They are generated by XPath when you launch Script Editor and they should not be changed. However, it is useful to understand their meaning when editing the script. Throughout the rest of the chapter, we will see examples of working with these events.

10.5 | Launching Script Editor

In our previous example, we used Script Editor to create the simple script function. Script Editor is a separate application that is launched from Info-Path when the user needs to create or edit a script function. In our example, we launched it from the **Button Properties** dialog, and it automatically created an empty function associated with that button.

There are a number of other ways to launch Script Editor, depending on the event that will trigger the function to be executed:

- If you are creating a script function associated with validation or modification of a particular field, you can launch Script Editor from the field's **Data Validation** dialog. This is explained in 10.7.2, "Launching Script Editor", on page 239.
- If you are creating a script function for the OnLoad or OnSwitchView event, you can click either of these events on the **Script** submenu of the **Tools** menu, shown in Figure 10-4.
- If you are creating a script function for the OnSubmitRequest event, you can launch Script Editor from the **Submitting**

Forms dialog that was described in 9.3.8, "Allowing users to submit forms", on page 220.

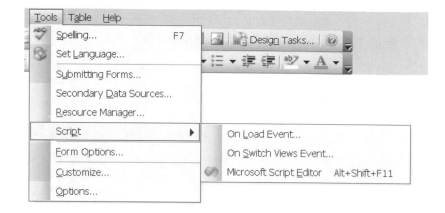

Figure 10-4   The Script submenu

In all these cases, InfoPath creates an empty "stub" function for you, and you just need to fill in the function body. Script Editor can also be launched directly from the **Script** submenu of the **Tools** menu.

10.6 | The InfoPath object model

Microsoft provides an object model for use in InfoPath scripts. The object model allows you to programmatically manipulate the underlying XML document, as well as the user interface itself. Figure 10-5 shows the basic hierarchy of the object model. Only the most commonly used objects are shown.

At the top of the object model hierarchy is the Application object which represents the application itself. From Application, you can access the open InfoPath windows via the Windows property, as well as the open XML documents, via the XDocuments property.

In most scripts you will be interested in performing some operation that involves the currently displayed XML document, which can be accessed via the XDocument object. For example, in 10.2, "A simple sample script", on

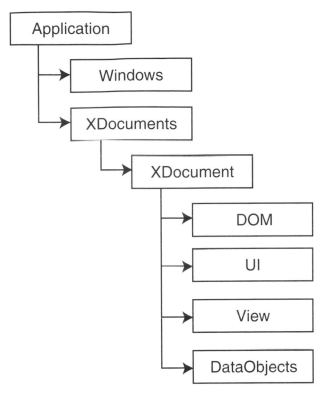

Figure 10-5 InfoPath object hierarchy

page 228, we used the method call XDocument.UI.Alert to display a message box within the current document. The XDocument object has a number of properties that are useful in scripts:

- DOM can be used to get an XML representation of the document. This is discussed further in the next section.
- UI can be used to display message boxes and other dialogs.
- View can be used to switch views, determine what view is currently displayed, and which fields are currently selected.
- DataObjects can be used to access secondary data sources, which are described in 11.1, "Defining a secondary data source", on page 252.

In addition, there are *event objects* that are passed to scripts as parameters when an event, such as clicking a button or changing a value, occurs.

10.6.1 *Using the XML document object model*

Many scripts involve querying or manipulating the XML document behind the form. This is accomplished by accessing the DOM (Document Object Model) of the XML document. DOM is an open W3C standard model for accessing XML documents. Microsoft implements the W3C standard and also provides some convenient extensions.

DOM is made up of quite a large number of objects, and therefore cannot be covered in a single chapter. However, we will provide you with a series of examples for common use cases. You can browse the complete DOM object model using Script Editor, as described in the next section.

You can access the DOM for the currently displayed XML document by specifying XDocument.DOM. The XDocument.DOM property represents the document as a whole. From there, you can access the nodes of the document.

Nodes are elements, attributes and other XML constructs such as comments and processing instructions. In addition, the character data content of an element is considered a node, specifically a *text node*. Nodes are arranged in a hierarchy and may have children and parents.

Using the DOM, you can select nodes from the document using an XPath expression. Alternatively, you can traverse the document via the nodes and their parent/child relationships to retrieve the elements and attributes of interest. You can also use the DOM to update the value of existing nodes, and insert new ones. We will look at each of these uses in turn.

10.6.2 *Browsing the object model*

The InfoPath object model is fully documented in the *InfoPath Developer's Reference*, which is included in the InfoPath help. This document is a reference guide for the various events and objects and their associated properties and methods.

In addition, you can browse the InfoPath object model interactively in Script Editor using Object Browser. If Object Browser is not already displayed, point to **Other Windows** on the **View** menu, then click **Object Browser**.

In Object Browser, you can traverse the object model much as you might in Windows Explorer. When an object is selected in the left-hand pane, its members (functions and properties) are displayed to the right, as shown in Figure 10-6. The pane at the bottom of Object Browser displays further information about the component, often including a description of its purpose.

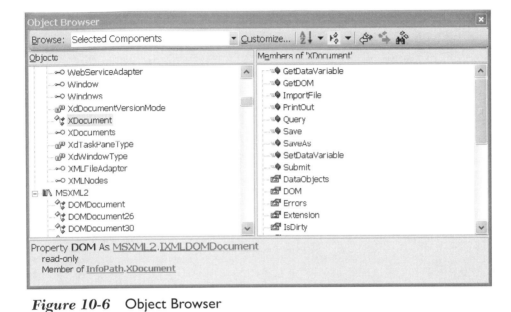

Figure 10-6   Object Browser

10.7 | Using scripts for validation

One of the most common uses for scripts is to perform validation, either because custom error messages are desired, or because the validation involves complex business rules. In this section we will look at three different examples of validation scripts. In the process, we will learn more about JScript as well as the InfoPath object model. All of the examples in this chapter can be found in the order_scripts.xsn example file. This form, shown in Figure 10-7, is a slightly modified version of our order form from the previous chapter.

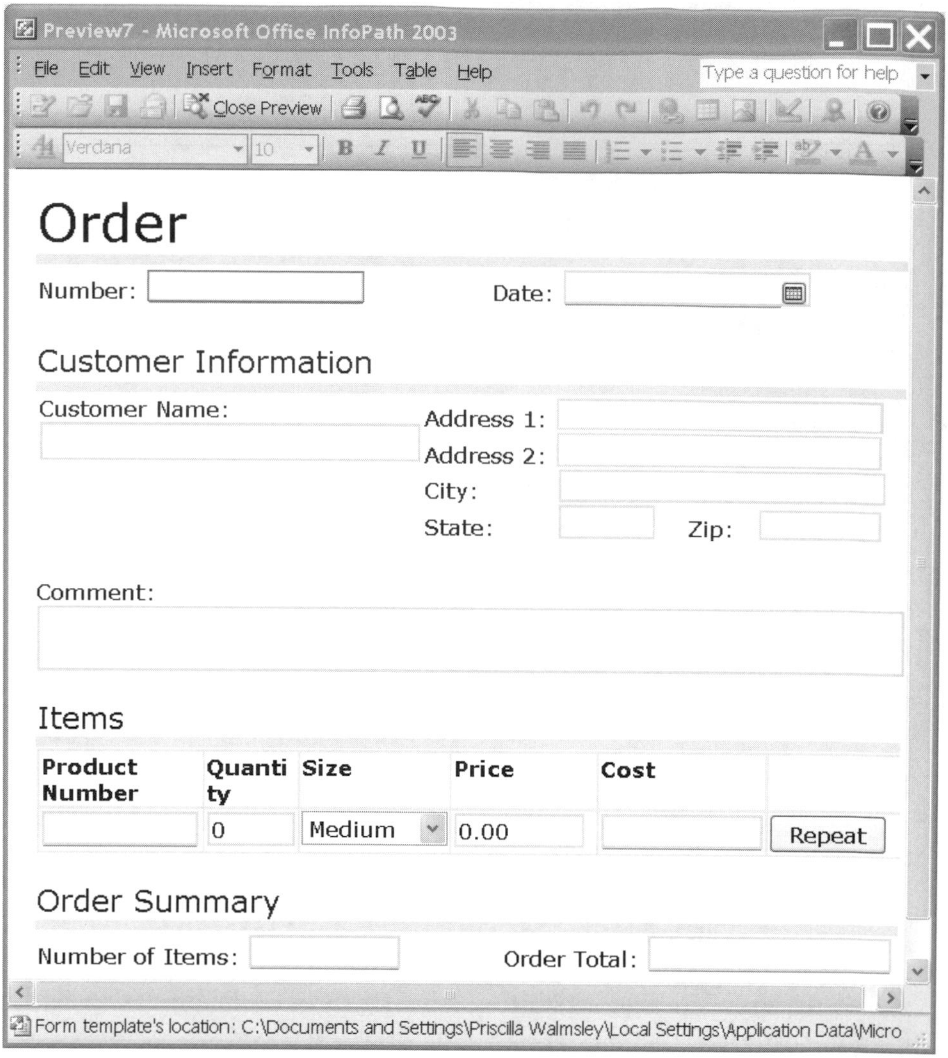

Figure 10-7   Revised Order Form (order_scripts.xsn)

10.7.1 *Validation-related events*

Validation is usually associated with either the OnBeforeChange event or the OnValidate event.

`OnBeforeChange`

> The `OnBeforeChange` event occurs after the user has made a change to a value, but before the change is accepted. If there is an error in the value, the change will be undone and the field will return to its previous value. This is useful if you want to prevent a user from specifying a field unless another field is specified or has a certain value. For example, you may want to prevent the user from specifying a second address line unless the first address line is completed.

`OnValidate`

> The `OnValidate` event occurs after the user has changed the value in the field, and after it has been validated against the schema. If an error is reported, the change will stay, but the field will be underlined in red to identify it as an error.

In addition to these events, it is possible to perform some validation when the user submits the form by relating the script to the `OnSubmitRequest` event. However, the user will not be warned of the error until the form is completed. Also, this works only for submit, not save. As a result, a user may unknowingly save a document with errors in it.

10.7.2 *Launching Script Editor*

To create or modify a script function associated with validation, you can launch Script Editor from the field's **Data Validation** dialog. If a script function already exists for that field, for that event, the cursor will be positioned at that script function. If one does not exist, a stub will be created, as we saw in our previous example.

To launch Script Editor to show our first example:

1. Open `order_scripts.xsn` in design mode.
2. Right-click the **Product Number** field and click **Text Box Properties**.
3. On the **Data** tab, click **Data Validation**. This brings up the **Data Validation** dialog shown in Figure 10-8.

4. At the bottom of the **Data Validation** dialog, select the event you wish to use as a trigger for the script, in this case `OnValidate`, and click **Edit** to launch Script Editor.

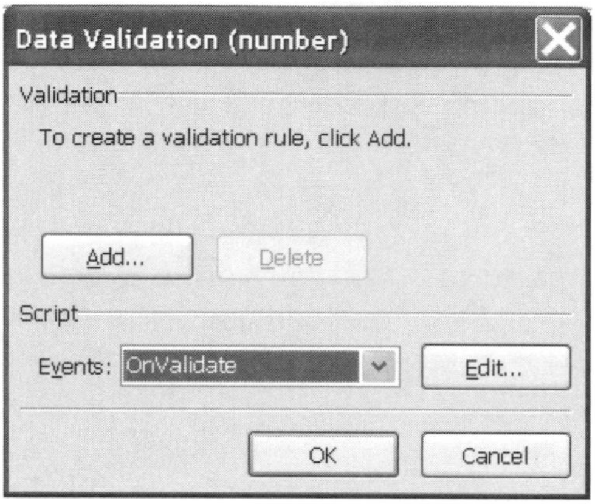

Figure 10-8   The Data Validation dialog

10.7.3   *A simple validation function*

You should now be in Script Editor with your cursor positioned on the first line of the script shown in Example 10-1. The purpose of this script is to ensure that the product number is less than 1000. This validation could also be done without a script, but we have chosen a simple example to start with.

Example 10-1. Product number validation

```
function msoxd__item_number_attr::OnValidate(eventObj)
{
  // Make sure it is less than 1000
  if (eventObj.Site.nodeTypedValue > 999)
    eventObj.ReportError(eventObj.Site,
      "Invalid product number: " +
      eventObj.Site.nodeTypedValue +
      "  The product number must be less than 1000.")
}
```

Line 1 indicates that the name of the function is `msoxd__item_number_attr::OnValidate`, which means that it is associated with the item number field and the `OnValidate` event. The function name is fixed and cannot be changed. Line 1 also tells us that a single parameter is passed to this function, `eventObj`. It provides information about the event, in particular the node that changed to trigger it (`eventObj.Site`).

Line 4 starts an `if` statement that determines whether the value in question is over 999. The value of the appropriate field is retrieved using the reference `eventObj.Site.nodeTypedValue`. If the value is greater than 999, an error is reported using the `ReportError` method of `eventObj`. We pass two parameters to the `ReportError` method: the node that is in error (`eventObj.Site`), and a string that is the error message.

You can test this script by entering a product number that is greater than 999. The field will be surrounded with a red-dashed line, and the custom error message will appear both when you hover over the field and when you right-click it.

10.7.4 *Validation involving multiple values*

Our last example simply checked the value of a field against a constant. However, some validation involves multiple fields. Suppose, for example, that the product number 999 is used for special promotions that have a limit of one per customer per order. As such, we don't want a user to be able to enter a quantity that is greater than 1 if the product number is 999. The script shown in Example 10-2 will enforce this constraint.

If you are still in Script Editor, you can simply scroll down to find this function. However, if you are not, you will have to launch Script Editor in a different way to get to it directly. This function is related to the entire item row, rather than an individual field. Specifically, it is associated with the `item` element. To get to a script function for an element that is not represented by one field in the form:

1. Select `item` in the **Data Source** task pane.
2. Right-click it and click **Properties**.
3. Click the **Validation and Script** tab.

Example 10-2. Multi-field validation

```
function msoxd_ns1_item::OnValidate(eventObj)
{
  // Retrieve the necessary nodes and values
  var itemNode = eventObj.Site
  var quantNode = itemNode.selectSingleNode("ns1:quant")
  var quant = quantNode.nodeTypedValue
  var prodNum = itemNode.selectSingleNode("@number").nodeTypedValue

  //test the condition and report error
  if (prodNum == 999 && quant > 1)
    eventObj.ReportError(quantNode,
      "Quantity cannot exceed 1 for product number 999.", false)
}
```

4. As before, select the event you wish to use as a trigger for the
   script, in this case OnValidate, and click **Edit** to launch
   Script Editor.

In our previous example, we used the reference
eventObj.Site.nodeTypedValue to get to the value of the element we
were validating. In this case, we instead want to work with nodes that are
related to the element we are validating, namely the quant child and the
number attribute of the item element.

line 4

On line 4, we assign the item element to a variable, namely
itemNode.

line 5

On line 5, we assign the quant node using the selectSingleNode
method of itemNode. The selectSingleNode method is passed
an XPath expression which selects the desired node. In our case,
we are using a *relative* XPath expression to select the ns1:quant
child of the item element. It is also possible to use absolute XPath
expressions, as we will see in our next example. Note that the
namespace prefix is required when referring to qualified elements
like quant. The prefix ns1 is generated by InfoPath. If you scroll
to the top of the script file, you will see the line that maps the ns1
prefix to the appropriate namespace (see Example 10-3).

line 6

On line 6 we extract the typed value of the node and assign it to the quant variable. Using a typed value allows it to be treated as a number rather than as a string. It would also be possible to specify `quantNode.text` to return the content of the quant element as a string.

line 7

Line 7 retrieves the product number value in a similar fashion to the quant child. However, since the number node is an attribute rather than an element, the @ character is used in the XPath expression to indicate this. In addition, the number attribute is unqualified, so it is not prefixed in the expression.

lines 9 through 12

Lines 9 through 12 test for the error condition and report an error if necessary. Note that the first parameter passed to the ReportError method is the quantNode node. This means that the error will show up as an error in the quantity field, even though the error involves two fields. If desired, we could have specified the product number field, or called ReportError twice to report errors in both fields.

Example 10-3. Declaring prefixes for namespaces

```
XDocument.DOM.setProperty("SelectionNamespaces",
        'xmlns:ns1="http://xmlinoffice.com/orders"
         xmlns:xhtml="http://www.w3.org/1999/xhtml"');
```

In this example, we could have associated the script function with the quantity field, rather than the entire row. However, associating it with the entire row, i.e. the item element, allows the script function to be executed each time any field in the row is changed.

10.7.5 *The* OnBeforeChange *event*

Up to this point, we have associated both of our validation examples with the OnValidate event. It is also possible to use the OnBeforeChange event for validation. For example, suppose we want to prevent users from entering a second address line if the first address line is not completed. We might use a script like the one shown in Example 10-4.

Example 10-4. Using the OnBeforeChange event

```
function msoxd_ns1_addr2::OnBeforeChange(eventObj)
{
  // Retrieve the necessary nodes and values
  var addr1 = XDocument.DOM.selectSingleNode(
                "/ns1:order/ns1:shipTo/ns1:addr")
  var addr2 = XDocument.DOM.selectSingleNode(
                "/ns1:order/ns1:shipTo/ns1:addr2")

  //test the condition and report error
  if (addr1.text == "" && addr2.text != "")
  {
    eventObj.ReturnMessage =
      "A second address line cannot be specified without a first."
    eventObj.ReturnStatus = false
    return
  }
  eventObj.ReturnStatus = true
  return
}
```

This script handles the error slightly differently, because calling the ReportError function is not allowed from an OnBeforeChange script function. Instead, it calls the ReturnMessage method of eventObj if there is an error. This results in a dialog that displays the error message after an invalid value is entered. In addition, the function sets the ReturnStatus property of eventObj to false if there is an error, and true if there is not an error.

If there is an error, the change to the field will be rolled back. You can test this by attempting to enter a second address line when the first address line is not specified. When you try to move the cursor from the **Address 2** field, you will get an error message and your change will be undone. Interestingly, because the function is related to the addr2 element only, this script does not prevent you from entering a first address line, then a second line, then deleting the first line. To do that, you would need to associate the script with a higher-level element, such as shipTo, which would be executed any time a change was made in any of its children.

There is another difference between this example and the previous examples. It uses absolute XPath expressions rather than relative ones. In the last example, we called the `selectSingleNode` method of the item node. The XPath expression we used was evaluated in the context of the item node. In this case, we are also executing the `selectSingleNode` method, but of the `XDocument.DOM` object itself, which represents the entire document. As a result, we need to specify the entire path to retrieve the node of interest, namely: `/ns1:order/ns1:shipTo/ns1:addr`

The slash at the beginning of the expression means that it starts at the root of the document and works its way down the hierarchy.

10.8 | Calculations

Another common use for scripts in InfoPath is to perform calculations, such as totals, averages, tax amounts, or currency conversions. Calculation scripts are often associated with the `OnAfterChange` event, which occurs after validation. This is useful for updating fields in response to changes in other fields, for example to update a total when a line item has changed.

Suppose we want each line item in our order form to reflect the total cost of that item, namely the quantity times the price. In addition, we want a summary section that shows the total number of items ordered, and the total cost of the order. We could associate script functions with the quantity and price fields, so that any time either of them change, the totals are updated. The script functions might look like Example 10-5.

Example 10-5. A calculation script

```
function msoxd_ns1_quant::OnAfterChange(eventObj) {
  if (eventObj.IsUndoRedo)
     return;
  updateCost(eventObj.Site.parentNode)
  updateTotals()
}

function msoxd_ns1_price::OnAfterChange(eventObj) {
  if (eventObj.IsUndoRedo)
     return;
  updateCost(eventObj.Site.parentNode)
  updateTotals()
}
```

This function just calls two other functions, `updateCost` and `updateTotals`, that are defined later in the script file. The `updateCost` function, shown in Example 10-6, calculates the cost of each line item.

Example 10-6. Calculating the cost

```
function updateCost(thisItemNode)
{
  var thisQuant = thisItemNode.selectSingleNode("ns1:quant")
  var thisPrice = thisItemNode.selectSingleNode("ns1:price")
  var thisCost = thisItemNode.selectSingleNode("ns1:cost")
  var nQuant = parseFloat(thisQuant.nodeTypedValue)
  var nPrice = parseFloat(thisPrice.nodeTypedValue)
  var nCost = nPrice * nQuant;
  thisCost.nodeTypedValue = nCost
}
```

On lines 3 through 5, it assigns the three relevant nodes to variables. Then, on lines 6 and 7, it extracts the typed value of the quantity and price nodes and converts them to JScript floating point numbers using the `parseFloat` function. This is necessary for them to be used in mathematical calculations. Line 8 calculates the cost and assigns it to the `nCost` variable, and finally the cost node is updated by setting the `thisCost.nodeTypedValue` equal to `nCost`.

Our second calculation function, `updateTotals`, appears in Example 10-7. It calculates the two values in the summary section, namely the number of items and the order total. The logic is similar to the `updateCost` function, except that it calls yet another function, `sum`, to calculate the sum.

Example 10-7. Calculating the totals

```
function updateTotals()
{
  var numItemsNode =
    XDocument.DOM.selectSingleNode("//ns1:numItems")
  var nNumItems = sum("//ns1:quant")
  numItemsNode.nodeTypedValue = nNumItems

  var orderTotalNode =
    XDocument.DOM.selectSingleNode("//ns1:orderTotal")
  var nOrderTotal = sum("//ns1:cost")
  orderTotalNode.nodeTypedValue = nOrderTotal
}
```

It passes the sum function XPath expressions that are used to retrieve the nodes whose values need to be included in the sum. The XPath expressions used in this function use a double slash notation, as in //ns1:quant. This essentially means "all the ns1:quant elements in the document, no matter where they appear."

The sum function is shown in Example 10-8. On line 3, it selects the nodes of interest using the selectNodes method of XDocument.DOM. In our previous examples, we used selectSingleNode because we only wanted to retrieve one node. The selectNodes method can be used instead to retrieve a list of nodes.

The function then iterates through the list of nodes using a while loop that assigns one node after another to the xmlNode variable. The value of each node in the list is added to the sum.

Example 10-8. The sum function

```
function sum(xpath)
{
  var nodeList = XDocument.DOM.selectNodes(xpath)
  var sum = 0
  var xmlNode

  while (xmlNode = nodeList.nextNode())
    if (xmlNode.nodeTypedValue > 0)
    sum += parseFloat(xmlNode.nodeTypedValue);

  return sum
}
```

In this example, we created a library of three functions that can be called from one or more other functions. You can add an unlimited number of such library functions to the script file. Unlike the functions that are specifically associated with fields and events, you can choose the names of your library functions.

10.9 | Inserting XML nodes

We have seen how to select nodes from a document using the selectSingleNode and selectNodes methods along with XPath expressions. We have also seen how to update a node's value, by assigning a value to the node's `nodeTypedValue` property.

There may be cases where you also want to insert or delete nodes from the hierarchy. In most cases, the standard InfoPath user interface will take care of this for you, in that it creates the basic structure of the document by default. The user can use the standard InfoPath functionality for inserting and deleting repeating or optional elements.

However, you may want to customize this functionality. Suppose we want a facility that allows users to repeat a line item in the order form, so that they can more easily enter similar items. We have accomplished this in our order form example by placing a **Repeat** button within the item row and associating it with the script shown in Example 10-9.

Example 10-9. Repeating an item

```
function RepeatButton::OnClick(eventObj) {
  //assign the current item node to a variable
  var currentItem = eventObj.Source;
  //copy the current item node
  var copyOfItem = currentItem.cloneNode(true);
  //insert the copy before the current item node
  currentItem.parentNode.insertBefore(copyOfItem,currentItem);
}
```

Three simple lines of code are all that is needed to insert a copy of an item. On line 3, the current item (the one whose row contains the **Repeat** button that was clicked) is assigned to the variable `currentItem`. In this case, we use `eventObj.Source` to access this node.

When using the `OnClick` event, there is no `eventObj.Site` property as there was in the validation and calculation examples. In its place, the `Source` property retrieves the node that directly contains the button. In this case, it is the `item` element because the button appears within an item's row.

Line 5 assigns a copy of the current item node to the variable `copyOfItem`. Finally, line 7 inserts the copy directly before the current item row. The `parentNode` property of the current item is used to access the item's parent, namely the `items` node. The `insertBefore` method is then used to insert the current item as a child of `items`.

10.10 | Additional features

This chapter has provided an overview of InfoPath scripts and how they can be used to query and modify XML documents. In addition to these features, there are a number of other InfoPath capabilities that were not covered in detail in this chapter. They include:

- Modifying the user interface. Using a script, it is possible to add a custom task pane, toolbar or menu.
- Integration with external code. Scripts can access any external COM component.
- Accessing external data. Scripts can be used to access data from files, databases or Web services. This is covered in detail in the next chapter.

A set of examples is provided with InfoPath. They can be found in the directory in which Microsoft Office is installed, in the OFFICE11\SAMPLES\INFOPATH subdirectory. Now that you have read this chapter, you will be in a good position to understand these examples and reuse parts of them in your own forms.

Using secondary data sources with forms

InfoPath Script Developer Task

- Secondary XML documents
- Databases
- SOAP Web services

Chapter

11

n the previous chapter, we learned how to use scripts to perform custom validation and calculation functions on the data in forms.

But the data in a form isn't the only data that's relevant. There is external data in documents, databases, and Web services that can help in form completion, validation, and process integration. In this chapter we'll show you how to work with these secondary data sources.

Skills required   This chapter builds on the InfoPath script-writing skills that were introduced in the previous chapter. You'll also need some background in Web services (see Chapter 19, "Web services introduction", on page 414 and Chapter 23, "Web services technologies", on page 484) and XPath (see Chapter 17, "XPath primer", on page 384 and Chapter 24, "XML Path Language (XPath)", on page 498).

11.1 | Defining a secondary data source

As we've learned, every InfoPath form has a primary data source that is either an XML file, a database or a SOAP Web service. This primary data source is the abstract XML document that is retrieved, edited, saved and/or submitted using the InfoPath form.

In completing a form, it is often useful to query or include data from other, secondary, data sources; for example:

- To validate the value of a field against a list of valid values stored in a database or file
- To bring in a list of values to be included in a drop-down list
- To automatically complete information in the form; for example, to fill in the city and state based on the ZIP code.

In InfoPath, this is accomplished by defining *secondary data sources* and accessing them from scripts. Setting up a secondary data source is not much different from setting up the primary data source.

1. On the **Tools** menu, click **Secondary Data Sources**. This will bring up the **Secondary Data Sources** dialog shown in Figure 11-1.
2. Click **Add**. This will bring up the **Data Source Setup Wizard**, which is also used to set up the primary data source.
3. Choose whether it is an XML file, a database, or a SOAP Web service, and follow the wizard instructions. These instructions were described in greater detail in 9.3.6.3, "Using an XML example", on page 205, 9.3.6.4, "Starting from a database", on page 206 and 9.3.6.5, "Starting from a SOAP Web service", on page 212.
4. When prompted, choose a name for the data source.
5. If the secondary source is an XML file, the wizard will prompt you to add it to the form template as a resource (unless it was previously added using Resource Manager). If you decline, other users of the form may not have access to the secondary source.

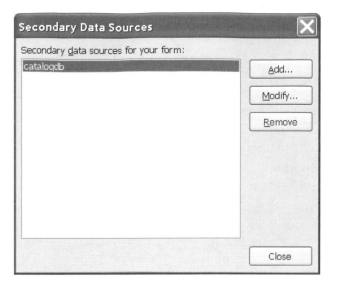

Figure 11-1   The Secondary Data Sources dialog

11.2 | Secondary XML documents

The Widget Wear product catalog is stored in an XML document. It looks something like Example 11-1.

11.2.1 *For validation*

When a user enters a product number, you want it to be checked against the product catalog to determine whether it is valid. The script functions shown in Example 11-2 will accomplish this. This script can be seen in action using the `order_xml.xsn` example file. The `OnValidate` function for the item number field calls another function, `lookupCatalog`, to determine whether the product number exists in the catalog. The line `if (!desc)` determines whether the `desc` variable contains a null value. If it does, it was not found in the catalog and an error is reported.

The `lookupCatalog` function first assigns the DOM of the `catalog` document to the variable `catDom` using the `GetDOM` method and referring to the document by the name specified for the secondary data source (`catalog`). It

Example 11-1. A product catalog in XML (catalog.xml)

```
<catalog>
  <product id="334">
    <name>Ten-Gallon Hat</name>
    <dept>ACC</dept>
  </product>
  <product id="356">
    <name>White Linen Blouse</name>
    <dept>WMN</dept>
  </product>
  <product id="522">
    <name>Deluxe Golf Umbrella</name>
    <dept>ACC</dept>
  </product>
  <product id="999">
    <name>Miscellaneous</name>
    <dept>NA</dept>
  </product>
</catalog>
```

Example 11-2. Script to validate product number against catalog

```
function msoxd__item_number_attr::OnValidate(eventObj) {
  var desc = lookupCatalog(eventObj.Site.nodeTypedValue)
  if (!desc)
    eventObj.ReportError(eventObj.Site,
      "Invalid product number.", false)
}

function lookupCatalog(prodNum) {
  var catDom = XDocument.GetDOM("catalog");
  var nameNode = catDom.selectSingleNode(
      "//product[@num='" + prodNum + "']/name");
  if (nameNode)
    return nameNode.nodeTypedValue;
}
```

then selects from the catalog the name node that has that product number. It does this by stringing together an XPath expression that will look, for example, like: //product[@num='334']/name

The brackets in the XPath expression surround what is known as a *predicate*, which limits results to nodes that meet a certain criterion; in this case, those whose num attributes are equal to 334.[1]

---

1. There is more on predicates in 24.2.1.2, "Predicates", on page 507.

If the function finds an appropriate node, it returns the node's typed value. If it does not find such a node, it returns a null value, signaling to the OnValidate function that the product was not found in the catalog.

11.2.2 *To complete fields*

Suppose that in addition to validating the product number, you want to fill in the product description automatically with the name data found in the catalog. The script function shown in Example 11-3 will accomplish this.

Example 11-3. Script to fill in the product name

```
function msoxd__item_number_attr::OnAfterChange(eventObj) {
  if (eventObj.IsUndoRedo) return;
  var descNode = eventObj.Site.selectSingleNode("../ns1:desc")
  var desc = lookupCatalog(eventObj.Site.nodeTypedValue)
  if (desc)
    descNode.nodeTypedValue = desc
  else
    descNode.nodeTypedValue = ""
}
```

The function is triggered by the OnAfterChange event, which occurs after the OnValidate event. It is very similar to the OnValidate function, in that it calls the lookupCatalog to retrieve the product description. This function, however, updates the description node with the name retrieved from the catalog. Note that it uses the relative XPath expression ../ns1:desc to retrieve the description. The .. step accesses the parent, while the ns1:desc step accesses the desc child of the parent.

11.2.3 *For drop-down lists*

Rather than validating a product number after it is entered, you could forestall errors by including the valid values in a drop-down list. This technique does not require a script; it is simply a matter of setting up the list control.

To test this out on our order form example:

1. Select the product number field and right-click.

2. On the resulting context menu, point to **Change To**, then click **Drop-Down List Box**.
3. Double-click the field to bring up its properties dialog, shown in Figure 11-2.
4. Under **List box entries**, click **Look up in a database, Web service, or file**.
5. Select the `catalog` data source from the drop-down list.
6. Use the button to the right of the **Entries** box to bring up the data source structure and select the `num` node.
7. Click **OK**. The **Entries** field should now say `/catalog/product/@num`.
8. Click **OK** again to return to the form.

11.3 | Databases

If the product catalog were in a relational database rather than an XML document, we could still perform similar validation and form completion functions. InfoPath has built-in support for Access and SQL Server databases, but also has a variety of techniques for supporting other databases.

11.3.1 *Access and SQL Server*

For example, suppose we have an Access database, `catalog.mdb`, which has a table named `CATALOG`, shown in Figure 11-3.

This process can be seen in action using the `order_db.xsn` example form. First, we set up a secondary data source for the database. This process is identical to the process for setting up a database as a primary data source, described in 9.3.6.4, "Starting from a database", on page 206. In our exam-

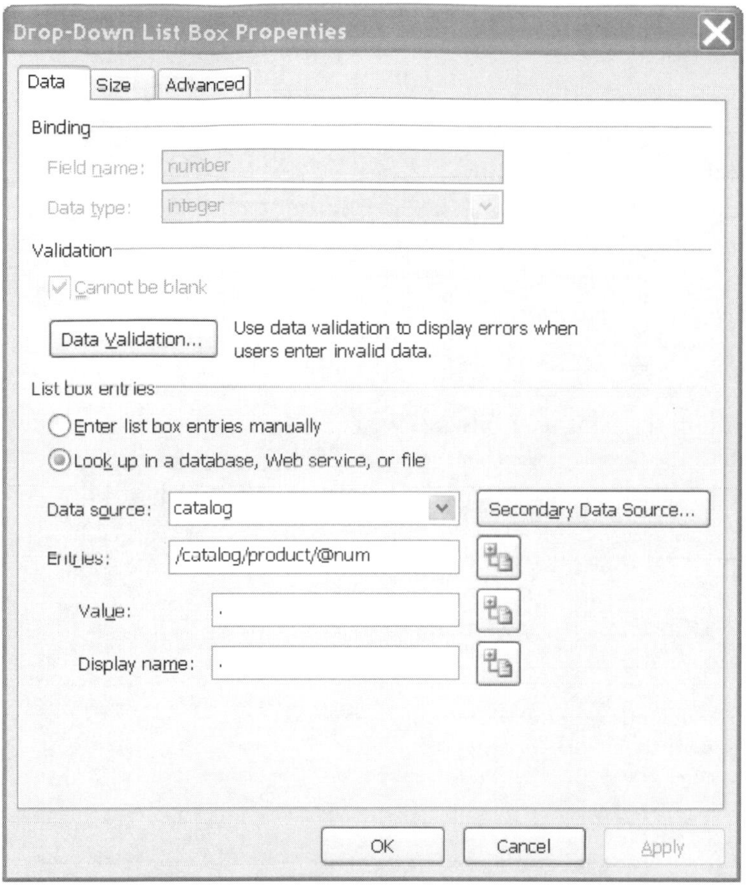

Figure 11-2   The Drop-Down List Box Properties dialog

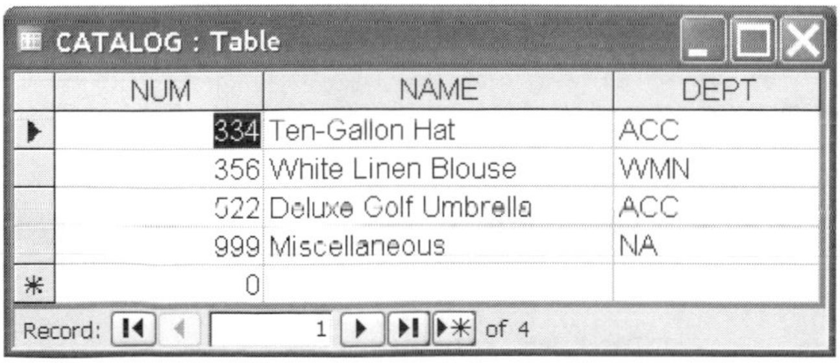

Figure 11-3   The CATALOG table

ple, we specified a secondary data source named catalogdb that pointed to the catalog.mdb database, and chose all the table columns.

Tip   *In general, you'll want to set up a secondary data source for each type of query that you will be performing on the data, rather than for each database or table. Doing so allows you to select only the tables, columns and joins that are relevant to the query, reducing the amount of data returned and ensuring that the data is joined appropriately.*

Once a secondary data source is set up, we can use a very similar script to what we used when selecting from a standalone XML document. The only changes required are to the lookupCatalog function, which is shown in Example 11-4.

Example 11-4. Script to check product number against database

```
function lookupCatalog(prodNum)
{
  var catdbDom = XDocument.GetDOM("catalogdb");
  catdbDom.setProperty("SelectionNamespaces",
  'xmlns:d="http://schemas.microsoft.com/office/infopath/2003/'
          + 'ado/dataFields"');
  var nameNode = catdbDom.selectSingleNode(
                  "//d:CATALOG[@NUM='" + prodNum + "']/@NAME");
  if (nameNode)
    return nameNode.nodeTypedValue;
}
```

InfoPath will convert the Access results into XML that can then be queried using the same methods we used to query the catalog XML document. An example of the XML output of the query is shown in Example 11-5.

The output document has a CATALOG element for each row in the CATALOG table, and each column is represented as an attribute. As this is a different structure from that of the catalog.xml file in Example 11-1, we use a different XPath expression in line 8 of Example 11-4 to retrieve the name.

In addition, because the CATALOG element is in its own namespace, we also need to use a prefix in the XPath expression. In order to map the prefix

Example 11-5. Output of the catalog database query

```
<dfs:myFields xmlns:dfs=
"http://schemas.microsoft.com/office/infopath/2003/dataFormSolution"
xmlns:d=
"http://schemas.microsoft.com/office/infopath/2003/ado/dataFields">
  <dfs:dataFields>
    <d:CATALOG NUM="334" NAME="Ten-Gallon Hat" DEPT="ACC"/>
    <d:CATALOG NUM="356" NAME="White Linen Blouse" DEPT="WMN"/>
    <d:CATALOG NUM="522" NAME="Deluxe Golf Umbrella" DEPT="ACC"/>
    <d:CATALOG NUM="999" NAME="Miscellaneous" DEPT="NA"/>
  </dfs:dataFields>
</dfs:myFields>
```

to the namespace, we call the setProperty method to set the SelectionNamespaces property, as shown in lines 4 through 6 of Example 11-4.

11.3.2 *Other databases*

The built-in database support described in the previous section will work for both Access and SQL Server databases. There are a number of techniques for accessing other kinds of databases using InfoPath, such as:

- building a SOAP Web service that accesses the data and returns it as XML (for example, using ADO.NET)
- writing scripts that access the database through any data access API, such as ADO, or a custom API provided by a vendor
- importing and exporting data from a database as XML files (most relational databases support this) and consuming the files in InfoPath[2]

11.4 | SOAP Web services

As we saw in 9.3.6.5, "Starting from a SOAP Web service", on page 212, InfoPath can send and receive data from SOAP Web services. When the

---

2. Refer to the documentation for your DBMS product to determine your options for accessing data as XML.

entire XML document is to be passed to (or retrieved from) the Web service, the setup is simply to design the form based on the Web service (as was described in that chapter). However, you may want to call a Web service as a secondary data source, for the purpose of validating or completing a form.

For example, Web services are available that will validate a ZIP code and return information about it, such as the city and state. We could set up our order form to allow the user to enter a ZIP code, then call a Web service to retrieve the city and state and fill them in automatically.

We will use the ZIP code Web service that was introduced in 6.2.1, "The ZIP code Web service", on page 123.[3] We set it up as a secondary data source in the same way we set up a Web service as a primary data source in 9.3.6.5, "Starting from a SOAP Web service", on page 212.

We chose the operation `GetInfoByZIP` from the list after entering `http://www.webservicex.net/uszip.asmx?WSDL` as the Web service URI. We named the secondary data source `GetInfoByZIP`.

For a working copy of this example, use the `order_ws.xsn` file.

11.4.1 *Web services interface document*

We won't be using the Office Web Services Toolkit that we used with Word. It doesn't – and doesn't need to – support InfoPath. That's because InfoPath hides the complexity of SOAP natively, with built-in support for parsing and generating SOAP messages.

InfoPath communicates with the Web service using SOAP documents whose envelopes contain the input and output message elements. To provide a SOAP-free interface to your scripts, it incorporates those message elements in a document that we refer to as a "Web services interface document".[4]

In our case, the document looks something like Example 11-6. It has two namespaces: one with the prefix `ws` for the Web service message elements, and one with the prefix `dfs` for InfoPath's housekeeping elements.

---

3. If you have not read that section of the book, you should do so before proceeding.

4. The document and its related schema documents are stored in the form template. The file names are based on the name you gave to the secondary data source.

We'll describe the document first, then show you how to write the script that creates and reads it.

11.4.1.1   Service request

Before the document is sent to the service, the input message is complete: there is an input parameter in `ws:USZip`. Although there is an element in the output message for the result (`ws:GetInfoByZIPResult`), it is empty.

Example 11-6. Interface document with message elements as sent to the Web service

```
<dfs:myFields xmlns:dfs=
"http://schemas.microsoft.com/office/infopath/2003/dataFormSolution"
            xmlns:ws="http://www.webserviceX.NET">
  <dfs:queryFields>
    <ws:GetInfoByZIP>
      <ws:USZip>49684</ws:USZip>
    </ws:GetInfoByZIP>
  </dfs:queryFields>
  <dfs:dataFields>
    <ws:GetInfoByZIPResponse>
      <ws:GetInfoByZIPResult/>
    </ws:GetInfoByZIPResponse>
  </dfs:dataFields>
</dfs:myFields>
```

11.4.1.2   Service response

After the Web service is called, the document has the service output in the content of the `GetInfoByZIPResult` element, roughly as shown in Example 11-7. The only change to the document is the `NewDataSet` element that was returned with the requested information.

11.4.2   *Writing the script*

Example 11-8 shows the script that causes InfoPath to invoke the Web service and update the form with the returned city and state.

Example 11-7. Interface document after output element is completed by the Web service

```
<dfs:myFields xmlns:dfs=
"http://schemas.microsoft.com/office/infopath/2003/dataFormSolution"
            xmlns:ws="http://www.webserviceX.NET">
  <dfs:queryFields>
    <ws:GetInfoByZIP>
      <ws:USZip>49684</ws:USZip>
    </ws:GetInfoByZIP>
  </dfs:queryFields>
  <dfs:dataFields>
    <ws:GetInfoByZIPResponse>
      <ws:GetInfoByZIPResult>
        <NewDataSet>
          <Table>
            <CITY>Traverse City</CITY>
            <STATE>MI</STATE>
            <ZIP>49684</ZIP>
            <AREA_CODE>616</AREA_CODE>
            <TIME_ZONE>E</TIME_ZONE>
          </Table>
        </NewDataSet>
      </ws:GetInfoByZIPResult>
    </ws:GetInfoByZIPResponse>
  </dfs:dataFields>
</dfs:myFields>
```

line 1

The function is executed when a change is made to the postal_code field of the primary document.

line 3

If the change is an undo or redo of a previous change, the script exits with no action.

line 6

A data object is constructed with the structure and properties of an empty Web service interface document for our data source (GetInfoByZIP). The variable webService is created to point to the object.

lines 8 through 11

The namespace prefixes for the interface document are declared and stored as properties of the webService object.

Example 11-8. Script that invokes the Web service

```
function msoxd_ns1_postal_code::OnAfterChange(eventObj)
{
  if (eventObj.IsUndoRedo) return;

  //Get a reference to the Web service data source
  var webService = XDocument.DataObjects.Item("GetInfoByZIP")

  webService.DOM.setProperty("SelectionNamespaces", "xmlns:dfs=" +
    "'http://schemas.microsoft.com/office/infopath/" +
    "2003/dataFormSolution'" +
    " xmlns:ws='http://www.webserviceX.NET' ")

  //Set the value of the ZIP code node in the input message
  var zipParm = webService.DOM.selectSingleNode(
    "/dfs:myFields/dfs:queryFields/ws:GetInfoByZIP/ws:USZip" )
  zipParm.text = eventObj.Site.text

  //call the Web service
  webService.Query()

  //Set the city and state values in the form
  XDocument.DOM.selectSingleNode( "//ns1:city" ).text =
    webService.DOM.selectSingleNode( "//CITY" ).text
  XDocument.DOM.selectSingleNode( "//ns1:state" ).text =
    webService.DOM.selectSingleNode( "//STATE" ).text
}
```

lines 14 and 15

The variable zipParm is created as a pointer to the (currently empty) ws:USZip node of the webService object.

line 16

The text of the postal_code node of the primary document (i.e. the ZIP code that was typed into the form by the user) is assigned to the USZip node of the input message through the pointer variable zipParm.

line 19

Line 19 calls the Web service. InfoPath copies the input message element from the webService object and includes it in a SOAP document that it sends to the service. When it receives the return SOAP document, it extracts the content of the output message element and inserts it into the webService object. The XML linearization of the `webService` object now looks like Example 11-7.

lines 21 through 24

The `CITY` and `STATE` values from the `webService` object are copied to the corresponding nodes in the primary XML document.

Access databases and XML

- Exporting Access tables as XML

- Transforming exported data

- Importing XML data to Access

Chapter

12

his chapter covers the XML features of Microsoft Access, specifically the tasks of importing and exporting XML. These features allow Access databases to be integrated into XML workflows with other enterprise systems.

> *Skills required*   Experience using Microsoft Access to create
> and query databases. To use transforms, you'll need to know about
> XSLT (see Chapter 18, "XSL Transformations (XSLT)", on page
> 392).

12.1 | Why use XML with Access?

The XML features of Microsoft Access consist of an export and import process.

12.1.1 *The export process*

XML can be generated from any Access tables, queries or forms. Doing so makes the data available for a variety of processes, such as:

- Reporting on the data in a Web page or Word document;
- Sending the data to a business partner as part of an e-commerce transaction;
- Analyzing the data in Excel; and
- Importing the data into a different database for business integration, reporting, and/or backup.

12.1.2 *The import process*

XML can be imported into Access tables. This is one way to interface the Access database with other applications, such as an e-commerce application that transmits orders as XML documents. It is also a means of populating Access tables when they are initially created.

12.2 | Our example database

Worldwide Widget Corporation is famous for its award-winning employee incentive program. Managers are given an incentive budget with which they can purchase discontinued Widget Wear items to reward outstanding people.

To keep track of these internal reward sales, the company maintains a small, simple Access database named order.mdb. Its design is shown in Figure 12-1. You can find the order.mdb database among the example files for this book.

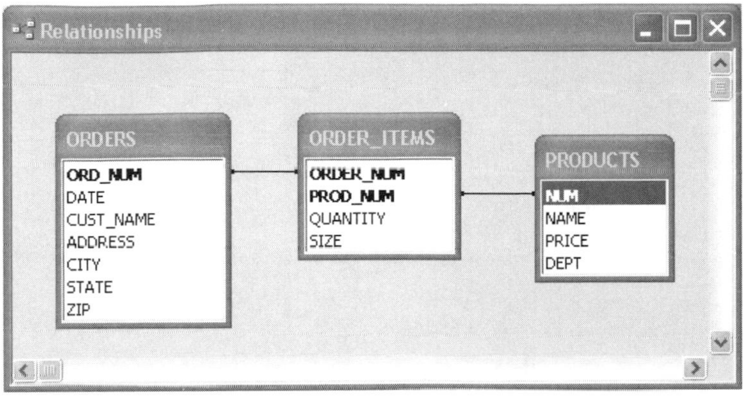

Figure 12-1   The order database design (order.mdb)

There are three tables: ORDERS, ORDER_ITEMS, and PRODUCTS. The ORDERS table contains such information as the order number, date, customer name, and shipping address. The primary key of the ORDERS table is the ORD_NUM column. The table contents are shown in Figure 12-2.

	ORD_NUM	DATE	CUST_NAME	ADDRESS	CITY	STATE	ZIP
+	1001	2/15/2004	Doug Jones	123 Main St.	Arlington	VA	22205
+	1002	3/23/2004	Monica Lyle	443 Elm Road	Traverse City	MI	49684
+	1003	4/12/2004	Marla Worthington	12 Jeremy Street	Moraga	CA	94556
▶	0						

Record: ◄◄ ◄ 4 ► ►◄ ►* of 4

Figure 12-2   The ORDERS table contents

The PRODUCTS table contains information such as product number, name, price and department. Its primary key is the NUM column. Its contents are shown in Figure 12-3.

PRODUCTS : Table

		NUM	NAME	PRICE	DEPT
	+	219	Cotton Rugby Shirt	$39.99	MEN
	+	233	Silk 2-Pocket Blouse	$59.99	WOMEN
	+	241	Deluxe Golf Umbrella	$39.99	ACCESSORY
	+	334	Wool Fisherman's Sweater	$129.99	MEN
	+	345	Corduroy Jumper	$25.99	CHILDREN
▶	+	766	Cotton Turtleneck	$18.99	WOMEN
*		0		$0.00	

Record: 6 of 6

Figure 12-3 The PRODUCTS table contents

The ORDER_ITEMS table contains the list of items for each order. Its primary key is a combination of the ORDER_NUM column, which has a foreign key relationship to the ORD_NUM column of ORDERS, and the PROD_NUM column, which has a foreign key relationship to the NUM column of PRODUCTS. Its contents are shown in Figure 12-4.

ORDER_ITEMS : Table

	ORDER_NUM	PROD_NUM	QUANTITY	SIZE
	1001	219	1	L
	1001	334	1	L
	1002	233	1	10
	1002	241	1	
	1002	345	2	M
▶	1003	345	1	2
*	0	0	0	

Record: 6 of 6

Figure 12-4 The ORDER_ITEMS table contents

12.3 | Exporting Access tables

Exporting Access table data as XML generates three kinds of files, all of them optional. They are:

1. A data file, with a .xml extension, that contains the data from the contents of the table(s).
2. A schema document, with a .xsd extension, which describes the structure of the data file.
3. A pair of presentation files, with the extensions .xsl and either .htm or .asp, which will display the data in a browser.

12.3.1 *A simple export*

First, let's look at a simple export of a single table using all the default settings. To do this:

1. Select the table you want to export from the list of tables. In this case, select ORDERS.
2. On the **File** menu, click **Export**.
3. Select **XML (*.xml)** from the **Save as type** list.
4. The **File name** box will default to the table name. Use the default value or type a different name into the box. Do not use a file extension; if you type a file extension other than **xml**, Access will append another file extension to it.
5. This will bring up the Export XML dialog shown in Figure 12-5. The three options shown in this dialog represent the three optional components to be generated. For now, leave the default settings (with the first two check boxes checked).

This simple export saves two files: in our example, ORDERS.xml and ORDERS.xsd.

12.3.1.1 The exported XML document

The generated XML data document, ORDERS.xml, is shown in Example 12-1.[1]

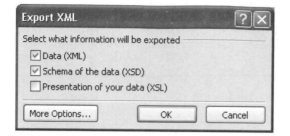

Figure 12-5   The Export XML dialog

The structure of the XML document closely parallels the structure of the table. There is a root element, dataroot, which contains one or more ORDERS elements. Each ORDERS element represents a row in the table. It contains a child element for each column in the table, for example ORD_NUM and DATE. The names used in the XML document (with the exception of dataroot) are taken directly from the Access table design.

Each of these children contains the data contained in that column for that row. If there is no value for that column in that row, an empty element is generated. The format of the data is dependent on the type of the column. In our example, the content of each DATE element is formatted as YYYY-MM-DDTHH:MM:SS, which is the XML Schema dateTime format that corresponds to the Date/Time type in Access.

12.3.1.2   The generated schema

The generated schema, ORDERS.xsd, is shown in Example 12-2.

The schema describes the structure of the generated XML document. It first contains the dataroot element declaration, which specifies that a dataroot element can contain zero, one or many ORDERS children. The ORDERS element declaration appears next, along with embedded declarations for the four allowed children.

The generated schema defines simple types for some of the elements that contain the data. For columns whose type is Text in Access, such as the CITY column, it generates a type that is a string whose length can be up to 50 characters. In other cases, for example the DATE column, it simply uses

---

1. Extra line breaks and spaces were added to make it easier to read.

Example 12-1. The exported XML (ORDERS.xml)

```
<?xml version="1.0" encoding="UTF-8"?>
<dataroot xmlns:od="urn:schemas-microsoft-com:officedata"
          xmlns:xsi="http://www.w3.org/2001/XMLSchema-instance"
          xsi:noNamespaceSchemaLocation="ORDERS.xsd"
          generated="2004-02-26T16:53:27">
  <ORDERS>
    <ORD_NUM>1001</ORD_NUM>
    <DATE>2004-02-15T00:00:00</DATE>
    <CUST_NAME>Doug Jones</CUST_NAME>
    <ADDRESS>123 Main St.</ADDRESS>
    <CITY>Arlington</CITY>
    <STATE>VA</STATE>
    <ZIP>22205</ZIP>
  </ORDERS>
  <ORDERS>
    <ORD_NUM>1002</ORD_NUM>
    <DATE>2004-03-23T00:00:00</DATE>
    <CUST_NAME>Monica Lyle</CUST_NAME>
    <ADDRESS>443 Elm Road</ADDRESS>
    <CITY>Traverse City</CITY>
    <STATE>MI</STATE>
    <ZIP>49684</ZIP>
  </ORDERS>
  <ORDERS>
    <ORD_NUM>1003</ORD_NUM>
    <DATE>2004-04-12T00:00:00</DATE>
    <CUST_NAME>Marla Worthington</CUST_NAME>
    <ADDRESS>12 Jeremy Street</ADDRESS>
    <CITY>Moraga</CITY>
    <STATE>CA</STATE>
    <ZIP>94556</ZIP>
  </ORDERS>
</dataroot>
```

XML Schema built-in types like `dateTime`. Additional Access-specific type information is included in the schema using attributes that are prefixed with `od`. These additional attributes are used by Access if you re-import the data into an Access database.

The generated schema also contains information about the primary keys and indexes on the table. This information is included in the `xsd:appinfo` element, within the declaration of ORDERS.

Example 12-2. The generated schema (ORDERS.xsd)

```xml
<?xml version="1.0" encoding="UTF-8"?>
<xsd:schema xmlns:xsd="http://www.w3.org/2001/XMLSchema"
            xmlns:od="urn:schemas-microsoft-com:officedata">
  <xsd:element name="dataroot"><xsd:complexType><xsd:sequence>
    <xsd:element ref="ORDERS" minOccurs="0" maxOccurs="unbounded"/>
  </xsd:sequence></xsd:complexType></xsd:element>
  <xsd:element name="ORDERS">
    <xsd:annotation><xsd:appinfo>
      <od:index index-name="PrimaryKey" index-key="ORD_NUM"
          primary="yes" unique="yes" clustered="no"/>
      <od:index index-name="CUST_NUM" index-key="CUST_NAME"
          primary="no" unique="no" clustered="no"/>
      <od:index index-name="ORDER_NUM" index-key="ORD_NUM"
          primary="no" unique="no" clustered="no"/>
    </xsd:appinfo></xsd:annotation>
    <xsd:complexType><xsd:sequence>
      <xsd:element name="ORD_NUM" minOccurs="0" od:jetType=
                  "longinteger" od:sqlSType="int" type="xsd:int"/>
      <xsd:element name="DATE" minOccurs="0" od:jetType="datetime"
                  od:sqlSType="datetime" type="xsd:dateTime"/>
      <xsd:element name="CUST_NAME" minOccurs="0" od:jetType="text"
                              od:sqlSType="nvarchar">
          <xsd:simpleType><xsd:restriction base="xsd:string">
                  <xsd:maxLength value="50"/>
          </xsd:restriction></xsd:simpleType></xsd:element>
      <xsd:element name="ADDRESS" minOccurs="0" od:jetType="text"
                              od:sqlSType="nvarchar">
          <xsd:simpleType><xsd:restriction base="xsd:string">
                  <xsd:maxLength value="50"/>
          </xsd:restriction></xsd:simpleType></xsd:element>
      <xsd:element name="CITY" minOccurs="0" od:jetType="text"
                          od:sqlSType="nvarchar">
          <xsd:simpleType><xsd:restriction base="xsd:string">
                  <xsd:maxLength value="50"/>
          </xsd:restriction></xsd:simpleType></xsd:element>
      <xsd:element name="STATE" minOccurs="0" od:jetType="text"
                          od:sqlSType="nvarchar">
          <xsd:simpleType><xsd:restriction base="xsd:string">
                  <xsd:maxLength value="50"/>
          </xsd:restriction></xsd:simpleType></xsd:element>
      <xsd:element name="ZIP" minOccurs="0" od:jetType="text"
                          od:sqlSType="nvarchar">
          <xsd:simpleType><xsd:restriction base="xsd:string">
                  <xsd:maxLength value="50"/>
          </xsd:restriction></xsd:simpleType></xsd:element>
    </xsd:sequence></xsd:complexType>
  </xsd:element>
</xsd:schema>
```

12.3.1.3 Additional options

You can have more control over how the XML-related components are generated by clicking **More Options** on the Export XML dialog. This brings up a new Export XML dialog with three tabs, one each for Data, Schema and Presentation. These options are discussed in following sections.

12.3.2 *Exporting data: a closer look*

In our previous example, we exported all the data from a single table. There are additional options which allow you to export data from more than one related table at once, and allow you to filter the data that is exported. These options are specified on the Data tab of the expanded Export XML dialog, shown in Figure 12-6.

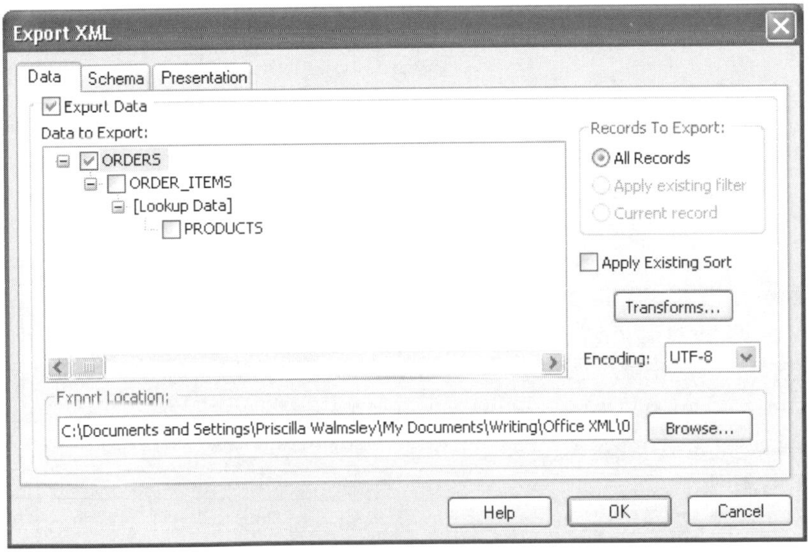

Figure 12-6 Export XML Data options

This dialog has several sections:

- The **Data to Export** section allows you to select the tables you want to export. This is described in 12.3.2.1, "Selecting tables to export", on page 276.
- The **Records To Export** section at the top right allows you to choose the specific records you want to export. This is described in 12.3.2.2, "Exporting using filters and sorts", on page 278.
- The **Apply Existing Sort** check box allows you to specify a sort. This is described in 12.3.2.2, "Exporting using filters and sorts", on page 278.
- The **Transforms** button allows you to select a transformation to apply to the data upon export. This is described in 12.5, "Applying a transform on export", on page 285.
- The **Encoding** list allows you to specify an encoding for your XML document.
- The **Export Location** section allows you to choose the location where your XML document will be saved.

12.3.2.1   Selecting tables to export

The **Data to Export** section of the **Data** tab shows the tables in the database in a tree structure. At the top is the table that was selected when you initiated the export. If you wish to start with a different table, you can exit the dialog, select a different table, and restart the export.

Access constructs the hierarchy of tables based on primary and foreign key relationships in the database. Only tables related to the table of interest are displayed in the hierarchy. A **[Lookup Data]** node appears when following a many-to-one relationship, for example from ORDER_ITEMS to PRODUCTS.

Each table is accompanied by a check box that allows you to select the tables that you want to export. You can select any or all of the tables to export, and it will export the data from all the selected tables to the same XML document. Access will join the tables based on the joins in the database. If you choose to export all three tables, a fragment of the resulting XML document is shown in Example 12-3.

The XML document contains ORDERS elements just as before. However, they now contain one or more ORDER_ITEMS elements that are related to that ORDERS row by the key relationship. In addition, PRODUCTS elements

Example 12-3. Generated XML data from related tables (ORDERS all tables.xml)

```
<ORDERS>
  <ORD_NUM>1001</ORD_NUM>
  <DATE>2004-02-15T00:00:00</DATE>
  <CUST_NAME>Doug Jones</CUST_NAME>
  <ADDRESS>123 Main St.</ADDRESS>
  <CITY>Arlington</CITY>
  <STATE>VA</STATE>
  <ZIP>22205</ZIP>
  <ORDER_ITEMS>
    <ORDER_NUM>1001</ORDER_NUM>
    <PROD_NUM>219</PROD_NUM>
    <QUANTITY>1</QUANTITY>
    <SIZE>L</SIZE>
  </ORDER_ITEMS>
  <ORDER_ITEMS>
    <ORDER_NUM>1001</ORDER_NUM>
    <PROD_NUM>334</PROD_NUM>
    <QUANTITY>1</QUANTITY>
    <SIZE>L</SIZE>
  </ORDER_ITEMS>
</ORDERS>
<!--...-->
<PRODUCTS>
  <NUM>233</NUM>
  <NAME>Silk 2-Pocket Blouse</NAME>
  <PRICE>59.99</PRICE>
  <DEPT>WOMEN</DEPT>
</PRODUCTS>
<PRODUCTS>
  <NUM>241</NUM>
  <NAME>Deluxe Golf Umbrella</NAME>
  <PRICE>39.99</PRICE>
  <DEPT>ACCESSORY</DEPT>
</PRODUCTS>
<PRODUCTS>
<!--...-->
```

contain the product information. The PRODUCTS are listed separately at the end of the document rather than contained in the ORDER_ITEMS elements. This is because of the cardinality of the relationship in the database design.

The newly generated schema reflects the new structure of the document. It contains declarations for all of the element types in ORDERS, ORDER_ITEMS and PRODUCTS.

12.3.2.2   Exporting using filters and sorts

The **Records To Export** section of the **Data** tab allows you to choose the specific records you want to export. There are three choices:

- **All Records** exports all the records in the table(s), as we have done in our previous examples.
- **Apply existing filter** allows you to apply a filter to the export. If a filter exists for the table you have chosen, and you choose this option, it will be applied on export. If no filter exists for the table, this option cannot be selected.
- **Current record** allows you to export the current record. You can only choose this option if you had a table open with a record selected when you initiated the export process. Access will export the current record, along with any related records in other tables (for example the ORDER_ITEMS elements that relate to that order). If you include a lookup table, as in PRODUCTS, it will still continue to export all the PRODUCTS records, not just the ones related to the exported ORDER_ITEMS.

The **Apply Existing Sort** check box allows you to specify whether to use the sort that currently exists on the table. A sort exists if, for example, you opened the datasheet view of the ORDERS table, sorted the records by CITY, and saved the table design. Checking the **Apply Existing Sort** box will cause the exported XML to also be sorted by CITY. If the box is unchecked, the records will be exported in the order in which they are physically stored in the table.

12.3.3   *Generating a schema*

The schema is useful as a guide to the structure of the exported document. In addition, if you plan to re-import the XML data into another Access database, the schema is essential to ensure that all of the table relationships and data types are preserved upon re-import.

The schema export options are shown in Figure 12-7.

The **Export Schema** check box indicates whether to export the schema at all; if you do not check this box, no schema will be generated.

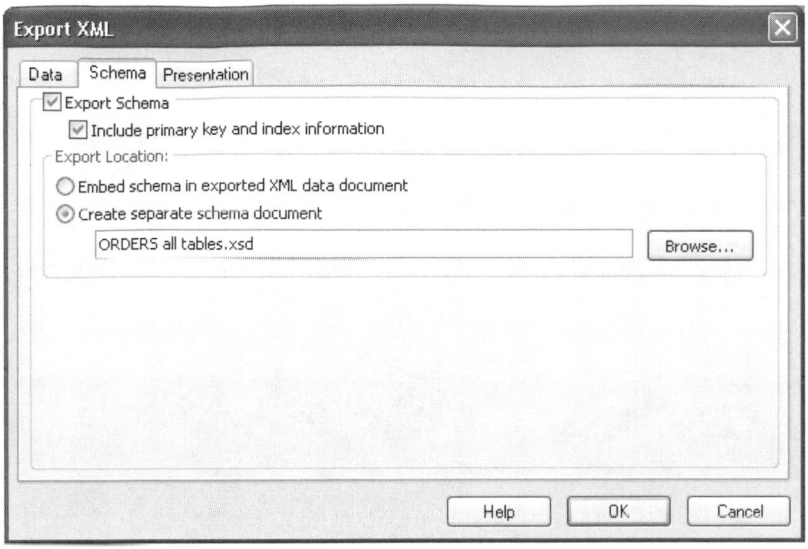

Figure 12-7   The Schema tab of the Export XML dialog

The **Include primary key and index information** check box indicates whether to include the primary key information as an annotation in the schema, as was shown in Example 12-2. This only matters if you want to re-import the data into another Access database, and you want Access to recreate those tables with their key relationships in the other database.

The **Export Location** section allows you to specify whether Access should embed the schema directly in the XML document that contains the data, or create a separate schema document (the default). In general, you should avoid embedding the schema, since this is not a customary practice and a schema processor may not be able to validate such a document.

12.3.4 *Generating a presentation*

When you choose to generate a presentation from a table, Access will generate documents that allow you to view the data in a tabular format in a Web browser. This involves two additional files:

1. an XSLT stylesheet, with the extension `.xsl`, that transforms the generated XML data to HTML for presentation; and

2. a file that is used by a Web server to apply the XSLT stylesheet. This file is either an HTML document containing a script, or an Active Server Page (ASP).

An example presentation is shown in Figure 12-8. Note that only the "main" ORDERS table is presented; the data from related tables is omitted. To include the data from the related tables, you would need to write a custom XSLT stylesheet, or use a tool like FrontPage to generate the XSLT based on your requirements.

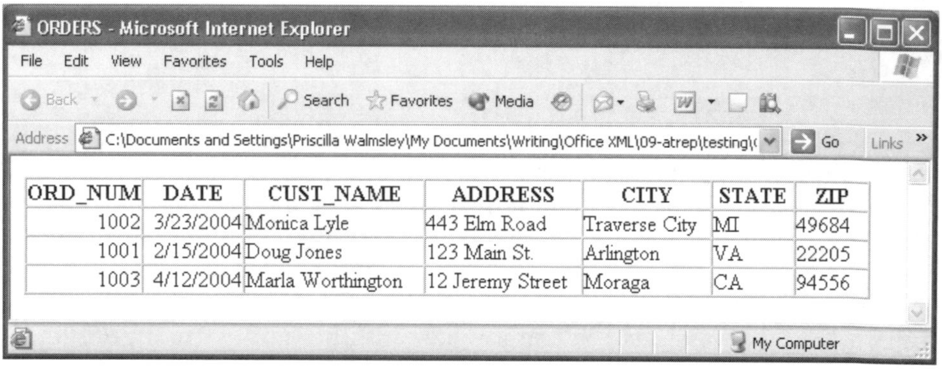

ORD_NUM	DATE	CUST_NAME	ADDRESS	CITY	STATE	ZIP
1002	3/23/2004	Monica Lyle	443 Elm Road	Traverse City	MI	49684
1001	2/15/2004	Doug Jones	123 Main St.	Arlington	VA	22205
1003	4/12/2004	Marla Worthington	12 Jeremy Street	Moraga	CA	94556

Figure 12-8 The Presentation file (ORDERS.htm) as shown in a Web browser

There are several options relating to generating the presentations. They can be set in the Presentation options dialog, shown in Figure 12-9.

The **Export Presentation** check box indicates whether to export the presentation files at all; if you do not check this, no presentation will be generated.

The **Run from** section allows you to specify whether the generated transformation is to be run from the client or server. If you choose **Client (HTML)**, it will generate an HTML page, with the file extension .htm. If you choose **Server (ASP)** it will generate an Active Server Page (ASP), with the file extension .asp.

The **Include report images** section indicates whether or not to include images. This is only relevant to exporting forms and reports, as described in 12.4.2, "Exporting forms", on page 284.

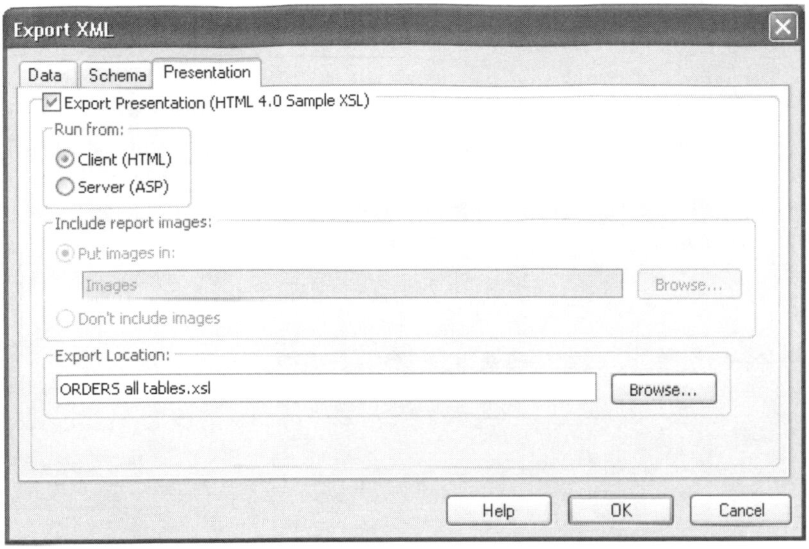

Figure 12-9   The Presentation tab of the Export XML dialog

The **Export Location** section allows you to specify the location for the XSLT stylesheet file. The related HTML or ASP document is always saved in the same directory as the data, regardless of the location of the stylesheet.

> *Tip*   The presentation generation capabilities of Access are useful for taking a quick look at the exported data. For more powerful presentation capabilities, FrontPage offers a GUI editor for generating Web pages from XML documents. These capabilities are described in Chapter 13, "Publishing XML to the Web with FrontPage", on page 294.

12.4 | Exporting other objects

In addition to exporting data directly from tables, you can also export queries, forms and reports from Access. This is useful when you want a different view of the data from what the table provides.

12.4.1 *Exporting queries*

Exporting a query is useful if you don't want to export all the columns of a table, if you want to join the tables on relationships other than the key relationships, or if you want to specify complex conditions that filter the exported rows.

Our orders database has a query named ORDERS WITH MENS DEPT ITEMS, shown in Figure 12-10.

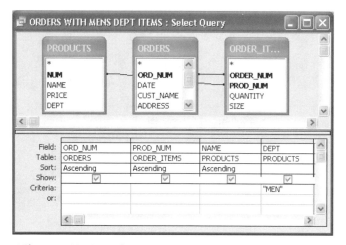

Figure 12-10   A query on the orders database

The query selects all the orders, along with their item information, that contain a product whose department is "MEN". We can export the results of this query using the exact same export procedure we used for tables. The result is the XML document shown in Example 12-4.

Each row is represented by an element whose element-type name matches the query name. In this case, since our query name has spaces, and spaces are not allowed in XML names, each space is replaced by the string _x0020_.

The row element has a child element for every column returned by the query. The element-type names are the column names from the tables used in the query. To change them, in the **Field** box of the query design view, you can specify an alias as a prefix, followed by a colon and a space as shown in Figure 12-11.

Example 12-4. Exported query data (ORDERS WITH MENS DEPT ITEMS.xml)

```xml
<?xml version="1.0" encoding="UTF-8"?>
<dataroot xmlns:od="urn:schemas-microsoft-com:officedata"
          xmlns:xsi="http://www.w3.org/2001/XMLSchema-instance"
          xsi:noNamespaceSchemaLocation=
          "ORDERS%20WITH%20MENS%20DEPT%20ITEMS.xsd"
          generated="2003-08-26T18:22:43">
  <ORDERS_x0020_WITH_x0020_MENS_x0020_DEPT_x0020_ITEMS>
    <ORD_NUM>1001</ORD_NUM>
    <PROD_NUM>219</PROD_NUM>
    <NAME>Cotton Rugby Shirt</NAME>
    <DEPT>MEN</DEPT>
  </ORDERS_x0020_WITH_x0020_MENS_x0020_DEPT_x0020_ITEMS>
  <ORDERS_x0020_WITH_x0020_MENS_x0020_DEPT_x0020_ITEMS>
    <ORD_NUM>1001</ORD_NUM>
    <PROD_NUM>334</PROD_NUM>
    <NAME>Wool Fisherman&apos;s Sweater</NAME>
    <DEPT>MEN</DEPT>
  </ORDERS_x0020_WITH_x0020_MENS_x0020_DEPT_x0020_ITEMS>
</dataroot>
```

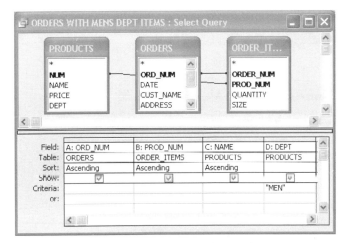

Figure 12-11   Using column aliases for queries

When the query is exported, the prefixes – A, B, C and D – are used as the element-type names.

12.4.2 *Exporting forms*

It is also possible to export the data behind a form as XML. This is useful if a user working with the form wants to export a single record. Our orders database contains a form named ORDERS, shown in Figure 12-12.

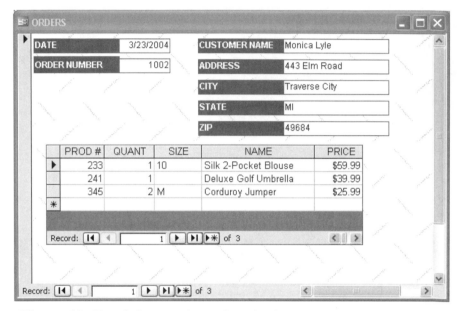

Figure 12-12   A form in the orders database

The structure of the exported data is exactly the same as that of data exported directly from the ORDERS table, as shown in Example 12-3. The export doesn't leave out the items that are not displayed on the form, nor does it structure the data any differently. You can, however, choose to only export the current order record by specifying that option on the **Data** tab of the **Export XML** dialog.

When saving a presentation with the form data, the HTML page that is generated has the same look and feel as the form, including the colors, fonts and general layout. You can also choose to export the images by selecting **Put images in** and specifying a directory. This will include all images, including any background pattern, that appear on the form.

Unfortunately, only the main form is displayed, and not the subforms. In our example, only the order header information is displayed, and not the individual items within an order. This limits the usefulness of the presentation somewhat.

12.4.3 *Exporting Access project objects*

In addition to exporting data from Access databases, it is possible to export data from Access *projects*. Access projects, files with the extension .adp, allow a user to access and report on Microsoft SQL Server data using the front-end tools of Access. XML data can be generated from an Access project table, view or form, in exactly the same way as it is generated from an Access database table or form.

If you are already using an Access project to manipulate or report on SQL Server data, this can be a convenient way to extract data. XML data can also be exported directly from SQL Server.

12.5 | Applying a transform on export

In some cases, you may want the exported XML to conform to a particular schema, rather than using the names and structure of the Access database. For example, if you are exporting an order that is to be used in an e-commerce transaction, you may need it to conform to a specific e-commerce schema.

Suppose you have agreed on such a schema with your customers. An example of a conforming exported order is shown in Example 12-5.

To accomplish this, you can transform the XML when you export it using an XSLT stylesheet. The stylesheet shown in Example 12-6 will transform the default export of the orders database into a new order that conforms to our desired schema.

You can specify the transform to be used on export on the Data tab of the Export XML dialog. Clicking **Transforms** takes you to the **Export Transforms** dialog, shown in Figure 12-13.

To add a transformation, simply click **Add** and specify the name of the XSLT stylesheet.

Example 12-5. Order conforming to a different schema (`order diff structure.xml`)

```
<?xml version="1.0" encoding="UTF-8"?>
<order xmlns="http://xmlinoffice.com/orders"
       number="1001">
  <date>2004-02-15T00:00:00</date>
  <customer>Doug Jones</customer>
  <shipTo>
    <addr>123 Main St.</addr>
    <city>Arlington</city>
    <state>VA</state>
    <postal_code>22205</postal_code>
  </shipTo>
  <items>
    <item number="219">
      <quant>1</quant>
      <size>L</size>
    </item>
    <item number="334">
      <quant>1</quant>
      <size>L</size>
    </item>
  </items>
</order>
```

The **Export Transforms** dialog lists all the *available* transforms. It is possible to add more than one transform to the list. However, only one will be applied on any given export: the one that is selected when **OK** is clicked.

12.6 | Importing XML data

It is also possible to import XML data into an Access database. This is a useful way to populate an Access database initially, or to add new data incrementally over time.

12.6.1 *A basic import*

First, let's perform a basic import of an entire set of tables. To do this:

1. Start with an empty, newly-created database.

Example 12-6. Transforming the order on export (order transform for export.xsl)

```xml
<?xml version="1.0" encoding="UTF-8"?>
<xsl:stylesheet version="1.0"
                xmlns:xsl="http://www.w3.org/1999/XSL/Transform"
                xmlns:ord="http://xmlinoffice.com/orders">
<xsl:template match="/dataroot">
  <ord:order number="1001">
    <xsl:attribute name="number">
      <xsl:value-of select="//ORD_NUM"/>
    </xsl:attribute>
    <ord:date><xsl:value-of select="//DATE"/></ord:date>
    <ord:customer>
      <xsl:value-of select="//CUST_NAME"/>
    </ord:customer>
    <ord:shipTo>
      <ord:addr><xsl:value-of select="//ADDRESS"/></ord:addr>
      <ord:city><xsl:value-of select="//CITY"/></ord:city>
      <ord:state><xsl:value-of select="//STATE"/></ord:state>
      <ord:postal_code>
        <xsl:value-of select="//ZIP"/>
      </ord:postal_code>
    </ord:shipTo>

    <ord:items>
      <xsl:apply-templates select="//ORDERS[1]/ORDER ITEMS"/>
    </ord:items>
  </ord:order>
</xsl:template>

<xsl:template match="ORDER_ITEMS">
  <ord:item>
    <xsl:attribute name="number">
      <xsl:value-of select="PROD_NUM"/>
    </xsl:attribute>
    <ord:quant><xsl:value-of select="QUANTITY"/></ord:quant>
    <ord:size><xsl:value-of select="SIZE"/></ord:size>
  </ord:item>
</xsl:template>

</xsl:stylesheet>
```

2. On the **File** menu, point to **Get External Data**, then click **Import**.
3. In the **Files of type** list, select **XML (*.xml;*.xsd)**.
4. Select the XML file containing the data you wish to import. For our example, use ORDERS all tables.XML.

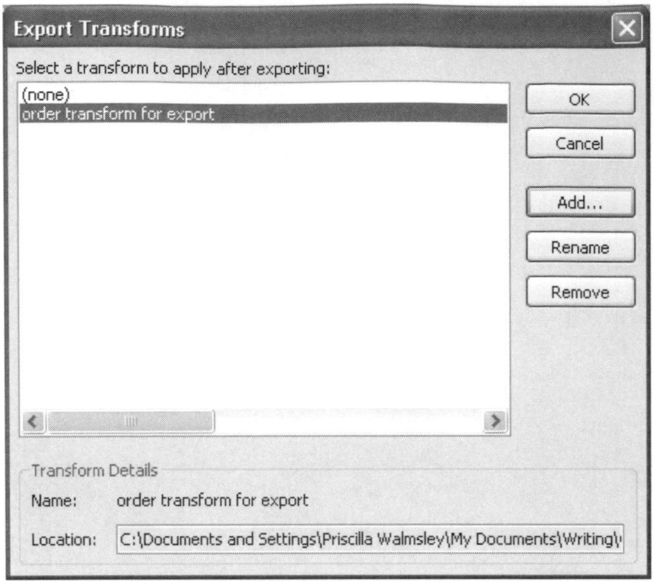

Figure 12-13   The Export Transforms dialog

5. Click **Import**.
6. This displays the **Import XML** dialog shown in Figure 12-14.

The large pane in the **Import XML** dialog shows the structure of the data to be imported. This is for informational purposes only; selecting table or column names has no effect on the import. At the bottom of the dialog (after you have clicked **Options**), you have three **Import Options**:

- **Structure Only** will create a table but will not populate it with data.
- **Structure and Data** (the default) will create a table and populate it with data. If a table by that name already exists, it will create a new table by appending a number to the name. For example, if the ORDERS table already exists, it will create ORDERS1.
- **Append Data to Existing Table(s)** will add the data to an existing table with the same name. If it cannot find a table with the appropriate name, it will create it.

Figure 12-14   The Import XML dialog

For this first example, click **Structure and Data**, then **OK**. You will see that it creates all three tables and populates them with all the existing rows.

The designs of the tables match the design of the tables in the `order.mdb` database. This is because the schema that is related to the `ORDERS all tables.xml` file, `ORDERS all tables.xsd`, contains information about the keys and column datatypes of the table. If the schema were not present, the import would still have created the tables, but it would not have defined keys for the tables, and it would have given every column the type **Text**.

12.6.2 *Appending data*

If you are interfacing your Access database with an e-commerce system, you may want to append data to existing tables rather than create new ones. For example, if a new order is received from a customer, you want to add it to the orders database. This can be accomplished checking the **Append Data to Existing Table(s)** box in the **Import XML** dialog.

The import process will generate errors for any records that have duplicate keys. For example, if your order contains products information that is already in the database, Access will raise an error message saying that it could not insert the row because of a duplicate key. It will not update the product row with the new information from the XML document.

12.6.3 *Creating your own XML document for import*

So far we have assumed that you already had a valid import file handy. However, you may be trying to map an existing XML document to Access, or creating one from scratch. In this case, it is helpful to understand how Access maps XML elements to tables and columns.

Access makes certain assumptions about the way the XML document is organized, namely that:

- The `dataroot` element contains all of the data.
- Any elements (other than the root element) that have child elements are assumed to represent rows in tables whose name is the same as the row's element-type name.

    For example, in Example 12-1, since ORDERS elements have children, Access assumes that it should create or use a table named ORDERS, and insert a row in this table for every ORDERS element in the XML document.

- The children of these row elements are assumed to represent columns. For example, in Example 12-1, Access creates columns for all the children of ORDERS, such as DATE and CITY.

Access will simply ignore elements that do not fit into this paradigm, such as elements that are children of the root element and do not have children of their own. Access will also ignore any data in attribute values.

Tip   There is a fairly easy way to determine how your XML document needs to be structured for import into Access. You can export an example from the database using the Export process described earlier in this chapter. You can then use the generated data file as an example, and use the generated schema to validate any incoming documents.

12.6.4 *Applying a transform on import*

The XML document you want to import will not always be structured as described in the previous section. You may have different element-type names in your XML document, or an entirely different structure from the one to be used in the database.

For example, suppose we were starting with the other kind of order document that was shown in Example 12-5, and we wanted to import it into our ORDERS database. We would need a transformation to change the element-type names and structure to match the Access tables. A simple XSLT stylesheet that accomplishes this transformation is shown in Example 12-7.

To specify that a transform should take place on import:

- From the **Import XML** dialog, click **Transform**. This brings up the **Import Transforms** dialog shown in Figure 12-15.
- Add a transform by clicking **Add**, browsing to the XSLT file name, and clicking **Add**. In our example, use order transform for import.xsl.
- Select the transform you want to use, and click **OK** to apply the transform.

The **Import Transforms** dialog lists all the *available* transforms. It is possible to add more than one transform to the list. However, only one will be applied on any given import: the one that is selected when the **OK** button is clicked. If the transform generates an XML document that cannot be

Example 12-7. Transforming the order on import (order transform for import.xml)

```xml
<?xml version="1.0" encoding="UTF-8"?>
<xsl:stylesheet version="1.0"
                xmlns:xsl="http://www.w3.org/1999/XSL/Transform"
                xmlns:ord="http://xmlinoffice.com/orders">
<xsl:template match="/ord:order">
  <dataroot xmlns:xsi="http://www.w3.org/2001/XMLSchema-instance">
   <ORDERS> <!--assumes only 1 order in the source document-->
     <ORD_NUM><xsl:value-of select="@number"/></ORD_NUM>
     <DATE><xsl:value-of select="ord:date"/></DATE>
     <CUST_NAME><xsl:value-of select="ord:customer"/></CUST_NAME>
     <ADDRESS><xsl:value-of select="ord:shipTo/ord:addr"/></ADDRESS>
     <CITY><xsl:value-of select="ord:shipTo/ord:city"/></CITY>
     <STATE><xsl:value-of select="ord:shipTo/ord:state"/></STATE>
     <ZIP><xsl:value-of select="ord:shipTo/ord:postal_code"/></ZIP>
     <xsl:apply-templates select="ord:items/ord:item"/>
   </ORDERS>
  </dataroot>
</xsl:template>

<xsl:template match="item">
<ORDER_ITEMS>
  <ORDER_NUM><xsl:value-of select="/ord:order/@number"/></ORDER_NUM>
  <PROD_NUM><xsl:value-of select="@number"/></PROD_NUM>
  <QUANTITY><xsl:value-of select="ord:quant"/></QUANTITY>
  <SIZE><xsl:value-of select="ord:size"/></SIZE>
</ORDER_ITEMS>
</xsl:template>

</xsl:stylesheet>
```

imported into Access, you will receive an appropriate error message. You will then be asked whether you want to save a copy of the transformed file to a temporary directory. It is useful to do this, since examining the transformed file often makes any errors in the stylesheet obvious.

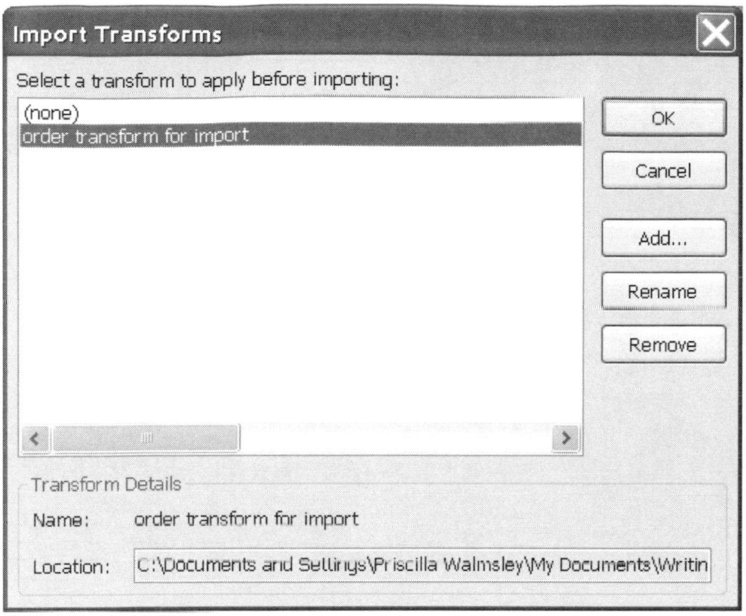

Figure 12-15   The Import Transforms dialog

Publishing XML to the Web with FrontPage

- Web design by example

- Setting up your website

- Choosing a data source

- Creating a data view

- Organizing the viewed data

- Formatting a data view

his chapter shows you how to use the XML-related features of
FrontPage in the creation of data-driven dynamic websites. Basic familiarity with FrontPage and Windows SharePoint Services isn't strictly necessary to understand this chapter, but will be required in order to actually build a FrontPage website.

> *Skills required*   Some techniques that we cover require
> knowledge of XPath (see Chapter 24, "XML Path Language
> (XPath)", on page 498) and XSLT (see Chapter 18, "XSL
> Transformations (XSLT)", on page 392).

13.1 | Why use FrontPage with XML?

We've seen that XML allows us to represent information in a purely abstract
way, separate from its presentation. In Chapter 4, "Creating and editing
XML documents", on page 60 we learned how XSLT stylesheets can be

used to transform abstract XML documents into WordML renditions so that they can be viewed, printed and edited as Word documents.

A more common transformation is from XML documents into HTML, to allow XML documents and data to be viewed on the Web. You can write such stylesheets by hand, as we did for WordML. For HTML output, though, FrontPage gives you a convenient alternative for many documents: a WYSIWYG editor that generates the XSLT for you.

Warning   The features of FrontPage described in this chapter are only available for websites that use Windows SharePoint Services. In order to run SharePoint, your Web server must run Windows 2003. FrontPage 2003 itself can run on Windows 2000, Windows XP, or Windows 2003.

13.2 | Web design by example

FrontPage uses a *design by example* paradigm, in which you design a Web page by inserting *data views* of representative data sources. You organize the data in the views and apply formatting styles. The product then generates an XSLT stylesheet that will produce the same Web page from any data source that conforms to the same schema as the representative.

Ellen, whom you may remember from 7.2, "The Worldwide Widget expense report", on page 134, decides to use FrontPage to create a Web page for the company intranet to expedite the expense approval process. In the following sections, we will go through the process step by step:

1. Set up a SharePoint website.
2. Define one or more representative data sources.
3. Create data views of the whole of the data sources or of selected elements.
4. Organize the viewed data by sorting, grouping, filtering, etc.
5. Format the data view from a choice of layouts and styles, including data-driven conditional formatting.

13.3 | Set up the website

The first order of business is to set up the website. To create a SharePoint website in FrontPage:

1. On the **File** menu, click **New**. This will display the **New** task pane.
2. From the task pane, click **SharePoint based team Web site**. This will display the **Web Site Templates** dialog.
3. Under **Options**, type the location of your new site. This will be the URL of your SharePoint site, plus a slash and the subdirectory that you would like to use for the new site.
4. You will be prompted to log into SharePoint. Enter your user ID and password and press Enter. This will show your new site in the Explorer window.

13.4 | Choose a data source

FrontPage allows you to define any *data source* that can be an XML document. These include all that we have encountered with other Office products, in other words:

- A local XML file
- A URL that returns an XML document
- A REST Web service (although you will have to construct the parameter string in the URL reference yourself)
- A SOAP Web service
- A database that can export XML

You can define multiple data sources to be combined in the same Web page. FrontPage allows you to create different data views for each of them.

 *Tip*   Remember that FrontPage doesn't understand schemas. The page design – and therefore the generated stylesheet – are based entirely on the representative data sources. Make sure that yours include all possible element types. You are not generating a static HTML page for that specific data, but a view that can be applied to any XML document that conforms to the same schema.

Ellen has chosen the file `sample expense report.xml` to represent Worldwide's expense reports. To upload it to your website:

1. On the **File** menu, point to **Import**, then click **Add File**.
2. Select the `sample expense report.xml` file and click **Open**.
3. Click **OK** to close the **Import** dialog.

13.5 | Create a data view

Your next step is to create a Web page into which you will insert data views of the expense report. To do this, you should start with a new Web page, as follows:

1. On the **File** menu, click **New**.
2. Click **Blank page** on the **New** task pane.
3. This will create a blank page named something like `new_page_1.htm`.

You can insert data views either in **Design** mode or in **Code** mode; it is your choice. For this exercise, click **Design** mode at the bottom of the window.

To see the data sources for which you can create data views:

1. On the **Data** menu, click **Insert Data View**. This will display the **Data Source Catalog** task pane, shown in Figure 13-1.

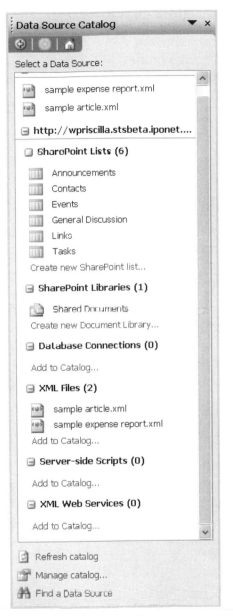

Figure 13-1   The Data Source Catalog task pane

2. Under **XML Files**, you should see the `sample expense report.xml` file you just imported. Right-click it, and click **Show Data** on the resulting context menu.
3. FrontPage will display the **Data View Details** task pane, shown in Figure 13-2. This task pane shows the structure of the data source, as well as any settings of the data view itself, such as styles, sorting and filtering.

You are now ready to begin inserting data views of the data source into your page. This is accomplished by selecting an element or elements in the task pane and clicking **Insert Data View**. For this example, we will focus on the repeating data (the expense items themselves).

1. Make sure the cursor is positioned in the Web page where you want to insert the data view.
2. Select the `expense` element, located about half way down the tree structure, and click **Insert Data View**.
3. This will display the expenses as a table, as shown in Figure 13-3.

The table contains a row for each `expense` element, and a column for each child of `expense`. The column headers are the child element-type names.

13.6 | Organize the viewed data

Once you have displayed repeating data in a view, FrontPage will allow you to massage that data in various ways, including inserting new columns, sorting and grouping, filtering, and conditional formatting.

13.6.1 *Inserting columns*

Our generated expense table automatically cuts the table off at five columns, but more columns can be added manually to reflect the rest of the child elements. To do this:

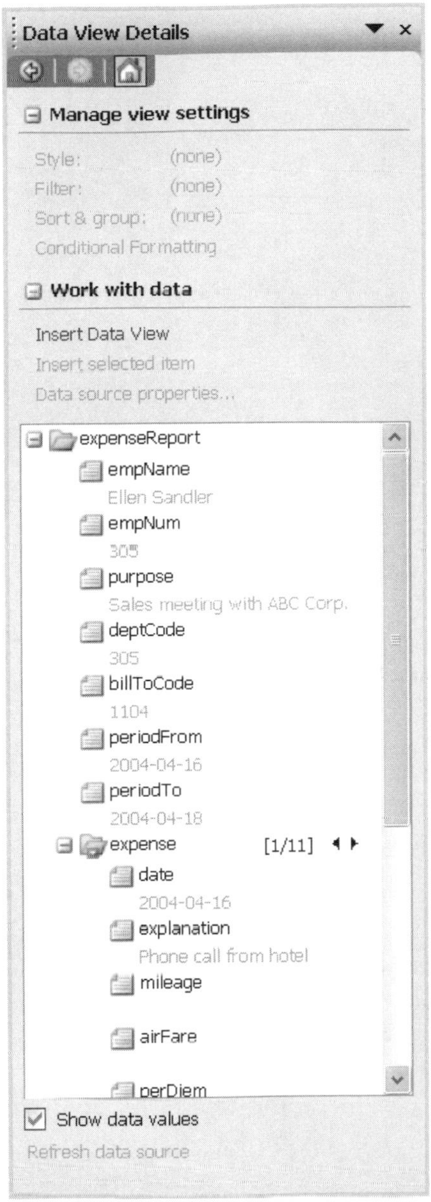

Figure 13-2   The Data View Details task pane

1. Position the cursor after the last column header, namely perDiem.

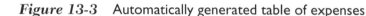

date	explanation	mileage	airFare	perDiem
2004-04-16	Phone call from hotel			
2004-04-16	Lodging			
2004-04-17	Lodging			
2004-04-16	Airfare		789.0	
2004-04-16	Cab to Hotel			
2004-04-18	Travel to/from airport	36		
2004-04-18	Parking at Airport			
2004-04-16	Per Diem			36.0
2004-04-17	Per Diem			36.0
2004-04-16	Dry Cleaning			

Design Split Code Preview

Figure 13-3   Automatically generated table of expenses

2. On the **Table** menu, point to **Insert**, then click **Rows or Columns**.
3. This brings up the **Insert Rows or Columns** dialog, as shown in Figure 13-4.
4. Click **Columns**, then **OK**. This will place a column after the `perDiem` column.
5. To specify a column header, type `Lodging` into the first row of the new column.
6. To populate the column, drag the `lodging` element into the *second* row of the new column. This will automatically populate all the rows of the table with the lodging data.

After you have added the rest of the columns, and revised the column headers, you are left with a table that looks like Figure 13-5.

13.6.2 *Sorting and grouping*

Suppose you want to sort our expense items by date. To do this:

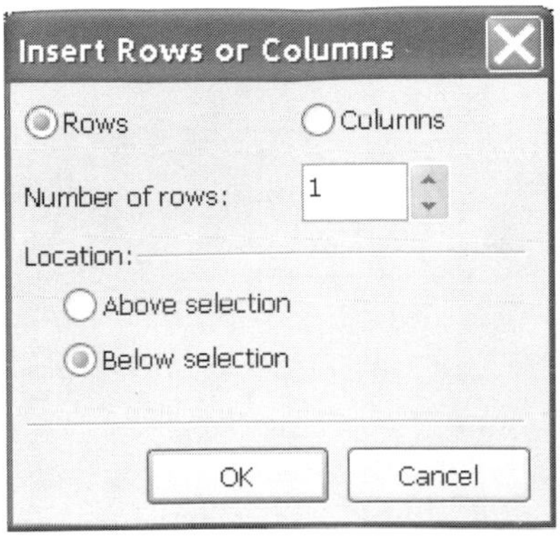

Figure 13-4   The Insert Rows or Columns dialog

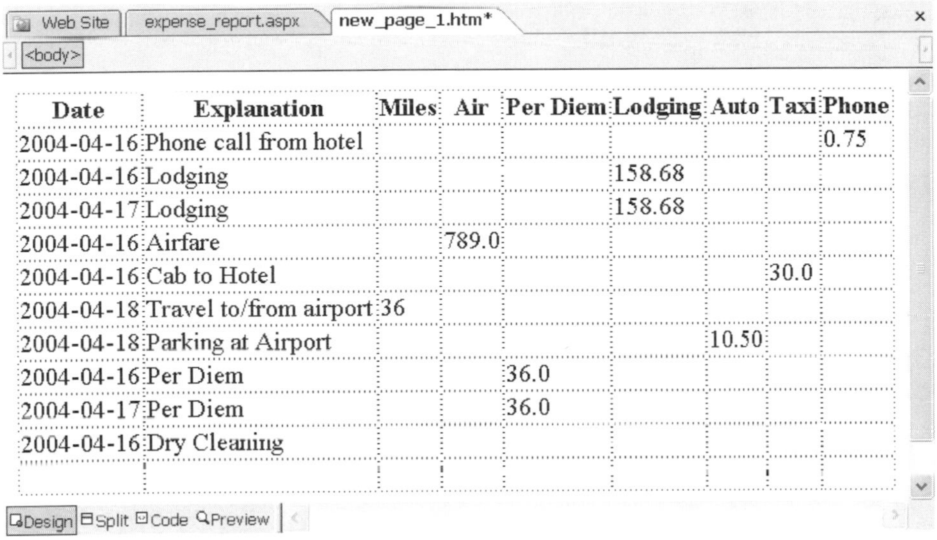

Figure 13-5   The revised table

1. Position the cursor anywhere in the table.
2. On the **Data** menu, click **Sort and Group**. This displays the **Sort and Group** dialog shown in Figure 13-6.
3. Select **date** from the list on the left, and click **Add**. This will add date to the list of columns to sort on.

4. Click **OK** and verify that the rows in the table are now sorted by date.

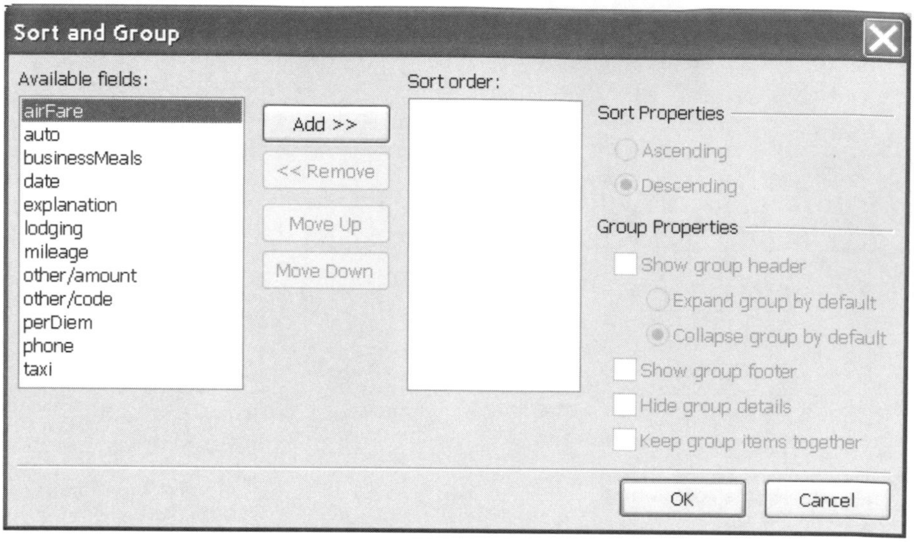

Figure 13-6   The Sort and Group dialog

In addition to sorting, rows can be grouped together by the column(s) on which they are sorted. This can be accomplished by checking the **Show group header** box on the **Sort and Group** dialog. This will result in a table that looks like Figure 13-7.

13.6.3 *Filtering*

It is also possible to filter the rows, based on conditions you specify. For example, suppose you want to show only the expenses where there is a lodging charge greater than $150. To do this:

1. Position the cursor anywhere in the table.
2. On the **Data** menu, click **Filter**. This displays the **Filter Criteria** dialog shown in Figure 13-8.
3. Click the row that says **Click here to add a new clause**.

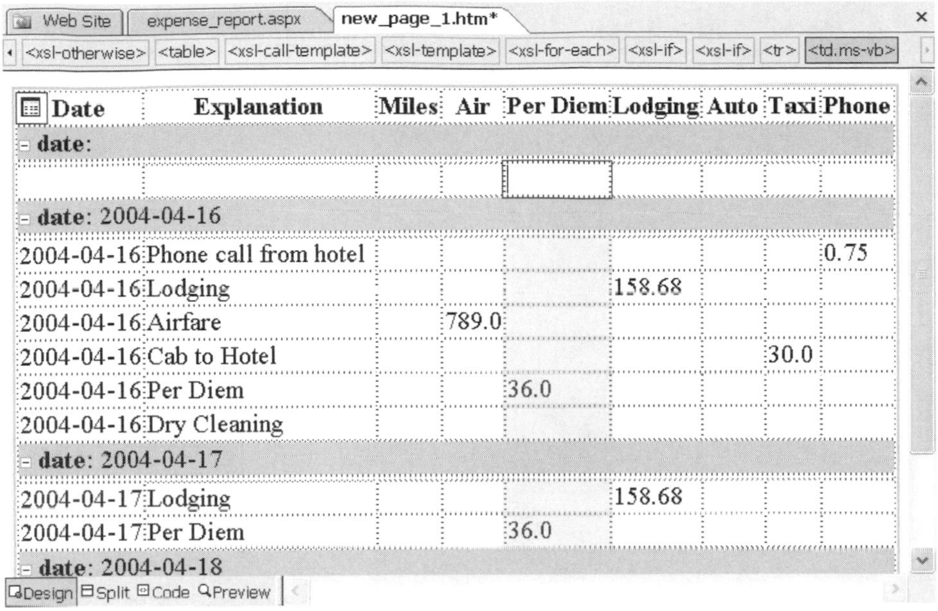

Figure 13-7 The sorted and grouped table

4. Select the field name **lodging (Number)**, comparison (**Greater Than**) and the value (**150**) and click **OK**.

This will limit the view to only those rows that have a value greater than 150 in the lodging element.

You can enter multiple criteria and join them using AND or OR operators. You can also specify criteria based on variables, such as the current date, and whether it is the first row in the table.

By clicking **Advanced** on the **Filter Criteria** dialog, you can also manually specify an XPath predicate that will be used to select the appropriate rows. For example, you could enter [number(ddw1:lodging) > '150'] to specify the same criteria as above. The ddw1 prefix was assigned by FrontPage to the expense report schema's target namespace. The number function instructs the processor to treat lodging like a number rather than a string. Using XPath provides more flexibility, allowing you to utilize functions such as count and max.

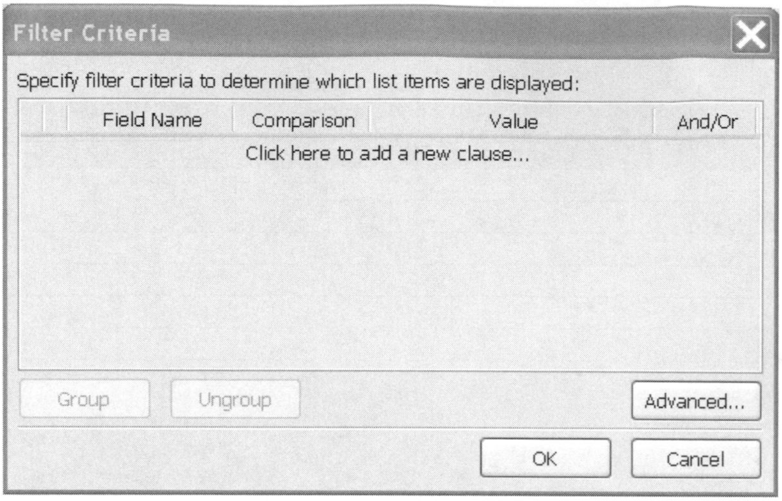

Figure 13-8   The Filter Criteria dialog

13.7 | Format the view

Once you have displayed the data you want, you can further refine the look of the view using the features of FrontPage. Once formatted, our table might look something like Figure 13-9.

The following sections describe two features for data-driven formatting: applying a style to the data itself, and conditional formatting.

13.7.1 *Applying a style to the data*

Our example has rows for expenses and columns for the various sub-elements of an expense. However, there may be occasions where you want to lay out the data differently. For example, in two columns, with the element-type names (e.g. date, explanation) on the left, and their content on the right. To do this:

1. Position the cursor anywhere in the table.
2. On the **Data** menu, click **Style**. This displays the **View Styles** dialog shown in Figure 13-10.

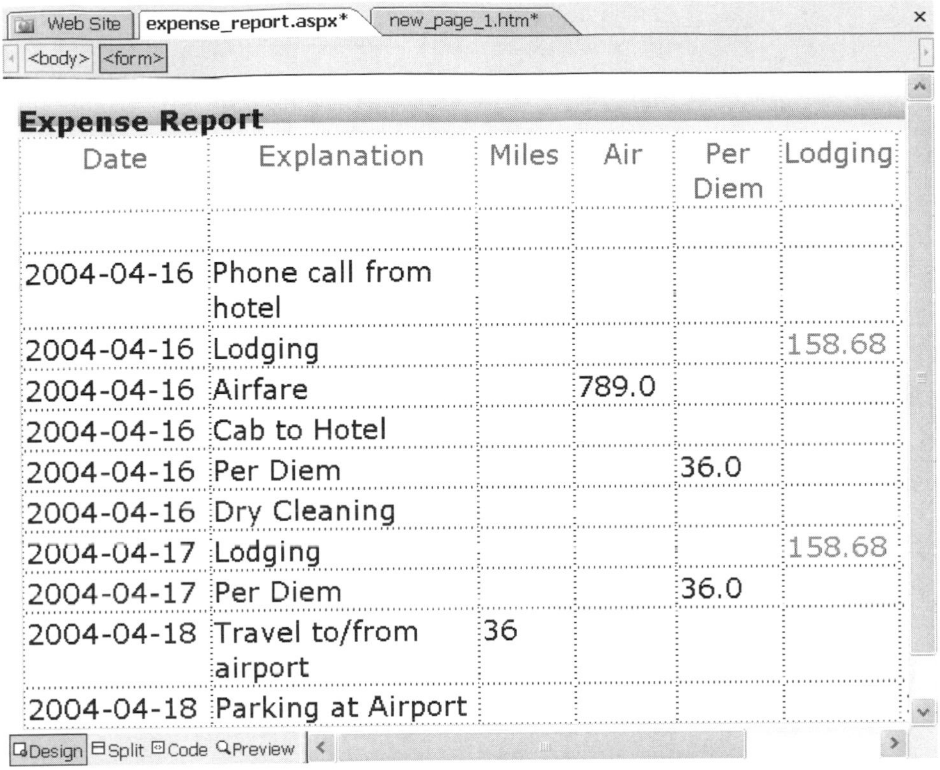

| Web Site | expense_report.aspx* | new_page_1.htm* | × |

`<body>` `<form>`

Expense Report

Date	Explanation	Miles	Air	Per Diem	Lodging
2004-04-16	Phone call from hotel				
2004-04-16	Lodging				158.68
2004-04-16	Airfare		789.0		
2004-04-16	Cab to Hotel				
2004-04-16	Per Diem			36.0	
2004-04-16	Dry Cleaning				
2004-04-17	Lodging				158.68
2004-04-17	Per Diem			36.0	
2004-04-18	Travel to/from airport	36			
2004-04-18	Parking at Airport				

Design   Split   Code   Preview

Figure 13-9   The formatted table

3. Select one of the styles from the list and click **OK**. The currently selected one produces the style in Figure 13-9, but there is another that would produce Figure 13-11.

13.7.2 *Conditional formatting*

You can format data differently based on criteria. For example, to have rows with a lodging charge of over $150 show up in red, to call attention to them during the manager's review of the expense report, do this:

1. On the **Data** menu, click **Conditional Formatting**. This displays the **Conditional Formatting** task pane shown in Figure 13-12.

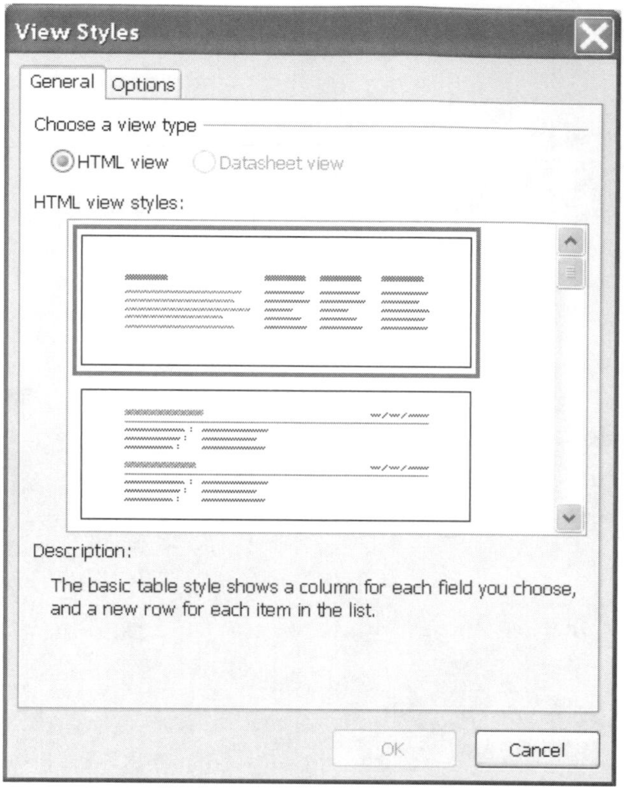

Figure 13-10   The View Styles dialog with a tabular layout selected

2. Select one of the lodging values (not the whole column), and click **Create**, then **Apply formatting** on the task pane.
3. This will bring up the **Condition Criteria** dialog which is similar to the **Filter Criteria** dialog in Figure 13-8.
4. Click the row that says **Click here to add a new clause**.
5. Enter the field name (**lodging (number)**), comparison (**Greater Than**) and the value (**150**) and click **OK**.
6. This will bring up the **Modify Style** dialog shown in Figure 13-13.
7. From there, you can choose a style for the data that meets the criteria by clicking **Format**. In our case, to modify the color of the text, click **Font** on the **Format** menu.

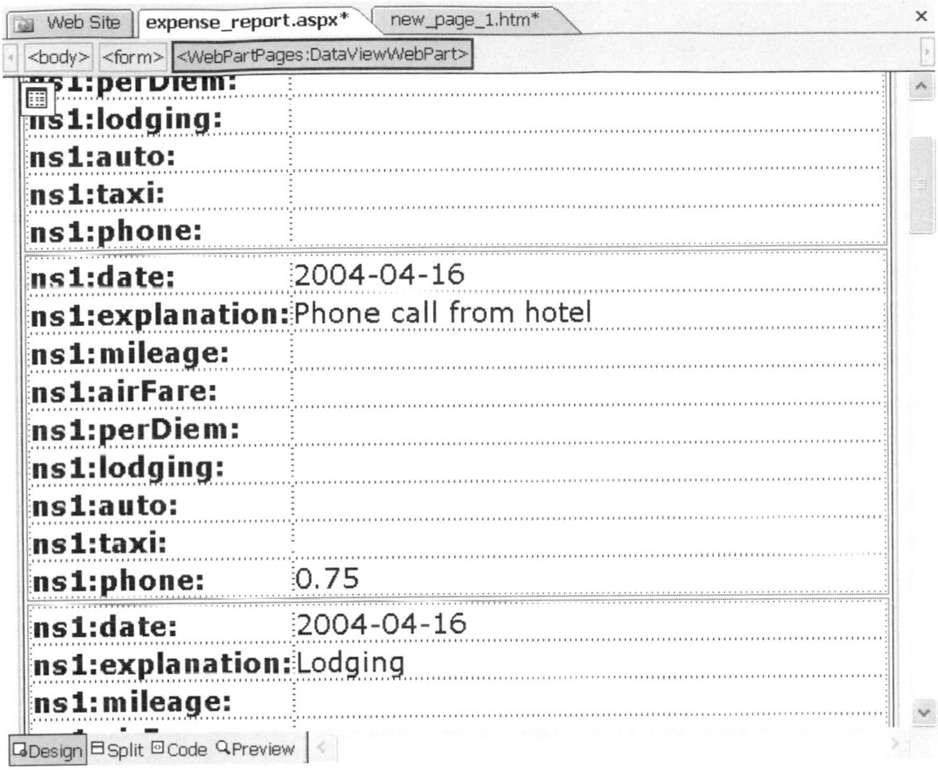

Figure 13-11   Restyled table

8. For **Color** select the red shade and click **OK**, then **OK** again to return to the main workspace.

As you can see, the lodging values are now displayed in red. Using the **Conditional Formatting** task pane, you can also choose to show or hide data based on criteria. This will result in the entire row (in this case, expense item) being shown or hidden, not just the value(s) being tested (e.g. lodging amount).

Figure 13-12   The Conditional Formatting task pane

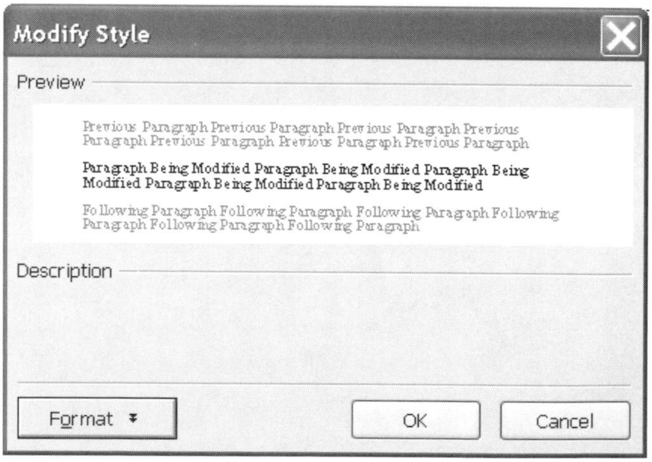

Figure 13-13   The Modify Style dialog

13.7.3 *Formatting freeform XML documents*

FrontPage's view styles are designed for predictable data that lends itself to tabular presentation (think "spreadsheet"). Our expense report is a typical example.

But what if you want to present a freeform XML document on a FrontPage site? For the most part you'll need to create your own XSLT stylesheets, as we'll describe shortly. But for some documents you can get some or all of the job done by using multiple data views.

For example, we can handle Doug's newsletter article in Figure 13-14 by dividing it into two different data views, hence two different styles.

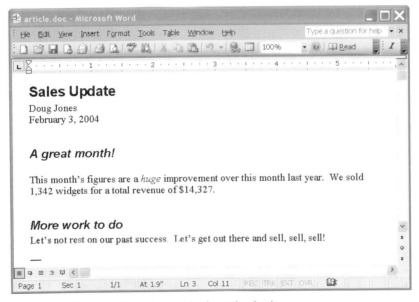

Figure 13-14   Doug's article (article.doc)

The first view, in tabular style, will include the elements that represent properties of the article, such as `title`, `author` and `date`. The body of the article will appear afterwards in a view styled more appropriately for freeform text.

To create the tabular view:

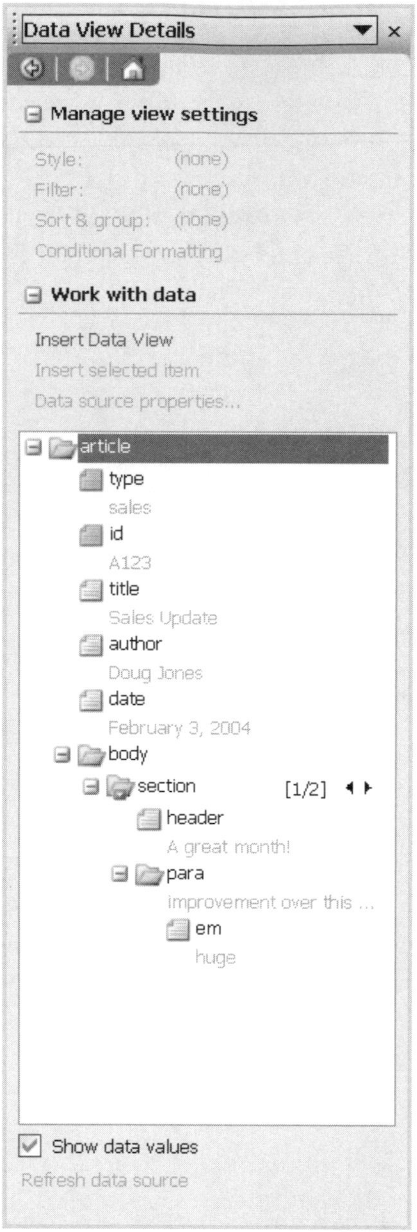

Figure 13-15 The Data View Details task pane for the article

1. Import the `sample article.xml`, select it in the **Data Source** task pane, and bring up its structure, shown in Figure 13-15, by right-clicking and choosing **View Data**.
2. Select the "property" elements `type`, `id`, `title`, `author` and `date`. Holding down the CTRL key will allow you to select multiple elements and attributes.
3. Click **Insert Data View** on the task pane.
4. This will insert the selected elements in a table with the element-type names in the first column, and the data content in the second, as shown in the top part of Figure 13-16. This is the default view for data that does not repeat.

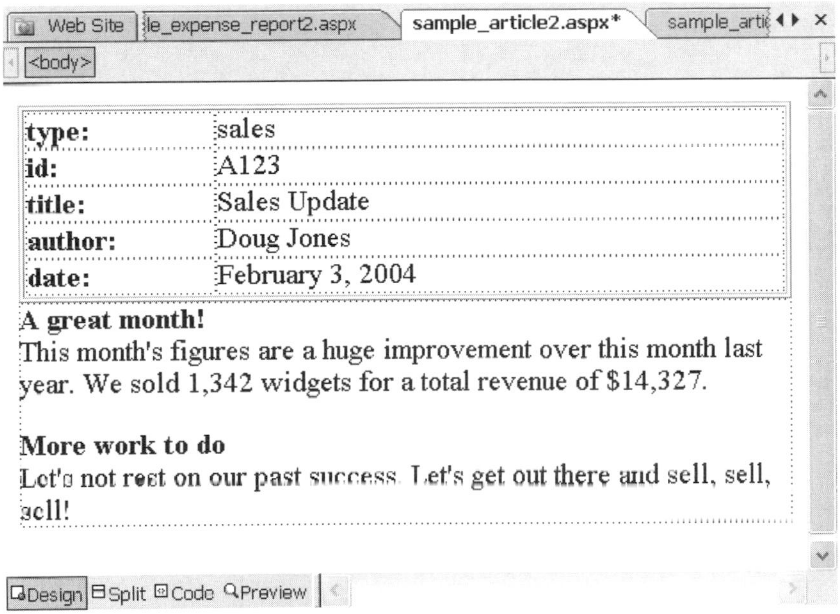

Figure 13-16   The article Web page

The next step is to insert the data view for the body of the article. Because the body has a simple structure that just alternates headers with paragraphs, we can use one of FrontPage's built-in styles. To specify the style of view we want:

1. Select the `section` element and click **Insert Data View**. This will insert the sections in the default style: as a table with two columns labeled `header` and `para` (the children of `section`).

2. For a style more suited to headers and paragraphs, click **Style** on the **Data** menu, and select the style shown in Figure 13-17.

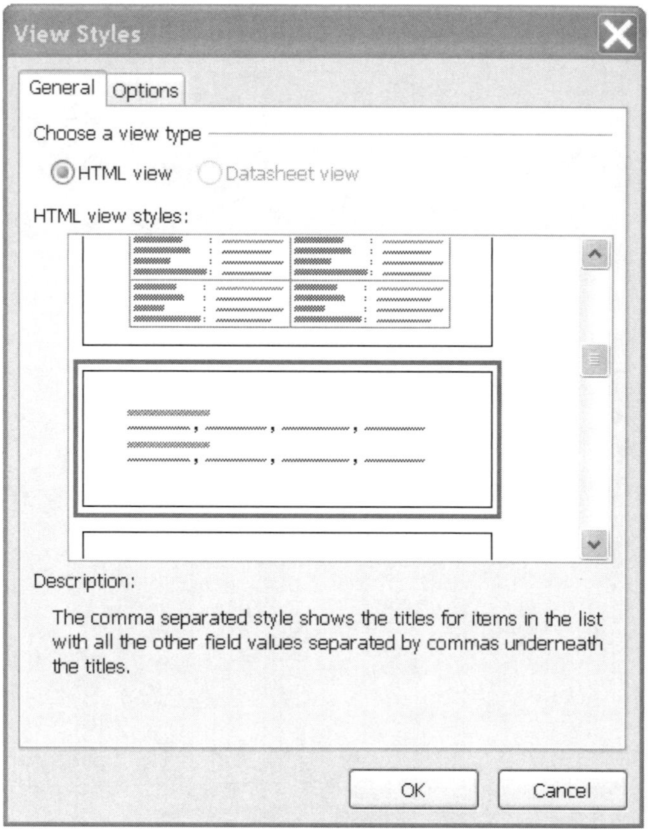

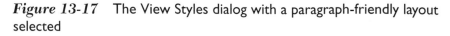

Figure 13-17   The View Styles dialog with a paragraph-friendly layout selected

This will display the headers followed by the paragraphs, as shown in Figure 13-16.

As before, you can modify the presentation of the article using the standard features of FrontPage, resulting in a document that looks like Figure 13-18.

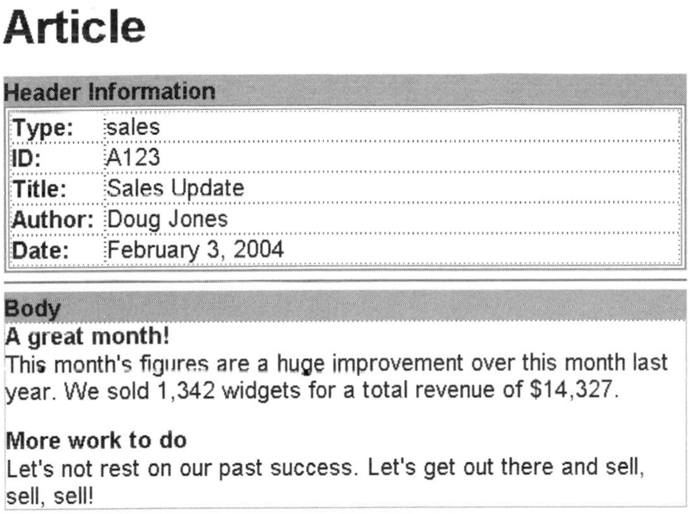

Article

Header Information	
Type:	sales
ID:	A123
Title:	Sales Update
Author:	Doug Jones
Date:	February 3, 2004

Body
A great month!
This month's figures are a huge improvement over this month last year. We sold 1,342 widgets for a total revenue of $14,327.
More work to do
Let's not rest on our past success. Let's get out there and sell, sell, sell!

Figure 13-18   The formatted article

13.7.4 *Editing and creating XSLT stylesheets*

FrontPage takes you a long way toward creating dynamic Web pages from XML documents. However, there may be cases where its WYSIWYG editor is not capable of displaying the data the way you want.

Behind the scenes, FrontPage is generating an XSLT stylesheet that transforms your XML data source into HTML. The XSLT is embedded in an ASPX Web page as a Web page part.

You can hand-modify the generated XSLT stylesheet from the **Code** view, which is shown in Figure 13-19. The ConnectionID element is the connection information for the data source, while the XSL element is a wrapper for the actual XSLT stylesheet.

Tip   *Even without FrontPage and SharePoint, you can create XSLT stylesheets to transform your XML documents into HTML or XHTML. You can use a plain text editor or one of the many tools available for this purpose.*

```
39 <ConnectionID>00000000-0000-0000-0000-000000000000</Connection
40 <XSL xmlns="http://schemas.microsoft.com/WebPart/v2/DataView">
41   <xsl:stylesheet version="1.0" exclude-result-prefixes="xsl c
42       <xsl:output method="html" indent="no"/>
43       <xsl:param name="dvt_adhocmode"></xsl:param>
44       <xsl:param name="dvt_fieldsort"></xsl:param>
45       <xsl:param name="dvt_sortfield"></xsl:param>
46       <xsl:param name="dvt_groupfield"></xsl:param>
47       <xsl:param name="dvt_sortdir"></xsl:param>
48       <xsl:param name="dvt_groupdir"></xsl:param>
49       <xsl:param name="dvt_grouptype"></xsl:param>
50       <xsl:param name="dvt_filterfield"></xsl:param>
51       <xsl:param name="dvt_filterval"></xsl:param>
52       <xsl:param name="dvt_firstrow">1</xsl:param>
53       <xsl:param name="dvt_nextpagedata"></xsl:param>
54       <xsl:template match="/">
55           <xsl:call-template name="dvt_1"/>
56       </xsl:template>
57       <xsl:template name="dvt_1">
58           <xsl:variable name="StyleName">RepForm3</xsl:variabl
59           <xsl:variable name="Rows" select="/*[name()='article
60           <xsl:variable name="RowCount" select="count($Rows)"/
61           <xsl:variable name="IsEmpty" select="$RowCount = 0"/
62           <xsl:choose>
63               <xsl:when test="$IsEmpty">
64                   <xsl:call-template name="dvt_1.empty"/>
65               </xsl:when>
```

Web Site | pense_report2.aspx | sample_article2.aspx* | **sample_article.aspx***

Design Split Code Preview

Figure 13-19   The XSLT stylesheet in the Code view

Developing Office XML applications

- Smart documents
- Smart tags
- The research pane
- XML expansion packs and manifests

P revious versions of Microsoft Office allowed developers to create custom applications that work within the Office environment. XML in Office 2003 improves Office custom applications, for two major reasons:

- Office can process more than its traditional binary .doc and .xls files. These days, almost any data is available as XML, which means it can be edited by Office. Complex applications can be built to perform completely customized tasks, but still provide the familiar features of the Office environment.
- XML allows the elements of a document to be identified unambiguously. Applications can therefore be accurately context-sensitive when interacting with the user.

A complete explanation of how to develop Office-based applications is outside the scope of this book. This chapter covers some of the key XML-enabled aspects, including:[1]

---

1. Microsoft refers to applications that use these features as *smart client solutions*.

- Smart documents, which allow specialized, context-sensitive task panes to appear, depending on the current element type. Users can interact with controls in the task pane.
- Smart tags, which allow context-sensitive menus to appear when a sequence of characters is recognized that matches a list or pattern.
- The research pane, which allows customized research services to be used from an Office task pane.
- XML expansion packs and manifests, which facilitate the deployment of Office applications.

14.1 | Smart documents

Smart documents are documents for which there are customized, context-sensitive, **Document Actions** task panes that assist the user in working with the document. They are context-sensitive in that the task pane changes depending on the type of element in which the cursor is positioned.

Some applications of smart documents include:

- Providing customized help for a specific set of users. Medical personnel filling out a health insurance claim form could be provided with a help pane whose content changes as they navigate from field to field.
- Allowing users to access data from a variety of sources by clicking on the task pane. Users preparing legal documents could include different types of boilerplate text from other documents or from a Web service.
- Guiding users through a process. Employees filling out an expense report can be guided step by step (calculate totals, validate, submit, etc.) based on the information that has already been completed in the worksheet.
- Providing context-sensitive data. Customer service representatives responding to a customer complaint can choose an explanation from a drop-down list in the task pane. The list members vary depending on the nature of the complaint.

- Allowing common actions to be performed at the click of a button. Smart document solutions can be configured to email the original author of a document when you have made revisions to it, or send a document to a Web service once it is complete.

This section explains smart documents, and provides an overview of how to build and use them in Word. We will revisit our customer letter example to illustrate the capabilities and walk you through the underlying code.[2]

A smart document solution is designed to work with XML documents that conform to a specific schema. Our letter solution, for example, will only work with documents that conform to the letter.xsd schema. You cannot use it with a non-XML Word document, or with an XML document that conforms to another schema.

Although the example uses Word, you can also use smart documents with Excel, in areas of worksheets that are mapped to the appropriate schema.

14.1.1 *The customer letter example, revisited*

In Chapter 6, "Using external XML data in documents", on page 114 we learned about Worldwide Widget's award-winning customer service program. The company prides itself on how quickly it responds to a customer complaint with a sincere personalized form letter. It decides to build a smart document solution to improve response time and the sincerity of the generated content.

We can add a variety of functions to the task pane, which will allow the user to:

- see different help text depending on where the cursor is positioned
- select a value for salutation or format from a group of radio buttons, as shown in Figure 14-1

---

2. Microsoft provides a Smart Documents Software Development Kit (SDK), downloadable from its website, which provides further detailed information and examples.

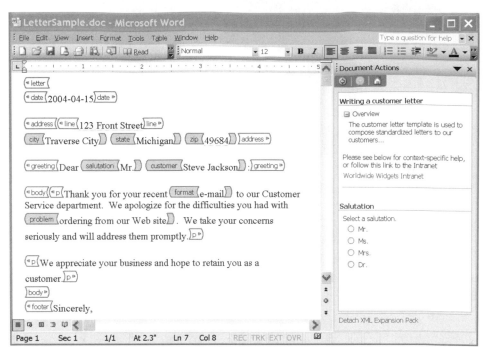

Figure 14-1　A smart document pane with radio buttons

- select boilerplate text to insert into the body of the document, as shown in Figure 14-2
- press a button to fill in the customer address based on the customer name
- link to websites for further assistance

A working customer letter example named LetterSample.doc can be found in the example files on the book's website.

14.1.2　*Installing a smart document solution*

Word documents and templates, and Excel workbooks, have to be associated with smart document solutions much like they need to be associated with schemas. Every smart document solution has a *manifest*, which is an XML document that lists all the components of the solution and their loca-

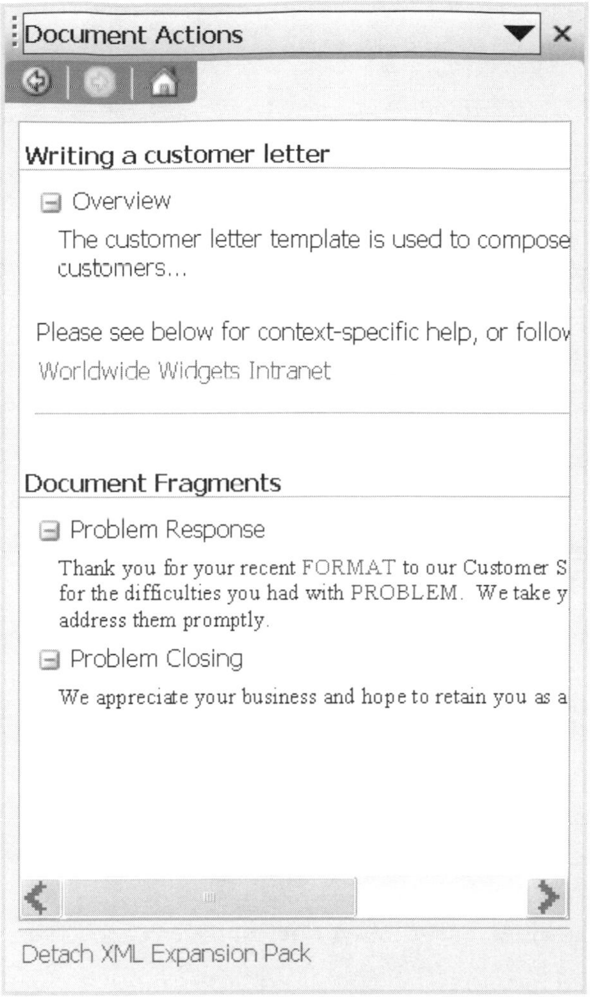

Figure 14-2   Listing document fragments for insertion

tions. We will look more closely at manifests in 14.4, "XML expansion packs and manifests", on page 346.

To associate a smart document solution with a Word document:

1. Open the document, in this case `letter_smart.doc`, in Word. It does not matter whether the `letter` schema has been added to the schema library yet.
2. Click **Templates and Add-ins** on the **Tools** menu.

Figure 14-3 The XML Expansion Packs tab of the Templates and Add-ins dialog

3. Click the **XML Expansion Packs** tab, which results in the dialog shown in Figure 14-3.
4. Click **Add**. In the resulting dialog, browse to the location of `letter_manifest.xml` and select it.
5. This will return you to the **Templates and Add-ins** dialog, this time with the attached solution listed as an available expansion pack, as shown in Figure 14-4.
6. Click **OK** to return to your document.

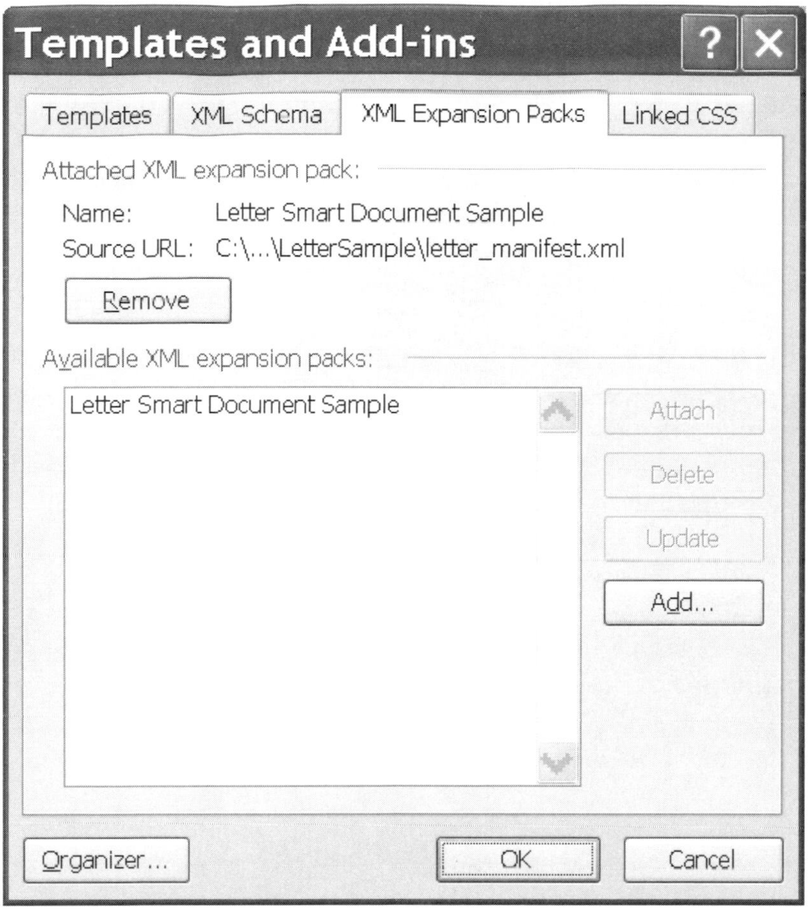

Figure 14-4   The XML Expansion Packs tab with expansion pack added

Attaching the manifest not only associated the smart document solution with your document, it associated a schema (which is listed in the manifest) with your document. You can now use the example to test out the capabilities of smart documents.

14.1.3 *How smart documents work*

The smart document solution is sensitive to element types. Whenever the mouse is clicked within an element, the **Document Actions** task pane displays user controls that are associated with that element type.

In Figure 14-1, for example, the cursor is currently positioned in the `salutation` element, which is associated with the radio button group at the bottom of the task pane. The four controls above that – help text, a hyperlink, etc. – belong to the ancestors of the current element, since the click occurred within them as well.

In this case there are two ancestors – `greeting` and `letter` – but all four of the other controls belong to `letter`.

Each of the two element types has a *caption* that introduces its controls. The caption for `letter` is "Writing a customer letter", while the caption for `salutation` is "Salutation".

The controls themselves may have captions and internal text. The caption for the radio group is "Select a salutation." Its internal text appears next to each of the buttons.

If the user interacts with a control, a *behavior* will occur. In our example, if a radio button is clicked, its text will be inserted into the document as the content of the `salutation`.

In order for the smart document processing to accomplish these things, your solution must provide it with the necessary information. Specifically:

1. The element-type names and captions for each element type that has controls.
2. The number of controls and types of control that are associated with each element type. The complete list of control types is found in Table 14-1.
3. The desired appearance of the controls, including their captions, display properties (such as fonts), and internal text such as the strings that appear with each radio button.
4. The behavior that occurs when a user interacts with the controls, for example by pressing a button or selecting an item from a list.

> *Tip*　If you are able to limit your solution to using only hyperlink, separator, label, image, embedded help, and button controls (with buttons limited to hyperlink actions), you can provide this information in XML without writing any program code. The Smart Documents SDK has the details on this. It is an extension of the smart tags list that we discuss in 14.2.1, "Using smart tag lists (MOSTL)", on page 338.

14.1.4 *The smart document interface*

The code for the letter solution is written in Visual Basic 6.0.[3] The Visual Basic project can be found in the example file `LetterSample.vbp`. It consists of a single class file, `clsActions.cls`, that is used to make `LetterSample.dll`.

The class implements the properties and methods of the `ISmartDocument` interface.[4] The interface has eight properties of element types and controls, and 17 methods for initializing controls and responding to interactions, as follows:

element-type properties

When a smart document is opened, or a smart document solution is attached to an open document, Office gets the values for element-type properties from your code. These include the number of element types that have controls, the element-type names and captions, and the number of controls for each element type.

control properties

Office also gets properties of each individual control, including its type, caption, and a numeric ID (`ControlID`).

---

3. Smart document solutions can also be developed in Visual Basic .NET, C# .NET and Visual C++.
4. The interface is in the Microsoft Smart Tags 2.0 Type Library.

Table 14-1   Control types

Control-type name constant	Description
C_TYPE_ACTIVEX	ActiveX control
C_TYPE_BUTTON	Command button
C_TYPE_CHECKBOX	Check box
C_TYPE_COMBO	Combo box
C_TYPE_DOCUMENTFRAGMENT	Document fragment that is specified as an XML string
C_TYPE_DOCUMENTFRAGMENTURL	Document fragment that is specified as a URL that returns an XML string
C_TYPE_HELP	Help text that is specified as an XHTML string
C_TYPE_HELPURL	Help text that is specified as a URL that returns an XHTML string
C_TYPE_IMAGE	Image
C_TYPE_LABEL	Label that is specified as a plain text string
C_TYPE_LINK	Hyperlink
C_TYPE_LISTBOX	List box
C_TYPE_RADIOGROUP	Radio button group
C_TYPE_SEPARATOR	Horizontal line
C_TYPE_TEXTBOX	Text box

control rendering methods

When the user clicks in an element, Office invokes a method for each of the element type's controls. The method supplies the information needed to render the control in the task pane. The method names are usually derived from the control type names; for example, `PopulateRadioGroup`, our implementation of which is shown in Example 14-8.[5]

control action methods

When the user interacts with a control, Office invokes a method that performs the desired behavior. The method name is usually derived from the control type name; for example, `OnRadioGroupSelectChange`, our implementation of which is shown in Example 14-10.

The number of properties and methods that your class needs to implement depends on the types of control you use. In the following sections we will see how our example class implements these properties and methods.[6]

14.1.4.1 Element-type properties

The beginning of the class code is shown in Example 14-1. The third line defines the constant `cTYPES` to be the number of element types with associated controls. Office gets this value from the `SmartDocXmlTypeCount` property. It is the basis for initializing the other element-type properties.

14.1.4.1.1 *Element-type names*

The smart document interface requires element-type names to be namespace-qualified. In XML that would mean declaring a namespace abbreviation and prefixing it with a colon to the element-type name. Smart document code doesn't have XML's syntactic constraints and doesn't need the abbreviation; the prefix is the complete namespace URI and a pound sign.[7]

---

5. In Visual Basic 6.0, the property and method names are prefixed with "`ISmartDocument_`".
6. Only enough of the code is included to show how it works.

In the code, the namespace URI is assigned to the constant cNAMESPACE, which is used to construct the qualified names for the ten element types that are to have controls associated with them (e.g. cLETTER, cSALUTATION).

Example 14-1. Defining constants for later reference

```
Option Explicit
Implements ISmartDocument
Const cTYPES As Integer = 10

Const cNAMESPACE As String = "http://xmlinoffice.com/letter"

Const cLETTER As String = cNAMESPACE & "#letter"
Const cDATE2 As String = cNAMESPACE & "#date"
Const cADDRESS As String = cNAMESPACE & "#address"
Const cSALUTATION As String = cNAMESPACE & "#salutation"
Const cCUSTOMER As String = cNAMESPACE & "#customer"
Const cBODY As String = cNAMESPACE & "#body"
Const cP As String = cNAMESPACE & "#p"
Const cFORMAT As String = cNAMESPACE & "#format"
Const cPROBLEM As String = cNAMESPACE & "#problem"
Const cEMP As String = cNAMESPACE & "#emp"
```

At this point, Office knows the number of element types that have controls, but not the element-type names. The property in Example 14-2 provides the names.

Tip   When you implement this property, you are in effect assigning sequential numeric IDs to the element types. Be sure to create a case for each element type that has associated controls. Any order is acceptable.

14.1.4.1.2 *Element-type captions*

Each element type has a caption, which is displayed before all the controls for that element type. In Figure 14-1, the caption for the salutation element type is **Salutation**.

---

7. For that reason, in smart document parlance an element-type name is called a *namespace#element name* or *smart document type name*.

Example 14-2. Get the relevant element-type names

```
Private Property Get
ISmartDocument_SmartDocXMLTypeName
  (ByVal SmartDocID As Long) As String

  Select Case SmartDocID
    Case 1
      ISmartDocument_SmartDocXMLTypeName = cEMP
    Case 2
      ISmartDocument_SmartDocXMLTypeName = cADDRESS
    Case 3
      ISmartDocument_SmartDocXMLTypeName = cLETTER
    'REST OF THE CASES GO HERE
    Case Else
  End Select
End Property
```

Office gets the captions from the property in Example 14-3, which functions the same way as the previous example.

Tip   Make sure the case numbers for the captions are the same as the case numbers for the corresponding element-type names in the previous example.

Example 14-3. Get the element-type captions

```
Private Property Get ISmartDocument_SmartDocXMLTypeCaption
  (ByVal SmartDocID As Long, ByVal LocaleID As Long) As String

  Select Case SmartDocID
    Case 1
      ISmartDocument_SmartDocXMLTypeCaption = "Employee Name"
    Case 2
      ISmartDocument_SmartDocXMLTypeCaption = "Look up address"
    Case 3
      ISmartDocument_SmartDocXMLTypeCaption = _
      "Writing a customer letter"
    'REST OF THE CASES GO HERE
    Case Else
  End Select
End Property
```

The LocaleID parameter indicates the location in which the code is running. You can use conditional logic with it to localize the captions.

14.1.4.1.3 *Control count*

In order to determine the control IDs for an element-type, Office needs to know how many controls there are. It uses the property in Example 14-4 to get the control count. For example, as we saw in 14.1.3, "How smart documents work", on page 326, letter has four controls.

Tip   When you implement this property, be sure to supply the correct quantity for each element type. Note that the argument is the element-type name (SmartDocName), *not the numeric ID as in the previous examples.*

Example 14-4. Get the control count for an element type

```
Private Property Get ISmartDocument_ControlCount
  (ByVal SmartDocName As String) As Long

  Select Case SmartDocName
    Case cEMP
      ISmartDocument_ControlCount = 1
    Case cADDRESS
      ISmartDocument_ControlCount = 1
    Case cLETTER
      ISmartDocument_ControlCount = 4
    'REST OF THE CASES GO HERE
    Case Else
  End Select
End Property
```

14.1.4.2   Control properties

Once Office knows the element types and the number of controls each has, it gets the property values for each control.

14.1.4.2.1 Control ID

At this point, Office does not have a unique identifier for each control. For any given element type, however, it knows the number of controls. It therefore knows a sequential index number that uniquely identifies each control among the others for its element type. For example, the four controls associated with the letter element type have the index numbers 1, 2, 3 and 4.

Office gets a solution-wide unique number from the ControlID property implemented in Example 14-5, by passing it the element type name and the control's sequential index number. For example, the one control associated with the address element type is assigned the control ID 101. The four controls associated with the letter element type are assigned 201, 202, 203 and 204.

Example 14-5. Get the unique numeric control ID

```
Private Property Get ISmartDocument_ControlID
  (ByVal SmartDocName As String, ByVal ControlIndex As Long) As Long

  Select Case SmartDocName
    Case cEMP
      ISmartDocument_ControlID = ControlIndex
    Case cADDRESS
      ISmartDocument_ControlID = ControlIndex + 100
    Case cLETTER
      ISmartDocument_ControlID = ControlIndex + 200
    'REST OF THE CASES GO HERE
    Case Else
  End Select
End Property
```

14.1.4.2.2 Control type

Office now has a numeric ID for each control, but not the control type. It gets that information from the property shown in Example 14-6.

In the example, the control whose ID is 202, which is the second control associated with the letter element type, is a label. A complete list of control types is shown in Table 14-1.

The ApplicationName parameter indicates the application in which the code is running. You can use conditional logic with it to specify different control types for Word and Excel.

Example 14-6. Get the control type

```
Private Property Get ISmartDocument_ControlTypeFromID
  (ByVal ControlID As Long, ByVal ApplicationName As String,
  ByVal LocaleID As Long) As SmartTagLib.C_TYPE

  Select Case ControlID
    Case 1
      ISmartDocument_ControlTypeFromID = C_TYPE_TEXTBOX
    Case 101
      ISmartDocument_ControlTypeFromID = C_TYPE_BUTTON
    Case 201
      ISmartDocument_ControlTypeFromID = C_TYPE_HELP
    Case 202
      ISmartDocument_ControlTypeFromID = C_TYPE_LABEL
    'REST OF THE CASES GO HERE
    Case Else
  End Select
End Property
```

14.1.4.2.3 *Control caption*

We have seen that each element type has a caption. Some control types also allow captions. In Figure 14-1, the caption for the `salutation` radio group is **Select a salutation.**

Office gets the control captions from the property implemented in Example 14-7. The control whose numeric ID is "1" has the caption "Please enter your name:".

Additional parameters that we have not yet seen allow more criteria for conditional logic to modify the captions.

- `Text` is the data content of the current element, concatenated with the data content of any subelements.
- `Xml` is the XML representation of the current element (which, by definition, includes its attributes and subelements).
- `Target` is the Word or Excel range object with the current element's content. By using `Target.Document` you can address the entire Word document; `Target.Worksheet` lets you address the entire Excel worksheet.

Example 14-7. Get the control caption

```
Private Property Get ISmartDocument_ControlCaptionFromID
  (ByVal ControlID As Long, ByVal ApplicationName As String,
   ByVal LocaleID As Long, ByVal Text As String,
   ByVal Xml As String, ByVal Target As Object) As String

  Select Case ControlID
    Case 1
      ISmartDocument_ControlCaptionFromID = _
          "Please enter your name:"
    Case 101
      ISmartDocument_ControlCaptionFromID = _
          "Look up address"
    Case 201
      ISmartDocument_ControlCaptionFromID = _
          "Overview"
    Case 202
      ISmartDocument_ControlCaptionFromID = _
          "Please see below for context-specific help, " + _
          "or follow this link to the Intranet"
    'REST OF THE CASES GO HERE
    Case Else
  End Select
End Property
```

14.1.4.3 Control initialization methods

As Office renders controls in the task pane, it invokes methods – usually specific to the control type – that specify their appearance and internal content. The method names begin with Populate and are typically derived from the control type name; for example, the method PopulateRadioGroup is called to initialize a radio group. An implementation of this method is shown in Example 14-8.

The same method is invoked for all controls of a type, regardless of where they occur in the smart document, so it is necessary to test for the control ID if you want to perform different actions for specific controls. In our example, control 401 is a radio group for the format element type, while control 501 belongs to the salutation element type.

The Props parameter points to a structure that can be used to set display properties for the control, such as:

- the size of the control (height and width);

Example 14-8. Initializing a control

```
Private Sub ISmartDocument_PopulateRadioGroup
  (ByVal ControlID As Long, ByVal ApplicationName As String,
  ByVal LocaleID As Long, ByVal Text As String,
  ByVal Xml As String, ByVal Target As Object,
  ByVal Props As SmartTagLib.ISmartDocProperties,
  List() As String, Count As Long, InitialSelected As Long)

  Select Case ControlID
      Case 401
          ReDim List(1 To 3) As String
          Count = 3
          List(1) = "letter"
          List(2) = "e-mail"
          List(3) = "phone call"
          InitialSelected = -1
      Case 501
          ReDim List(1 To 4) As String
          Count = 4
          List(1) = "Mr."
          List(2) = "Ms."
          List(3) = "Mrs."
          List(4) = "Dr."
          InitialSelected = -1
  End Select
End Sub
```

- positioning of the control (alignment, indentation and spacing between controls); and
- fonts of text labels (face, size, style and weight).

For example, to set the properties for a label, you might use the code shown in Example 14-9.

Example 14-9. Setting the properties of a control

```
With Props
        .Write Key:="FontFace", Value:="Arial"
        .Write Key:="FontWeight", Value:="bold"
        .Write Key:="Align", Value:="left"
  End With
```

In addition to parameters like Props and the others we have seen, which are passed to all the control initialization methods, there are parameters that are passed only to specific control types. For example, the `List()`, `Count` and `InitialSelected` parameters are passed only to methods that initialize controls that have lists.

The initialization methods are executed each time the user moves between element types. Your implementations can therefore use conditional logic and the appropriate parameters to display the controls differently depending on the state of the document. For example, if the user has already inserted a `type` attribute of `body` with a value of `problem`, you can display document fragments that differ from those displayed for a body type of `sales`.

14.1.4.4   Control action methods

When the user interacts with a control in the **Document Actions** task pane, Office performs the control's built-in behavior if it has one. Clicking a hyperlink, for example, will always result in a browser being pointed toward the specified URL.

For other control types, Office calls the appropriate action method. For example, if a user clicks on a radio button, Office invokes the `OnRadioGroupSelectChange` method. An example implementation of this method is shown in Example 14-10.

Example 14-10. Setting the properties of a control

```
Private Sub ISmartDocument_OnRadioGroupSelectChange
  (ByVal ControlID As Long, ByVal Target As Object,
   ByVal Selected As Long, ByVal Value As String)

  Dim objRange As Word.Range
  Set objRange = Target.XMLNodes(1).Range
  objRange.Text = Value
  Set objRange = Nothing
End Sub
```

As with the initialization methods, there is only one action method for all controls of the same type. In our example, we want the same behavior regardless of which radio group control is clicked, so we do not test for the control ID. We simply copy the selected `Value` into the current XML element.

However, we are not limited to such a simple action. In this method, we could change any part of the current element or the document in any way, access external code or a database or Web service, perform Word tasks such as applying styles or printing, or any other action that can be expressed in code.

14.2 | Smart tags

Smart tags allow actions to be associated with words and phrases in a document. The "tags" don't have to be delimited, as XML tags are. Instead, they are defined by a program or by a lookup table that contains character strings and their associated actions. The product recognizes the matching strings in the document.

Instead of a specific character string, recognition could be based on a kind of pattern for strings that computer scientists call a *regular expression*. In this case, any character string in the document that matched the pattern would be recognized and considered a smart tag.

Alternatively, program code could be used to create more sophisticated recognition tests.

In all cases, though, when a user inserts or mouses over recognized text a small button appears. When clicked, a context menu pops up that contains actions relating to the recognized text.

Figure 14-5 is an example of the stock symbol smart tag that is built into Excel. The string "MSFT" in cell A1 has been recognized as a stock ticker symbol, so the smart tag **i** button is displayed next to the cell. Clicking the button caused the context menu to appear. The menu allows you to insert the stock price in the worksheet or to go to the MSN website for more information about the stock or the company.

Another built-in smart tag for Word recognizes full names of your Microsoft Outlook contacts. The context menu lets you send that person an e-mail or schedule a meeting with her.

14.2.1 *Using smart tag lists (MOSTL)*

The simplest way to implement smart tags is by creating an XML document that complies with the Microsoft Office Smart Tag Lists (MOSTL)

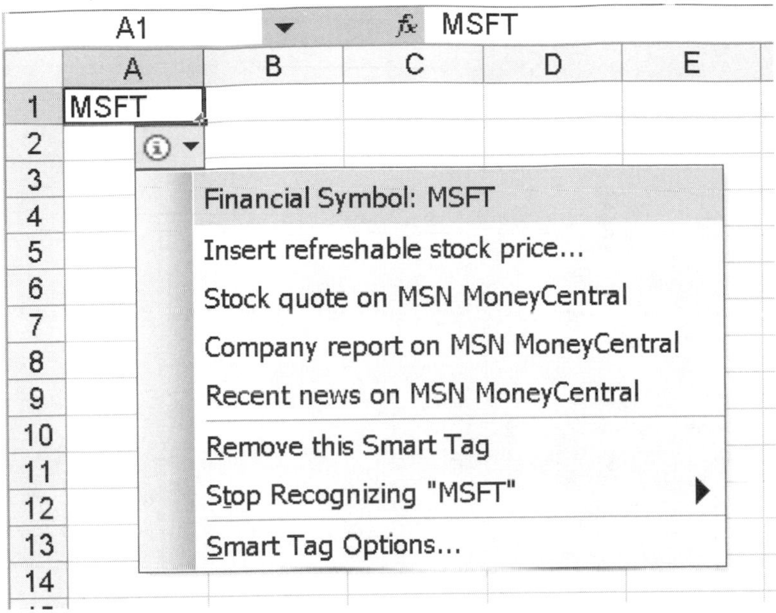

Figure 14-5   A smart tag menu

schema. This document lists the text strings or patterns to look for, and the actions to show in the context menu when a smart tag is recognized.

An example of a MOSTL document for recognizing ZIP codes is shown in Example 14-11. While some MOSTL documents list literal text strings to recognize, this document specifies a pattern. The regular expression (\d{5}), which represents five digits, is the content of the exp element. This means that any five consecutive digits will be recognized as a ZIP Codes smart tag.

Each menu item is specified with an action element that contains a caption (the text that will appear on the menu) and a url that is referenced when you click the menu item. Our example might allow users to look up shipping rates to that ZIP code, or to determine the time zone of the ZIP code. The expression {TEXT} is used within the URL to mean that the recognized string (in this case the 5-digit number) will be included in the URL at that point.

Implementing this smart tag list is a simple matter of placing the XML document in your local smart tag lists directory, and restarting all

Example 14-11. A MOSTL document to implement smart tags

```
<FL:smarttaglist
    xmlns:FL="urn:schemas-microsoft-com:smarttags:list">
 <FL:name>ZIP Codes</FL:name>
 <FL:lcid>1033</FL:lcid>
 <FL:description>Recognizes ZIP codes</FL:description>
 <FL:moreinfourl>http://xmlinoffice.com</FL:moreinfourl>

 <FL:smarttag
type="urn:schemas-microsoft-com:smarttags#msproducts">
    <FL:caption>ZIP Code</FL:caption>
    <FL:re>
       <FL:exp>(\d{5})</FL:exp>
    </FL:re>
    <FL:actions>
       <FL:action id="ship">
          <FL:caption>Look up shipping rates</FL:caption>
          <FL:url>http://xmlinoffice.com/ship/{TEXT}</FL:url>
       </FL:action>
       <FL:action id="tz">
          <FL:caption>Determine time zone</FL:caption>
          <FL:url>http://xmlinoffice.com/tz/{TEXT}</FL:url>
       </FL:action>
    </FL:actions>
 </FL:smarttag>
</FL:smarttaglist>
```

smart-tag-compliant applications. The directory path is normally:

```
Program Files\Common Files\Microsoft Shared\Smart Tag\Lists\
```

14.2.2 *Using program code*

Smart tags can also be implemented using program code, written with either Visual Studio.NET or Visual Studio 6.0.

While MOSTL documents can only specify actions as URLs, program code allows you to perform almost any action you can imagine. You can access Web services and databases, send emails, and insert or edit text or XML elements, among other things.

More sophisticated recognizers can also be written using program code, for example to only recognize valid ZIP codes, or only ZIP codes that appear in certain areas of a document.

Unlike smart documents, smart tags have no direct relationship with the Office features that allow the editing and viewing of XML documents.

Smart tags can therefore be used in any Word and Excel documents, regardless of whether the documents are associated with a schema. Smart tags can also be used in PowerPoint, Access, Outlook, and Internet Explorer.

However, in Word and Excel documents that are associated with a schema, it can be useful to create smart tag solutions that are sensitive to the XML context. For example, you could write a smart tag recognizer that only recognizes ZIP codes when they appear inside a `ZIP` element, or client codes when they appear inside a `billTo` element.

A smart tag recognizer could be written to respond when a user types the word "problem" into the `body` element of a letter. The context menu could allow a choice among different canned "problem letter" phrases, which would be inserted automatically into the document.

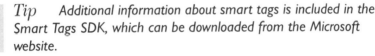

Tip   Additional information about smart tags is included in the Smart Tags SDK, which can be downloaded from the Microsoft website.

14.3 | The research pane

The *research pane* feature of Office 2003 allows you to query a variety of research services on the Web from the task pane, without leaving your document. For example, you could look up word definitions, review stock quotes and information, perform Google searches, check the prices of goods for sale, or find journal articles related to a topic (as shown in Figure 14-6).

You display the research pane by clicking **Research** on the task pane list. You interact with it by typing your search terms into the **Search for:** box, selecting a research service, and clicking the green arrow icon. Alternatively, you can press **Alt** plus a word to query the research service automatically. The research service will return a set of results in the bottom part of the pane.

The research pane can be used with Word, Excel, PowerPoint, Outlook, Publisher and Visio. Unlike smart documents, the research pane does not require your Word documents or Excel workbooks to be associated with a schema; it is independent of the XML editing features of Office.

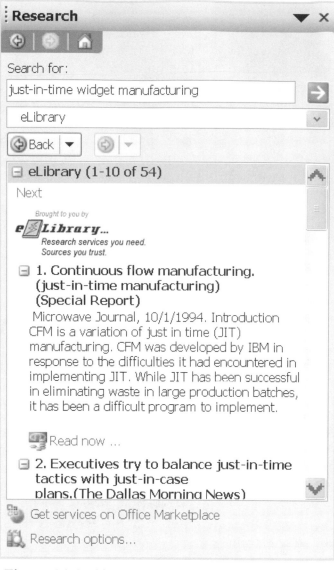

Figure 14-6   Using the research pane

14.3.1 *Available research services*

A number of research services are provided with Office 2003. These include dictionaries, thesauri, encyclopedias, language translators, Web searches, and stock quotes. The complete list can be viewed by clicking **Research options** on the task pane, which brings up the Research Options dialog shown in Figure 14-7.

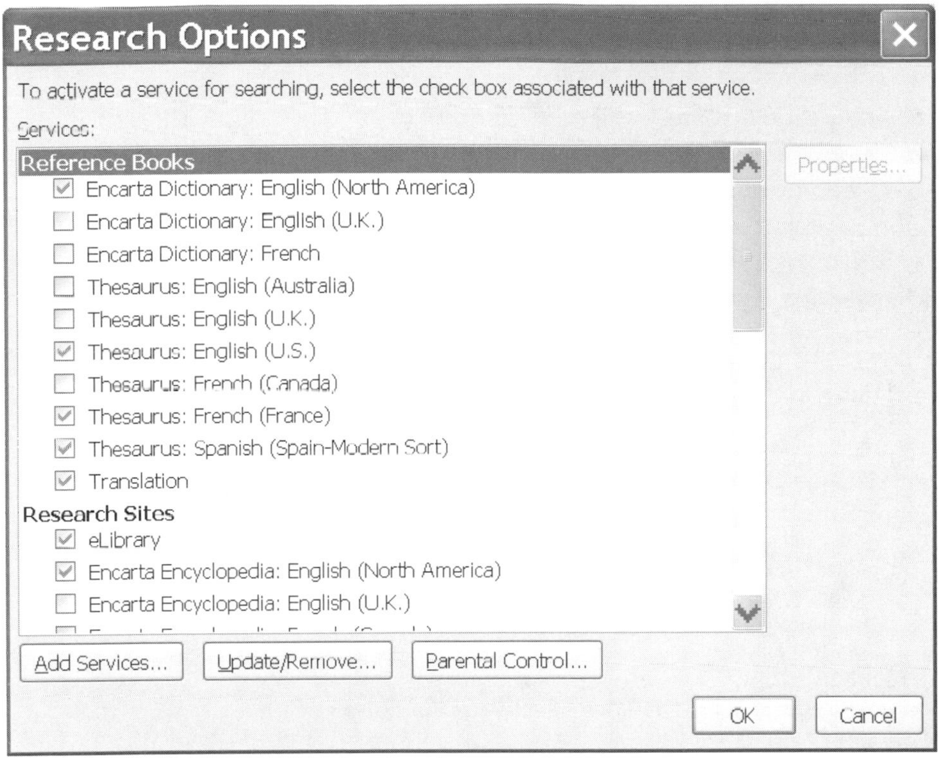

Figure 14-7   The Research Options dialog

There are additional research services written by third parties that can be added to Office, sometimes for a fee. These services can be found on the Office Marketplace Web site, which can be accessed from the task pane by clicking **Get services from Office Marketplace**. To add to your available services, click **Add services** on the Research Options dialog and enter the URL provided by the research service documentation.

You can also write your own research service by implementing it as a SOAP Web service. While the term "research" usually implies accessing public reference sources, the research pane can be used for any information that a user might want to look up.

For example, you could develop a private company-only research service that returns background information on a customer in response to a query using its name or customer number. This would be useful to customer service representatives who are writing letters.

14.3.2   *How it works*

Research services are implemented as SOAP Web services that are specifically designed to work with the Office research pane. The Web services have two operations: `Registration` and `Query`. The `Registration` operation is performed when a user first adds the research service in Office. The `Query` operation is performed each time the user looks something up using that service.

Example 14-12. XML document sent to the Query operation

```
<QueryPacket xmlns="urn:Microsoft.Search.Query"
             revision="1" build="(11.0.5308)">
  <Query>
    <SupportedFormats>
      <Format revision="1">
urn:Microsoft.Search.Response.Document:Document</Format>
    </SupportedFormats>
    <Context>
      <QueryText type="STRING" language="en-us">just-in-time
widget manufacturing</QueryText>
      <LanguagePreference>en-us</LanguagePreference>
    </Context>
  </Query>
</QueryPacket>
```

A number of parameters may be passed to the `Query` operation, such as the search text, the preferred language, and the maximum number of items to retrieve. An example of an XML document that might be passed to the Web service is shown in Example 14-12.

The research service returns an XML document with the results. The results can be rendered using a variety of techniques, including rich text,

Example 14-13. XML returned from the Query operation

```xml
<ResponsePacket revision="1" xmlns="urn:Microsoft.Search.Response">
  <Response>
    <Range>
      <StartAt>1</StartAt>
      <Count>2</Count>
      <TotalAvailable>738</TotalAvailable>
      <Results>
        <Content xmlns="urn:Microsoft.Search.Response.Content">
          <Image source="http://www.elibrary.com/Logo.gif"/>
          <Heading collapsible="true">
            <Text>Continuous flow manufacturing...</Text>
            <P>Microwave Journal... </P>
            <Hyperlink url="http://ask.elibrary.com/login.asp...">
              <Text>Read now ...</Text>
            </Hyperlink>
          </Heading>
          <Heading collapsible="true">
            <Text>Executives try to balance...</Text>
            <!-- etc. -->
          </Heading>
        </Content>
      </Results>
    </Range>
    <Status>SUCCESS</Status>
  </Response>
</ResponsePacket>
```

images, tables, hyperlinks, horizontal lines, collapsible sections, and even smart tags. An example of the result XML is shown in Example 14-13.[8]

> *Tip*   For more information on developing custom research services, download the *Office Research SDK* from the Microsoft website. It provides detailed specifications for the Web services, as well as a number of examples.

---

8. Some information is truncated for legibility.

14.4 | XML expansion packs and manifests

An *XML expansion pack* is a group of related files that make up one or more related Office XML solutions. It may include schemas, XSLT stylesheets, smart tag lists, DLLs for smart documents, external files used in smart document solutions, and other types of files.

Each XML expansion pack contains a *manifest*: an XML document that lists all of the files in the pack, their "types" (i.e. their roles in an Office solution, such as `solutionActionHandler`), and their locations. In 14.1.2, "Installing a smart document solution", on page 322, we installed a smart document solution using the manifest shown in Example 14-14.

Example 14-14. Manifest for the smart document solution (letter_manifest.xml)

```
<?xml version="1.0" encoding="UTF-8"?>
<manifest xmlns=
"http://schemas.microsoft.com/office/xmlexpansionpacks/2003">
  <version>1.1</version>
  <updateFrequency>20160</updateFrequency>
  <uri>http://xmlinoffice.com/letter</uri>
  <solution>
    <solutionID>{15960625-1612-46AB-877C-BBCB59503FCF}</solutionID>
    <type>smartDocument</type>
    <alias lcid="*">Letter Smart Document Sample</alias>
    <file>
      <type>solutionActionHandler</type>
      <version>1.0</version>
      <filePath>LetterSample.dll</filePath>
      <CLSID>{F854ADAA-A8A2-40EC-B31A-A2DB811FD7F3}</CLSID>
    </file>
  </solution>
  <solution>
    <solutionID>schema</solutionID>
    <type>schema</type>
    <alias lcid="*">letter</alias>
    <file>
      <type>schema</type>
      <version>1.0</version>
      <filePath>letter.xsd</filePath>
    </file>
  </solution>
</manifest>
```

- The `manifest` element defines the namespace for the manifest document.
- The `uri` element contains the target namespace for the solutions.
- The first `solution` element describes a solution whose `type` is `smartDocument`. It uses the file `LetterSample.dll`, whose `type` is `solutionActionHandler`. The `alias` element's content is the name that appears in the XML Expansion Pack dialog.
- The second `solution` element describes a solution whose `type` is `schema`. It uses the file `letter.xsd` – whose `type` is also `schema` – as its schema document. (Other valid values of `type` for files are `transform` and `other`.) The `alias` element's content is used in the Schema Library as a nickname for the schema.

Other element types may be included in a manifest; a detailed reference is provided in the Smart Documents SDK.

When this expansion pack is installed, both the smart document solution and the schema are added to the library locally.

When an expansion pack is associated with a document, a link to the manifest is stored within the document's metadata, which allows the solution to be centrally maintained. The manifest can be stored on a file server or in SharePoint, or even be returned by a Web service. To upgrade to the latest version of a solution, a user can select it and click **Update** in the **XML Expansion Packs** dialog.

Alternatively, a solution can be set up for automatic installations and updates. If a user who does not have the latest version of an expansion pack installed tries to open an associated document, he will be prompted to allow the expansion pack to be installed automatically. This approach greatly simplifies deployment of changes and upgrades to solutions.

XML expansion packs are not just for smart documents. They can be used simply to add schemas and stylesheets to Word documents, rather than requiring that users do this manually. XML expansion packs can also be used in Excel, by clicking **XML Expansion Packs** on the **XML** submenu.

XML Tutorials

- The XML language
- Web services
- XML Path Language (XPath)
- XSL Transformations (XSLT)
- XML Schema (XSDL and datatypes)
- Jargon Demystifier

Part Three

After you've read Chapter Two, this Part will provide the information you need to go deeper into XML. Chapters 15 through 20 can be read in order to learn the XML language and the key technologies that are used with it: XPath, XSLT, and Web services.

Chapters 21 and 22 will teach you both parts of the XML Schema standard: datatypes and the XML Schema definition language. We go into enough detail that you will be able to create practical schemas and understand those that are provided for your use.

Chapters 23 and 24 provide more advanced information about Web services and XPath.

The XML language

Friendly Tutorial

- Syntactic details
- The prolog and the document instance
- XML declaration
- Elements and attributes

Chapter 15

XML's central concepts are quite simple, and this chapter outlines the most important of them. Essentially, it gives you what you need to know to actually create XML documents. In subsequent chapters you will learn how to combine them, share text between them, format them, and validate them.

Before looking at actual XML markup (don't worry, we'll get there soon!) we should consider some *syntactic constructs* that will recur throughout our discussion of XML documents. By *syntax* we mean the combination of characters that make up an XML document. This is analogous to the distinction between sounds of words and the things that they mean. Essentially, we are talking about where you can put angle brackets, quote marks, ampersands, and other characters and where you cannot! Later we will talk about what they mean when you put them together.

After that, we will discuss the components that make up an XML document instance[1]. We will look at the distinction between the prolog (information XML parsers need to know about your document) and the instance (the representation of the actual document itself).

---

1. Roughly, what the XML spec calls the "root element".

15.1 | Syntactic details

XML documents are composed of characters from the *Unicode* character set. Any such sequence of characters is called a *string*. The characters in this book can be thought of as one long (but interesting) string of text. Each chapter is also a string. So is each word. XML documents are similarly made up of strings within strings.

Natural languages such as English have a particular *syntax*. The syntax allows you to combine words into grammatical sentences. XML also has syntax. It describes how you combine strings into well-formed XML documents. We will describe the basics of XML's syntax in this section.

15.1.1 *Case-sensitivity*

XML is *case-sensitive*. That means that if the XML specification says to insert the word "ELEMENT", it means that you should insert "ELE-MENT" and not "element" or "Element" or "ElEmEnT".

So mind your "p's" and "q's" and "P's" and "Q's". Our authoritative laboratory testing by people in white coats indicates that exactly 74.5% of all XML errors are related to case-sensitivity mistakes. Of course XML is also spelling-sensitive and typo-sensitive, so watch out for these and other products of human fallibility.

Note that although XML is case-sensitive it is not case-prejudiced. Anywhere that you have the freedom to create your own names or text, you can choose to use upper- or lower-case text, as you prefer.

For instance, when you create your own document types you will be able to choose element-type names. A particular name could be all upper-case (SECTION), all lower-case (section) or mixed-case (SeCtION). But because XML is case-sensitive, all occurrences of a particular element-type name would have to use the same case. It is good practice to create a simple convention such as all lower-case or all upper-case so that you do not have to depend on your memory.

15.1.2 *Markup and data*

The constructs such as tags, entity references, and declarations are called *markup*. These are the parts of your document that are supposed to be understood by the XML parser. The parts that are between the markup constitute the *character data*. While the XML parser rips apart and analyzes markup, it merely passes the character data to the application.

Recall that the parser is the part of the program dedicated to separating the document into its constituent parts. The application is the "rest" of the program. In a word processor, the application is the part that lets you edit the document; in a spreadsheet it is the part that lets you crunch the numbers.

We haven't explained all of the parts of markup yet, but they are easy to recognize. All of them start with less-than (<) or ampersand (&) characters. Everything else is character data.

15.1.3 *White space*

There is a set of characters called *white space* characters that XML parsers treat differently in XML markup. They are the "invisible" characters: space (Unicode/ASCII 32), tab (Unicode/ASCII 9), carriage return (Unicode/ASCII 13) and line feed (Unicode/ASCII 10). These correspond roughly to the spacebar, tab, and Enter keys on your keyboard.

When the XML specification says that white space is allowed at a particular point, you may put as many of these characters as you want in any combination. Just as you might put two lines between paragraphs in a word processor to make a printed document readable, you may put two carriage returns in certain places in an XML document to make your source file more readable and maintainable. When the document is processed, those characters will be ignored.

In other places, white space will be significant. For instance you would not want the parser to strip out the spaces between the words in your document! Thatwouldmakeithardtoread. So white space outside of markup is always preserved.

15.1.4 *Names*

When you use XML you will often have to give things names. You will name logical structures with element-type names, particular elements with IDs, and so forth. XML names have certain common features. They are not nearly as flexible as character data.

Letters or underscores can be used anywhere in a name. There are thousands of characters that XML version 1.0 considers a "letter" because it includes characters from every language including ideographic ones like Japanese Kanji. XML version 1.1 is even more liberal: it treats a character as a "letter" unless it is from a small list designated as punctuation.[2] Characters that can be used anywhere in a name are known in XML terms as *name start* characters. They are called this because they may be used at the start of names as well as in later positions.

This implies that there must be characters that can go in a name but cannot be the first character. You may include digits, hyphens and full-stop (.) characters in a name, but you may not start the name with one of them. These are known as *name characters*. Other characters, like various white space and Western punctuation characters, cannot be part of a name at all. Examples of these non-name characters include the tilde (~), caret (^) and space ( ).

You cannot make names that begin with the string "xml" or some case-insensitive variant like "XML" or "XmL".

Like almost everything else in XML, names are matched case-sensitively. Names may not contain white space, punctuation or other "funny" characters other than those listed above. The remaining "ordinary" characters (including letters from non-Latin alphabets) are called *name characters* because they may occur anywhere in a name.

15.2 | Prolog vs. instance

Most document representations start with a header that contains information about the actual document and how to interpret its representation. This is followed by the representation of the real document.

For instance, HTML has a HEAD element that can contain the TITLE and META elements. After the HEAD element comes the BODY. This is where the representation of the actual document resides. Similarly, email messages have "header lines" that describe who the message came from, to whom it is addressed, how it is encoded, and other things.

---

2. The two versions differ only in some character set details, which is why XML 1.1 hasn't been mentioned before.

An XML document is similarly broken up into two main parts: a *prolog* and a *document instance*. The prolog provides information about the interpretation of the document instance, such as the version of XML and the document type to which it conforms. The document instance follows the prolog. It contains the actual document data organized as a hierarchy of elements.

15.3 | The document instance

The actual content of an XML document goes in the document instance. It is called this because if it has a document type definition or schema definition, it is an *instance* of the *class* of documents defined by that DTD or schema. Just as a particular person is an instance of the class of "people", a particular memo is an instance of the class of "memo documents".

The formal definition of "memo document" is in the memo DTD or schema definition.

15.3.1 *What the tags reveal*

Example 15-1 is an example of a small XML document.

15.3.1.1   Tree structure

Because a computer cannot understand the data of the document, it looks primarily at the *tags*, the markup beginning with the less-than and ending with the greater-than symbol. The tags delimit the beginning and end of various elements. The computer thinks of the elements as a sort of tree. It is the XML parser's job to separate the markup from the character data and hand both to the application.

Figure 15-1 shows a graphical view of the logical structure of the document. The memo element is called either the *document element* or the *root element*.

The document element (memo) represents the document as a whole. Every other element represents a component of the document. The from and to elements are meant to indicate the sender and recipient of the

Example 15-1. Small XML document

```
<?xml version="1.0"?>
<!DOCTYPE memo SYSTEM "memo.dtd">
<memo>
<from>
   <name>Paul Prescod</name>
   <email>papresco@prescod.com</email>
</from>
<to>
   <name>Charles Goldfarb</name>
   <email>charles@sgmlsource.com</email>
</to>
<subject>Another Memo Example</subject>
<body>
<paragraph>Charles, I wanted to suggest that we
<emphasis>not</emphasis> use the typical memo example in
our book. Memos tend to be used anywhere a small, simple
document type is needed, but they are just
<emphasis>so</emphasis> boring!
</paragraph>
</body>
</memo>
```

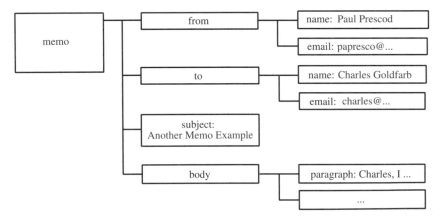

Figure 15-1   The memo XML document viewed as a tree

memo. The name elements represent people's names. Continuing in this way, the logical structure of the document is apparent.

15.3.1.2   Semantics

Experts refer to an element's real-world meaning as its *semantics*. In a particular vocabulary, the semantics of a P element might be "paragraph" and in another it might mean "pence".

If you find yourself reading or writing markup and asking: "But what does that *mean*?" then you are asking about semantics.

Computers do not yet know anything about semantics. They do not know an HTTP protocol from a supermodel. Vocabulary designers must describe semantics to authors some other way. For instance, they could send email, write a book or make a major motion picture (well, maybe some day).

What the computer does care about is how an element is supposed to look when it is formatted, or how it is to behave if it is interactive, or what to do with the data once it is extracted. These are specified in *stylesheets* and computer programs.

15.3.2   *Elements*

XML elements break down into two categories. Most have content, which is to say they contain characters, elements or both, and some do not. Those that do not are called *empty elements*. Elements within other elements are called *subelements*.

15.3.2.1   Elements with content

Example 15-2 is an example of an element with content.

Example 15-2. Simple element

```
<title>This is the title</title>
```

Elements with content begin with a start-tag and finish with an end-tag. The "stuff" between the two is the element's content. In Example 15-2, "This is the title" is the content.

XML start-tags consist of the less-than (<) symbol ("left angle bracket"), the name of the element's type (sometimes termed a *generic identifier* or

GI), and a greater-than (>) symbol ("right angle bracket"). Start-tags can also include attributes. We will look at those later in the chapter. The start-tag in Example 15-2 is `<title>` and its element-type name is "title".

XML end-tags consist of the string "`</`", the same generic identifier (or *GI*) as in the start-tag, and a greater-than (>) symbol. The end-tag in Example 15-2 is `</title>`.

You must always repeat the generic identifier in the end-tag. This helps you to keep track of which end-tags line up with which start-tags. If you ever forget one or the other, the parser will know immediately, and will alert you that the document is not well-formed.

Note that less-than symbols in content are always interpreted as beginning a tag. If the characters following them would not constitute a tag, then the document is not well-formed.

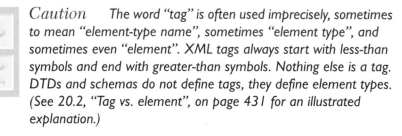

Caution   The word "tag" is often used imprecisely, sometimes to mean "element-type name", sometimes "element type", and sometimes even "element". XML tags always start with less-than symbols and end with greater-than symbols. Nothing else is a tag. DTDs and schemas do not define tags, they define element types. (See 20.2, "Tag vs. element", on page 431 for an illustrated explanation.)

15.3.2.2   Empty elements

It is possible for an element to have no content at all. Such an element is called an *empty element*. One way to denote an empty element is to merely leave out the content. But as a shortcut, empty elements may also have a different syntax. Because there is no content to delimit, they may consist of a single empty-element tag. That looks like this: `<MyEmptyElementTag/>`.

The slash at the end indicates that this is an empty-element tag, so there is no content or end-tag coming up. The slash is meant to be reminiscent of the slash in the end-tag of an element with both tags. This is just a shortcut syntax. XML parsers do not treat empty-element tags differently from elements that merely have no content between the start- and end-tag.

Usually empty elements have *attributes*. Occasionally an empty element without attributes will be used to flag a particular location in a document. Example 15-3 is an example of an empty element with an attribute.

Example 15-3. Empty element with attribute

```
<EMPTY-ELEMENT ATTR="ATTVAL"/>
```

Remember what the slash at the end means! You will see it often and it is easy to miss when there are attributes like this. The slash indicates that this is an empty element so that the parser need not look for a matching end-tag.

15.3.2.3   Summary

In summary, elements are either empty or have content. Elements with content are represented by a start-tag, the content, and an end-tag. Empty elements can either have a start-tag and end-tag with nothing in between, or a single empty-element tag. An element's type is always identified by the generic identifiers in its tags.

The reason we distinguish element types from generic identifiers is because the term "generic identifier" refers to the syntax of the XML document – the characters that represent the actual document. The term "element type" refers to a property of a component of the actual document.

15.3.3 *Attributes*

In addition to content, elements may have *attributes*. Attributes are a way of attaching characteristics or properties to elements of a document. Attributes have *names*, just as real-world properties do. They also have *values*. For instance, two possible attributes of people are their "shoe size" and "IQ" (the attributes' names), and two possible values are "12" and "112" (respectively).

In a DTD or schema definition, each attribute is defined for a specific element type and is allowed to exhibit a certain type of value. Multiple element types could provide attributes with the same name and it is sometimes convenient to think of them as the "same attribute" even though they technically are not.[3]

---

3. Unless they are in the same namespace, a situation we discuss in Chapter 16, "Namespaces", on page 376.

Attributes have semantics also. They always *mean* something. For example, an attribute named `height` might be provided for `person` elements (allowed occurrence), exhibit values that are numbers (allowed values), and represent the person's height in centimeters (semantics).

Here is how attributes of `person` elements might look:

Example 15-4. Elements with attributes

```
<person height="165cm">Dale Wick</person>
<person height="165cm" weight="165lb">Bill Bunn</person>
```

As you can see, the attribute name does not go in quotes, but the attribute value does because it is a *literal string*.

15.3.3.1   Literal strings

The data (text other than markup) can contain almost any characters. Obviously, in the content of your document you need to use punctuation and white space characters! But sometimes you also need data characters *within* markup. For instance, an element might represent a hyperlink and need to have a URL attribute.

Literal strings allow users to use (non-name) data characters within markup. For instance, to specify the URL in the hyperlink, we would need the slash character. Example 15-5 is an example of such an element.

Example 15-5. Literal string in attribute value

```
<REFERENCE URL="http://www.documents.com/document.xml">...
</REFERENCE>
```

The string that defines the URL is the literal string. This one starts and ends with double quote characters. Literal strings are always surrounded by either single or double quotes. The quotes are not part of the string. For example, see Example 15-6.

Example 15-6. Quotes within quotes

```
"This is a double quoted literal."
'This is a single quoted literal.'
"'tis another double quoted literal."
'"And this is single quoted" said the self-referential example.'
```

15.3.3.2   ID and IDREF attributes

Sometimes it is important to be able to give a name to a particular occurrence of an element type; that is, to a single element. For instance, to make a simple hypertext link or cross-reference from one element to another, you can name a particular section or figure. Later, you can refer to it by its name.

The target element is labeled with an *ID* attribute. The other element refers to it with an *IDREF* attribute. This is shown in Example 15-7.

Example 15-7. Using ID and IDREF attributes

```
<BOOK>
. . .
<SECTION ID="Why.XML.Rocks"><TITLE>Features of XML</TITLE>
. . .
</SECTION>


. . .
If you want to recall why XML is so great, please see
the section entitled <CROSS-REFERENCE IDREF="Why.XML.Rocks"/>.
. . .
</BOOK>
```

Caution   *You may see an element-type name, such as* SECTION *in the above example, referred to as an element name. The real element name — the name of this individual* SECTION *element — is the value of the element's* ID *attribute; in this case,* Why.XML.Rocks. *(See 20.2, "Tag vs. element", on page 431.)*

15.4 | The prolog

XML documents may start with a prolog that describes the XML version ("1.0" or "1.1", for now), document type, and other characteristics of the document.

The prolog is made up of an *XML declaration* and a *document type declaration*, both optional.

Caution   Some Microsoft Office applications require an XML declaration in order to recognize and process the document as XML.

The XML declaration must precede the document type declaration if both are provided. Also, comments, processing instructions, and white space can be mixed in among the two declarations. The prolog ends when the first start-tag begins.

Example 15-8 is a simple prolog.

Example 15-8. A simple prolog

```
<?xml version="1.0"?>
<!DOCTYPE book SYSTEM "http://www.oasis-open.org/.../docbookx.dtd">
```

This prolog says that the document conforms to XML version 1.0 and declares adherence to a particular document type, book.

15.4.1 *XML declaration*

The XML declaration has three parts; the last two are optional. A minimal XML declaration looks like this:

Example 15-9. Minimal XML declaration

```
<?xml version="1.0"?>
```

Example 15-10 is a more expansive one, using all of its parts.

Example 15-10. More expansive XML declaration

```
<?xml version="1.0" encoding="UTF-8" standalone="yes"?>
```

Although the parts have the same syntax as attributes, there is an important difference. The parts are strictly ordered whereas attributes can be specified in any order.

The third part, the *standalone document declaration*, is rarely used and arguably useless; we'll say no more about it!

15.4.1.1   Version info

The *version info* part of the XML declaration declares the version of XML that is in use. It is required in all XML declarations, although the XML declaration itself is optional. At the time of writing, the only permitted version strings are "1.0" and "1.1". If you leave out the entire XML declaration (thereby leaving out the version) then your document is presumed to be an XML 1.0 (not 1.1) document.

The XML version information is part of a general trend towards information representations that are *self-identifying*. This means that you can look at an XML document and (if it has the declaration) know immediately both that it is XML and what version of XML it uses. As more and more document representations become self-identifying, we will be able to stop relying on error-prone identification schemes like file extensions.

15.4.1.2   Encoding declaration

The *encoding declaration* part describes the character encoding that is used. If omitted, it defaults to a Unicode encoding called *UTF-8* which incorporates the commonly-used 7-bit ASCII. Therefore, you need only use the encoding declaration for a national or regional encoding like Russia's KOI8-R, Western Europe's ISO-8859-1 or Japan's Shift-JIS, as shown in Example 15-11.

Example 15-11. Encoding declaration

```
<?xml version="1.0" encoding="KOI8-R"?>
```

15.4.2   *Document type declaration*

After the XML declaration (if present) and before the first element, there may be a *document type declaration* which declares the document type that is in use in the document. A "book" document type, for example, might be made up of chapters, while a letter document type could be made up of element types such as ADDRESS, SALUTATION, SIGNATURE, and so forth.

The document type declaration is at the heart of the concept of *validity*, which makes applications based on XML robust and reliable. It includes the markup declarations that express the *document type definition (DTD)*.

The DTD is a formalization of the intuitive idea of a document type. The DTD lists the element types available and can put constraints on the occurrence and content of elements and other details of the document structure. This makes an information system more robust by forcing the documents that are part of it to be consistent.

A schema definition can also be used for this purpose, but other means must be used to associate it with documents. There are several schema languages; we discuss the official W3C one in Chapter 22, "XML Schema (XSDL)", on page 466.

15.5 | Entities: Breaking up is easy to do

XML allows flexible organization of document text. The XML constructs that provide this flexibility are called *entities*. They allow a document to be broken up into multiple storage objects and are important tools for reusing and maintaining text. Entities are used in many publishing-oriented applications of XML but are much less common in machine-to-machine applications.

In simple cases, an entity is like an abbreviation in that it is used as a short form for some text. We call the "abbreviation" the *entity name* and the long form the *entity content*. That content could be as short as a character or as long as a chapter. For instance, in an XML document, the entity XSL could have the phrase "Extensible Style Language" as its content. Using a reference to that entity is like using "XSL" as an abbreviation for that phrase – the parser replaces the reference with the content.

You create the entity with an *entity declaration*. Example 15-12 is an entity declaration for an abbreviation.

Example 15-12. Entity used as an abbreviation

```
  <!ENTITY XSL "Extensible Style Language">
]>
```

Like other markup declarations, entity declarations occur in the document type declaration section of the document prolog (Example 15-13).

> *Note*   You can use entities with schemas. In that case your "DTD" would consist solely of declarations needed for the entities.

Example 15-13. Entity declarations occur in the document type declaration

```
<!DOCTYPE mydoc ...[
  <!ENTITY XSL "Extensible Style Language">
  ... other markup declarations ...
]>
```

Entities can be much more than just abbreviations. Another way to think of an entity is as a box with a label. The label is the entity's name. The content of the box is some sort of text or data. The entity declaration creates the box and sticks on a label with the name. Sometimes the box holds XML text that is going to be *parsed* (interpreted according to the rules of the XML notation), and sometimes it holds data, which should not be.

15.5.1 *Parsed entities*

If the content of an entity is XML text that the parser should parse, the XML spec calls it a *parsed entity*.

If the content of an entity is data that is not to be parsed, the XML spec calls it an *unparsed entity*.

The abbreviation in Example 15-12 is a parsed entity. Parsed entities, being XML text, can also contain markup. Example 15-14 is a declaration for a parsed entity with some markup in it.

Example 15-14. Parsed entity with markup

```
<!ENTITY XSL "<title>Extensible Style Language</title>">
```

Because the entity content in the example is in the entity declaration, the entity is called an *internal entity*. Only parsed entities can be internal entities.

15.5.2 *External entities*

The parser can also fetch content from somewhere on the Web and put that into the box. This is an *external* entity. For instance, it could fetch a chapter of a book and put it into an entity. This would allow you to reuse the chapter between books. Another benefit is that you could edit the chapter separately with a sufficiently intelligent editor. This would be very useful if you were working on a team project and wanted different people to work on different parts of a document at once. Example 15-15 illustrates.

Example 15-15. External entity declaration

```
<!ENTITY intro-chapter SYSTEM "http://www.megacorp.com/intro.xml">
```

Entities also allow you to edit very large documents without running out of memory. Depending on your software and needs, either each volume or even each article in an encyclopedia could be an entity.

15.5.3 *Entity references*

An author or DTD designer refers to an entity through an *entity reference*. The XML parser replaces the reference by the content, as if it were an abbreviation and the content was the expanded phrase. This process is called *entity inclusion* or *entity replacement*. After the operation we say either that the entity reference has been *replaced* by the entity content or that the entity content has been *included*.

Which you would use depends on whether you are talking from the point of view of the entity reference or the entity content. The content of parsed entities is called their *replacement text.*[4]

Example 15-16 is an example of a parsed entity declaration and its associated reference.

Example 15-16. Entity declaration

```
<!DOCTYPE MAGAZINE[
...
<!ENTITY title "Hacker Life">
...
]>
<MAGAZINE>
<TITLE>&title;</TITLE>
...
<P>Welcome to the introductory issue of &title;. &title; is
geared to today's modern hacker.</P>
...
</MAGAZINE>
```

Anywhere in the document instance that the entity reference "&title;" appears, it is replaced by the text "Hacker Life". It is just as valid to say that "Hacker Life" is included at each point where the reference occurs.

The ampersand character starts all general entity references and the semi-colon ends them. The text between is an entity name.

15.5.4 *How entities are used*

Here are some examples of what you can do with entities:

■ You could store every chapter of a book in a separate file and link them together as entities.

---

4. If you are a programmer, you might think of entities as macros and call the process *entity expansion*.

■ You could "factor out" often-reused text, such as a product name, into an entity so that it is consistently spelled and displayed throughout the document.

■ You could update the product name entity to reflect a new version. The change would be instantly visible anywhere the entity was used.

■ You could create an entity that would represent "legal boilerplate" text (such as a software license) and reuse that entity in many different documents.

Note   We have explained only the basics about entities. For the full story, see the XML Recommendation or The XML Handbook.

15.6 | Character references

It is not usually convenient to type in characters that are not available on the keyboard. With many text editors, it is not even possible to do so. XML allows you to insert such a character with a *character reference*.

If, for instance, you wanted to insert a character from the "International Phonetic Alphabet", you could spend a long time looking for a combination of keyboard, operating system and text editor that would make that straightforward. XML simply allows you to refer to the character by its *Unicode number*.

15.6.1 *Reference by decimal number*

Here is an example:

Example 15-17. Decimal character reference

```
<P>Here is a reference to Unicode character 161: &#161;.</P>
```

Unicode is a character set. The character numbered 161 in Unicode happens to be the inverted exclamation mark.

15.6.2 *Reference by hexadecimal number*

Alternatively, you could use the *hexadecimal (hex)* value of the character number to reference it:

Example 15-18. Hex character reference

```
<P>Here is a different reference to Unicode character 161: &#xA1;.
```

Hex is a numbering system often used by computer programmers that translates naturally into the binary codes that computers use. The *Unicode Standard book* uses hex, so those that have that book will probably prefer this type of character reference over the other (whether they are programmers or not).

Note that character references are not entity references, though they look similar to them. Entities have names and values, but character references only have character numbers. In an XML document, all entities except the predefined ones must be declared. But a character reference does not require a declaration; it is just a really verbose way to type a character (but often the only way).

15.6.3 *Reference by name (via an entity)*

Because Unicode numbers are hard to remember, it is often useful to declare entities that stand in for them:

Example 15-19. Entity declaration for a Unicode character

```
<!ENTITY inverted-exclamation "&#161;">
```

15.7 | Suppressing markup recognition

Sometimes when you are creating an XML document, you want to protect certain characters from being interpreted as markup. Imagine, for example, that you are writing a user's guide to HTML. You would need a way to include an example of markup. Your first attempt might be to create an `example` element and do something like Example 15-20.

Example 15-20. An invalid approach to HTML examples in XML

```
<p>HTML documents must start with a DOCTYPE, etc. etc. This
is an example of a small HTML document:
<sample>

  <!DOCTYPE HTML PUBLIC "-//W3C//DTD HTML 3.2 Final//EN">
  <HTML>
  A document's title
  <H1>A document's title</H1>
  </HTML>

</sample>
```

This will not work, however, because the angle brackets that are supposed to represent HTML markup will be interpreted as if they belonged to the XML document you are creating, not the mythical HTML document in the example. Your XML parser will complain that it is not appropriate to have an HTML DOCTYPE declaration in the middle of an XML document!

There are two solutions to this problem: CDATA sections and predefined entities.

15.7.1 *CDATA sections*

A construct called a *CDATA section* allows you to ask the parser to suspend markup recognition in a large chunk of text: "Hands off! This isn't meant to be interpreted."

CDATA stands for "character data". You can mark a section as being character data using the syntax shown in Example 15-21.

The first and last lines mark the start and end, respectively, of the CDATA section. The last line is a delimiter called *CDEnd* (`]]>`). It may only be used to close CDATA sections. It must not occur anywhere else in an XML document.

Example 15-21. Writing about HTML in a CDATA section

```
<![CDATA[
<HTML>
This is an example from HTML for Dumbbells!
<p>It may be a pain to write a book about HTML in HTML,
but it is easy in XML!
</HTML>
]]>
```

15.7.2 *Predefined entities*

Predefined entities allow an author to represent individual data characters that would otherwise be interpreted as markup. There are five of them, shown in Table 15-1, along with the markup interpretations that they avoid.

Table 15-1 Predefined entities

Entity reference	Character	Markup not recognized
&amp;	&	Entity or character reference
&lt;	<	Tag
&gt;	>	CDend
&apos;	'	Literal
&quot;	"	Literal

We can use references to the predefined entities to insert these characters, instead of typing them directly. Then they will not be interpreted as markup. Example 15-22 demonstrates this.

When your XML parser parses the document, it will replace the entity references with actual characters. It will not interpret the characters it inserts as markup, but as "plain old data characters" (character data).

Predefined entities and CDATA sections only relate to the interpretation of the markup, not to the properties of the real document that the markup represents.

Example 15-22. Writing about HTML with predefined entities

```
<p>HTML documents must start with a DOCTYPE, etc. etc. This
is an example of a small HTML document:
<sample>
    &lt;!DOCTYPE HTML PUBLIC "-//W3C//DTD HTML 3.2 Final//EN">
    &lt;HTML>
    &lt;HEAD>
    &lt;TITLE>A document's title
    &lt;/TITLE>
    &lt;/HEAD>
    &lt;/HTML>
</sample>
```

15.8 | Comments

Sometimes it is useful to embed information about a document or its markup in a manner that will be ignored by computer processes and renditions of the document. For example, you might insert a note to yourself to clean up the wording of a section, a note to a co-author explaining the reason for a particular section of the document, or a note in a DTD describing the semantics of a particular element. This information can be hidden from the application in a *comment*. Comments should never be displayed in a browser, indexed in a search engine, or otherwise processed as part of the data of the actual document.

Example 15-23. A comment

```
<!-- This section is really good! Let's not change it. -->
```

Comments consist of the characters "<!--" followed by almost anything and ended by "-->". The "almost anything" in the middle cannot contain the characters "--". This is a little bit inconvenient, because people often use those two characters as a sort of dash, to separate thoughts. This is another point to be careful of, lest you get bitten.

Comments can go just about anywhere in the instance or the prolog. However, they are not permitted within declarations, tags, or other comments.

Markup is not recognized in comments. You can put less-than and ampersand symbols in them, but they will not be recognized as the start of elements or entity references.

15.9 | Processing instructions

An XML comment is for those occasions where you need to say something to another human being without reference to the DTD or schema, and without changing the way the document looks to readers or applications. A *processing instruction* (PI) is for those occasions where you need to say something to *a computer program* without reference to the DTD or schema and without changing the way that the document is processed by other computer programs. This is only supposed to happen rarely.

Processing instructions start with a fixed string "<?". That is followed by a name and, after that, any characters except for the string that ends the PI, "?>". The XML declaration shown in Example 15-10 is an example.

The name at the beginning of the PI is called the *PI target*. This name would typically be specified in the documentation for the tool or specification. In this case, the PI target is the XML processor itself.

After the PI target comes white space and then some totally proprietary command. This command is not parsed in the usual way at all. Characters that would usually indicate markup are totally ignored. The command is passed directly to the application and it does what it wants to with it.

The command ends when the processor sees the string "?>". There is absolutely no standard for the characters in the middle. PIs could use attribute syntax for convenience, as the XML declaration does, but they could also choose not to.

Processing instructions are appropriate when you are specifying information about a document that is unrelated to its structure and content. As we describe in 18.10, "Referencing XSLT stylesheets", on page 412, XSL provides a processing instruction for associating stylesheets. Similarly, Office uses a PI to determine which application to use to open an XML document:

```
<?mso-application progid="Word.Document"?>
```

Note that this sort of processing instruction does not really add anything to the content or structure of the document. It says something about how to *process* the document. It says: "This document has an associated style-sheet (or application)."

It is not always obvious what is abstract information and what is merely processing information. If your information must be embedded in documents of many types, or with DTDs or schemas that you cannot change, then processing instructions are typically the appropriate technique.

15.10 | Office support for the XML language

Office can read and write XML documents that have declarations and other markup besides tags. However, most markup cannot be entered directly; the user interfaces of the products must be used, and they do not support some features of the XML language.

These support characteristics (shown in Table 15-2) may be significant when working with XML documents that are generated or processed by systems other than Office.

In many cases, lack of support for a construct can be overcome by simple generic transforms when opening and saving the document.

For example, an opening transform that tagged the CDATA sections with, for example, `<saveMarkup:CDATA>` tags and end-tags would preserve the section boundaries. The original markup could then be restored by transforming the document when it is saved: replacing the tags with the CDATA start and end.

Entity references could be handled similarly by adding an attribute for the system identifier URL, so that the closing transform can restore the entity declaration.

15.11 | Summary

An XML document is composed of a prolog and a document instance. The prolog is optional, and provides information about how the document is structured both physically (where its parts are) and logically (how its ele-

Table 15-2   Degree of support for XML language constructs

Construct	Open and Import	User	Save and Export
Tags	Full: includes tags with attributes and empty-element tags	Full	Full: all tags read in or created through user interface
User-defined parsed entities	Full: references to internal and external entities replaced with entity content	None	None: entity content merged into document
Processing instructions	Full: PIs allowed anywhere	None	Partial: saves PIs that precede root element
Predefined entities	Full: entity references replaced with their data characters	No need	Full: prohibited data characters converted to entity references
Character references	Full: entity references replaced with their data characters	None	None: characters merged into document; declarations not saved
CDATA sections	Full: markup in section content treated as data	None	None: section content merged into document; protected with predefined entity references
DTDs	Full (non-validating): default attribute values are processed	None	None: DTD not saved
Comments	Full: comments allowed anywhere	None	None: comments not saved

ments fit together). Elements and attributes describe the logical structure while *entities* describe the physical structure.

Namespaces

- Unique names
- URI-based namespaces
- Attributes with namespaces

Chapter

16

he *Namespaces in XML* specification is an extension to XML that answers the burning question: Are we talking about the same subject?

Since anyone can define element-type names, and elements from different documents can be mixed together, we need a way to clearly separate our names from other people's names. We need to have different so-called *namespaces*.

We do this in the real world all of the time.

What would you do if you needed to refer to a particular John Smith without confusing him with any other John Smith. You qualify the name: "John Smith from London." That sets up a namespace that separates Londoners from everyone else.

If that isn't sufficient then you further qualify the namespace: "John Smith from East London". That makes a namespace that separates Easterners from everyone else. You could narrow it down even more: "John Smith from Adelaide Street in East London." The trick is qualifying names in order to separate them from other names. The separate groups of names are known as "namespaces."

16.1 | The namespaces solution

Given that what we want to do is qualify names, the most obvious idea is to have a prefix that does the qualification, as in `myBrowserProgram:email` or `myEmailProgram:email`. This seems to work at first, but eventually two people will make program names that clash.

In the real world people constantly choose names that other people also choose. Even city names can clash: consider how many there are named "Springfield"! If people are allowed to choose names without any central authority then they will eventually choose names that clash.

The World Wide Web Consortium could set up a registry of these prefixes, but a suitable registry already exists – the domain name registry. It has the extra benefit that the domains can be subdivided into multiple prefixes by using the familiar URI mechanism (typically `http:` URLs).

Example 16-1 shows what URI-based namespace prefixes might look like.

Example 16-1. Mythical (illegal!) URI-based namespace prefix

```
<http://www.aol.com/EmailAppGuy:email>email@machine.com
</http://www.aol.com/EmailAppGuy:email>
```

There are two problems with these prefixes. First, they are not legal XML names because of all of the funny characters such as slashes and dots. Second, they are ugly and incredibly verbose.

The solution is to set up a local abbreviation, like an entity reference for the prefix. The *Namespaces in XML* specification defines the mechanism for setting up such abbreviations.

16.1.1 *Namespace prefixes*

The *Namespaces in XML* specification defines a rule that attributes that start with the prefix `xmlns:` should be interpreted as prefix-defining attributes. The name immediately following the prefix is a local abbreviation for the namespace.

The attribute value is a URI reference. You can use any URI (typically a URL) that you would normally have control over. Throughout the element exhibiting that attribute, the prefix stands for the namespace. Example 16-2 demonstrates.

Example 16-2. Using XML namespaces

```
<eag:email xmlns:eag="http://www.aol.com/EmailAppGuy">
email@machine.com
</eag:email>
```

The actual prefix you use is not relevant. It is just a stand-in for the URI. So, for example, when creating an XSL stylesheet you do not need to use the xsl: prefix for names defined in the XSL spec. Doing otherwise might be confusing, but it is totally legal.

Note that the details of the URI are not relevant either. It does not matter whether there is a document at that location or whether the client machine is Internet-connected. There is no need to connect to the Internet to check the contents of the document at that address.

That's an important point! Namespaces work with broken URIs because namespaces only disambiguate names, they don't define names. The only requirement is that you really do control the URI that you use.

16.1.2 *Scoping*

The prefix scheme is still pretty verbose, but it is some improvement. It looks better when you realize that namespace declarations are *scoped* by their declaring elements. That means that they apply to the element, its children, and the children's children and so forth unless some child has a declaration that specifically overrides the first declaration. Example 16-3 shows a document that uses a namespace associated with the myns prefix many times despite declaring it only once.

Therefore you could declare namespaces in the document (root) element and have them apply throughout the entire document! Example 16-4 demonstrates.[1]

---

1. Note that .con is the new high-level domain for Internet scams.

Example 16-3. Using an ancestor's namespace

```
<myns:a xmlns:myns="http://www.someurl.com/2002">
    <myns:b>
    </myns:b>
    <myns:c>
        <myns:d>
        </myns:d>
    </myns:c>
</myns:a>
```

Example 16-4. XML namespace scope

```
<html:html
    xmlns:eag="http://www.aol.com/EmailAppGuy"
    xmlns:html="http://www.w3.org/TR/WD-HTML40"
    xmlns:math="http://www.w3.org/TR/REC-MathML/">
  <html:title>George Soros Personal Wealth Page</html:title>
  <html:h2>Counting My Cash</html:h2>
  <html:p>As you know, my cash rivals the gross national
product of some small countries. Consider the following equation:
  <math:reln>
    <math:eq/>
    <math:ci>wealth</math:ci>
    <math:ci>gnp</math:ci>
  </math:reln>
If you have any ideas of how I could spend this money. Please
contact
  <eag:email>georges@aol.con</eag:email>.
</html:p>

</html:html>
```

16.1.3 *Default namespace*

We can minimize namespace clutter even more by removing some of the prefixes. There is a special namespace called the *default namespace*. This namespace is defined without a prefix, so element-type names in the scope of the definition that have no prefix are considered to be in this namespace.[2] If you expect to use many elements from a particular namespace, you can make it the default namespace for the appropriate scope. In fact, you can even have a document in which the namespaces correspond cleanly

---

2. You can think of the default namespace as having a null prefix, if that helps any.

to the elements and there are no prefixes at all, as Example 16-5 demonstrates.

Example 16-5. Two default namespaces: HTML and MathML

```
<html
    xmlns="http://www.w3.org/TR/WD-HTML40">
  <title>George Soros Personal Wealth Page</title>
  <h2>Counting My Cash</h2>
  <p>As you know, my cash rivals the gross national
product of some small countries. Consider the following equation:
  <reln xmlns="http://www.w3.org/TR/REC-MathML/">
    <eq/>
    <ci>wealth</ci>
    <ci>gnp</ci>
  </reln>
If you have any ideas of how I could spend this money.</p>
</html>
```

Note that the default namespace is HTML both before and after the `reln` element. Within the `reln` element the default namespace is MathML. As you can see, we can eliminate many of the prefixes but still keep the relationship between the element-type names and the namespaces.

We can also establish a scope in which names without prefixes have no namespace, by using an empty string instead of a URI. In Example 16-6, `notes` and `todo` are not in the MathML namespace.

Example 16-6. A scope for local names

```
<reln xmlns="http://www.w3.org/TR/REC-MathML/">
  <eq/>
  <ci>wealth</ci>
  <ci>gnp</ci>
  <notes xmlns="">
    <todo>check the math</todo>
  </notes>
</reln>
```

16.1.4 *Attribute names*

Attribute names can also come from a namespace, which is indicated in the usual way by prefixing them with a namespace prefix. For instance, the

XML Linking Language (XLink) uses the namespace mechanism to allow XLink attributes to appear on elements that themselves come from some other namespace. Example 16-7 shows such attributes.

Example 16-7. Attributes in XLink namespace

```
<myLink xmlns:xlink="http://www.w3.org/1999/xlink"
   xlink:type="simple">
...
</myLink>
```

It does not matter what the namespace of the element type is. The XLink attributes are in the XLink namespace even when they are exhibited by an element type that is not in the XLink namespace.

In fact, even attributes without prefixes are not in the same namespace that their element type is in. Nor are they in the default namespace. Attributes without prefixes are in no namespace at all.

From a processing standpoint, the lack of a namespace doesn't matter. The attribute name can still be specified in a stylesheet pattern or utilized by the template for the element type's template rule.

XPath primer

Friendly Tutorial

- Location paths
- Addressing multiple objects
- Children and descendants
- Attributes
- Predicates

Chapter

17

Path is a notation for addressing information within a document. That information could be:

- An "executive summary" of a longer document.
- A glossary of terms whose definitions are scattered throughout a manual.
- The specific sequence of steps, buried in a large reference work, needed to solve a particular problem.
- The customized subset of information that a particular customer subscribes to.
- All the sections and subsections of a book that were written by a particular author or revised since a specific date.
- For documents holding information from relational databases, all the typical queries made of relational databases: a particular patient's medical records, the address of the customer with the most orders, the inventory items with low stock levels, and so on.
- For documents that are containers for document collections, all the typical queries made in a library catalog or on a website:

articles about Abyssinian cats, essays on the proper study of mankind, etc.

A programmer working with an XML-aware programming or scripting language could write code to search the document for the information that meets the specified criteria. The purpose of XPath is to automate this searching so that a non-programming user can address the information just by writing an expression that contains the criteria.

17.1 | Location paths

In order to retrieve something, you need to know where to find it – in other words, its *address*.

An address doesn't have to be an absolute location; you can address things relatively ("two doors down from 29 Jones St."). It doesn't have to be an explicit location at all: you can address things by name ("Lance") or description ("world's greatest athlete").

You can address several things at once ("Monty and Westy"), even if you don't know exactly what they are or whether they even exist ("inexpensive French restaurant downtown").

All those forms of address can be used to locate things in XML documents, by means of an *XPath expression*.

The most important form of XPath expression is called a *location path*. You may already be familiar with location paths because they are used to address your computer's files by specifying the path from the file system's root to a specific subdirectory. For example, the path `/home/bob/xml/samples` identifies a particular one of the four `samples` subdirectories shown in Figure 17-1.

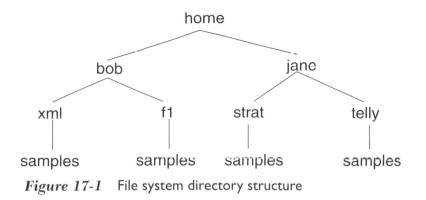

Figure 17-1   File system directory structure

17.2 | Addressing multiple objects

A location path is capable of addressing multiple objects. For example, the expression in Example 17-1 addresses all `caption` elements within `figure` elements that are within `chapter` elements within `book` elements.

Example 17-1. Location path

```
/book/chapter/figure/caption
```

In the book whose structure is shown in Figure 17-2, the expression in Example 17-1 would address the first two `caption` elements, because they are children of `figure` elements. It would not address the third, which is the child of an `example` element.

Example 17-2 shows the XML representation of the book.

17.3 | Children and descendants

The `/book/chapter/figure/caption` expression addresses two elements with no children other than data. The expression `/book/chapter/figure`,

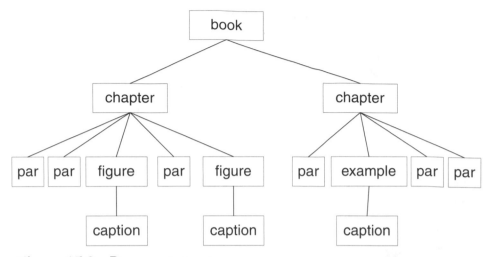

Figure 17-2   Document structure

Example 17-2. A short book in XML

```
<?xml version="1.0"?>
<book>
  <chapter>
    <par author="bd">First paragraph. <emph>Really.</emph></par>
    <par author="cg">Second paragraph.</par>
    <figure picfile="one.jpg">
      <caption>The first figure's caption</caption>
    </figure>
    <par>Third paragraph.</par>
    <figure picfile="two.jpg">
      <caption>The second figure's caption.</caption>
    </figure>
  </chapter>
  <chapter>
    <par author="pp">Chapter 2, first paragraph.</par>
    <example>
      <caption>The first example.</caption>
    </example>
    <par>Chapter 2, second paragraph.</par>
    <par author="bd">Chapter 2, third paragraph.</par>
  </chapter>
</book>
```

however, addresses the `figure` elements with their `caption` children, as shown in Example 17-3.

Example 17-3. Figure elements with their caption children

```
<figure picfile="one.jpg">
  <caption>The first figure's caption</caption>
</figure>
<figure picfile="two.jpg">
  <caption>The second figure's caption.</caption>
</figure>
```

The location path `/book` addresses the entire document.

In a location path, the slash character (`/`) means "child of." A double slash (`//`) means "descendant of," which is more flexible as it includes children, grandchildren, great-grandchildren, and so on. For example, `/book//caption` addresses any `caption` element descended from a `book` element. In the book shown in Figure 17-2 it would address the `example` element's `caption` from the book's second chapter along with the figure elements' two `caption` elements:

Example 17-4. Caption elements descended from the book element

```
<caption>The first figure's caption</caption>
<caption>The second figure's caption.</caption>
<caption>The first example.</caption>
```

17.4 | Attributes

An address in XML document navigation is not a storage address like a file system path, despite the similarity in syntax. An XPath expression locates objects by their position in a document's structure and other properties, such as the values of attributes.

A diagram like Figure 17-2 should not present an attribute's information as a child of the element exhibiting the attribute. To do so would be incorrect, because attributes are not siblings of subelements. For this reason, XPath uses `/@` to show the element/attribute relationship.

For example, the expression in Example 17-5 addresses all the values of the par elements' author attributes.

Example 17-5. Expression with an attribute

```
/book//par/@author
```

Example 17-6. Objects addressed by Example 17-5

```
bd
cg
pp
bd
```

17.5 | Predicates

A *predicate* is an expression that changes the group of objects addressed by another expression that precedes it. A predicate expression is delimited by square brackets and is either true or false. If true, it adds to the objects addressed; if false, it removes objects.

For example, the expression in Example 17-7 addresses all chapters that have a figure element in them.

Example 17-7. Addressing chapters with a figure element

```
/book/chapter[figure]
```

The predicate expression figure is true for any chapter that contains a figure. If true, that chapter is included among the addressed objects. Note that the figure itself is not among the objects addressed (although it is contained within the addressed chapter object).

A predicate expression can be a comparison. For example, .= lets you address an element by comparing its content data to a specific character string. Example 17-8 uses this technique to address all the par elements that have "Second paragraph." as their content data.

Example 17-8. Addressing par elements with specific content data

```
/book//par[.="Second paragraph."]
```

Example 17-9. Objects addressed by Example 17-8

```
<par author="cg">Second paragraph.</par>
```

17.6 | The XPath data model

We have been talking informally about the "objects" that XPath addresses, but what are they?

One thing they certainly are not is the unparsed text of an XML document. That's because there are several alternative text strings that could mean the same thing, so addressing them would be ambiguous.

For example, an apostrophe in data and the predefined entity reference ' are equivalent to an XML parser. XPath addresses the *result* of parsing.

Computer scientists call the structure in Figure 17-2 a tree, even though it seems to be growing upside down! In fact, they usually speak of it as a family tree, as we have been doing, with ancestors, children, descendants, siblings, and so on.

The objects in a computer science tree are called *nodes*, and nodes are the objects that XPath addresses. There are nodes that represent elements, textual data, attributes, and other things found by the parser.

> *Tip*   An advanced tutorial on XPath can be found in Chapter 24, "XML Path Language (XPath)", on page 498.

XSL Transformations (XSLT)

Friendly Tutorial

- Template rules
- Patterns
- Templates
- Referencing stylesheets

Chapter

18

We have seen XSLT used at a high level in other chapters, now we'll look at the details of how it works. But be aware that the full details on XSLT could fill a book[1] and we don't cover them all here. The objective of this chapter is to provide a basic understanding for the way that XSLT stylesheets cause XML documents to be processed.

18.1 | Transforming vs. rendering

XSL was designed to apply style to an XML document by using XSLT to *transform* it into a rendition, represented by XSL formatting objects (XSL-FO). The XSL processor may then display the rendered document on a screen, print it, or convert it to some other rendition representation, such as PDF, PostScript, or even voice synthesis!

---

1. The one we recommend is *Definitive XSLT and XPath* by Ken Holman, published in this series.

But "style" in the world of generalized markup encompasses every kind of processing. The transformation could be very powerful and complex, as XSLT can reorder, duplicate, suppress, sort, and add elements. There are many applications besides formatting where such transformations would be useful.

Consider an electronic commerce application where many companies must communicate. Each of their internal systems may use similar but different document types. To communicate they need to translate their various document types into a common one. An XSLT transformation provides a sophisticated but straightforward way to do so.

To summarize: name notwithstanding, XSLT is more than just a style language. While it can fulfill its original design goal of transforming documents into XSL-FO renditions, it can do far more than that. XSLT can transform XML documents into other XML abstractions, and into other rendered representations as well – such as WordML.

18.2 | XSLT stylesheets

Most XSLT looks more or less like ordinary XML. Simple XSLT stylesheets are merely a specialized form of XML markup designed for specifying the transformation of other XML documents. You can think of XSLT as just another document type.

A stylesheet that transforms a document into another XML document might have a root element that looks like Example 18-1.

Example 18-1. XSLT stylesheet using XML output elements

```
<xsl:stylesheet xmlns:xsl="http://www.w3.org/1999/XSL/Transform"
                version="1.0">
<xsl:output method="xml"/>
    <!-- template rules go here -->
</xsl:stylesheet>
```

The root element is `xsl:stylesheet`.[2] It must have a namespace declaration for XSLT. It makes sense to use the same declaration and `xsl:` prefix

---

2. The spec also allows the root element to be called `xsl:transform`, presumably for the benefit of people with no style sense!

every time. You can also specify the output method to be used by the processor, choosing between XML, HTML and plain text.

The `xsl:stylesheet` element is usually filled with template rules. The template rules describe how to transform elements in the source document. Of course almost every element type could be processed differently from every other element type so there are many rules in an XSLT stylesheet. Particular elements could even be processed differently if they share a type but have different attributes or occur in a different context.

18.3 | Using HTML with XSLT

Many XSLT implementations allow transformations from XML into HTML. This is good for serving to today's mainstream browsers (6.x and up) and the legacy (3.x-5.x) browsers that most websites must still support.

It also takes advantage of many Web designers' knowledge of HTML. If you format a document using element types from HTML, the page will look to a browser as if it had been created in HTML directly. You can think of this process as a conversion from XML markup to HTML markup. It is a useful way to publish XML documents to the Web.

Because basic HTML is widely understood, we will use HTML element types in most of our examples. We will restrict our usage to only a few HTML types, namely:

- h1 and h2 element types for top-level and second-level headings;
- p element type for paragraphs;
- body element type to contain the document's content; and the
- em element type to emphasize a series of characters.

A stylesheet that generates HTML elements might have a root element that looks like Example 18-2.

Example 18-2. XSLT stylesheet using HTML elements

```
<xsl:stylesheet xmlns:xsl="http://www.w3.org/1999/XSL/Transform"
                version="1.0">
<xsl:output method="html"/>
    <!-- template rules go here  >
</xsl:stylesheet>
```

18.4 | Rules, patterns and templates

A *template rule* defines a mapping of parts of a source document into a result document. During XSLT processing every element, character, comment and processing instruction in an XML document is processed by some template rule. Some of them will be handled by template rules that the stylesheet writer created. Others are handled by *built-in* template rules that are hard-coded into every XSLT processor.

Template rules consist of two parts, the *pattern* and the *template*. Be careful with the terminology: a template is not a template rule. The pattern describes which source nodes (elements, textual data strings, comments or processing instructions) should be processed by the rule. The template describes the structure to generate when nodes are found that match the pattern.

In an XSLT stylesheet, a template rule is represented by an `xsl:template` element.[3] The pattern is the value of the `xsl:template` element's `match` attribute, and the template proper is the element's content.

Template rules are simple. You do not have to think about the order in which things will be processed, where data is stored or other housekeeping tasks that programming languages usually require you to look after. You just declare what you want the result to look like and the XSLT processor figures out how to make that happen. Because everything is done through declarations we say that XSL is a *declarative* language.

18.5 | Creating a stylesheet

XSLT's processing model revolves around the idea of *patterns*. Patterns are XPath expressions designed to test nodes. Patterns allow the XSLT processor to choose which elements to apply which style rules to. XSLT's pattern language is basically XPath with a few extensions and restrictions. Patterns are used in the `match` attribute of template rules to specify which nodes the rule applies to.

---

3. It would have been clearer had they called it an `xsl:template-rule` element, but they didn't.

18.5.1 *Document-level template rule*

Consider a document whose root element-type is book and that can contain title, section and appendix element types. section and appendix elements can contain title, para and list subelements. Titles contain #PCDATA and no subelements. Paragraphs and list items contain emph and #PCDATA. Example 18-3 is a DTD that represents these constraints and Example 18-4 is an example document.

Example 18-3. DTD for book example

```
<!ELEMENT book (title, (section|appendix)+)>
<!ELEMENT section (title, (para|list)+)>
<!ELEMENT appendix (title, (para|list)+)>
<!ELEMENT title (#PCDATA)>
<!ELEMENT para (#PCDATA|emph)*>
<!ELEMENT emph (#PCDATA)>
<!ELEMENT list (item)+>
<!ELEMENT item (#PCDATA|emph)*>
```

Example 18-4. Book document instance

```
<book>
   <title>Chicken Soup for the Chicken's Soul</title>
   <section>
       <title>Introduction</title>
       <para>I've always wanted to write
             this book.</para>
   </section>
</book>
```

First the XSLT processor would examine the root element of the document. The XSLT processor would look for a rule that applied to books (a rule with a *match pattern* that matched a book). This sort of match pattern is very simple. Example 18-5 demonstrates.

Example 18-5. Simple match pattern

```
<xsl:template match="book">
  <!-- describe how books should be transformed -->
</xsl:template>
```

We can choose any basic structure for the generated book. Example 18-6 shows a reasonable one.

Example 18-6. Generated book structure

```
<xsl:template match="book">
  <body>
    <h1><!-- handle title --></h1>
    <!-- handle sections -->
    <hr/> <!-- HTML horizontal rule -->
    <h2>Appendices</h2>
    <!-- handle appendices -->
    <hr/>
    <p>Copyright 2004, the establishment.</p>
  </body>
</xsl:template>
```

The template in this template rule generates a body to hold the content of the document. The tags for the body element are usually omitted in HTML but we've generated them here so we can add some attributes to the element later. The body is called a *literal result element*.

18.5.2 *Literal result elements*

The XSLT processor knows to treat body as a *literal result element* that is copied into the output because it is not an XSLT instruction (formally, it is not in the XSLT namespace). Elements in templates that are not part of the XSLT namespace are treated literally and copied into the output. You can see why these are called templates! They describe the form of the result document both by ordering content and by generating literal result elements. If the XSLT processor supports legacy HTML output, and the HTML output method is being used to serialize the result, then it will know to use legacy HTML conventions.

The h1, h2 and hr elements are also literal result elements that will create HTML headings and horizontal rules. As the stylesheet is represented in XML, the specification for the horizontal rule can use XML empty-element syntax. Finally the document has a literal result element and literal text representing the copyright. XSLT stylesheets can introduce this sort of *boilerplate* text.

18.5.3 *Extracting data*

The template also has comments describing things we still have to handle: the document's title, its sections and the appendices.

We can get the data content from the `title` element with the `xsl:value-of` instruction. It has a `select` attribute which is a pattern. If this pattern names a simple element type then it will match a subelement of the *current* element.

In this case the current element is the `book` element as that is the element matched by the template rule. Example 18-7 shows what the data extraction would look like.

Example 18-7. Extracting data from a subelement

```
<h1><xsl:value-of select="title"/></h1>
```

18.5.4 *The* `apply-templates` *instruction*

The next step is to handle sections and appendices. We could do it in one of two ways. We could either create a new template rule for handling sections or we could handle sections directly in the `book` template rule.

The benefit of creating a new rule is that it can be used over and over again. Before we create the new rule we should ensure it will get invoked at the right point. We will use a new instruction, `xsl:apply-templates`. Example 18-8 shows this instruction.

Example 18-8. The `xsl:apply-templates` instruction

```
<xsl:apply-templates select="section"/>
```

The `xsl:apply-templates` instruction does two important things.

1. It finds all nodes that match the `select` attribute pattern.
2. It processes each of these in turn. It does so by finding and applying the template rule that matches each node.

This important principle is at the heart of XSLT's processing model.

In this case, the *select* pattern in the `xsl:apply-templates` element selects all of the book's subelements of type `section`. The `xsl:apply-templates` instruction always searches out the rule that is appropriate for each of the selected nodes. In this case the `xsl:apply-templates` instruction will search out a rule that applies to sections. The expanded `book` template rule is in Example 18-9.

Example 18-9. Handling section elements

```
<xsl:template match="book">
  <body>
    <h1><xsl:value-of select="title"/></h1>
    <xsl:apply-templates select="section"/>
    <hr/>
    <h2>Appendices</h2>
    <xsl:apply-templates select="appendix"/>
    <p>Copyright 2004, the establishment</p>
  </body>
</xsl:template>
```

18.5.5 *Handling optional elements*

Our sample document does not have appendices but the stylesheet should support anything that the DTD or schema allows. Documents of this type created in the future may have appendices.

Our stylesheet generates the title element followed by section elements (in the order that they occurred in the document) followed by appendix elements (also in *document order*).

If our DTD allowed more than one title subelement in a book element then this stylesheet would generate them all. There is no way for a stylesheet to require that the document have a single title. These sorts of constraints are specified in a DTD or schema.

Our DTD does permit documents to have no appendices. Our "Appendices" title and horizontal rule separating the appendices from the sections would look fairly silly in that case. XSLT provides an instruction called `xsl:if` that handles this situation. We can wrap it around the relevant parts as shown in Example 18-10.

The `xsl:if` instruction goes within a template. We could drop it into our `book` template as a replacement for our current appendix handling.

Example 18-10. Using `xsl:if`

```
<xsl:if test="appendix">
  <hr/>
  <h2>Appendices</h2>
  <xsl:apply-templates select="appendix"/>
</xsl:if>
```

The instruction also contains another template within it. The contained template is only instantiated (generated) if there is some element that matches the pattern exhibited by the test attribute – in this case, an appendix element.

As with the select attribute, the context is the current node. If there is no node that matches the pattern in the test attribute then the entire contained template will be skipped.

There is another instruction called `xsl:choose` that allows for multiple alternatives, including a default template for when none of the other alternatives match.

18.5.6 *Reordering the output*

If the DTD had allowed titles, sections and appendices to be mixed together our stylesheet would reorder them so that the title preceded the sections and the sections preceded the appendices.

This ability to reorder is very important. It allows us to use one structure in our abstract representation and another in our rendition. The abstract structure is optimized for editing, validating and processing convenience. The rendered structure is optimized for viewing and navigation.

Reordering is easy when you know exactly the order in which you want elements of various types to be processed. In the case of the body, for example: titles before sections before appendices. But within a section or appendix, reordering is somewhat trickier because we don't know the complete output order.

That is, we need to process titles before any of the paragraphs or lists, but we cannot disturb the relative order of the paragraphs and lists themselves. Those have to be generated in the document order.

We can solve this fairly easily. In XPath pattern syntax the vertical bar (|) character means "or". So we can make a rule like the one in Example 18-11.

Example 18-11. The section rule

```
<xsl:template match="section">
    <h2><xsl:value-of select="title"/></h2>
    <xsl:apply-templates select="para|list"/>
</xsl:template>
```

This rule forces titles (in our DTD there can be only one) to be handled first and paragraphs and lists to be processed in the order that they are found. The rules that are defined for paragraphs and lists will automatically be selected when those types of element appear. We'll create those rules next.

18.5.7 *Data content*

Next we can handle paragraphs. We want them each to generate a single HTML element. We also want them to generate their content to populate that element in the order that the content occurs, not in some order pre-defined by the template.

We need to process all of the paragraph's *subnodes*. That means that we cannot just handle emph subelements. We must also handle ordinary character data. Example 18-12 demonstrates this.

Example 18-12. Paragraph rule

```
<xsl:template match="para">
    <p><xsl:apply-templates select="node()"/>
    </p>
</xsl:template>
```

As you can see, the rule for paragraphs is very simple. The xsl:apply-templates instruction handles most of the work for us automatically. The select attribute matches all nodes: element nodes, text nodes, etc. If it encounters a text node it copies it to the result; that is a *default* rule built into XSLT. If it encounters a subelement, it processes it using the appropriate rule.

XSLT handles much of the complexity for us but we should still be clear: transformations will not always be this easy. These rules are so simple because our DTD is very much like HTML. The more alike the source and result DTDs the simpler the transformation will be. It is especially helpful to have a very loose or flexible result DTD. HTML is perfect in this regard.

18.5.8 *Handling inline elements*

The rule for emph follows the same basic organization as the paragraph rule. Mixed content (i.e. character-containing) elements often use this organization. The HTML element-type name is em (Example 18-13). Note that in this case we will use an abbreviated syntax for the xsl:apply-templates element: Because the select attribute defaults to node(), we can leave it out.

Example 18-13. Handling emphasis

```
<xsl:template match="emph">
    <em><xsl:apply-templates/></em>
</xsl:template>
```

List items also have mixed content, so we should look at the rules for lists and list items next. They are in Example 18-14.

Example 18-14. List and item rules

```
<xsl:template match="list">
    <ol>
        <xsl:apply-templates/>
    </ol>
</xsl:template>
<xsl:template match="item">
    <li><xsl:apply-templates/></li>
</xsl:template>
```

The rules in Example 18-13 and Example 18-14 work together. When a list is detected the literal result element is processed and an ol element is generated. It will contain a single li element for each item. Each li will in turn contain text nodes (handled by the default rule) and emph (handled by the emph rule).

18.5.9 *Sharing a template rule*

We still need a template rule for appendices. If we wrote out the rule for appendices we would find it to be identical to sections. We could just copy the sections rule but XSLT has a more elegant way. We can amend our rule for sections to say that the rule applies equally to sections *or* appendices. Example 18-15 demonstrates.

Example 18-15. The rule in Example 18-11 revised to handle appendices as well as sections

```
<xsl:template match="section|appendix">
    <h2><xsl:value-of select="title"/></h2>
    <xsl:apply-templates select="para|list"/>
</xsl:template>
```

18.5.10 *Final touches*

We now have a complete stylesheet but it is rather basic. We might as well add a background color to beautify it a bit. HTML allows this through the bgcolor attribute of the body element. We will not go into the details of the HTML color scheme but suffice to say that Example 18-16 gives our document a nice light purple background.

Example 18-16. Adding a background color

```
<xsl:template match="book">
  <body bgcolor="#FFDDFF">
    <!-- Handling of body content is unchanged -->
    ...
  </body>
</xsl:template>
```

There is also one more detail we must take care of. We said earlier that the more flexible a document type is the easier it is to transform to. Even though HTML is pretty flexible it does have one unbreakable rule. Every document must have a title element, but "title" means something different in the HTML vocabulary from what it does in our book DTD.

We've handled the title element from the source as a heading, but in HTML the title shows up in the window's title bar, in the bookmark list and in search engine result lists. We need the document's title to appear as both the HTML title and as an HTML heading element. Luckily XSLT allows us to duplicate data.

With these additions our stylesheet is complete! It is shown in Example 18-17.

As you can see, simple transformations can be quite simple to specify in XSLT – evidence of the language's good design. The important thing to keep in mind is that the basic XSLT processing model is based on template rules, patterns and templates. Flow of control between rules is handled by special instructions.

18.6 | Top-level instructions

XSLT also allows you to do more complex things. It supports all of XPath, sophisticated selections, stylesheet reuse and many other advanced features. We will introduce a few of these in this section.

Top-level instructions are those that go directly in the `xsl:stylesheet` element. They do not apply to any particular template rule but rather declare behaviors, variables and other things that affect the entire stylesheet. Except for `xsl:import` instructions, which we'll describe shortly, the order of top-level statements is not important.

18.6.1 *Combining stylesheets*

There are two ways to combine stylesheets: inclusion and import.

18.6.1.1 Including other stylesheets

The `xsl:include` instruction includes another stylesheet. Stylesheets may not include themselves directly or indirectly. The instructions in an included stylesheet are treated exactly as if they had been typed directly in the including stylesheet. They are not second-class in any sense. Example 18-18 demonstrates the inclusion of other stylesheets through both absolute and relative URIs.

Example 18-17. Complete stylesheet

```
<?xml version="1.0"?>
<xsl:stylesheet xmlns:xsl="http://www.w3.org/1999/XSL/Transform"
                version="1.0">
<xsl:output method="html"/>

<xsl:template match="book">
  <body bgcolor="#FFDDFF">
    <title><xsl:value-of select="title"/></title>
    <h1><xsl:value-of select="title"/></h1>
    <xsl:apply-templates select="section"/>
    <hr/>
    <xsl:if test="appendix">
      <hr/>
      <h2>Appendices</h2>
      <xsl:apply-templates select="appendix"/>
    </xsl:if>
    <p>Copyright 2004, the establishment</p>
  </body>
</xsl:template>

<xsl:template match="para">
    <p><xsl:apply-templates/></p>
</xsl:template>

<xsl:template match="emph">
    <em><xsl:apply-templates/></em>
</xsl:template>

<xsl:template match="list">
    <ol>
        <xsl:apply-templates/>
    </ol>
</xsl:template>

<xsl:template match="item">
    <li><xsl:apply-templates/></li>
</xsl:template>

<xsl:template match="section|appendix">
    <xsl:apply-templates select="title"/>
    <xsl:apply-templates select="para|list"/>
</xsl:template>
</xsl:stylesheet>
```

Example 18-18. Including another stylesheet

```
<xsl:include href="http://.../currency.xsl"/>
<xsl:include href="bonds.xsl"/>
```

18.6.1.2 Importing from other stylesheets

Importing is a little bit different from *including*. Just as in the real world, there are restrictions on imports! In the XSLT context that means imports are second-class. Imported rules only take effect when no rule in the main stylesheet matches. Also, import statements earlier in the document take precedence over later ones.

Import instructions *must* go at the top of a stylesheet, preceding any other top-level instructions and the `xsl:template` elements. A stylesheet must not directly or indirectly import itself. Example 18-19 demonstrates the importation of other stylesheets through both absolute and relative URIs.

Example 18-19. Importing another stylesheet

```
<xsl:import href="http://.../stocks.xsl"/>
<xsl:import href="credit-cards.xsl"/>
```

18.6.2 *Whitespace handling*

Whitespace nodes are ordinary text nodes that happen to have only whitespace (tab, space, newline) characters in them.

In machine-to-machine applications, whitespace nodes are usually irrelevant. Even in publishing applications, some whitespace is not important for processing. A blank line between two section elements is just intended to make the source XML easier to read. It is not intended to affect what is seen by the ultimate readers of the rendered document.

XSLT has a feature that allows you to strip out these whitespace-only nodes based on the elements in which they occur. The `xsl:strip-space` instruction strips space from elements of specified types in the source document. Example 18-20 shows how you would strip space from address and date elements.

Example 18-20. Stripping space

```
<xsl:strip-space elements="address date"/>
```

In some vocabularies, all element types are so-called *space-stripping*. You can accomplish this by using an asterisk in the `xsl:strip-space` instruction (Example 18-21).

Example 18-21. Strip space from all elements

```
<xsl:strip-space elements="*"/>
```

If a vocabulary has only a few non-whitespace stripping elements (*whitespace-preserving elements*), you can selectively override the blanket stripping statement with the `xsl:preserve-space` instruction. By default, whitespace is preserved.

18.6.3 *Output descriptions*

The `xsl:output` instruction sets various options that control what the stylesheet should generate as output. The main attribute in the instruction is the `method` attribute, which typically takes a value like "xml", "html" or "text".

"xml" is appropriate for (surprise!) generating XML; it is the default. "html" uses html conventions for empty-elements, processing instructions and similar constructs. The "text" output is useful when you want to generate plain text without the XSLT processor representing delimiter characters such as less-than signs (<) as `&lt;`, and so forth.

Other attributes can control whether the output is indented for "pretty printing", what character encoding to use, whether to add an XML declaration and/or document type declaration and other (even more obscure) output options. Most XSLT stylesheets will not need to change these options from their defaults.

But if you find that the output of your stylesheet is not quite what you would expect, then `xsl:output` may have the answer for you.

18.6.4 *Numeric formats*

The `xsl:decimal-format` instruction allows you to describe how decimal numbers will be printed by your stylesheet. For instance, you can use this to change the character that separates the decimals from the integral part of the number. You could set that option to period for North Americans and comma for Europeans.

Other options allow you to change the "grouping-separator" between the billions, millions and thousands and to choose characters or strings to represent "infinity", "minus", "percent", "per-mille" (per thousand), "the zero digit" and "Not a number". The latter is used for error handling.

18.6.5 *Attribute sets*

xsl:attribute-set allows you to define a reusable set of attributes. If you have several different types of images that must share certain attributes then it is more efficient to define those in an attribute set than to repeat them all in each template rule. Example 18-22 demonstrates the basic idea.

Example 18-22. Reusable set of attribute values

```
<xsl:attribute-set name="big-image">
    <xsl:attribute name="width">500px</xsl:attribute>
    <xsl:attribute name="height">500px</xsl:attribute>
</xsl:attribute-set>
<xsl:attribute-set name="small-image">
    <xsl:attribute name="width">100px</xsl:attribute>
    <xsl:attribute name="height">100px</xsl:attribute>
</xsl:attribute-set>

... in a template ...
<img xsl:use-attribute-sets="big-image">
```

18.6.6 *Namespace alias*

Just as xsl:output helps you to solve the problem of how to treat a less-than sign as an ordinary data character, xsl:namespace-alias helps you to treat a namespace prefixed literal result element as just a literal result element, even if the namespace happens to be XSLT! This sounds strange but it could happen if you were writing an XSLT stylesheet that generates an XSLT stylesheet. Needless to say, this is not a common situation so we will not dwell on it further.

18.6.7 *Keys*

Keys are a performance-enhancement concept borrowed from the database world. Their main use is to provide a (possibly) faster way to reference elements by the values of their attributes or subelements. You get to decide which attribute or element values form the key by declaring it, as shown in Example 18-23.

Example 18-23. Declaring a key

```
<xsl:key name="employees-by-ssn"
         match="employee"
         use="social-security"/>
```

Keys don't let you do anything that can't be done with normal XPath addressing, which is why we're not explaining them in detail. Their major benefit is to allow the XSLT processor to build a lookup table to attempt to speed up keyed references. Whether the attempt succeeds depends on the number of keys, how often they are referenced, and the complexity of the XPath expressions they replace.

Keys can also simplify a stylesheet by letting you use simple key names in place of possibly complex XPath expressions. Not all XSLT processors support keys.

18.7 | Variables and parameters

XSLT variables and parameters are closely related in that both involve replacing a name with an associated value (much like an XML entity).

18.7.1 *Variables*

An *XSLT variable* is a value that a stylesheet creator stores away for use in some other part of the stylesheet. A top-level variable is one defined outside any template rule. The value is automatically available for use in any template. For instance a variable could hold the company name. The value that the variable holds could even be extracted from the input XML document. Example 18-24 demonstrates.

Example 18-24. Defining a variable

```
<xsl:variable name="company-name" select="/doc/creator/company"/>
```

Variables can be referred to in XPath expressions by preceding the variable name with a dollar-sign ($). Example 18-25 demonstrates.

Example 18-25. Referencing a variable

```
<xsl:value-of select="$company-name"/>
```

18.8 | Parameters

An *XSLT parameter* is just like a variable except that the value can be overridden. How it would be overridden depends on your XSLT implementation. Command-line XSLT transformation engines typically use command-line options. Graphical environments might use options in a graphical user interface. In other words, parameters are user options that change the stylesheet's behavior. They are declared and referenced just as variables are. Example 18-26 demonstrates.

Example 18-26. Defining a parameter

```
<xsl:param name="company-name" select="/doc/creator/company"/>
```

The `select` attribute of a parameter is used as a *default value*. If the user fails to supply a parameter, the default value is used when the stylesheet is processed.

It is also possible to define template rules that have parameters. In that case, the parameters are only available within that template. Template rule parameters are passed not from the user, but from other templates. For instance a template for a chapter might use a parameter to pass the chapter number to a template rule for a section. That way the section number could be derived from the chapter number (e.g. section number 5.4 within chapter 5).

18.9 | Extending XSLT

XSLT permits customized extensions (the "X" in "XSLT") to be supported by an XSLT processor.

The XSLT language has a mechanism that allows you to call into a component written in any programming language. You could refer to a *Java* class file, Python program, Perl script or an ActiveX control. You could even embed a small script from a scripting language such as *Javascript* or *Python*. The script can be defined right in your stylesheet!

18.10 | Referencing XSLT stylesheets

There is a W3C Recommendation that specifies how XML documents should refer to their stylesheets. Here is the relevant text:

Model (xml-ss) 18-1. The `xml-stylesheet` processing instruction

The `xml-stylesheet` processing instruction is allowed anywhere in the prolog of an XML document. The processing instruction can have pseudo-attributes `href` (required), `type` (required), `title` (optional), `media` (optional), `charset` (optional).

These are called *pseudo-attributes* because, although they use attribute syntax, they do not describe properties of an element. The only real syntactic difference between pseudo-attributes and attributes is that you must use pseudo-attributes in the order they are defined. You can use attributes in any order.

The most important pseudo-attributes for this processing instruction are `href`, which supplies a URI for the stylesheet, and `type`, which says whether the stylesheet is in XSLT, DSSSL, CSS, or some other stylesheet language.

Example 18-27 is a sample stylesheet processing instruction (PI).

Example 18-27. Stylesheet PI

```
<?xml-stylesheet href="http://www.xmlbooks.com/memo.xsl"
                 type="text/xsl"?>
```

You can provide multiple PIs to allow for different output media or stylesheet language support. You could, for example, have different stylesheets for print (with footnotes and page breaks), online (with clickable links), television (large text and easy scroll controls) and voice (read aloud using inflection to render emphasis). In such cases, you would want to specify a `media` pseudo-attribute and possibly a `title` that the browser might use when offering a list of stylesheet choices. Example 18-28 demonstrates this.

Example 18-28. Alternative stylesheets

```
<?xml-stylesheet rel=alternate
                 href="mystyle1.xsl"
                 title="Fancy"
                 media="print"
                 type="text/xsl"?>
<?xml-stylesheet
                 rel=alternate
                 href="mystyle2.css"
                 title="Simple"
                 media="online"
                 type="text/css"?>
<?xml-stylesheet
                 rel=alternate
                 href="mystyle2.aur"
                 title="Aural"
                 media="voice"
                 type="text/aural"?>
```

Web services introduction

Introductory Discussion

- Communication protocols
- Service discovery
- REST
- XML Signature

If you are involved with information technology – and haven't spent the last five years installing Wi-Fi access points on Mars – you've heard of Web services.

In fact, you may have heard of it in breathless terms as a "revolution". The last time there was so much revolutionary talk in the air, there was also tea in Boston harbor.

You can understand the hype if you look back at recent history. Before the Web, it was very difficult to distribute information so that anybody could access it using any computer system. The Web standards made computer-to-human communication easy and automatic. XML has begun to make computer-to-computer communication easier as well.

Web services is trying to go further in this direction. It is a term for services supported by a new set of XML-based protocols intended to make computer-to-computer communications not just easy, but standardized and automatic.[1]

19.1 | Communication protocols

Computers are like humans in that they cannot communicate with each other except by means of a shared language. Just like humans, they also cannot communicate if both parties speak at the same time. There must be some concept of back and forth, send and receive, talk and listen. The specification of how this happens is termed a *protocol*.

XML is not a protocol. XML is the shared language; it helps define what the terms of discussion are. But XML does not itself say anything about who speaks first, what they may say, what is appropriate in response, and other requirements of transmission.

Protocols are seldom used in isolation. They build on other protocols and standards. For example, the Web services protocols use XML as the data representation. They use Web communication protocols such as HTTP to move the XML around the Internet, but offer additional functions.

The SOAP messaging protocol is an example.[2] The SOAP spec defines a standardized carrier document – sort of an envelope – in which another document – the *payload* – is transported.

SOAP is the protocol beloved of large software companies. For many, the use of SOAP is implied by the term "Web services", but others do without it. We'll look at two well-known Web services, one SOAPless and one SOAPy.

19.2 | Amazon.com

Amazon's Web service has an interesting business model. The service is free to use; it earns its money by increasing Amazon's sales. It is essentially a

---

1. These services are sometimes referred to by Microsoft as *XML Web Services*, no doubt to distinguish them from the general class of Web-based services – such as online psychic readings! However, the rest of the IT industry, with its usual aversion to the precise use of English, seems happy with *Web services* alone. So despite the ambiguity, we too use the shorter term.
2. SOAP is considered a Web services protocol even though it has other uses and actually pre-dates the Web services hype by several years.

search service for Amazon's product line, but because the line in many areas is comprehensive, the service has research value as well: "How many books did Paul Prescod write? Did he ever record a DVD?"

19.2.1 *Amazon Associates*

Amazon has long had a model whereby "associates" can earn money by directing book buyers to the Amazon site. Amazon's Web service allows these vendors to integrate more tightly with Amazon's underlying databases.

Some even set up their own virtual store-fronts, selling books as if they were full-service retailers but allowing Amazon to do the actual fulfillment and billing. Entrepreneurial developers have created software that allows anyone to build a virtual storefront on top of the Amazon Web service in hours.

One innovative associate allows people to choose things from Amazon and then purchase them using currencies that Amazon does not support. The associate does the appropriate currency trading for you behind the scenes.

Everyone benefits from the Web service. The associates make more money by selling more products. The Web service gives them very accurate and timely information. When Amazon changes a price, they know quickly. Amazon makes a profit on most books it sells, so it benefits from giving the associates the tools they need to build their storefronts and sell books.

19.2.2 *Why not HTML?*

From the earliest days of the Amazon associates program, Amazon supplied HTML graphics and search boxes for associates to include on their Web pages. The links created by that HTML markup caused HTML pages to be displayed. That was o.k. for end users who wanted to buy books, but it was a nuisance for programmers who needed to integrate Amazon search results into complex Web pages or other applications.

In a nutshell: Amazon delivered renditions when the programmers needed abstractions!

Amazon's browser style is pretty elaborate, as you can see from the search results page in Figure 19-1. It shows that the most popular book about the keyword "genome" is called "Genome" and is by "Matt Ridley". It costs $11.20 at Amazon.

Figure 19-1   Amazon.com search results in a Web browser

It follows from the elaborate formatting that the corresponding HTML source is pretty elaborate as well, as you can see in Example 19-1. A programmer looking for the facts about the top search result has to ignore things in the HTML pages that are helpful to people but irrelevant to computers, such as fonts, tabular layouts, line breaks, and so forth.

A program that analyzes a rendition to find abstract data is said to be *screen scraping*. Such programs are difficult to write because there is no guaranteed pattern of formatting markup. Worse yet, the program might break any time that Amazon decides to change the layout of the search results.

Example 19-1. Partial HTML source of Figure 19-1

```
<table border=0 cellpadding=3 width=100%>
<tr valign=top> <td> <font size=-1><b>1.</b></font></td>
<td align=center width=60>
<font face=verdana,arial,helvetica size=-1>
<a href=/exec/.../sr=2-1/ref=sr_2_1/103-5013077-5501429>
<img src="http://...PIt.arrow,TopLeft,-1,-17_SCTHUMBZZZ_.jpg"
    width=42 height=66 align=left border=0></a>
</font>
</td>
<td width=100% valign=top>
<font face=verdana,arial,helvetica size=-1>
<a href=/exec/.../sr=2-1/ref=sr_2_1/103-5013077-5501429>
<b>Genome</b></a>
-- by Matt Ridley (Author); Paperback
<br>
<span class=small>
<a href=/exec/.../ref=sr_2_1/103-5013077-5501429>
Buy new</a></span>: <b class=price>$11.20</b>
--
<a
href=http://.../all/ref=sr_pb_a/103-5013077-5501429>
Used & new from</a>: <b class=price>$3.95</b>
 
</font>
</b>
```

19.2.3 *The Amazon Web service*

The Amazon Web service eliminates the need for screen scraping by returning abstract XML documents. That makes it easy for programs to find the desired information elements.

Using the Web service, it is possible to construct queries similar to those that Amazon's user interface allows: search by author, search by ISBN, search by keyword, and so forth.

Consider Example 19-2, which shows the Web service query for books about "genome". You can actually type this query in a browser's address pane and see a rendition of the XML document that the service would return to a program.[3]

---

3. Well, you once could have. As we went to press, Amazon changed its Web service interface and now requires a "developer's token" in its queries.

Example 19-2. Web service query (split into two lines to fit page width of this book)

```
http://rcm.amazon.com/e/cm?t=encyclozine&l=st1
&search=genome&mode=books&pk102&o=1&f=xml
```

If you ask the browser to "View Source", you will see the XML source of the search result, as shown in Example 19-3.[4]

Example 19-3. Partial XML source of Example 19-2 search result

```
<?xml version="1.0" encoding="ISO-8859-1"?>
<catalog>
<keyword>genome</keyword>
<product_group>Books</product_group>
  <product>
    <ranking>1</ranking>
    <title>Genome</title>
    <asin>0060932902</asin>
    <author>Ridley, Matt</author>
    <image>
      http://images.amazon.com/images/P/0060932902.01.MZZZZZZZ.jpg
    </image>
    <small_image>
      http://images.amazon.com/images/P/0060932902.01.TZZZZZZZ.jpg
    </small_image>
    <our_price>$11.20</our_price>
    <list_price>$14.00</list_price>
    <release_date>20001003</release_date>
    <binding>Paperback</binding>
    <availability> </availability>
    <tagged_url>http://www.amazon.com:80/exec/obidos/redirect?
      tag=encyclozine&amp;creative=9441&amp;camp=1793
      &amp;link_code=xml&amp;path=ASIN/0060932902</tagged_url>
  </product>
  -- more products here --
</catalog>
```

As you can see, Example 19-3 yields much of the same information as Example 19-1. The top-ranked book about the keyword "genome" is called "Genome" and is by "Matt Ridley". It costs $11.20 at Amazon, which is a few dollars cheaper than its $14.00 list price. But unlike the HTML, this XML is about as straightforward as you could hope for.

---

4. Note that in reality the content of `tagged_url` has no white space. It was broken into three lines in order to fit this book's page width.

This Web service is SOAPless; Amazon offers a SOAPy version as well, which returns a substantially more complex document. We'll look at a SOAP-based service next, but instead of Amazon we'll use the equally famous Google.

19.3 | Google

The Google Web service allows programmers to treat Google as if it were a massive database of information about the Web. Or to be more precise, they now have access to the real database that underlies the Google search engine. Now, for example, a programmer can write a program that compares the change in popularity of different slang terms from day to day.

Google provides three different operations:

search

performs a traditional Google search

spelling

checks the spelling of a word and returns a suggestion if it is misspelled: Did you mean "handbook"?

cache

returns the version of a page that Google stored the last time its spider crawled the Web

Example 19-4 illustrates the result of a search query for "XML Handbook". The return element is the payload of a SOAP message. It contains the Google search result.

Example 19-4 is clearly not the poster child for XML's simplicity and elegance. But computers have an easier time reading it than do humans.

For example, if you examine the document carefully you can see an estimatedTotalResultsCount element containing the number of hits for this query. A program or XPath expression can find it much more easily than you can. Still, the complexity required by SOAP has somewhat tarnished a mostly positive reaction to Google's service.

Example 19-4. Google query result

```
<?xml version='1.0' encoding='UTF-8'?>
<SOAP-ENV:Envelope
  xmlns:SOAP-ENV="http://schemas.xmlsoap.org/soap/envelope/"
  xmlns:xsi="http://www.w3.org/1999/XMLSchema-instance"
  xmlns:xsd="http://www.w3.org/1999/XMLSchema">
<SOAP-ENV:Body>
<ns1:doGoogleSearchResponse
  xmlns:ns1="urn:GoogleSearch"
  SOAP-ENV:encodingStyle=
    "http://schemas.xmlsoap.org/soap/encoding/">
  <return xsi:type="ns1:GoogleSearchResult">
    <documentFiltering
      xsi:type="xsd:boolean">false</documentFiltering>
    <estimatedTotalResultsCount
      xsi:type="xsd:int">120000</estimatedTotalResultsCount>
    <directoryCategories
      xmlns:ns2="http://schemas.xmlsoap.org/soap/encoding/"
      xsi:type="ns2:Array"
      ns2:arrayType="ns1:DirectoryCategory[0]">
    </directoryCategories>
    <searchTime xsi:type="xsd:double">0.071573</searchTime>
    <resultElements
      xmlns:ns3="http://schemas.xmlsoap.org/soap/encoding/"
      xsi:type="ns3:Array"
      ns3:arrayType="ns1:ResultElement[0]">
    </resultElements>
    <endIndex xsi:type="xsd:int">0</endIndex>
    <searchTips xsi:type="xsd:string"></searchTips>
    <searchComments xsi:type="xsd:string"></searchComments>
    <startIndex xsi:type="xsd:int">0</startIndex>
    <estimateIsExact
      xsi:type="xsd:boolean">false</estimateIsExact>
    <searchQuery
      xsi:type="xsd:string">xml handbook</searchQuery>
  </return>
</ns1:doGoogleSearchResponse>
</SOAP-ENV:Body>
</SOAP-ENV:Envelope>
```

And yet Google's result format is considered simple for a SOAP service. So why get involved with SOAP's complexity in the first place? We'll explore that question next.

19.4 | Service discovery

One of the more advanced ideas underpinning Web services is that of *service discovery*. At present, humans generally decide with whom a program should share information. The purchasing agent for Miracle Cleanser tells his computer that the order for the "free if you act now" scrub brushes should be sent to the High-on-the-Hog Bristle Company.

Some believe that with Web services, that won't be necessary. The purchasing program can search for a supplier using an elaborate registry system called *Universal Description, Discovery, and Integration (UDDI)*.[5] A UDDI registry contains three classes of information:

white pages
They contain general contact information about organizations.

yellow pages
These list organizations by business category or location.

green pages
These include the technical aspects of conducting business, including Web service descriptions and schemas.

The green page Web Service descriptions are expressed in XML conforming to the *Web Services Description Language (WSDL)*.

A WSDL service description in turn affects the structure of the SOAP messages that are used in conjunction with the service. It indicates the operations that the service performs, the message structure for requesting each operation, and the message structures that the operation returns.

This dynamic interaction between SOAP and WSDL is what makes this model of service discovery possible. (We discuss UDDI and WSDL in detail in Chapter 23, "Web services technologies", on page 484.)

---

5. Given the problems that even humans have in evaluating service offerings and providers – plus the many intangibles often involved in a decision – some skepticism may be warranted. Full realization of service discovery would seem to require both artificial intelligence from the computer and genuine faith from the humans!

19.5 | Web services for the REST of us!

SOAP is not without its critics, who argue that it doesn't do enough to warrant its complexity and attendant costs. They observe that in most SOAP services the HTTP Web protocol is doing the heavy work of moving data from place to place, and XML is describing the data that is being moved.

Worse yet, they point out that SOAP doesn't use HTTP and XML in the way they were designed to be used. Instead of treating XML documents as persistent resources with Web addresses (URIs), SOAP treats them as transient messages sent to objects that are completely outside the Web or XML framework.

A second generation of Web services is now being developed that is integrated with the architecture of the Web: Web URIs address XML documents that can be retrieved via the Web's HTTP. This architecture has been named *REST*. (You don't want to know why.)[6] It is also referred to as *XML over HTTP*.

Developers who use REST techniques say it is a more productive way to build Web Services because it builds on techniques that are known to work.

Users seem to agree. The Amazon.com Web service is available in both the REST form that we discussed earlier and in a SOAP version. At the time of writing, Amazon reports that the REST service gets 85% of the use!

19.6 | Security

It takes a good deal of trust to rely on a Web service from outside your company, possibly from a supplier who is known only to your computer! In fact, the software industry may have to scale back its (revenue) hopes and ambitions for Web services for precisely that reason.

But it's not going to quit without trying, so there has been a flurry of development in security standards and tools. Two security issues that are vital for Web services messages concern hiding them from prying eyes and verifying whom they're from: encryption and identification.

---

6. Web pages are *representations* of resources. An application changes *state* as it traverses links to *transfer* from one page to another, hence *Representational State Transfer (REST)*. We warned you that you didn't want to know why!

19.6.1 *Encryption*

You may have created a ZIP archive with a tool that gives you the option of protecting the archive with a password. If you send such a password-protected archive to a friend, he'll be prompted for the password in order to open the archive. Without the password, the archive is indecipherable.

In cryptographic terms, that password is a *key* with which the sending system encrypts the ZIP archive. Since the sender and recipient both use the same key, the process is called *symmetric cryptography* – the fastest kind.

The problem with symmetric cryptography is communicating the key. How can you do that securely? You could encrypt it, but then you would need to transmit the key to the original key, and so on.

And what if the key is stolen?

A popular solution to this, er, key problem is called *public key cryptography*, which is *asymmetric cryptography*. Instead of a single *symmetric key*, shared by both parties, there is a mathematically-related pair of keys. You keep your own *private key* and you distribute a related *public key* to your friends so they can send you encrypted email. They encrypt their messages to you by using your public key, but you decrypt them using your private key.[7]

A system for deploying public key cryptography is called a *public key infrastructure (PKI)*. It requires a means of managing public keys. The *certificates* that are the cause of so many mysterious messages from your Web browser are actually descriptions of public keys, digitally signed by a *Certification Authority (CA)*.

19.6.2 *Identification*

One of the most basic security questions is "Who goes there?" – the question of user *identification*.

---

7. At least that's the way it seems, but because symmetric cryptography is so much faster, the sender's software actually encrypts the message with a randomly-generated symmetric key. It then encrypts the symmetric key with your public key so your software can decrypt it with your private key, and then use the decrypted symmetric key to decrypt the message. Whew!

For documents, the classic means of identification is the signature. The signed name provides identification and the uniqueness of handwriting provides a (less-than-perfect!) means of authentication.

Just as in the written world, the digital signature is intended to identify and authenticate the author of a machine-readable document. The authentication is provided by public key encryption – but operating in reverse! A digital signature is encrypted with the signer's private key and decrypted with the public key.

XML Signature is a W3C specification for representing digital signatures in XML. With XML Signature, it is possible to attach signatures to any object, whether it be XML or binary, standardized or proprietary.

When you sign a printed contract, your signature goes on the last or only piece of paper of the contract (and perhaps you also initial every page). That way, the signature cannot be shifted to a different contract from the one you signed originally. This procedure maintains the *integrity* of the signed contract.

Similarly, an XML signature is generated in a way that binds it to a single object. The receiver can check that the object has not changed by looking at a summary (*hash*) of it embedded in the signature. The digital signature acts as a *seal*, but without the messy hot wax!

The receiver can also, of course, use the sender's public key to check that the signature was generated by his private key. If both tests are successful, then the recipient has got exactly the message that was signed and knows exactly who sent it.

Just as with printed signatures, digital signatures serve as a basis for *non-repudiation*. In other words, they prove that you endorsed the signed content. If you claim that you did not agree to a (digital) contract that has your (digital) signature, you had better have proof that your (private) key was stolen!

XML Jargon Demystifier™

- Structured vs. unstructured

- Tag vs. element

- Document type, DTD, and markup declarations

- Schema and schema definitions

- Documents and data

Chapter

20

ne of the problems in learning a new technology like XML is getting used to the jargon. A good book will hold you by the hand, introduce terms gradually, and use them precisely and consistently.

Out in the real word, though, people use imprecise terminology that often makes it hard to understand things, let alone compare products. And, unlike authors,[1] they sometimes just plain get things wrong.

For example, you may see statements like "XML documents are either well-formed or valid." As you've learned from this book, that simply isn't true. *All* XML documents are well-formed; some of them are also valid.

In this book, we've taken pains to use consistent and accurate terminology. However, for product literature and other documents you read – even Office help! – the mileage may vary. So we've prepared a handy guide to the important XML jargon, both right and wrong.

---

1. We should be so lucky!

20.1 | Structured vs. unstructured

Structured is arguably the most commonly used word to characterize the essence of markup languages. It is also the most ambiguous and most often misused word.

There are four common meanings:

structured = abstract

XML documents are frequently referred to as structured while other text, such as renditions in notations like RTF, is called *unstructured*. Separating "structure from style" is considered the hallmark of a markup language. But in fact, renditions can have a rich structure, composed of elements like pages, columns, and blocks. The real distinction being made is between "abstract" and "rendered".

structured = managed

This is one of the meanings that folks with a database background usually have in mind. Structured information is managed as a common resource and is accessible to the entire enterprise. Unfortunately, there are also departmental and individual databases and their content isn't "structured" in quite the same sense.

structured = predictable

This is another alternative for relational database people. Structured data is captured from business transactions, comes in easily identified granules, and has metadata that identifies its semantics. In contrast, *freeform data* is normally buried in reports, with no metadata, and therefore must be "parsed" (by reading it!) to determine what it is and what it means. If an essentially freeform document has islands of structured data within it, the document might be termed *semi-structured*. See 20.8, "Documents and data", on page 436 for more on this.

structured = possessing structure

This is the dictionary meaning, and the one used in this book. There is usually the (sometimes unwarranted) implication that the structure is fine-grained (rich, detailed), making components accessible at efficient levels of granularity. A structure can be very simple – a single really big component – but nothing is unstructured. All structure is well-defined and "predictable" (in the sense of consistent), it just may not be very granular.

These distinctions aren't academic. It is very important to know which "structured" a vendor means.

What if your publishing system has bottlenecks because you are maintaining four rendered versions of your documents in different representations? It isn't much of a solution to "structure" them in a database so that modifying one version warns you to modify the others.

You'll want to have a single "structured" – that is, abstract – version from which the others can be rendered. And if you find that your document has scores of pages unrelieved by sub-headings, you may want to "structure" it more finely so that both human readers and software can deal with it in smaller chunks.

Keep these different meanings in mind when you read about "structured" and "unstructured". In this book, we try to confine our use of the word to its dictionary meaning, occasionally (when it is clear from the context) with the implication of "fine-grained".

20.2 | Tag vs. element

Tags aren't the same thing as elements. Tags describe elements and delimit them.

In Figure 20-1 the pet carrier, metaphorically speaking, is an element. The contents of the carrier is the *content* of an element. It is bounded by two tags.

The start-tag, at the left, describes the element. It contains three names:

- The *element-type name* (dog), which says what type of element it is.
- A *unique identifier*, or id (Spike), which says which particular element it is.
- The name of an attribute that describes some other property of the element: weight-"8 lbs".

Figure 20-1   Tags aren't elements!

The end-tag, at the right, marks the end of the element. It repeats the element-type name.

When people talk about a *tag name*:

1. They are referring to the element-type name (in this case, dog).
2. They are making an error, because tags aren't named.

And when they talk about an *element name*:

1. They are again referring to the element-type name.
2. They are again making an error, because an element is named by its unique identifier (in this case, Spike).

20.3 | Content

We know that formally the *content* of an element is what occurs between the start-tag and the end-tag. Therefore, the content of a document is what occurs between the first start-tag and the last end-tag of the document.

So when people say that "XML separates content from presentation", they really mean that XML lets you separate abstract data (in the document) from rendition information (in a stylesheet).

When they say "an XML document has content and structure", they mean it has data and structure.

People also refer to "content" or "XML content" as a commodity: "Our website has dynamic, involving, interactive, rich, multimedia XML content". We do that as well in this book when the context is clear (but without the adjectives!).

Some people – not us – also use the term "content" when making a principled distinction between data intended for people ("content") and data intended for machines ("data").

20.4 | Document type, DTD, and markup declarations

A *document type* is a class of similar documents, like telephone books, technical manuals, or (when they are marked up as XML) inventory records.

A *document type definition* (*DTD*) is the set of rules for using XML to represent documents of a particular type. These rules might exist only in your mind as you create a document, or they may be written out.

Markup declarations, such as those in Example 20-1, are XML's way of writing out DTDs.

Example 20-1. Markup declarations in the file greeting.dtd.

```
<!ELEMENT greeting (salutation, addressee) >
<!ELEMENT salutation (#PCDATA) >
<!ELEMENT addressee  (#PCDATA) >
```

It is easy to mix up these three constructs: a document type, XML's markup rules for documents of that type (the DTD), and the expression of those rules (the markup declarations). It is necessary to keep the constructs separate if you are dealing with two or more of them at the same time, as when discussing alternative ways to express a DTD. But most of the time, even in this book, "DTD" will suffice for referring to any of the three.

20.5 | Schema and schema definition

The programming and database worlds have introduced some new terminology to XML.

We now speak of a document type as a kind of *schema*, a conception of the common characteristics of some class of things. Similarly, a DTD is a *schema definition*, the rules for using XML to represent documents conforming to the schema.

Schema definitions are invariably written out in a notation called a *schema definition language*, or simply a *schema language*. And as with DTDs, the word "schema" can serve for all these purposes when there is no ambiguity.

20.6 | Document, XML document, and instance

The term *document* has two distinct meanings in XML.

Consider a really short XML document that might be rendered as:

Hello World

The *conceptual document* that you see in your mind's eye when you read the rendition is intuitively what you think of as the document. Communicating that conception is the reason for using XML in the first place.

In a formal, syntactic sense, though, the complete text (markup + data, remember) of Example 20-2, is the *XML document*. Perhaps surprisingly, that includes the markup declarations for its DTD (shown in Example

20-1). The XML document, in other words, is a character string that *represents* the conceptual document.[2]

In this example, much of that string consists of the markup declarations, which express the `greeting` DTD. Only the last four lines describe the conceptual document, which is an instance of a `greeting`. Those lines are called the *document instance*.

Example 20-2. A greeting document.

```
<?xml version="1.0"?>
<!DOCTYPE greeting SYSTEM "file://greeting.dtd">
<greeting>
<salutation>Hello</salutation>
<addressee>World</addressee>
</greeting>
```

That term gets flipped around when schema languages are involved. Unlike DTD declarations, schema languages are XML-based, so a schema definition must be stored as an XML document in its own right (a *schema document*). That means an instance of a schema definition is a separate document, so it is known as an *instance document*.

20.7 | What's the meta?

Nothing. What did you think was the meta?[3]

There are two "meta" words that come up regularly when computer types talk about XML: metadata and metalanguage.

---

2. After a program parses the string it usually keeps an *object model* in memory so that it can navigate and access data directly in terms of the conceptual document structure. During processing it usually updates the object model, then *serializes* it as the result XML document.

3. Sorry about that!

20.7.1 *Metadata*

Metadata is data about data. The date, publisher's name, and author's name of a book are metadata about the book, while the data of the book is its content. The DTD and markup tags of an XML document are also metadata. If you choose to represent the author's name as an element, then it is both data and metadata.

If you get the idea that the line between data and metadata is a fluid one, you are right. And as long as your document representation and system let you access and process metadata as though it were data, it doesn't much matter where you draw that line.

Be careful when talking to database experts, though. In their discipline "metadata" typically refers only to the schema.

20.7.2 *Metalanguage*

You may hear some DTDs or schemas referred to as languages, rather than document types. HTML is a prominent example. There's nothing special about them, it is just another way of looking at the way a markup language works.

Remember that an XML document is a character string that represents some conceptual document. The rules for creating a valid string are like the rules of a language: There is a *vocabulary* of element type and attribute names, and a *grammar* that determines where the names can be used.

These language rules come from the DTD or schema, which in turn follows the rules of XML. A language, such as XML, which you can use to define other languages (such as DTDs), is called a *metalanguage*. XML document types are sometimes called *XML-based languages*.

20.8 | Documents and data

For many decades, data processing got the big budgets while document processing got a room in the basement with a copying machine. While the data processors relished their importance to the organization, the document processors basked in their importance to humanity. They were preservers of human knowledge, not just high-speed bean counters.

No wonder the two never got along!

Markup languages are changing all that. With XML, documents and databases both store data and can share it, so document processing and data processing can be performed at the same time, by the same people.

20.8.1   *It's all data!*

In an XML document, the text that isn't markup is data. You can edit it directly with an XML editor or plain text editor. With a stylesheet and a rendering system you can cause it to be displayed in various ways.

In a database, you can't touch the data directly. You can enter and revise it only through forms controlled by the database program. However, rendition is similar to XML documents, except that the stylesheet is usually called something like "report template".

The important thing is that, in both cases, the data can be kept in the abstract, untainted by the style information for rendering it. This is very different from word processing documents, of course, which normally keep their data in rendered form. Even WordML is a rendition, despite its use of XML.

20.8.2   *Data-centric vs. document-centric*

Documents, data, and processes are sometimes characterized as "data-centric" in contrast to "document-centric". Since all XML documents (except empty ones) contain data, these terms are actually a misleading shorthand. Worse, they are applied in two very different contexts:

- how much the XML resembles relational data; and,
- whether you have to deal with the whole document at once.

20.8.2.1   How relational is it?

The *data-centric* misnomer is common among database hackers trying to describe structures that map easily onto relational tables and primitive datatypes. Structures that don't are called *document-centric*.

The intended meaning of data-centric is that the document structure – really element structure, since a document is essentially just the largest element – is *fully predictable*.

An element has a *fully predictable structure* if it and its subelements are constrained to contain either:

- type-sequenced elements (e.g., a sequence of elements of the types: `quantity`, `itemNum`, `description`, `price`),
- data characters only (i.e., #PCDATA), or
- nothing at all.

Fully predictable elements can easily be visualized as forms. A business transaction document such as a purchase order is more likely to be fully predictable than a memo.

In addition to "data-centric", the misnomer *highly structured* is sometimes used. However, *highly predictable* would be more precise, particularly as many documents that aren't fully predictable are still much more predictable than they are freeform.

20.8.2.2   How granular is it?

Another (mis)use of *data-centric* is to characterize the storage and/or access of documents at the level of individual elements, rather than the entire document at once (*document-centric*). Once again, the usage is misleading because what it describes has nothing to do with data per se, and because it implies a contradiction between data and documents that does not exist.

20.8.3 *Document processing vs. data processing*

While "data-centric" and "document-centric" aren't rigorous terms for characterizing information, they are quite meaningful when applied to processing. XML, however, because it can preserve abstract data (like a database) but still be interchanged and processed as a character string (like a document), is starting to break down the historic separation of the two paradigms. Applications can now intermix data processing and document processing techniques to get the job done.

20.8.4 *Comparing documents to data*

Since documents contain data, what are people doing when they compare or contrast documents and data?

They are being human. Which is to say, they are using a simplified expression for the complex and subtle relationship shown in Table 20-1. They are comparing the typical kind of data that is found in XML and word processing (WP) documents with business process (BP) transactional data (*operational data*), which usually resides in databases.

Table 20-1   Typical traits of data

	XML data	**BP data**	**WP data**
Presentability	Abstraction	Abstraction	Rendition
Source	Written	Captured	Written
Structure	Hierarchy+ links	Tables	Paragraphs
Purpose	Processing	Processing	Presentation
Location	Document	Database	Document

Note that the characteristics in the table are typical, not fixed. For example, XML data can be a rendition (HTML and WordML are examples). In addition, XML data could:

- Be captured from a data entry form or a program (rather than written);
- Consist of simple fields like those in a relational table (rather than a deeply nested hierarchy with links among the nodes); and

■   Be intended for presentation as well as processing.

Caution   The true relationship between documents and data isn't as widely understood as it ought to be, even among experts. That is in part because the two domains existed independently for so long. This fact can complicate communication.

20.9 | And in conclusion

The matrix in Figure 20-2 ties together a number of the concepts we've been discussing.

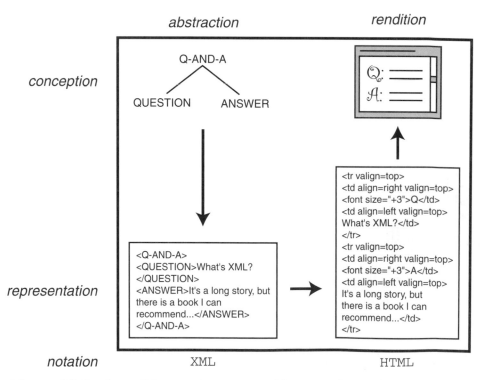

Figure 20-2   A rendition can be generated from an abstraction

The top row contains two conceptual documents, as they might appear in your mind's eye. Actually, they are two states of the same document. The left column shows the document in its abstract state, while the right column shows it rendered.

The bottom row shows the computer representations of the abstraction and the rendition. The abstraction uses XML notation while the rendition uses HTML. The horizontal arrow indicates that the rendition was generated from the abstraction.

The diagram illustrates some important points:

- Abstraction and rendition are two *presentability* states that a document can be in. Renditions are ready to be presented; abstractions aren't.
- Renditions can be generated from abstractions automatically.
- Markup languages can represent both abstractions and renditions; "structuring in XML" is no guarantee that you'll get an abstraction.
- The *computer representation* of a document incorporates two ideas: presentability and notation. In other words, the representation of a document is either an abstraction or a rendition, and is either in an XML-based language or some other notation.

Datatypes

- Built-in datatypes
- Primitive datatypes
- Derived datatypes
- User-derived datatypes

P erhaps the most widely used product of the W3C *XML Schema* project is the datatype work. It was made a separate Part 2 of the *XML Schema* spec, with the intention "that it be usable outside of the context of *XML Schema* for a wide range of other XML-related activities".

In this chapter, we describe the basic concepts of XML datatypes, with an emphasis on those that are built into the specification.

21.1 | Built-in datatypes

The *XML Schema Datatypes* spec defines two categories of datatype: primitive and derived. All primitive datatypes are defined in the spec and are therefore among the *built-in datatypes*. You may not create your own primitive datatype.

A derived datatype is defined in terms of one or more existing datatypes. It might be a specialized or extended version of another datatype. You may make your own derived datatypes. The spec also includes several among its built-in datatypes, which are therefore supported by every implementation.

Figure 21-1 illustrates the built-in datatypes, showing the derivations.

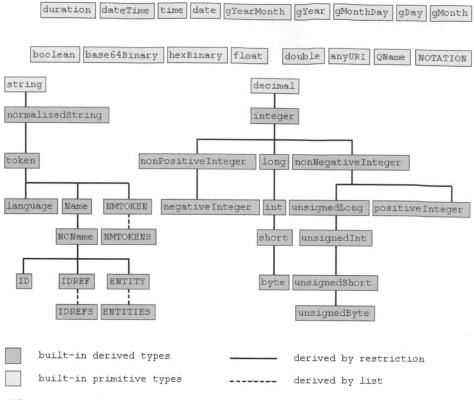

Figure 21-1   Built-in datatypes

21.1.1 *Primitive datatypes*

The *primitive datatypes* are the building blocks of all others. Most are also useful just by themselves.

21.1.1.1 Common programming datatypes

The first five we will cover include common datatypes in most programming languages and database management systems.

string

> An arbitrarily long sequence of characters. You might use this for a `title` element's datatype.

boolean

> True and false values. The data may be any one of the following strings: `false` or `0` for false values or `true` or `1` for true values. You might use this for a datatype that represented whether a checkbox in a graphical user interface should be turned on by default (true) or turned off by default (false).

decimal

> Arbitrary precision decimal numbers. These can represent anything numerical: height, weight, financial amounts, etc. Decimal numbers may have a fractional part that follows a period as in `5.3`. Decimal numbers may be preceded by a plus (+) or minus (–) sign to represent whether they are negative or positive.

float

> Single precision 32-bit floating point numbers. This is a form of number that is very efficient for numerical computation on 32-bit computers. Floats may have a fractional part and may also be preceded by a plus or minus sign. Compared to decimals, floats are less precise. They are an approximation. Sometimes the number you put into the computer will not be exactly the number you get out later![1]

double

> Double precision 64-bit floating point numbers. These numbers are more precise than single-precision floats but are still approximations.[2]

---

1. If you do use them, they may have exponents (preceded by "e" or "E", as in "2.5E5") and may take the values "NaN", "INF" and "-INF".
2. And the same footnote applies!

21.1.1.2   XML datatypes

anyURI

This extremely important primitive datatype is used for URIs (typically URLs). These may include so-called *fragment identifiers* after a pound sign.

QName

This primitive datatype is based on the XML namespaces specification. It stands for a namespace-qualified name. In other words, a QName is a name that may have a colon in it. If it does, the text before the colon should be a namespace prefix for a namespace that has been declared. If it does not, the names should be interpreted as belonging to the default namespace. See Chapter 16, "Namespaces", on page 376 for more information on namespaces.

NOTATION

This datatype corresponds to the XML NOTATION attribute type.

21.1.1.3   Binary datatypes

There are two datatypes for representing binary data. The first is called hexBinary because it uses the *hex* notation, popular among practitioners of the occult and programmers of the UNIX operating system. There are sixteen hex digits.[3] The digits 0 through 9 represent the same thing they do in ordinary decimal numbers. The letter a represents 10, b represents 11 and so forth through f representing 15. Hex is popular not only because of its mystical powers but also because a few simple calculations can turn two hex digits into a value between 0 and 255, which is exactly the amount that can be held in a single byte.

The other datatype is called base64Binary because it represents base64-encoded data. Base64 is not as simple to translate into bytes without a computer but uses less space than hex. Hex doubles the size of the data. Base64 increases it by only a third, approximately.

---

3. In fact, hex is short for hexadecimal, which is the base-16 numbering system.

21.1.1.4   Durations

The remaining primitive datatypes are all related to time: durations in this section and absolute dates and times in the next.

The `duration` datatype is based on the ISO 8601 date format standard. It represents a length of time, such as an hour or 3.56 seconds. Durations can be represented with a precision of seconds or fractions of a second. They can also span thousands of years.

A duration always starts with P; for example, P2Y. The 2Y that follows the P means two years (the gestation period for some elephants!).

Instead of measuring in years, you could measure in months: P3M would be three months (the amount of time it takes to get a new phone line installed in some cities).

You can also measure in years and months: P1Y3M means one year and three months (the shelf-life of a boy band). You can also count in days (with or without years or months): P3D (length of the Battle of Gettysburg).

But wait...that's not all. Durations can get as fine grained as a fraction of a second. If you want to deal in time units shorter than a day you use the designator T after you've listed all of the day/month/year parts (or directly after the P if you are interested only in hour/minute/second units).

For instance P1YT1M represents one year and one minute (which is the amount of time that a VCR with a P1Y warranty is likely to survive). As you can see, M represents both month and minute, which is why you must include the T designator that separates the date part from the time part. If you have an hour, a minute or a second part you must have the T.

In addition to minutes you may use H for hour and S for second. S is the only part of the duration that may have a fractional part. PT3M43.13S represents three minutes and 43.13 seconds (the world record for running a mile).

The different parts of the date and time must always come in the same order: P, years, months, days, T, hours, minutes, seconds. Remember that the P is always required and the T is required if there are hours/minutes/seconds. Everything else is optional.

21.1.1.5   Dates and times

The `date` datatype represents a specific calendar date in the form YYYY-MM-DD. For instance the date of the Beatles' debut on Ed Sullivan would be `1964-02-09` – February 9th, 1964.

Negative dates are also allowed, to represent BCE (BC) dates. For instance `-0133-06-01` represents the approximate date of a Roman slave revolt lead by a man called Aristonicus – June 1, 133 BCE.

The `time` datatype represents a time that recurs every day. Times have the form hh:mm:ss. The seconds may have a fractional part. So `14:12:34.843` represents 2:12 and 34.843 seconds in the afternoon. It is *not* legal to leave the seconds out, even if they are not relevant: `14:12:00`.

To indicate that the time is expressed in *coordinated universal time (UTC)*, also known as Greenwich mean time (GMT), add a z to the end of the time: `14:20:00Z`.

It is also possible (and a good idea!) to specify a time zone for a time, as an offset from GMT. Do this by appending a - or + sign and a number of hours and minutes in the form hh:mm, such as `08:15:00-08:00` (8:15 Pacific time) or `11:20:00+03:30` (11:20 Tehran time). The time zone is optional but if you leave it out then it will be impossible to compare times across time zones.

As you might guess, it is possible to combine a date and time into a `dateTime`. A `dateTime` has a T between the date and time parts: `1929-10-29T11:00:00-05:00`.

21.1.1.6   Recurring dates and times

The `gDay`, `gMonth` and `gMonthDay` datatypes represent a day that recurs every month (e.g. the first or fifteenth day of each month), a month that recurs every year (let's say July – or any other month!) and a particular date that recurs every year (such as Valentine's day). The g in their names indicates that they are based on the Gregorian calendar.

The `gDay` datatype is in the form ---DD. There are three leading dashes, so the 8th of every month would be `---08`.

The `gMonth` datatype, --MM, is similar. However, there are only two leading dashes, so every June would be `--06`.

The gMonthDay datatype is in the form --MM-DD. For instance, Caesar's "Ides of March" (March 15th) would be --03-15 and a gMonth of --02 represents the month of February of every year.

These datatypes represent durations from the very first instant of the date to the very last. To improve precision, any of them may be followed by a time zone indicator.

The gYear and gYearMonth represent particular years or months in history or in the future. The year is a four-digit number and a gYearMonth is a four-digit number followed by a two-digit number: 2002-06. Either may be preceded by a negative sign (-) to represent BCE dates. They may also be followed by a time zone indicator.

21.1.2 *Derived datatypes*

The *derived datatypes* are based on the primitive ones. The *XML Schema Datatypes* spec defines some derived datatypes and provides facilities for users to define their own.

The ones defined in the spec are listed below. They fall into several categories.

21.1.2.1 Restricted numeric datatypes

These are numeric datatypes more specific (*restricted*) than the primitive datatypes.

21.1.2.1.1 *Integers*

integer
  Decimal number (no matter how large or small) with no fractional part.

positiveInteger
  Integer greater than zero.

negativeInteger
  Integer less than zero.

nonPositiveInteger
> Integer less than or equal to zero.

nonNegativeInteger
> Integer greater than or equal to zero.

21.1.2.1.2 *Computer word lengths*

This group allows data to be restricted to values that specific computers can handle efficiently. Most modern computers handle everything from 8-bits to 32-bits well. A 64-bit computer handles `long` and `unsignedLong` most efficiently and other values less so.

byte
> 8-bit signed number (between -128 and 127)

unsignedByte
> 8-bit non-negative number (between 0 and 255)

short
> 16-bit number (between -32768 and 32767)

unsignedShort
> 16-bit non-negative number (between 0 and 65535)

int
> 32-bit number (between -2147483648 and 2147483647)

unsignedInt
> 32-bit non-negative number (between 0 and 4294967295)

long
> 64-bit number (between -9223372036854775808 and 9223372036854775807)

unsignedLong
> 64-bit non-negative number (between 0 and 18446744073709551615) (whew!)

21.1.2.2   Derived XML datatypes

Several derived datatypes are based on XML attribute types and other constructs. We list only the basic ones.

21.1.2.2.1   *XML attribute types*

Some derived datatypes emulate XML attribute types. They are easy to recognize because they are the only built-in datatypes with upper-case names.

ID
> An identifier unique to a single element in a document.

IDREF
> A reference to a unique ID in the document.

21.1.2.2.2   *Other XML constructs*

There are other datatypes for XML constructs.

normalizedString
> This datatype is for strings in which whitespace characters such as carriage return and tab characters should be replaced by spaces. If you use this datatype or derive from it, the schema processor will handle this normalization for you.

21.2 | Defining user-derived datatypes

The XML Schema definition language (XSDL) provides a facility for defining user-derived datatypes, using the simpleType definition element.

The element must contain a child element for the desired form of derivation: list, union, or restriction.

derivation by list
> Derivation by list is quite straightforward. You merely take an existing datatype (like gYear) and create a new datatype that accepts a list of them (we could call it gYears).

derivation by union

> This sort of derivation merges two or more datatypes into one that supports values of either sort. For instance a datatype representing months might allow either `gMonth` integers or string names by deriving by union from `Name` and `gMonth`.

derivation by restriction

> This form of derivation narrows down the values allowed by an existing datatype. For instance you could take the datatype `gYear` and restrict it to years in a particular century.

The child element might optionally be preceded by an `annotation` element, as shown in Example 21-1.

Note   Annotation elements can hold more than documentation, and XSDL elements in general have other properties that support self-documentation and application processing of schema definitions. As these facilities are not germane to deriving datatypes for general use, they are discussed in 22.3.2, "Schema components", on page 472.

Example 21-1. A `simpleType` definition

```
<xsd:simpleType name="mynewType">
   <xsd:annotation>
      <xsd:documentation>Important new type</xsd:documentation>
   </xsd:annotation>
   <xsd:restriction base="someOtherType">
      ...
   </xsd:restriction>
</xsd:simpleType>
```

21.2.1 *Derivation by list*

You derive by list when you want to allow occurrences of the datatype in the document to contain multiple values rather than just one. For instance to allow multiple dates you could derive a dates datatype[4] from the primitive date datatype, as in Example 21-2.

Caution   *Items in lists are always separated by whitespace. If a datatype allows embedded whitespace (such as string), deriving a list from it may produce unexpected results.*

Example 21-2. Deriving a list from a named datatype

```
<xsd:simpleType name="dates">
  <xsd:annotation>
    <xsd:documentation>Multiple dates</xsd:documentation>
  </xsd:annotation>
  <xsd:list itemType="xsd:date"/>
</xsd:simpleType>
```

In Example 21-2, the list was derived from an existing named datatype. It is also possible to derive a list from a newly-defined anonymous datatype. Rather than putting an itemType attribute on the list, you would merely put a simpleType element in the list element content.

The embedded simpleType will be used just as if you had defined it elsewhere, given it a name and referred to it with the itemType attribute. Example 21-3 demonstrates.

Example 21-3. Deriving a list from an anonymous datatype

```
<xsd:simpleType name="pubDates">
  <xsd:list>
    <xsd:simpleType>
        ... derivation of pubDate ...
    </xsd:simpleType>
  </xsd:list>
</xsd:simpleType>
```

---

4. XSDL would call this a simple type, rather than a datatype, but in this chapter it is clearer to call it a datatype.

21.2.2 *Derivation by union*

Derivation by union is a way of combining existing datatypes into one datatype. For instance you might want to allow dates to be specified according to any one of:

- the built-in Gregorian `date` datatype,
- a notation based on the ancient Aztec calendar, or
- the Hebrew calendar.

If we define our datatypes so that they are syntactically distinct then we can easily create a union of them. One way to easily distinguish Aztec and Hebrew dates is to start them with the letters A and H, respectively, because we know that built-in dates start with a number. Example 21-4 demonstrates such a union datatype.

Example 21-4. Union datatype

```
<xsd:simpleType name="AnyKindaDate">
  <!-- we could put an annotation here -->
  <xsd:union memberTypes="myns:AztecDate myns:HebrewDate xsd:date">
     <!-- we could put another annotation here -->
  </xsd:union>
</xsd:simpleType>
```

If we carelessly defined our notations so that some Aztec dates could also be recognized as Hebrew or Gregorian dates, then the Aztec interpretation would win over the other ones because it is listed first in the `memberTypes` attribute.

Instead of – or in addition to – a `memberTypes` attribute, you could also put `simpleType` elements within the union to define anonymous in-line datatypes, just as we did for lists. Unlike lists, however, which are derived from a single datatype, we can define as many anonymous datatypes as we like. Each of them contributes to the union just as if it had been defined externally and referenced.

If we wanted to, we could define a union of two different kinds of lists. Perhaps we would allow a list of Hebrew dates or a list of Aztec dates. Conversely, we could define a list of a union datatype. For instance, a list derived from `AnyKindaDate` would be a list of a union.

Many complex combinations of different kinds of derivation are possible.

21.2.3 *Deriving datatypes by restriction*

Another way to derive a datatype is by restriction. In this case, you add constraints to an existing datatype, either built-in or user-derived.

By definition, a datatype derived by restriction is more constraining than its base datatype. Any value that conforms to the new derived datatype would also have to conform to the original base datatype.

Restrictions are created with the `restriction` element. You may have a single `restriction` as a child of the `simpleType` element. You can refer to a named base datatype with the `base` attribute, or define an anonymous base datatype by including a simple type in the content.

There is a fixed list of ways that you can constrain a given datatype. These are called *constraining facets*. There are twelve of them, each represented by a specific element type. They occur as sub-elements of the `restriction` element. The allowable ones depend on the base datatype.

They have several points in common:

- They all allow a single optional `annotation` sub-element and no other.
- Each has a required `value` attribute that specifies the constraining value. The exact meaning and allowable values of the attribute depend on the specific facet and the base datatype.
- They work together.

The last item requires some explanation.

If you define a datatype with a minimum value and then refine it by restriction to make a new datatype with a maximum value, the new datatype has *both* the minimum value constraint from the base datatype *and* the maximum value constraint from the derived datatype. If you defined yet a third datatype by restriction based on the new datatype, it would add still other restrictions.

This principle applies even when the same facet is applied at two different levels. So you could define a datatype that represents the set of numbers greater than 10,000 by setting a minimum value constraint. In a datatype derived from that you could set another minimum value constraint raising the minimum value to 20,000.

Values must now be both greater than 10,000 and greater than 20,000, which is the same as saying just that they must be greater than 20,000. In one sense both restrictions apply, but really the more constraining derived datatype overrides the base datatype.[5]

21.3 | Constraining facets

This section describes the twelve `facet` elements that are used when deriving by restriction. They fall into six categories: range, length, decimal digit, enumeration, white space, and pattern.

21.3.1 *Range restrictions*

The simplest kind of restriction available for numeric and date datatypes is a range restriction. For instance we might want to define a user-derived datatype called "publication year" as a year that must fall between 1000 and 2100. Example 21-5 defines a `pubYear` datatype with these characteristics.

Example 21-5. Defining a restricted range integer datatype

```
<xsd:simpleType name="pubYear">
  <xsd:annotation>
    <xsd:documentation>A publication year</xsd:documentation>
  </xsd:annotation>
  <xsd:restriction base="xsd:gYear">
      <xsd:minInclusive value="1000"/>
      <xsd:maxInclusive value="2100"/>
  </xsd:restriction>
</xsd:simpleType>
```

The `minInclusive` element sets the minimum value allowed for the new `pubYear` datatype and the `maxInclusive` element sets the maximum value allowed.

---

5. There is a way to prevent such overrides, but as it is rarely needed, we don't cover it here.

Alternatively, we could use the maxExclusive and minExclusive elements. They also set upper and lower bounds, but the bounds exclude the named value. In other words, a maxExclusive value of 2100 allows 2099 but not 2100.

21.3.2 *Length restrictions*

There are three length constraining facets: minLength and maxLength, which work together or separately to set lower and upper bounds on a value's length, and a facet called simply length which requires a specific fixed length.

Length means slightly different things depending on the datatype that it is restricting.

list

If the datatype is a list (e.g. IDREFS) then the length facets constrain the number of items in the list.

string

If the datatype derives from string (directly or through multiple levels of derivation) then the length facets constrain the number of characters in the string.

binary

Applied to a binary datatype, length facets constrain the number of bytes of decoded binary data.

21.3.3 *Decimal digit restrictions*

There are two facets that only apply to decimal numbers and types derived from them. These are totalDigits and fractionDigits.

The first constrains the maximum number of digits in the decimal representation of the number and the second constrains the maximum number of digits in the fractional part (after the .). For instance it would make sense when dealing with dollars to constrain the fractionDigits to two.

21.3.4 *Enumeration restrictions*

You can also define a datatype as a list of allowable values by using several enumeration elements. In Example 21-6, we define a dayOfWeek datatype.

Example 21-6. Defining an enumerated datatype

```
<xsd:simpleType name="workday">
  <xsd:restriction base="xsd:string">
    <xsd:enumeration value="Sunday"/>
    <xsd:enumeration value="Monday"/>
    <xsd:enumeration value="Tuesday"/>
    <xsd:enumeration value="Wednesday">
      <xsd:annotation>
        <xsd:documentation>Halfway there!</xsd:documentation>
      </xsd:annotation>
    </xsd:enumeration>
    <xsd:enumeration value="Thursday"/>
    <xsd:enumeration value="Friday">
      <xsd:annotation>
        <xsd:documentation>Almost done!</xsd:documentation>
      </xsd:annotation>
    </xsd:enumeration>
    <xsd:enumeration value="Saturday"/>
  </xsd:restriction>
</xsd:simpleType>
```

Note that an enumeration element, like all facet-constraining elements, may have an annotation sub-element.

Enumeration elements work together to restrict the value to one of the enumeration values. Enumeration elements are so strict that they supersede any of the base datatype's constraints. Where other constraints say things like "the value must be higher than X or look like Y", enumerations say: "the value must be one of these values and not anything else".

The enumeration values must be legal values of the base datatype. Therefore, if an enumeration datatype derives from another enumeration datatype, the derived datatype may only have values that the base datatype has.

21.3.5 *The* whiteSpace *facet*

The whiteSpace facet is a little bit different from the others. Rather than constraining the value of a datatype, it constrains the processing. The facet can have one of three values:

preserve
> The datatype processor will leave the whitespace alone.

replace
> Whitespace of any kind is changed into space characters.

collapse
> Sequences of whitespace are collapsed to a single space and leading and trailing whitespace is discarded.

The built-in datatypes all use the value collapse, except for string and types derived from it. Those types include normalizedString, which in turn is a base type for token. As we discussed in 21.1.2.2.2, "Other XML constructs", on page 451, all of the datatypes that represent names of things (language, Name, NMTOKEN, etc.) derive from tokens.

21.3.6 *The pattern facet*

The most sophisticated and powerful facet is the pattern facet. Patterns have a value attribute that is a *regular expression.*

The regular expressions that constrain datatypes are based on those used in various programming languages. They have especially close ties to the Perl programming language which integrates regular expressions into its core syntax.

Note The full regular expression language is quite complicated because of deep support for Unicode. There are also shortcuts to reduce the size of regular expressions. We do not cover all of these. Instead we concentrate on those regular expression features that are used most of the time.

Example 21-7 illustrates some interesting patterns. We'll explain what goes into them in the following sections.

Example 21-7. Pattern examples

```
<xsd:simpleType name="even-number">
    <xsd:restriction base="xsd:decimal">
        <xsd:pattern value="\d*[02468]"/>
    </xsd:restriction>
</xsd:simpleType>

<xsd:simpleType name="old-fashioned-domain-name">
    <xsd:restriction base="xsd:string">
        <xsd:pattern value="\w+\.(com|net|org|gov)"/>
    </xsd:restriction>
</xsd:simpleType>

<xsd:simpleType name="phone-number">
    <xsd:restriction base="xsd:string">
        <xsd:pattern value="(\d{3}-)?\d{3}-\d{4}"/>
    </xsd:restriction>
</xsd:simpleType>
```

21.3.6.1   Constructing regular expressions

The simplest regular expression is just a character. a is a regular expression that matches the character "a". There is only one string in the world that matches this string.

If we put other letters beside the "a" then the regular expression will match them in order. abcd matches "a" and then "b" and then "c" and then "d". Once again there is only one string that matches that expression.

21.3.6.1.1   *Quantifiers*

A slightly more sophisticated regular expression will match one or more occurrences of the last letter "d": abcd+. The plus symbol means "one or more of this thing", where "this thing" is whatever comes just before the plus symbol – typically a character. There are also ? and * symbols available. They stand for "zero or one of the thing" and "zero or more of the thing". We call these quantifiers.

There is another quantifier that uses curly braces ({}) with one or two numbers between them. The quantifier {3} means that there should be three occurrences of the thing.

So ba{3}d matches "baaad". It is also possible to express a range: ba{3,7}d matches "baaad", "baaaad", "baaaaad", "baaaaaad" and "baaaaaaad". The lower bound can go as low as zero, in which case the item is optional (just as if you had used a question mark).

The upper bound can be omitted like this: ba{3,}d. That means that there is no upper bound. That expression is equivalent to baaaa*d which is itself equivalent to baaa+d. All three expressions match three or more occurrences of the middle letter "a".

We can put these ideas together. For instance ab{2,5}c+d{4} matches one "a" followed by two to five "b"s followed by one or more "c"s followed by exactly 4 "d"s. Example 21-8 demonstrates.

Example 21-8. Quantifiers in a regular expression

```
<xsd:simpleType name="reg-exp-example">
    <xsd:restriction base="xsd:string">
        <xsd:pattern value="ab{2,5}c+d{4}"/>
    </xsd:restriction>
</xsd:simpleType>
```

21.3.6.1.2 *Alternatives and grouping*

Regular expressions use the | symbol to represent alternatives.

Consider the regular expression yes+|no+. It matches "yes", "yess", "yesss", "no", "noo", "nooo" and so forth.

If we want to repeat the whole word yes, we can use parentheses. The regular expression (yes)+|(no)+ matches the strings "yes", "yesyes", "yesyesyes", "no", "nono", "nonono".

We can even use parentheses to group the whole expression: (yes|no)+. This expression allows us to match multiple occurrences of "yes" and "no". For example: "yes", "no", "yesyes", "yesno", "noyes", "nono", "yesyesyes", "yesnoyes" and so forth.

21.3.6.1.3 *Special characters*

There are ways to refer to function characters:

- \n represents the newline (or line-feed) character.
- \r represents the return character.
- \t represents the tab character.

So a\nb represents the letter "a" followed by a newline followed by "b".

There are also ways to refer to the characters that would normally be interpreted as symbols. For instance the + character might be necessary in a regular expression involving mathematics.

- Convert a symbol into an ordinary character by preceding it with the symbol \. So \? is translated into the ordinary character (not special symbol) ?.
- Convert a backslash symbol to a character like this: \\. Convert two of them like this: \\\\.
- The symbol characters you need to handle in this way are:

  \ | . - ^ ? * + { } ( ) [ ]

21.3.6.2   Character classes

It is often useful to be able to refer to lists of characters without explicitly listing all of the characters. For instance it would be annoying to need to enter (1|2|3|4|5|6|7|8|9|0) whenever you want to allow a digit.

Plus there are many Unicode characters that are considered digits that are not in this set. Examples include TIBETAN DIGIT ZERO, GUJARATI DIGIT TWO and DINGBAT NEGATIVE CIRCLED DIGIT NINE. It would not be internationally correct to ignore those!

These sets of reusable characters are known as *character classes*. They are represented by a backslash character followed by a letter.[6]

21.3.6.2.1   *Built-in character classes*

This particular character class, digits, is represented by \d. So \d+ means one or more digits, while \d+a\d{2,5} means one or more digits, and then the letter "a", and then two to five more digits. The opposite of this character class is indicated by an upper-case \D, meaning anything that is not a digit.

Another major character class is indicated simply by a period (.). It matches any character except a newline or linefeed character. So d.g

---

6. Note that the backslash does two different jobs. It turns symbol (punctuation) characters into ordinary characters and ordinary letters into character classes.

matches "dig" and "dog" but also "d~g" and "d%g". The middle character could even be Kanji or Cherokee (both components of Unicode!).

The character class \s represents any whitespace character (space, tab, newline, carriage return). \S is its opposite. It represents any non-whitespace character.

\i represents the set of "initial name" characters – basically letters, the underscore and the colon.[7] \I is its opposite: anything that is not an initial name character. \c represents the set of all name characters. \C is its opposite.[8]

\w represents what you might call "word" characters: basically letters, digits, and some symbols (e.g. currency, math). That is to say, characters that are not punctuation, separators or the like. \w+ will roughly match a word; \W represents the opposite – the characters that are not considered word characters.

21.3.6.2.2 *Constructing a character class*

You can also create character classes in your regular expressions (though you cannot give them fancy backslash-prefixed names!). The syntax to do this is called a *character class expression* and it uses square brackets ([]).

For instance to represent the first four characters in the alphabet you would say [abcd]. This simple example could just as easily be represented as (a|b|c|d) but the character class notation allows a couple of tricks that are difficult to emulate with the | symbol.

When you construct a character class expression you can specify ranges. For instance [a-z] represents the characters from "a" through "z" in Unicode (which are the same as in the English alphabet). You can even put multiple ranges together: [a-zA-Z0-9].

Inside square brackets, the characters *, +, (,), {, } and ? are just characters. They have no special meaning. Backslash (\) remains special because we use that to refer to the built-in character classes (\d for digits and so forth). Here is a character class that matches all of them and also matches Unicode digit and word characters: [*+(){}\d\w].

---

7. The class was renamed from the proper XML terminology of *name start characters* so that \n could have its common regular expression meaning of "newline".

8. See 15.1.4, "Names", on page 353 for a refresher on both of these character classes.

It is also possible to construct a "negative" character class which includes all of the characters that you do not list. You do this by starting your character class expression with a caret (^) symbol. So to match every character except "a" and "z", you would use the regular expression: [^az]. If you wanted to match everything except the characters *from* "a" *to* "z", you could do that like this: [^a-z].

21.4 | Conclusion

XML Schema Datatypes provides a useful library of built-in datatypes and a powerful facility for deriving your own from them. These datatypes can be used in XSDL schema definitions, in DTDs, and with non-XSDL schema languages.

XML Schema (XSDL)

- ▌ *XML Schema* definition language

- ▌ Syntax and declarations

- ▌ Simple and complex types

- ▌ Locally-scoped elements

- ▌ Schema inclusion

Chapter

22

An XML DTD is a specific case of a more general concept called a schema definition. The dictionary defines *schema* as a "general conception of what is common to all members of a class." A *schema definition* takes that "conception" and turns it into something concrete that can be used directly by a computer.

There are many types of schema in use in the computer industry, chiefly for databases. DTDs are different in that the class for which they declare "what is common to all members" is a class of XML documents.

The popularity of XML has brought DTDs to entirely new constituencies. The database experts and programmers who are taking to XML in droves are examining it from the standpoint of their own areas of expertise and familiar paradigms.

All of these creative folks have ideas about what could be done differently. The World Wide Web Consortium has incorporated these ideas into a design for an enhanced schema definition facility called the *XML Schema definition language (XSDL)*.

The name of the language is often shortened to "XML Schema", but we reserve that phrase for the name of the W3C spec. We call the language XSDL so you'll know when we are referring to the "schema definition language" as opposed to:

- a particular "schema definition",
- a conceptual "schema", or
- the *XML Schema* specification.

The words "XML schema", unfortunately, could refer to any of those three things.

Caution   The XML Schema spec is several times longer than the XML specification itself. It is also quite intricate and formal. This chapter will informally teach a subset that is sufficiently functional for most projects and yet simple enough that we can teach it all in one chapter.

22.1 | A simple sample schema

Let's start our explanation of XSDL by introducing a sample schema definition.

Example 22-1. Poem document

```
<?xml version="1.0"?>
<poem xmlns="http://www.poetry.net/poetns"
    publisher="Boni and Liveright" pubyear="1922">
<title>The Waste Land</title>
<picture href="pic1.gif"/>
<verse>April is the cruellest month, breeding</verse>
<verse>Lilacs out of the dead land</verse>
</poem>
```

The sample XSDL definition in Example 22-2 demonstrates some of the most important features of the language. Example 22-1 shows a document that conforms to that schema.

The schema defines a `poem` element type that consists of a `title` element followed by a `picture` and one or more `verse` elements. The `poem` element type has two optional attributes: `publisher` and `pubyear`.

The `picture` element type's required `href` attribute is declared with a type of `xsd:anyURI`, which indicates that the value of `href` must have a URI datatype.

Example 22-2. Poem schema definition in XSDL

```xml
<?xml version="1.0"?>
<xsd:schema xmlns:xsd="http://www.w3.org/2001/XMLSchema"
        xmlns:poem="http://www.poetry.net/poetns"
   targetNamespace="http://www.poetry.net/poetns">
  <xsd:element name="poem">
    <xsd:complexType>
      <xsd:sequence>
        <xsd:element ref="poem:title"/>
        <xsd:element ref="poem:picture"/>
        <xsd:element ref="poem:verse" maxOccurs="unbounded"/>
      </xsd:sequence>
      <xsd:attribute name="publisher" type="xsd:string"/>
      <xsd:attribute name="pubyear" type="xsd:NMTOKEN"/>
    </xsd:complexType>
  </xsd:element>
  <xsd:element name="title" type="xsd:string"/>
  <xsd:element name="verse" type="xsd:string"/>
  <xsd:element name="picture">
    <xsd:complexType>
      <xsd:attribute name="href" use="required" type="xsd:anyURI"/>
    </xsd:complexType>
  </xsd:element>
</xsd:schema>
```

There are several notable characteristics of the syntax:

- Perhaps the most obvious is that a schema definition is represented as an XML document.
- There is a dependency on namespaces, which are heavily utilized.[1] The `schema` element declares the prefix `xsd` for names defined in XML Schema and `poem` for names that are defined within this schema definition.
- There is a built-in syntax that can be used to declare datatypes: the `type` attribute. Actually, it is used for more than datatypes; it is arguably the most important concept in XSDL, as we'll soon see.

---

1. Namespaces are discussed in Chapter 16, "Namespaces", on page 376.

22.2 | Elements and types

Notice the four `element` elements[2] in Example 22-2: `poem`, `title`, `verse` and `picture`. They declare the properties of a class of elements:

1. the element-type name;
2. the data structure of the content; and
3. attributes provided for the class, including attribute types and default values.

In XSDL, a `complexType` element can define *and name* a data structure and attributes *independently of declaring an element type*. There is also a `simpleType` element, but it can define and name only the simplest data structures: various forms of character strings, such as datatypes.

The unqualified word *type* in XSDL is reserved for just these two types: complex types and simple types.[3]

An `element` element, then, declares the element-type name and data structure type of a class of elements. The type could be defined within the content of the `element` element, as in the case of `poem` in Example 22-2, in which case the type itself is not named.

Alternatively, if the type was defined and named elsewhere, the declaration could use a `type` attribute, as shown for the `title` element. As the `xsd` prefix in the attribute value suggests, the `string` type is not actually defined within this schema. XSDL automatically provides named simple type definitions for all of the built-in datatypes. Those names are in the *XML Schema* namespace.

The two methods of declaring data structure types for elements are equivalent, and are equally applicable to complex and simple types. That includes user-derived datatypes, which, as we saw in 21.2, "Defining user-derived datatypes", on page 451, are actually simple types.

---

2. Yes, `element` elements.
3. In fact the XSDL spec barely mentions any other types (element, attribute, data, etc.), perhaps to avoid confusion with the unqualified use of "type".

22.3 | Structure of a schema definition

A schema is defined by one or more *schema documents*. Their root element is a `schema` element. Its attributes can define applicable namespaces, and its content components include elements like those we have been discussing, plus annotation elements.

22.3.1 *Namespaces*

The `schema` element must have a declaration for the XML schema namespace, `http://www.w3.org/2001/XMLSchema`. It could either assign a prefix (`xsd` and `xs` are two popular ones) or it could make *XML Schema* the default namespace. The prefix (if any) is used both for schema component elements and in references to built-in datatypes.

To validate documents that use namespaces, you can specify a `targetNamespace` for the schema, as shown in Example 22-2. Components that are children of the `schema` element are called *global schema components*. They declare and define items in the schema's target namespace.

The example also declares the `poem` prefix for the schema's target namespace. It is used within the schema definition to refer to the elements, attributes and types declared (or defined) by global schema components.

The instance document in Example 22-1 utilizes the same namespace, `http://www.poetry.net/poetns`. However, as it is declared as the default namespace, no prefix is declared or used.

Note that the value of the `name` attribute of a component, such as a type definition or element declaration, does not have a namespace prefix. A component name always belongs to the target namespace. It is only when the declared or defined objects are referenced that the prefix may be used.

Within a namespace different kinds of components can normally have the same name. The exception is simple and complex types, as there are many places where they are treated interchangeably. Elements, however, are not types, so an element declaration component may use the same name as a complex or simple type. There is no more relationship between them than between a guy named Bob at your office and the guy named Bob on your favorite television show (unless you work in Hollywood!).

22.3.2   *Schema components*

The XSDL elements we have been discussing, such as `element` and `simpleType`, occur in the content of a `schema` element and are collectively known as *schema components*. Those, like `element`, that correspond to DTD declarations, are also called (surprise!) *declaration components*.

As XSDL schemas are themselves defined in XML documents, it was possible to provide techniques to make them self-documenting and capable of being processed by applications other than schema processors. These include unique identifiers, extension attributes, and annotation elements.

22.3.2.1   Unique identifiers

All schema components are defined with an optional `id` attribute. You can therefore assign unique identifiers to make the components easier to refer to using XPath expressions. Each value assigned to an `id` attribute must be different from any other assigned anywhere in the schema document.

22.3.2.2   Extension attributes

Schema components may be extended with arbitrary attributes in any namespace *other* than the *XML Schema* namespace. For instance you could add attributes from the XLink namespace or from the RDF namespace.

If you had software that helped you to visualize the schema, extension attributes could be used to store the graphical coordinates of the various elements. If you used software that converted XML schemas to a relational database schema, you might use the extension attributes to guide that process.

22.3.2.3   The `annotation` element

Any XSDL component may have an `annotation` element as its first sub-element. The `schema` element, however, goes above and beyond the call of duty! It may have as many `annotation` sub-elements as you like. It is good practice to have at least one annotation at the beginning as an introduction to the document type.

An annotation element may have zero or more documentation and appinfo children elements.

The documentation element is used to add user-readable information to the schema. Any elements are permitted; they needn't be defined in the schema. The benefit of using annotation elements rather than XML comments is that it is much easier to use rich markup such as XHTML or Docbook. Application software can extract this documentation and use it for online help or other purposes.

An appinfo element adds some information specific to a particular application. These are extension elements; they work like the extension attributes we discussed earlier. You may use them for the same sorts of tasks, but the elements can have an internal structure while attributes can only contain data characters. Your extension elements should be in a namespace that will enable your applications to recognize them.

22.3.3 Complex types

Example 22-3 shows the definition of an address type. It also shows two element declarations that utilize it.

Example 22-3. Elements built on an address type

```
<xsd:complexType name="address">
   <xsd:sequence>
     <xsd:element ref="myns:line1"/>
     <xsd:element ref="myns:line2"/>
     <xsd:element ref="myns:city"/>
     <xsd:element ret="myns:state"/>
     <xsd:element ret="myns:zip"/>
   </xsd:sequence>
   <xsd:attribute name="id" type="xsd:ID"/>
</xsd:complexType>
<xsd:element name="billingAddress" type="myns:address"/>
<xsd:element name="shippingAddress" type="myns:address"/>
```

In XSDL, types are definable independently of elements and may be associated with more than one element-type name. In the example, the address type is used by both billingAddress and shippingAddress.

This example shows some of the power of complex types: we can create structural definitions as reusable units that make element declaration and maintenance easier. Types are similar to the virtual or abstract classes used in object-oriented programming.

Types do not themselves define elements that will be used directly. Example 22-3 would not permit an address element in a valid document. Instead the type is a set of reusable constraints that can be used as a building block in element declarations and other type definitions.

XSDL does not require you to give every type a name. If you only intend to use a type once, you could put the definition for it right in an element declaration, as in Example 22-4.

Example 22-4. Inline type definition

```
<xsd:element name="address">
  <xsd:complexType>
   <xsd:sequence>
     <xsd:element ref="myns:line1"/>
     <xsd:element ref="myns:line2"/>
     <xsd:element ref="myns:city"/>
     <xsd:element ref="myns:state"/>
     <xsd:element ref="myns:zip"/>
   </xsd:sequence>
   <xsd:attribute name="id" type="xsd:ID"/>
  </xsd:complexType>
</xsd:element>
```

Example 22-4 was created from Example 22-3 by wrapping the complexType in an element and moving the name attribute. You could do the same with a simpleType. Note that the element declaration has no type attribute. You need to choose whether to refer to a named type or embed an unnamed type definition.

To create a type that allows character data in addition to whatever is specified in its content model, you may add a mixed="true" attribute value to the complexType element.

To declare the element-type empty, we could have left out the sequence element.

22.3.4 *Content models*

Content models allow us to describe what content is allowed within an element.

22.3.4.1 Sequences

A sequence is specified in Example 22-5. It indicates that there must be an A element followed by a B element followed by a C element.

Example 22-5. sequence element

```
<xsd:sequence>
   <xsd:element ref="myns:A"/>
   <xsd:element ref="myns:B"/>
   <xsd:element ref="myns:C"/>
</xsd:sequence>
```

An element element might declare things directly, or else indirectly by referencing an existing element declaration. The declarations in the example do the latter, as indicated by the use of ref attributes instead of name attributes. Note that an element reference must be prefixed if it lives in a namespace (which it will if declared in a schema with a targetNamespace).

22.3.4.2 Choices

Example 22-6 shows the XSDL code that defines a choice of element types. It means the element must contain either an A or a B or a C.

Example 22-6. choice element

```
<xsd:choice>
   <xsd:element ref="myns:A"/>
   <xsd:element ref="myns:B"/>
   <xsd:element ref="myns:C"/>
</xsd:choice>
```

22.3.4.3 Nested model groups

For more complex content models, model groups can be nested. For example, we can specify a choice element within a sequence element, as shown in Example 22-7.

The declaration for verse states that it may have multiple occurrences through its maxOccurs attribute. There is a corresponding minOccurs that defaults to "1" – meaning at least one is required by default.

Example 22-7. Sequence with nested choice

```
<xsd:sequence>
  <xsd:element ref="poem:title"/>
  <xsd:element ref="poem:picture"/>
  <xsd:element ref="poem:verse" maxOccurs="unbounded"/>
  <xsd:choice>
    <xsd:element ref="poem:footnotes"/>
    <xsd:element ref="poem:bibliography"/>
  </xsd:choice>
</xsd:sequence>
```

Inside of sequences and choices it is also possible to use `any` and `group` elements. An `any` element means that any content is allowed. It has various bells and whistles to allow you to narrow down what you mean by "any". Most document types do not require this feature so we will not go into any detail.

The `group` element allows you to refer to a named "model group definition". You can use these model group definitions to reuse parts of content models by referencing them.

22.3.4.4   `all` elements

The `all` element specifies that all of the contained elements must be present, but their order is irrelevant. So you could enter "A B C", "A C B", "B A C" and all of the other combinations of the three. Example 22-8 demonstrates.

Example 22-8. `all` element

```
<xsd:complexType name="testAll">
  <xsd:all>
    <xsd:element ref="myns:A"/>
    <xsd:element ref="myns:B"/>
    <xsd:element ref="myns:C"/>
  </xsd:all>
</xsd:complexType>
```

`all` must only be used at the top level of a complex type definition. `all` is also unique in that it may only contain `element` elements, not sequences, choices, groups, etc.

22.3.5 *Attributes*

The poem and picture element declarations in Example 22-2 both contain attribute declarations. Example 22-9 shows the declarations for the poem element's optional publisher and pubyear attributes.

Example 22-9. Attribute declarations

```
<xsd:attribute name="publisher" type="xsd:string"/>
<xsd:attribute name="pubyear" type="xsd:NMTOKEN"/>
```

They are optional because there is no use attribute in their definitions. You can also make them required with use="required".

Example 22-10 shows two attribute declarations. One uses a built-in datatype and the other a user-defined simple type.

Example 22-10. Built-in and user-defined types

```
<xsd:attribute name="href" use="required" type="xsd:anyURI"/>
<xsd:attribute name="pubdate" type="myns:pubyear"/>
```

Attribute declarations can also occur within a named attributeGroup element, which allows them to be reused in complex type definitions and in other attribute groups.

attribute elements have a default attribute that allows you to specify a default value for optional attributes. To supply a default value that cannot be overridden, supply it using the fixed attribute rather than the default attribute.

22.4 | Declaring schema conformance

How does an XML document tell a processor that it conforms to a particular XSDL schema definition? Usually it doesn't!

In theory, you can determine which schema definition to use from the root element type, file type, or other cues. In practice, the namespace is typically used.

There is a convention specified in the *XML Schema* specification to allow the document author to give a more explicit hint to the receiver. Example 22-11 demonstrates.

Example 22-11. Referring to a schema definition

```
<myns:mydoc
    xmlns:myns="http://www.myns.com/myns"
    xmlns:xsi="http://www.w3.org/2001/XMLSchema-instance"
    xsi:schemaLocation="http://www.myns.com/myns
                        http://www.mysite.com/myxsdl.xsd">

</myns:mydoc>
```

Note the declaration of the `xsi` namespace prefix. It identifies a namespace that is specifically for putting *XML Schema* information into instance documents. There is a global attribute in this namespace called `schemaLocation` that allows a document to point to an appropriate schema definition.

The attribute value is defined as a list of paired URIs. The first one in each pair is a namespace URI. The second one is the URI for a schema document. As the schema processor works its way through the instance document, it can find the applicable schema for an element or attribute by looking up its namespace.

The sender of a document may also provide the receiver with a schema through an API, command line, or graphical interface.

Although there is nothing wrong with using these hints just to check whether a document is valid, often you want to check whether it validates against some particular schema. In that case you don't want your software to use hints, you want it to use the schema you've provided.

The manner in which you tell the software what schema to use for a particular namespace will depend on the software. One convention is merely to configure the software with a list of schemas. The software can read the schemas and collect the list of target namespaces from the `targetNamespace` attributes. Then, when it sees a particular namespace in a document it can use the appropriate schema to validate it. Because *you* provide the list of schemas in the beginning, you know exactly what schemas are being used to validate no matter what is in the document.

22.5 | Schema inclusion

The *schema inclusion* facility allows a schema definition to treat another schema definition's contents as part of its own. Example 22-12 uses the `include` element to incorporate declarations from the schema in Example 22-13. The declarations are thenceforth treated as part of the `book.xsd` schema.

Example 22-12. `book.xsd` schema definition including declarations from `common.xsd`

```
<xsd:schema xmlns:xsd="http://www.w3.org/2001/XMLSchema"
        xmlns:myns="http://www.myns.net/myns"
  targetNamespace="http://www.myns.net/myns">
 <xsd:include schemaLocation="common.xsd"/>
 <xsd:element name="book">
   <xsd:complexType>
     <xsd:sequence>
       <xsd:element ref="myns:title"/>
       <xsd:element ref="myns:chapter" maxOccurs="unbounded"/>
     </xsd:sequence>
   </xsd:complexType>
 </xsd:element>
 <xsd:element name="chapter">
   <xsd:complexType>
     <xsd:sequence>
       <xsd:element ref="myns:title"/>
       <xsd:element ref="myns:par" maxOccurs="unbounded"/>
     </xsd:sequence>
   </xsd:complexType>
 </xsd:element>
</xsd:schema>
```

Example 22-13. `common.xsd` schema definition

```
<xsd:schema xmlns:xsd="http://www.w3.org/2001/XMLSchema"
        xmlns:myns="http://www.myns.net/myns"
  targetNamespace="http://www.myns.net/myns">
 <xsd:element name="title" type="xsd:string"/>
 <xsd:element name="par" type="xsd:string"/>
</xsd:schema>
```

In addition to inclusion, XSDL also has support for importing and redefinition of other schemas. Importing is for combining schemas that describe different namespaces. A redefinition allows you to include another schema and override bits and pieces of the included schema. For instance you could redefine the type of an element or attribute that you are including.

22.6 | Additional capabilities

We'll now describe some additional functions briefly. We'll try to provide just enough detail to allow you to decide whether to investigate them further.

22.6.1 *Locally-scoped elements*

Element-type names in a schema are normally global; any element type can be referenced in any other element type's content model. So if you define title you can use it in chapters, sections and anywhere else you see fit.

Once you have defined your schema, authors can use the title element in each of the contexts that you have specified. In each of those contexts the element type is exactly the same: it has the same name, attributes and allowed content.

XSDL has a facility that allows you to say that titles in one context should have a different attribute set and content model from titles in another – even if they are in the same namespace! In effect, you can declare two element types with the same name. The name is *bound* to a different element-type definition in each context.

You can do this by declaring an element type within the declaration for another element type. Example 22-14 shows two different title element types declared within the same schema. They each use a different user-derived datatype.

In documents conforming to this schema, a title element within a book element must conform to the title element declared within the book element declaration, complete with the required ISBN and booktitle attribute values.

A title element within an employee element, however, must conform to the title element declared inside the example's employee element declaration.

Example 22-14. Two locally-scoped `title` declarations

```
<xsd:element name="book"><xsd:complexType>
  <xsd:sequence>
    <xsd:element name="title"><xsd:complexType>
      <xsd:attribute name="booktitle" use="required"
                     type="xsd:string"/>
      <xsd:attribute name="ISBN" use="required"
                     type="myns:ISBNFormat"/>
    </xsd:complexType></xsd:element>
    <xsd:element ref="myns:chapter"/>
  </xsd:sequence>
</xsd:complexType></xsd:element>

<xsd:element name="employee"><xsd:complexType>
  <xsd:sequence>
    <xsd:element name="empId"/>
    <xsd:element name="title"><xsd:complexType>
      <xsd:sequence>
        <xsd:element ref="myns:jobtitle"/>
        <xsd:element ref="myns:company"/>
      </xsd:sequence>
    </xsd:complexType></xsd:element>
  </xsd:sequence>
</xsd:complexType></xsd:element>
```

22.6.2 *Type derivation*

Type derivation is the creation of a new type as a variation of an existing one (or a combination of several existing ones). This is much like the way object-oriented classes inherit from other classes. The derived type will have a content model that is an extension of the base type's.

We discussed derivation of simple types in 21.2, "Defining user-derived datatypes", on page 451. In Example 22-15 we see the derivation of a complex type, `internationalAddress`. It adds a new child element, called `countryCode`, to the `address` type we defined in Example 22-3.

With this definition, an `internationalAddr` is just like an `address`, but after specifying the details of the `address` you must also specify a `countryCode`.

You can also derive a type by *restriction*. That means that you add constraints, such as making an attribute or subelement required when it was previously optional. This is very similar to the equivalent concept for datatypes.

Example 22-15. One type extends another

```
<xsd:complexType name="internationalAddr">
  <xsd:complexContent>
    <xsd:extension base="myns:address">
      <xsd:sequence>
          <xsd:element ref="myns:countryCode"/>
      </xsd:sequence>
    </xsd:extension>
  </xsd:complexContent>
</xsd:complexType>
```

22.6.3 *Identity constraints*

There could be several elements in a document that logically represent a set. For example, records of the employees in a company might be represented as elements in an XML document.

Each element in a set must have a unique name or *key* that distinguishes it from all other elements in the set. For example, the employee records key could be an `empid` attribute or sub-element.

These *identity constraints* can get even more complicated: we might wish to declare that there must be no two customers with the same first name, last name, and address.

XSDL has sophisticated features for defining unique keys and the means of referencing them. It uses XPath for this purpose. For instance you could define the list of customers with one XPath expression and use a second to describe how each member of the set is unique.[4]

22.7 | Conclusion

XSDL is a sophisticated tool in the toolbox of schema developers. It has the virtue of supporting modern ideas of inheritance and namespaces. At the same time it is controversial because it is so large and complex. The subset described in this chapter should be both useful and manageable.[5]

---

4. The discussion in 18.6.7, "Keys", on page 410 gives an idea of the problem and the approach to solving it.
5. For the whole story, we recommend Priscilla Walmsley's *Definitive XML Schema*, published in this series.

Web services technologies

Tad Tougher Tutorial

- Service discovery
- Web Services Description Language (WSDL)
- Universal Description, Discovery, and Integration

Chapter

23

omputer programs are brittle. It is easier for applications to talk
to people than to other applications. That's why Web services
specifications are less mature than pure Web specifications.

There are three major Web services technologies: SOAP, WSDL, and
UDDI. We covered SOAP in Chapter 19, "Web services introduction", on
page 414. Now we'll take a closer look at the other two.

23.1 | Web Services Description Language

If I agree to provide you with some XML documents, we will also agree on
the document type. That agreement is usually recorded formally in a DTD
or schema definition. The definition is like a recipe: It lists the ingredients
of a dish – in this case, the data elements of the documents that I'm serving.

If I agree to provide you information through an XML-based protocol,
you'll want to know the offerings I have available and how to request each
one. For this you'll need a description of my service, which I can express

formally using the Web Services Description Language (WSDL). The service description is like a menu from a take-out restaurant: It tells you in great detail what is available and your options for getting it.

Figure 23-1 shows the components of WSDL in the form of a stack. Ignore the details for now; just focus on the middle column.

23.1.1 *Starting at the top: service*

WSDL is a layered specification. Each layer depends upon the layer directly below it. There is a certain elegance to layered designs. When you are working with them, you can concentrate on one layer at a time. Using this technique, let's explore WSDL by working from the top down with an application example.

Logically enough for a language that describes Web services, the top concept is the *service*. In our case, it is a global meteorological service offered to subscriber corporations. It might, in turn, get its information from other Web services run by national meteorological departments.

23.1.2 *Dividing up work: port*

A service could offer multiple functions, called *operations*. To balance the resources for supporting them, the service could span multiple physical computer systems. Access to particular groups of operations is provided by *ports*. Each port could exist on a different machine or multiple ports could be on the same machine. That is totally up to the Web service creator.

Each port has a name. Perhaps one port would serve the temperatures, another the humidity and a third the barometric pressure. It would all depend on what was most convenient for the person constructing the service. Let's call our ports `temperature`, `humidity` and `pressure`. They might have Web addresses such as:

- `http://temperature.weatherworld.com/`
- `http://humidity.weatherworld.com/` and
- `http://pressure.weatherworld.com`

We could have put two ports on the same machine if that was convenient.

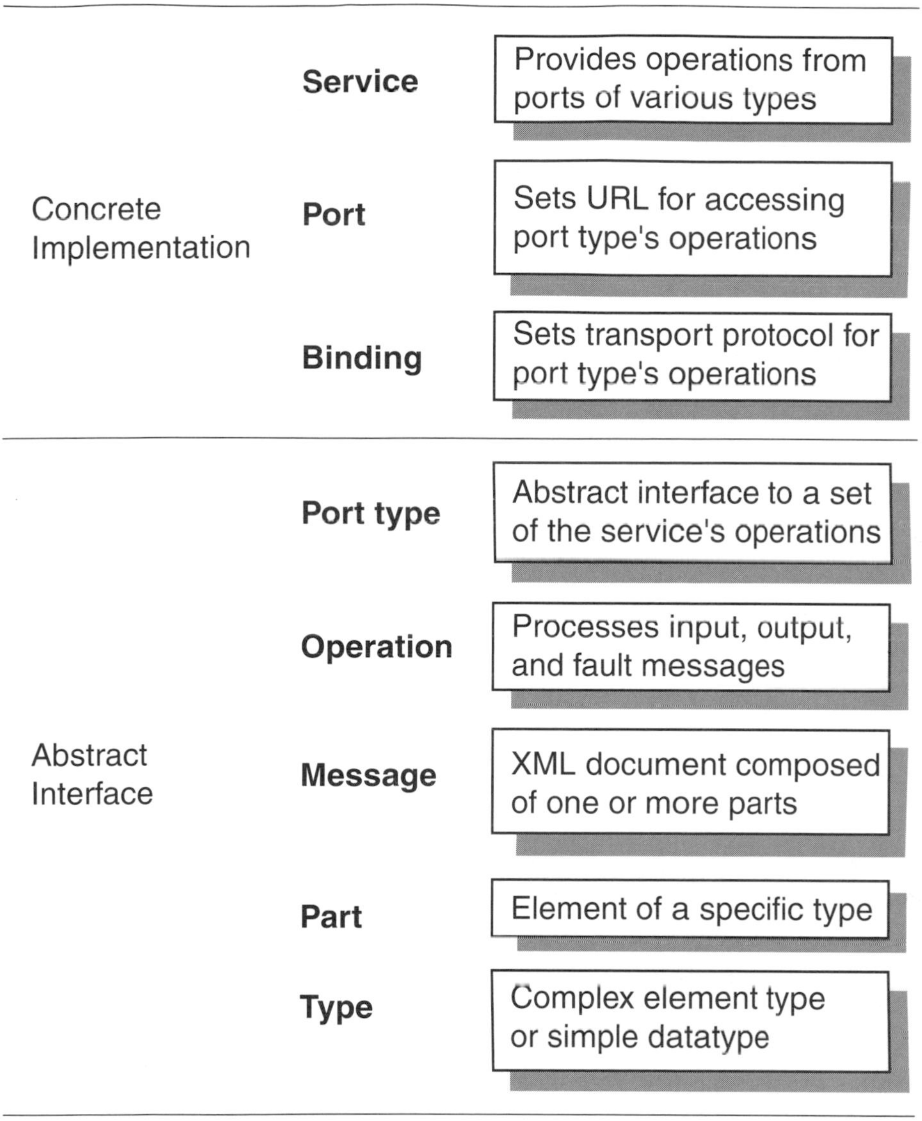

	Service	Provides operations from ports of various types
Concrete Implementation	**Port**	Sets URL for accessing port type's operations
	Binding	Sets transport protocol for port type's operations
	Port type	Abstract interface to a set of the service's operations
	Operation	Processes input, output, and fault messages
Abstract Interface	**Message**	XML document composed of one or more parts
	Part	Element of a specific type
	Type	Complex element type or simple datatype

Figure 23-1   The WSDL stack

Because ports are URL-specific, it makes no sense for this part of a Web service to be defined in an industry standard, as you might define an industry-standard DTD or schema. The other parts of a WSDL definition are more reusable than the ports.

23.1.3 *Choosing a transport protocol: binding*

Now that we know where on the Internet to go for the ports that give access to different operations of the service, we need to know how to communicate with them. For that, each port must specify a *binding*.

Protocols tend to build on one another. A binding is basically a way of defining a new protocol based on an existing one. In this case, the existing protocol is the *transport protocol* that is used to transport the messages from place to place. It makes sense to build on top of an existing transport protocol because otherwise you would have to specify the exact order of the bits travelling down the wire. That would be a total waste of time!

In this case we are going to build our new meteorological protocol on top of SOAP. We could also specify a binding based on the HTTP protocol that is used by Web browsers. However, each port may support only one binding. For the service to support both transport protocols, we would have to define separate ports, with names like `temperature_soap`, and `temperature_http`. Both ports would support the same operation; only the transport protocol would differ.

The WSDL spec describes how to use WSDL with SOAP and HTTP. Third parties could define how to use WSDL with (for example) the popular mail protocol SMTP. Any existing transport protocol could be used, but somebody, somewhere would have to write a document explaining how WSDL and the protocol fit together.

The binding does more than just choose the transport protocol. It also specifies some details about how to use the transport protocol for each operation. These details depend upon which transport protocol you have chosen. For instance if you choose SOAP, you get to choose options that are available in the SOAP specification and generally tweak the layout of the SOAP messages that are sent across the network.

23.1.4 *Getting abstract: port type*

Each binding is associated not only with a transport protocol but also with a *port type*, which is a set of operations provided by the service. All the operations of a service are grouped into one or more port types. In our example, we've created three port types with one operation each, `temperature`, `humidity` and `pressure`.

This is the layer at which we start to lift off from the very concrete into the land of the abstract. The bindings and ports were concrete in that they defined how the information would be laid out in terms of SOAP messages (or HTTP messages) and where on the Internet the messages would physically go.

Port types are abstract. They do not say what exactly should go on the wire nor where that information should go. Rather they define in the abstract what sort of things can be said. That means, for example, that an industry group could define a single port type for handling temperatures and then specify a variety of bindings for it.

Doing so would allow some Web services to handle temperatures using SOAP and some to use HTTP (the protocol for the existing Web and REST Web services). Service providers could compete based on which concrete bindings they provide for the same abstract port types.

23.1.5 *Defining behavior: operation*

Each port type has a name and a set of *operations*. Any Web service that claims to support the port type must have concrete bindings for each of the operations. Just as a DTD or schema requires many XML documents to have the same element structure, all ports of the same type must support the same operations.

Operations are defined in terms of input, output, and faults.

Imagine a real-world service for delivering pizza. To place an order, you must give the pizzeria a list of toppings, an address and a credit card number. In WSDL terms these are the *input* to the process.

Hopefully you will eventually get a pizza. This is called the *output*. If something goes wrong, you can expect a phone call along the lines of "we could not find your house" or "we could not process your credit card." These error messages are called *faults*.

23.1.6 *The information unit: message*

In our meteorological example, the output certainly is not a pizza and a fault is not a phone call. Web services deal in information represented as XML. The unit of information sent back and forth between programs is an

XML document called a *message*. Operations define their input, output and faults in terms of messages.

The operation `query_temperature` would have as its input a geographical location. Users are probably interested in the temperature where they live! We would therefore define a message type for asking about the temperature at a particular point on the globe. It might also allow the user to specify whether the result should be in Celsius or Fahrenheit. The output would be another XML message, containing the temperature represented as an integer.

We might send fault messages for requesting an unsupported location (e.g. Antarctica) and for requesting an unsupported temperature unit (e.g. Kelvin).

Let us say we called our output message type `temperature_report`. The interesting thing about this element type is that it could be useful in a totally different operation, wherein a remote weather station reports the temperature to our server. For that operation, it would be an input message rather than an output.

In other words, the remote station would contact us and send a `temperature_report` message as input. Later, an end-user could request the neighborhood temperature and we would send another `temperature_report` message, this time as output.

23.1.7 *Composing messages: part and type*

Each message has one or more components, called *parts*. Every part is an element, either one whose content is a datatype defined in the *XML Schema* specification, or one that conforms to a defined complex element type.

For instance the input to our `query_temperature` operation would need a latitude and longitude. Each of these could be a part with data content conforming to the *XML Schema* integer datatype.

Alternatively, we could define a single complex `position` element type with subelements or attributes for the latitude and longitude. We would then refer to that one element type in our message part definition.

It is possible to define new element types by embedding their definitions right in the Web service description, or else by referring to external schema definitions. You can define types that are very simple, such as credit card number, or very complex, such as purchase order.

Creating definitions in WSDL is easiest with the *XML Schema* definition language (XSDL), but other schema languages can be used as well.

23.1.8 *Summary of WSDL*

Here is a summary of the WSDL hierarchy shown in Figure 23-1, working from the top down. Now the details we encouraged you to skip the first time should be meaningful.

service
> A Web service performs operations.[1] These are grouped into one or more sets, called "port types". Each port type is accessed from one or more ports.

ports
> A port establishes a binding between a port type and a Web address for accessing the port type's operations. There could be several ports of the same type, each bound to a different transport protocol. The addresses of a service's ports could point to the same or different machines.

bindings
> Bindings are the links between the physical implementation of a Web service and the abstract interface. Each binding specifies how a particular transport protocol is used for the operations of a given port type.

port types
> The operations provided by a Web service are grouped into one or more port types. Port types define the abstract interface to a Web service.

operations
> An operation could consume a particular input and/or produce a particular output. If errors occur, it could also produce faults. Inputs, outputs, and faults are types of messages.

---

1. If you think of a Web service as an object, the operations are its methods.

messages

Messages are XML documents. They are made up of parts.

parts

A part is an element of a specific type.

types

Part types can be complex element types (with subelements and/or attributes) or simple datatypes. They are typically defined in XSDL.

The layers obviously go from most complex ("a complete Web service") to simplest ("a single element"). They also go from concrete implementation ("send these bits, to this URL, on this machine, using this transport") to abstract interface ("the types of things we are talking about are temperatures and air pressures").

Most importantly, the layers go from most specific to most reusable. Compare the definition "Sal's Pizza on the corner of Main Street and First Avenue" with the generic term "pizzeria". The first is very specific because it includes a concrete location. Web services also have one or more concrete locations because they are provided by the ports.

It is the lower layers that are reusable and might be defined by an industry consortium rather than a specific company. There is not necessarily anything company-specific about bindings, operations, messages or element types. In many circumstances it would make sense to share these and have multiple competing implementations.

But it would never make sense to share ports themselves. It is no more possible to "compete" by sharing a port than it would be to open two pizzerias at the same address!

23.2 | UDDI

Now we know how to check the temperature or order a pizza. But from whom? What if you wanted to find a weather information service or pizzeria? You might know in the abstract what sort of service (bindings, operations, etc.) you want, but you wouldn't necessarily know how to find all of the relevant service providers.

23.2.1 *Finding a service provider*

Universal Description, Discovery, and Integration (UDDI) is a set of OASIS specifications for the Web services world's equivalent of phone books. When you want to find a service in your town, you pick up the **Universal** yellow pages business **Description** listings and scan through them to **Discover** one that meets your requirements. Then you might **Integrate** the listing with your wallet by using the "scissors" protocol!

UDDI is based on SOAP and WSDL. Service providers use it to let Web services consumers know that their services exist, just as yellow pages help off-line consumers to know that businesses exist.

UDDI is different from existing business directories because of its integration with Web services. For instance, a UDDI business registry is actually a Web service itself, so programmers can contact it and ask it questions through SOAP. UDDI and SOAP are also integrated in a more important way. The UDDI registry can report which Web services are available from a particular business.

In theory a computer could connect to a UDDI registry, use SOAP to search it for a Web service implementing a "real-time currency conversion" operation, connect to that service and do the conversion without human intervention.

The information available through UDDI is typically described as falling into one of three categories, based on the telephone book metaphor:

white pages
> These describe an organization's name, address and contact information.

yellow pages
> Yellow pages categorize businesses by industrial category and geographical location.

green pages
> The so-called green pages are technical descriptions of how to interact with each organization's services.

23.2.2 *UDDI data structures*

A UDDI *registry* is a database of *business entities, business services, binding templates* and *tModels*. These are known as the UDDI *data structures*.

23.2.2.1   Business entities

Business entities are records of corporations or departments. They contain names, contacts, descriptions and other identifying information.

A business entity is uniquely identified by a `businessKey`, which is a long random-looking string of numbers and letters known as a *Universally Unique ID (UUID)*.

23.2.2.2   Business services

Business services are records of the services provided by a business entity. These can be true Web services. However, they can just as easily be traditional offline services, such as phone lines, or non-automated services, such as email.

Each service has a UUID called a `serviceKey`. It also has other identifying information, such as a name and a description. Most importantly, each service refers to one or more `bindingTemplates`.

23.2.2.3   Binding templates

Binding templates specify how to contact the company and consume the service. The most important subelement of the binding template is the access point, which tells how to communicate with the service.

Valid types of access point are:

- `mailto` for email,
- `http` for Web browsers or SOAP,
- `https` for secure HTTP,
- `ftp` for File Transfer Protocol,
- `fax` for fax machine, and
- `phone` for telephone.

23.2.2.4   tModels

tModels[2] are typically used as assertions that a service meets a certain specification. As UDDI is designed to be extremely general, the structure of tModels will vary widely.

tModels can be used to refer to almost any kind of service description. The description can be as technically precise as a WSDL definition or as informal as a prose document.

For Web services, of course, the formal tModels are the useful ones. Other businesses, however, simply cannot be described in that way. What is the input and the output of a dentist? Is biting his finger a fault?

23.2.3   *Will it work?*

The original emphasis in UDDI was on a single public registry for service discovery, now dubbed a *Universal Business Registry (UBR)*.[3]

The Fourth Edition of *The XML Handbook* cautioned:

> Some wonder whether there is even a good reason to think that service discovery will be any different in the Web services world. Perhaps businesses will continue to find one another through advertisements in magazines, introductions through social networks, and other traditional means. Business does require a certain level of trust after all!

The UDDI developers appear to have wondered the same thing. UDDI 3.0 recognizes that most of today's Web services are intended for use either internally or among existing trusted trading partners. Accordingly, it provides for multiple registries – private and shared, as well as public – and for their technical interoperability.

---

2. The word tModel does not really stand for anything.
3. A UBR actually exists; it is operated jointly by IBM, Microsoft, NTT Com, and SAP.

23.3 | Implementation

It is important to keep in mind that no matter how related they may seem, Web services technologies and Web-based delivery of services are two different things. This is particularly confusing right now because the industry is moving on both fronts at once, which causes people to think that they are the same thing.

Obviously there are already services on the Web that are not based on the new Web services technologies. *HotMail* and *Kazaa* are two examples.

Similarly, Web services technologies have nothing technically to do with subscription-based content syndication services, although some of those services are being built *using* Web services technologies.

23.4 | Conclusion

Although the specifications are under active development, much of the promise of Web services remains a dream of the future, not a here-and-now reality. Retain a degree of skepticism.

On the other hand, you can understand why this prospect has so excited the executives of every major software company.

Computers already talk to each other, with and without human supervision. The complexity of this communication will only increase in the future. Just as XML helps you manage the complexities of data representation, the new XML-based Web services technologies will help you with the complexities of computer communication.[4]

---

4. And remember that in one sense at least, Web services is a proven concept: Churches in L.A. have been holding them for years!

XML Path Language (XPath)

Tad Tougher Tutorial

- XPath applications
- XPath data model
- Location expressions

A ll XML processing depends upon the idea of *addressing*. In order to do something with data you must be able to locate it. To start with, you need to be able to actually find the XML document on the Web. Once you have it, you need to be able to find the information that you need within the document.

The Web has a uniform solution for the first part. The XML document is called a *resource* and *Uniform Resource Identifiers* are the Web's way of addressing resources. The most popular form of Uniform Resource Identifier is the ubiquitous Uniform Resource Locator (URL).

The standard way to locate information *within* an XML document is through a language known as the *XML Path Language* or *XPath*. XPath can be used to refer to textual data, elements, attributes and other information in an XML document.

As we have seen, both XSLT and XSDL make use of XPath for addressing.

24.1 | The XPath data model

It is only possible to construct an address – any address – given a model. For instance the US postal system is composed of a model of states containing cities containing streets with house numbers. To some degree the model falls naturally out of the geography of the country but it is mostly artificial. State and city boundaries are not exactly visible from an airplane. We give new houses street numbers so that they can be addressed within the postal system's model.

Relational databases also have a model that revolves around tables, records, columns, foreign keys and so forth. This "relational model" is the basis for the SQL query language. Just as SQL depends on the relational model, XPath depends on a formal model of the logical structure and data in an XML document.

24.1.1 *Why do we need a model?*

You may wonder if XML really needs a formal model. It seems so simple: elements within elements, attributes of elements and so forth. It *is* simple but there are details that need to be standardized in order for addresses to behave in a reliable fashion. The tricky part is that there are many ways of representing what might seem to be the "same" information. We can represent a less-than symbol in at least four ways:

- a predefined entity reference: `&lt;`
- a CDATA section: `<![CDATA[<]]>`
- a decimal Unicode character reference: `&#60;`
- a hex Unicode character reference: `&#x3c;`

We could also reference a text entity that embeds a CDATA section and a text entity that embeds another text entity that embeds a character reference, etc. In a query you would not want to explicitly search for the less-than symbol in all of these variations. It would be easier to have a processor that could magically *normalize* them to a single model. Every XPath-based query engine needs to get exactly the same data model from any particular XML document.

24.1.2 *Tree addressing*

The XPath data model views a document as a tree of nodes, or *node tree*. Most nodes correspond to document components, such as elements and attributes.

It is very common to think of XML documents as being either families (elements have child elements, parent elements and so forth) or trees (roots, branches and leaves). This is natural: trees and families are both hierarchical in nature, just as XML documents are. XPath uses both metaphors but tends to lean more heavily on the familial one.[1]

XPath uses genealogical taxonomy to describe the hierarchical makeup of an XML document, referring to children, descendants, parents and ancestors. The parent is the element that contains the element under discussion. The list of ancestors includes the parent, the parent's parent and so forth. A list of descendants includes children, children's children and so forth.

As there is no culture-independent way to talk about the first ancestor, XPath calls it the "root". The root is not an element. It is a logical construct that holds the document element and any comments and processing instructions that precede and follow it.

Trees in computer science are very rarely (if ever) illustrated as a natural tree is drawn, with the root at the bottom and the branches and leaves growing upward. Far more typically, trees are depicted with the root at the top just as family trees are. This is probably due to the nature of our writing systems and the way we have learned to read.[2] Accordingly, this chapter refers to stepping "down" the tree towards the leaf-like ends and "up" the tree towards the root as the tree is depicted in Figure 24-1. One day we will genetically engineer trees to grow this way and nature will be in harmony with technology.

24.1.3 *Node tree construction*

A *node tree* is built by an XPath processor after parsing an XML document like that in Example 24-1.

---

1. Politicians take note: in this case, family values win out over environmentalism!
2. To do: rotate all tree diagrams for Japanese edition of this book!

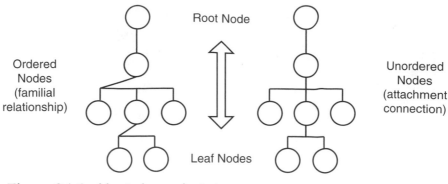

Figure 24-1   Vertical tree depictions

Example 24-1. Sample document

```
<?xml version="1.0"?>
<!--start-->
<part-list><part-name nbr="A12">bolt</part-name>
<part-name nbr="B45">washer</part-name><warning type="ignore"/>
<!--end of list--><?cursor blinking?>
</part-list>
<!--end of file-->
```

In constructing the node tree, the boundaries and contents of "important" constructs are preserved, while other constructs are discarded. For example, entity references to both internal and external entities are expanded and character references are resolved. The boundaries of CDATA sections are discarded. Characters within the section are treated as character data.

The node tree constructed from the document in Example 24-1 is shown in Figure 24-2. In the following sections, we describe the components of node trees and how they are used in addressing. You may want to refer back to this diagram from time to time as we do so.

24.1.4 *Node types*

The XPath data model describes seven types of nodes used to construct the node tree representing any XML document. We are interested primarily in

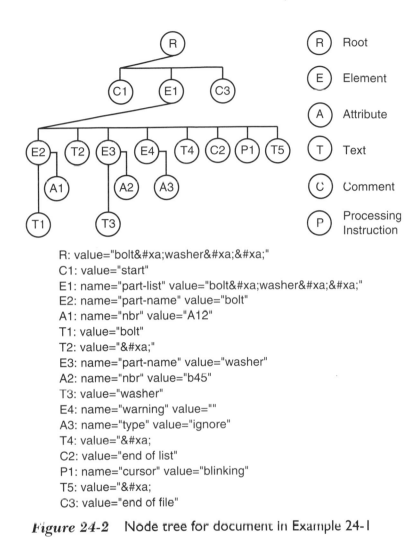

R: value="bolt
washer

"
C1: value="start"
E1: name="part-list" value="bolt
washer

"
E2: name="part-name" value="bolt"
A1: name="nbr" value="A12"
T1: value="bolt"
T2: value="
"
E3: name="part-name" value="washer"
A2: name="nbr" value="b45"
T3: value="washer"
E4: name="warning" value=""
A3: name="type" value="ignore"
T4: value="

C2: value="end of list"
P1: name="cursor" value="blinking"
T5: value="

C3: value="end of file"

Figure 24-2 Node tree for document in Example 24-1

the root, element, attribute and text node types, but will briefly discuss the others.

For each node type, XPath defines a way to compute a *string-value* (labeled "value" in Figure 24-2). Some node types also have a "name".

24.1.4.1 Root node

The top of the hierarchy that represents the XML document is the root node.

It is important to remember that in the XPath data model the root of the tree representing an XML document is *not the document (or root) element of the document.* A root *node* is different from a root *element.* The root node *contains* the root element.

The nodes that are children of the root node represent the document element and the comments and processing instructions found before and after the document element.

24.1.4.2 Element nodes

Every element in an XML document is represented in the node tree as an element node. Each element has a parent node. Usually an element's parent is another element but the document element has as its parent the root node.

Element nodes can have as their children other element nodes, text nodes, comment nodes and processing instruction nodes.

An element node also exhibits properties, such as its name, its attributes and information about its active namespaces.

Element nodes in documents with DTDs may have unique identifiers. These allow us to address element nodes by name. IDs are described in 15.3.3.2, "ID and IDREF attributes", on page 361.

The string-value of an element node is the concatenation of the string-values of all text node descendants of the element node in the document order. You can think of it as all of the data with none of the markup, organized into one long character string.

24.1.4.3 Text nodes

The XML Recommendation describes character data as all text that is not markup. In other words it is the textual data content of the document and it does not include data in attribute values, processing instructions and comments.

XPath does not care how a character was originally represented. The string "<>" in an XML document is simply "<>" from the data model's point of view. The same goes for "`&#60;&#62;`" and "`<![CDATA[<>]]>`". The characters represented by any of these will be grouped with the data characters that precede and follow them and called a "text node." The individual characters of the text node are not considered its children: they are just part of its value. Text nodes do not have any children.[3]

Remember that whitespace is significant. A text node might contain nothing else. In Figure 24-2, for example, nodes T2, T4, and T5 contain line feed characters, represented by hexadecimal character references.[4]

24.1.4.4 Attribute nodes

If an element has attributes then these are represented as attribute nodes. These nodes are not considered children of the element node. They are more like cousins who live in the guest house.

An attribute node exhibits name, string-value, and namespace URI properties. Defaulted attributes are reported as having the default values. The data model does not record whether they were explicitly specified or merely defaulted. No node is created for an unspecified attribute that had an `#IMPLIED` default value declared. Attribute nodes are also not created for attributes used as namespace declarations.

Note that an XML processor is not required to read an external DTD unless it is validating the document. This means that detection of ID attributes and default attribute values is not mandatory.

24.1.4.5 Other node types

Namespace nodes keep track of the set of namespace prefix/URI pairs that are in effect at a particular point in a document. Like attribute nodes, namespace nodes are attached to element nodes and are not in any particular order.

---

3. As the word "text" means something different in XPath from its meaning in the XML Recommendation, we try always to say "text node", even when the context is clear, reserving "text" as a noun for its normal meaning.
4. Character references are described in 15.6, "Character references", on page 368.

Each comment and processing instruction in the XML document is instantiated as a comment or processing instruction node in the node tree. The string-value property accesses the content of these constructs, as you can see in Figure 24-2.

24.2 | Location paths

An instance of the XPath language is called an *expression*. XPath expressions can involve a variety of operations on different kinds of operands. In this chapter we will focus on two operand types: function calls and location paths.

A *location path* is the most important kind of expression in the XPath notation. Its syntax is similar to the familiar path expressions used in URLs and in Unix and Windows systems to locate directories and files.[5]

24.2.1 *Basic concepts*

A location path has a starting point, which XPath calls its *context node*. In a file system path, it might be a computer, a disk drive, or a directory. In an XPath location path it could be, for example, the document element node or some other element node.

The purpose of the location path is to select nodes from the document by locating the desired nodes relative to the initial context node.

Arguably, the simplest location path is "/". This selects the root node (not the document element node).

24.2.1.1   Stepping down the hierarchy

We can extend this location path to select the document element node instead of the root node. "/mydoc" will select a document element node

---

5. There is an illustrated tutorial on path expressions in Chapter 17, "XPath primer", on page 384.

named "mydoc". The name of an element node is the element-type name of the element it represents.

 Note   *From now on, as long as we are discussing node trees, we'll often just say "element" instead of "element node".*

We have taken a step "down" the tree. We can take another step: "/mydoc/section". This will select every section element that is a child of the mydoc element.

Each slash-separated (/) path component is a *step*.

Any amount of whitespace can be present between the parts of a location path. Steps can be written across a number of lines or spaced apart to be more legible to a reader.

24.2.1.2   Predicates

So far we have seen how to build single and multi-level location paths based on element-type names. However, the type name is not the only thing that is interesting about an element. For example, we might want to filter out elements that have (or do not have) particular attributes with particular values. Or we may be interested in the first or seventh element, or just the even-numbered ones.

We can express these constraints with qualifiers called *predicates*. Any step can be qualified. The location path in Example 24-2, for example, selects the seventh paragraph from each section with a security attribute whose string-value is "public".

Example 24-2. Selecting the seventh para from each public section

```
/mydoc/section[@security="public"]/para[7]
```

24.2.1.3   Selection

Note that we use the word *select* carefully. We could say that the expression *returns* certain nodes but that might put a picture in your head of nodes being ripped out of the tree and handed to you: "Here are your nodes!"

Rather, what you get back is a set of locations – pointers to the nodes. Imagine the result of a location path as a set of arrows pointing into the node tree, saying: "Your nodes are here!"

24.2.1.4   Context

The context node keeps changing as we step down the path. As each step is evaluated, the result is a set of nodes – in XPath talk, a *node-set*. The node-set could have one or more nodes, or it could be empty.

The next step is then evaluated for each member of that node-set. That is, each member is used as the context node for one of the evaluations of the next step. The node-sets selected by each of those evaluations are combined (except for any duplicates) to produce the result node-set.

Consider what happens in Example 24-2.

1. The XPath processor first evaluates the "/". The root node becomes the initial context node.
2. Next it looks for every child of the context node with the name "mydoc". There will be only one member of that node-set because XML allows only a single root element. It becomes the context node for the next step, which is evaluated only once.
3. Next the processor looks for all of the section children in the context of the mydoc element that have the appropriate attribute value and returns their node-set. The next step will be evaluated once for each selected section node, which is the context node for that evaluation.
4. We're almost done. The processor looks for the seventh para several times, once for each section in the node-set. It puts the selected para nodes together into the final node-set and returns a set of pointers to them: "Your nodes are here!".

The initial context does not always have to be the root node of the document. It depends on the environment or application. Whatever application (e.g. database or browser) or specification (e.g. XSLT or XPointer) is using XPath must specify the starting context.

In XSLT there is always a concept of the *current node*. That node is the context node for location paths that appear in XSLT transforms. In XPointer, the starting context is always the root node of the particular document, selected by its URI. In some sort of document database, we might be allowed to do a query across thousands of documents. The root node of each document would become the context node in turn. XPath itself does not have a concept of working with multiple documents but it can be used in a system that does.

In addition to the current node, an application could specify some other details of the context: it could supply some values for variables and functions that can be used in the XPath expression. It could also include namespace information that can be used to interpret prefixed names in a location path.

24.2.1.5   Axes

But wait. That's not all! Up to now we've always stepped down the tree, to a child element. But we can also step *up* the tree instead of down and step many levels instead of one.

We can step in directions that are neither up nor down but more like sideways. For example we can step from elements to attributes and from attributes to elements.

We can also step from an element directly to a child of a child of a child (a descendant).

These different ways of stepping are called *axes*.

For example, the *descendant axis* (abbreviated `//`) can potentially step down all the levels of the tree. The location path "`/mydoc//footnote`" would select all footnotes in the current document, no matter how many levels deep they occur.

The *parent axis* uses an abbreviated syntax (`..`) that is similar to that for going up a directory in a file system. For instance we could select all of the elements *containing* a footnote like this: "`/mydoc//footnote/..`".

The *attribute axis* (abbreviated "`@`") steps into the attribute nodes of an element.

The *namespace axis* is used for namespace information associated with an element node.

There are a number of less commonly used axes as well. You can find out more about them in the XPath specification.

24.2.1.6   Node tests

The attribute and namespace axes each have only one type of node, which is (necessarily!) its principal node type.

The other axes, however, have element as the principal node type but have comment, processing instruction, and text node types as well. We'll refer to such an axis as a *content axis* and its nodes as *content nodes*.

A step normally selects nodes of the principal type. In the case of content axes, a node test can be used to select another type. For example, the node test `text()` selects text nodes.

24.2.2   *Anatomy of a step*

We've now seen enough of the basics to take a formal look at the parts of a location step. There are three:

- An axis, which specifies the tree relationship between the context node and the nodes selected by the location step. Our examples so far have used the child axis.
- A node test, which specifies the node type of the nodes selected by the location step. The default type is element, unless the axis is one that can't have element nodes.
- Zero or more predicates, which use arbitrary expressions to further refine the set of nodes selected by the location step. The expressions are full-blown XPath expressions and can include function calls and location paths. In Example 24-2 the first predicate is a location path and the second uses an abbreviation for the `position()` function.

In this tutorial, we've only been using abbreviated forms of the XPath syntax, in which common constructs can often be omitted or expressed more concisely. Example 24-3 shows the unabbreviated form of Example

24-2. Note the addition of explicit axis names (`child` and `attribute`) and the `position()` function call.

Example 24-3. Unabbreviated form of Example 24-2

```
/child::mydoc/child::section[attribute::security="public"]
              /child::para[position()=7]
```

In the remainder of the chapter, we'll take a closer look at each of the three parts: node tests, axes, and predicates.

24.2.2.1   Node tests

Some node tests are useful in all axes; others only in content axes.
Node tests for all axes are:

`*`

any node of the principal type; i.e., element, attribute, or namespace.[6]

`node()`

any node of any type

Node tests solely for content axes are:

`text()`

any text node

`comment()`

any comment node

`processing-instruction()`

any processing-instruction node, regardless of its target name

`processing-instruction(target-name)`

any processing-instruction node with the specified target name

---

6. The asterisk *cannot* be used as a prefix (`"*ara"`) or suffix (`"ara*"`) as it is in some regular-expression languages.

Here are some examples of node tests used in a *content* axis:

`processing-instruction(cursor)`
> all nodes created from a processing instruction with the target name "cursor"

`part-nbr`
> all nodes created from an element with the element-type name `part-nbr`

`text()`
> all text nodes (contrast below)

`text`
> all nodes created from an element with the element-type name `text`

`*`

> all nodes created from elements, irrespective of the element-type name

`node()`
> all nodes created from elements (irrespective of the element-type name), contiguous character data, comments or processing instructions (irrespective of the target name)

24.2.2.2   Axes

The most important axes are described here.

24.2.2.2.1   Child

The default axis is the child axis. That means that if you ask for "`/section/para`" you are looking for a `para` in a `section`. If you ask merely for "`para`" you are looking for the `para` element children of the context node, whatever it is.

24.2.2.2.2 *Attribute*

When using the symbol "@" before either an XML name or the node test
"*", one is referring to the attribute axis of the context node.

The attribute nodes are attached to an element node but the nodes are
not ordered. There is no "first" or "third" attribute of an element.

Attribute nodes have a string-value that is the attribute value, and a name
that is the attribute name.

Some examples of abbreviated references to attribute nodes attached to
the context node are:

`@type`
> an attribute node whose name is "`type`"

`@*`
> all attributes of the context node, irrespective of the attribute
> name

24.2.2.2.3 *Descendant*

We can use the double-slash "`//`" abbreviation in a location path to refer to
the descendant axis. This axis includes not only children of the context
node, but also all other nodes that are descendants of the context node.

This is a very powerful feature. We could combine this with the wildcard
node test, for example, to select all elements in a document, other than the
document element, no matter how deep they are: "`/doc//*`".

Some examples:

`/mydoc//part-nbr`
> all element nodes with the element-type name `part-nbr` that are
> descendants of the `mydoc` document element; that is, all of the
> `part-nbr` elements in the document

`/mydoc//@type`
> all attribute nodes named `type` attached to any descendant
> element of the `mydoc` document element; i.e., all of the `type`
> attributes in the document

```
/mydoc//*
```

> all elements that are descendants of the mydoc document element; i.e., every element in the document except the mydoc element itself

```
/mydoc//comment()
```

> all comment nodes that are descendants of the mydoc document element

```
/mydoc//text()
```

> all of the text nodes that are descendants of the mydoc document element; i.e., all of the character data in the document!

We do not have to start descendant expressions with the document element. If we want to start somewhere farther into the document we can use "//" in any step anywhere in the location path.

We could also begin with "//". A location path that starts with "//" is interpreted as starting at the root and searching all descendants of it, including the document element.

24.2.2.2.4 Self

The self axis is unique in that it has only one node: the context node. This axis can solve an important problem.

For instance in an XSLT transformation we might want to search for all descendants of the current node. If we begin with "//" the address will start at the root. We need a way to refer specifically to the current node.

A convenient way to do this is with an abbreviation: a period (.) stands for the context node.[7]

So ".//footnote" would locate all footnote descendants of the context node.

24.2.2.2.5 Parent

The parent axis (..) of a content node selects its parent, as the axis name suggests. For a namespace or attribute node, however, it selects the node's attached element.

---

7. This "dot-convention" also comes from the file system metaphor. Unix and Windows use "." to mean the current directory.

You could therefore search an entire document for a particular attribute and then find out what element it is attached to: "`//@confidential/..`". You could go on to find out about the element's parent (and the parent's parent, etc.): "`//@confidential/../..`".

24.2.2.2.6 *Ancestor*

There is also a way of searching for an ancestor by name, but it does not have an abbreviated syntax. For example, "`ancestor::section`" would look for the ancestor(s) of the context node that are named "`section`".

This location path locates the titles of sections that contain images: "`//image/ancestor::section/title`".

24.2.3 *Our story so far*

Here are some examples of location paths using features we have covered so far:

`item`
> `item` element nodes that are children of the context node

`item/para`
> `para` element nodes that are children of `item` element nodes that are children of the context node; in other words, those `para` grandchildren of the context node whose parent is an `item`

`//para`
> `para` element nodes that are descendants of the root node; in other words, all the `para` element nodes in the entire document

`//item/para`
> `para` element nodes that are children of all `item` element nodes in the entire document

`//ordered-list//para`
> `para` element nodes that are descendants of all `ordered-list` element nodes in the entire document

```
ordered-list//para/@security
```
> `security` attribute nodes attached to all `para` element nodes that are descendants of all `ordered-list` element nodes that are children of the context node

```
*/@*
```
> attribute nodes attached to all element nodes that are children of the context node

```
../@*
```
> attribute nodes attached to the parent or attached node of the context node

```
.//para
```
> `para` element nodes that are descendants of the context node

```
.//comment()
```
> comment nodes that are descendants of the context node

24.2.4 *Predicates*

It is often important to filter nodes out of a node-set. We might filter out nodes that lack a particular attribute or subelement. We might filter out all but the first node. This sort of filtering is done in XPath through *predicates*. A predicate is an expression that is applied to each node. If it evaluates as false, the tested node is filtered out.

We'll discuss some common types of predicate expressions, then look at some examples.

24.2.4.1   Expression types

24.2.4.1.1   *Node-sets*

A location path expression can be used as a predicate. It evaluates to true if it selects any nodes at all. It is false if it does not select any nodes. So Example 24-4 would select all paragraphs that have a footnote child.

Example 24-4. Using a location path as a predicate

```
//para[footnote]
```

Recall that the evaluation of a step in the path results in a node-set, each member of which is a context node for an evaluation of the next step.[8]

One by one, each member of the result node-set, which in this case is every paragraph in the document, would get a chance to be the context node. It would either be selected or filtered out, depending on whether it contained any footnotes. Every paragraph would get its bright shining moment in the sun when it could be ".".[9]

A number of predicates can be chained together. Only nodes that pass all of the filters are passed on to the next step in the location path. For example, "//para[footnote][@important]" selects all paragraphs with important attributes and footnote children.

Like other location paths, those in predicates can have multiple steps with their own predicates. Consider the complex one in Example 24-5. It looks for sections with author child elements with qualifications child elements that have both professional and affordable attributes.

Example 24-5. A complex location path predicate

```
section[author/qualifications[@professional][@affordable]]
```

---

8. In other words, Example 24-4 is really an abbreviation for "//para[./footnote]".
9. Unfortunately, the moment is brief and the price of failure is exclusion from the selection set.

24.2.4.1.2 *String-values*

Not all predicates are location path expressions. Sometimes you do not want to test for the existence of some node. You might instead want to test whether an attribute has some particular value. That is different from testing whether the attribute exists or not.

Testing an attribute's value is simple: "`@type='ordered'`" tests whether the context node has a `type` attribute with value "ordered".

In XPath, every node type has a string-value. The value of an element node that is the context node, for example, is the concatenation of the string-values from the expression: "`.//text()`". In other words, it is all of the character data content anywhere within the element and its descendants.

So we can test the data content of a section's `title` child element with "`section[title='Doo-wop']`" and both of the sections in Example 24-6 would match.

Example 24-6. Matching sections

```
<section><title>Doo-wop</title>
...
</section>

<section><title>Doo-<emph>wop</emph></title>
...
</section>
```

24.2.4.1.3 *Context position*

There is more to the context in which an expression is evaluated than just the context node. Among the other things is the node's *context position*, which is returned by a function call: `position()=number`.

In practice, an abbreviation, consisting of the number alone, is invariably used. A number expression is evaluated as `true` if the number is the same as the context position.

Context position can be a tricky concept to grasp because it is, well, context-sensitive. However, it is easy to understand for the most common types of steps.

In a step down the child axis (`a/b`) the context position is the position of the child node in the parent node. So "`doc/section[5]`" is the fifth section in a `doc`. In a step down the descendant axis (`a//b[5]`) it still refers to the position of the child node in its *parent node*, not its numerical order in the list of matching nodes.

XPath also has a function called "last()". We can use it to generate the number for the last node in a context: "a//b[last()]". We can also combine that with some simple arithmetic to get the next-to-last node: "a//b[last()-1]".

24.2.4.2 Predicate examples

Here are some examples, using the predicate types that we've discussed:

item[3]
> third item element child of the context node

item[@type]/para
> para element children of item elements that exhibit a type attribute and are children of the context node

//list[@type='ordered']/item[1]/para[1]
> first para element child of the first item element child of any list element that exhibits a type attribute with the string-value "ordered"

//ordered-list[item[@type]/para[2]]//para
> para elements descended from any ordered-list element that has an item child that exhibits a type attribute and has at least two para element children (whew!)

This last example is illustrated in Figure 24-3.

The XPath spec includes numerous other examples of using predicates. XPath is a powerful expression language, including operators and functions that operate on node-sets, numbers, strings, and booleans.

24.3 | ID function

The most common high-level expression in XPath is the location path, which we have explored in some detail. And, as we have seen, a location

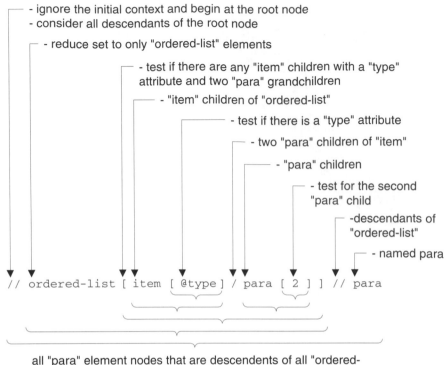

- ignore the initial context and begin at the root node
- consider all descendants of the root node

- reduce set to only "ordered-list" elements

- test if there are any "item" children with a "type" attribute and two "para" grandchildren

- "item" children of "ordered-list"

- test if there is a "type" attribute

- two "para" children of "item"

- "para" children

- test for the second "para" child

-descendants of "ordered-list"

- named para

```
// ordered-list [ item [ @type ] / para [ 2 ] ] // para
```

all "para" element nodes that are descendents of all "ordered-list" element nodes of the entire document node tree that have at least two "para" element node children of an "item" child that has a "type" attribute specified or defaulted

Figure 24-3   Evaluating multiple steps

path can also be used at lower levels – as a predicate expression, for example.

Another form of expression that returns a node-set is a function call to the id(string) function. The main use of the function is to select the element node whose ID is the same as the string. For example, "id('final')". selects the element node whose unique identifier is "final".

An ID function and a location path can be used in the same expression. One way is to create the union of the two, as in Example 24-7. The result node-set is the element whose ID is "final", plus all para elements descended from ordered-list elements.

Another way to combine the two is to use the ID function as the initial context node of a location path, to create a path expression like that in

Example 24-7. Union expression

```
id('final') | /ordered-list//para
```

Example 24-8. It locates the `title` child of the element whose ID is "A12345".

Example 24-8. Path expression

```
id('A12345')/title
```

Instead of a literal string, the argument could be a node whose string-value would be used, as in "`id(@IDREF)`". This expression locates the element referenced by the IDREF attribute of the context node.

24.4 | Conclusion

XPath is an extremely powerful language for addressing an XML document. Although it has depths that we could not address even in a "tad tougher" tutorial, we have covered all of the most common features.

Hint   For the complete details on XPath, we recommend *Definitive XSLT and XPath by G. Ken Holman of Crane Softwrights Ltd.,* `http://www.CraneSoftwrights.com`. *We also thank Ken for his expert contributions to this chapter.*

Index

Symbols

--, in comments 372
_ (underscore), in names 354
, (comma), in numbers 409
- (hyphen, minus)
    in names 354
    in numbers 445
    in regular expressions 463
; (semicolon), in entities 367
: (colon)
    in axes 446
    in names 446
? (question mark), in regular expressions 460, 462
?>, in PIs 373
/ (slash)
    in attribute values 360
    in location paths 389, 506–508, 515–519
    in tags 358–359
/ / (double slash), in location paths 247, 389, 509, 513–519
. (full-stop)
    in location paths 514, 516
    in names 354
    in numbers 409
    in regular expressions 462
. ., in location paths 255, 509, 514, 516
^ (caret)
    in names 354
    in regular expressions 464
~ (tilde), in names 354
' (single quote)
    in attributes 360–361
    in character data 371
" (double quote)
    in attributes 360–361
    in character data 371

[ ] (square brackets)
    in location paths 254, 390, 517–519
    in regular expressions 463
]] > (CDEnd) 370
{ } (curly braces), in regular expressions 460
@ (at), in location paths 389, 509, 513, 516–519
$ (dollar-sign), in XSLT 411
* (asterisk)
    node test 408, 511–514, 516
    in regular expressions 460
\ (backslash), in regular expressions 461–463
& (ampersand)
    in character data 371
    in entities 353, 367
+ (plus sign)
    in numbers 445
    in regular expressions 460
< (less-than)
    in character data 370–371, 408, 500, 504
    in tags 353, 355, 357–358
< ! --, in comments 372
<?, in PIs 373
-->, in comments 372
> (greater-than)
    in character data 370–371, 504
    in tags 355, 358
| (vertical bar)
    in patterns 401–402, 404
    in regular expressions 461

A

Abramatic, Jean-Francois xxx
abstraction
    definition 29
Access xxiii, xxviii, 267–293, 341
    databases 256
        exporting data 285

M

N

X

Z

LICENSE AGREEMENT AND LIMITED WARRANTY